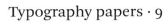

Typography papers · 9

G000255294

Front cover stencils cut by Fred Smeijers, based on Des Billettes (see pp. 28 ff).

Back cover Letters marked out from stencils, based on Des Billettes (see pp. 28 ff); (paired images at left, from top left) self-portrait of Gerlachus, *c.* 1150 (see pp. 5 ff); stenciller, from an engraving by Louis Simonneau, 1701 (see pp. 28 ff); detail of a specimen cover, Brüder Butter typefoundry, *c.* 1913 (see pp. 91 ff); Matthew Luckiesh lecturing, *c.* 1940s (see pp. 117 ff); illustrated entry from the *Longman Dictionary of Contemporary English* (1995) (see pp. 153 ff); specimen for Linotype Yakout, formerly Mrowa-Linotype Simplified Arabic (see pp. 173 ff).

Inside front cover Relief sculpture, Toulouse, *c.* 1120, formerly part of the Basilica of St. Sernin (see pp. 5 ff).

Inside back cover Ornaments designed by Hahnemann, Schütze, and Sigrist, 'Buchschmuck' specimen, Brüder Butter typefoundry, 1920 (see pp. 91 ff).

Typography papers · 9

Typography papers is edited, designed, and prepared for press in the Department of Typography & Graphic Communication, University of Reading (www.reading.ac.uk/typography) and published by Hyphen Press, London (www.hyphenpress.co.uk).

editors Eric Kindel & Paul Luna

editorial support for this volume Mary Dyson, Robin Kinross, Ole Lund, Alice Savoie

designer Eric Kindel

Typeset and made-up using Adobe InDesign cs6 with typefaces from the OurType Arnhem Pro, Arnhem Fine, and Fresco Sans families by Fred Smeijers, Antwerp; and from the Adobe Arabic family. Thanks to OurType for supplying additional transliteration glyphs used in Nemeth.

production at Reading image editing by Michael Johnston, Design & Print Studio, University of Reading.

Printed in Belgium by Die Keure, Bruges, on Lessebo Design Smooth Natural, 115 gsm. Bound by Sepeli nv, Evergem.

ISBN 978-0-907259-48-0

Gerard Unger is a graphic designer, type designer, and a Professor in the Department of Typography & Graphic Communication, University of Reading.

ungerard@wxs.nl

Eric Kindel is an Associate Professor in the Department of Typography & Graphic Communication, University of Reading.

e.t.kindel@reading.ac.uk

Fred Smeijers is a Dutch type designer, researcher, writer, and Professor of Type Design at the Hochschule für Grafik und Buchkunst, Leipzig.

info@fredsmeijers.com

James Mosley is a Professor in the Department of Typography & Graphic Communication, University of Reading.

j.m.mosley@reading.ac.uk

Maurice Göldner is the designer of OurType Stan and other typefaces, living in Leipzig.

goeldner@kurs26.de

William Berkson is a philosopher and the designer of Williams Caslon, living in Virginia.

berkson@mentsh.com

Peter Enneson is an art director and graphic designer, working in Toronto.

peter@enneson.com

Paul Luna is the designer of several Oxford dictionaries and a Professor in the Department of Typography & Graphic Communication, University of Reading.

p.luna@reading.ac.uk

Titus Nemeth is a type designer, typographer, and researcher.

tn@tntypography.com

In this ninth volume of *Typography papers*, we range widely over time and topic in pursuit of compelling narratives.

Some scholars have argued that letterforms called 'Romanesque' lack stable characteristics of their own, and are only transitional between Carolingian and Gothic letterforms. Gerard Unger counters this view by drawing together identifiable Romanesque characteristics traceable across much of Europe, and which were remarkably durable, if bewilderingly varied and interchangeable.

In the 1690s, an encyclopedic 'description of trades' was begun by the Académie royale des Sciences in Paris. The first trade examined was printing. Texts about it were written by two 'technicians', one of whom was Gilles Filleau des Billettes. Among the topics he addressed was stencilling. Eric Kindel presents a reconstruction of the equipment described, and reflects on its use. Four appendices, including two by Fred Smeijers, explore related matters in detail. The reconstruction is accompanied by Des Billettes's text, which is published now for the first time. More information about Des Billettes and the *Description des arts et métiers* is provided by James Mosley.

Maurice Göldner assembles a history of the Dresden typefoundry Brüder Butter, partly from meagre archival resources that survived the Second World War, but also from a wealth of inventive type specimens issued by the foundry. Themes of international marketing and a fascination with decorative typographic ornaments and modular systems – from Jugendstil to outright Modernist – emerge from this rich resource, allowing us to reconsider Brüder Butter's reputation among German typefoundries.

A dispute, often vehement, between two psychologists about readability, legibility, and their definition forms the narrative presented by William Berkson and Paul Enneson. By comparing the methodologies and publications of Matthew Luckiesh and Miles Tinker, they uncover the origins of the distinction (or confusion?) between readability and legibility, as understood by typographers and psychologists. Reappraising Luckiesh's approach to readability, they believe, will expand our understanding of the complexity of reading.

Dictionaries are thought of as books of words, but Paul Luna concentrates on the illustrations that accompany dictionary definitions. While the most common form of illustration from the 1850s to the 1960s was the small black-and-white wood engraving or line drawing, he shows that innovative colour illustrations in recent dictionaries explain the relationships between words as well as define objects.

Simplification of the Arabic script for quicker and more efficient typesetting has brought advantages – and compromises – to Arabic language publishing. Titus Nemeth investigates the most successful project of simplification, a collaboration between a Lebanese newspaper owner-editor and the British Linotype company. He assesses the typeface that resulted, Mrowa-Linotype Simplified Arabic.

More than four years have passed since the previous volume of *Typography papers*, edited by our esteemed colleague, the late Paul Stiff. He began the venture in 1996 with the notice that 'Whatever else it is claimed to be, typography is design for reading.' We hope to continue with Paul's generous idea of typography, and dedicate this volume to his memory.   EK & PL   *Reading, October 2013*

Gerard Unger

Romanesque capitals in inscriptions

This essay presents an overview of Romanesque capitals in inscriptions. They are first placed in the scene of the Romanesque period, then discussed in respect of their characteristics, both as individual letterforms and as part of inscriptions. Their origins are considered, as are relationships between manuscript and inscriptional uses. Explanations for the positioning and distribution of capitals in inscriptions are also proposed. An album provides additional examples of inscriptions from the period. The essay concludes with a brief review of revivals of Romanesque capitals that have appeared in subsequent centuries, up to the present day.

Romanesque capitals in inscriptions are a mix of three kinds of letters: the descendants of the Roman imperial square capital (*capitalis quadrata*), uncials, and angular versions of round letters, known as insular. The three were harmonised in some details, such as stroke width, in order that they work together. Romanesque capitals otherwise feature uncials and insular letters that are continuously and arbitrarily interchanged, and letters of all three kinds that are variously ligatured, intertwined, nested, or reversed. Letter widths and the spaces between them also vary, again often arbitrarily, though sometimes to fill a given space. Capitals that can be described as Romanesque first appear in inscriptions shortly before AD 1000, and for the next 200 or so years they were carved in stone, painted on walls, chased in metal and executed in various other ways. They are found in many parts of Europe, from Sicily to Norway, from the British Isles to eastern Europe, and indeed as far east as Novgorod, Constantinople, and Jerusalem; (figure 1, overleaf).[1]

In the literature of letterform history, the Roman imperial square capital has received generous attention; so, too, have its renaissance revivals. Gothic capitals from the intervening period are also relatively well-known, as are early renaissance capitals such as those found in Florence.[2] Romanesque capitals, which served as models for early renaissance capitals, have by contrast received comparatively little attention. Some commentators have assumed that the forms of Romanesque capitals were not fixed but instead represented only the gradual change from Carolingian to Gothic,[3] or that they were experiments leading to the Gothic capital but little more.[4] But when a relatively large group of examples is assembled, it becomes clear that common characteristics can be identified that determine the appearance of Romanesque capitals. These characteristics, combined with an extraordinary variety of individual letterforms used in surprising and idiosyncratic ways, give Romanesque capitals their particular significance in the history of letterforms.

In the pages that follow, the principal sources and features of Romanesque capitals are introduced.

1. Romanesque capitals spread beyond Constantinople to Jerusalem and the Holy Land in the wake of the crusaders, carried there on objects such as the seals of Godfrey of Bouillon and the Knights Templar. See Prawer (1970), vol. 1, pp. 203, 243, 478, 482, 492; also Rozenberg (1999) for illustrations of funeral monuments (p. 295) and a tomb fragment (cover), all with Romanesque capitals.

2. Bibliographies compiling representative studies of the Roman imperial square capital and its revival can be found in *Typography papers*, 6 (2005), London: Hyphen Press, *passim*; Stiff (2005) discusses Florentine capitals in detail.

3. Koch (2007), p. 149.

4. Gray (1986), pp. 88, 107.

Figure 1. Romanesque capitals.

(a) Detail of the tomb of Gundrada, wife of William of Warenne, comrade-in-arms of William the Conqueror, St. John's church, Lewes, England, *c.* 1145. The letter N with a curved diagonal, a treatment that was rare in continental Europe, suggests that this tomb slab was made locally. Other letters are typically Romanesque, including A with a flat top, spiralling G, and R with a double-curved leg.

(b) Detail of bronze doors, Bonanno Pisano, Monreale cathedral, Sicily, 1186. The text runs: D(OMI)N(U)S PLASMAVI(T) ADA(M) DE LIMO TERE (the Lord formed Adam out of clay and earth). Typical Romanesque letters include A with a cross bar at its apex, composite DE, uncial M formed from an O-like shape with a large attached curl, minuscule N whose height matches the other capitals, and uncial U similar to the minusule N but flipped on a horizontal axis.

(c) Late Romanesque capitals from the Akaleptos Monastery church, Constantinople, painted after the fourth crusade (1202–4) but before 1250. Archaeological Museum, Istanbul. From a fresco depicting the life of St. Francis of Assisi (d. 1226).

The Romanesque scene

The 'Romanesque' period ran from the middle of the tenth century to the end of the twelfth, without a clear beginning or end.[5] In the preceding centuries, Europe was beleaguered on all sides: in the south by the Saracens, in the north and west by the Vikings, and in the east by the Magyars. The Magyar threat was eventually lifted following their defeat by the army of Otto I at the battle of Lechfeld near Augsburg in 955. The Vikings were pacified by a treaty with the French king Charles the Simple in 911, and by their settlement in northwest France (though as Normans they remained occupiers in the south of Italy and on Sicily, and invaded England in 1066). The Saracen threat remained for considerably longer, and it was not until 1491 and the surrender of Granada that they were expelled entirely from western Europe.

A generally safer and more stable Europe in the second half of the tenth century led to increases in commerce and travel and a revival of towns and cities. Although churches and convents had frequently been plundered by marauders, the western Christian church had

5. This demarcation is derived from Fernie (1996), p. 568; Timmers (1969) places its start around 950. Petzold (1995), p. 7, in agreement with other specialists, states that 'the term "Romanesque" is used to describe both the art and architecture of Western Europe from 1050 to 1200'. For the period 950 to 1050, the term 'First Romanesque' is often used; in Britain this period is called Saxon and the succeeding period, Norman; in Germany, art and architecture from immediately before 1050 is designated 'Ottonian'.

survived and now began to expand. Part of its expansion involved new construction activities that encompassed religious buildings and secular structures such as castles, bridges, and market halls.[6] This work was needed for several reasons: to repair damaged buildings, to provide more and bigger churches to service growing populations, and to satisfy cravings for prestige and power among the aristocracy and higher clergy. The period was also marked by growing numbers of pilgrims travelling long distances to commune with saints and relics housed in imposing shrines.

A consequence of much of this activity was a blossoming of Romanesque sculpture, to be found among other places on capitals and tympanums. Sculptures and architectural structures were frequently provided with inscriptional texts that sometimes include the names of their makers (figure 2, a–b). Letters and texts were also integrated into stained-glass windows, altars, fonts, reliquaries, pulpits, and other objects adorning buildings.

Characteristics

When studying the characteristics of Romanesque inscriptions it is instructive to draw a parallel with Romanesque buildings. Buildings from the period vary greatly. There seem to be more differences than similarities between St. Mark's Basilica in Venice, for example, the cathedral at Pisa, and the Basilica of St. Servatius in Maastricht (figure 3, a–c, overleaf). What many Romanesque buildings do have in common is that from the outside it is evident how their interiors

6. Le Goff (2006), p. 91.

Figure 2. Letter carvers.
(a) Signature of HARTMANNUS, inscription on a capital from the porch of the demolished collegiate church of St. Simon and St. Jude, Goslar, c. 1150. Notable is the double N comprised of a capital, followed by a minuscule N of the same height.

(b) Inscription, church of Santa Maria de Iguácel, north of Jaca (Spanish Pyrenees), c. 1094. The front of the church incorporates an inscription across its entire width. On a side wall, the letter carver Azenar has recorded his own name and the name of the man responsible for the paintings inside the church. The text runs: SCRITOR HARVM LITTERARV(M) N(OM)I(N)E AZENAR MAGISTER HARV(M) PICTVRARV(M) N(OM)I(N)E CALINDO GARCES (The name of the carver of these letters is Azenar, the name of the painter of these pictures is Calindo Garces). Notable is the use of upside-down A for V (see, for example, HARVM at top right).

Figure 3. Buildings of the
Romanesque period.
(a) St. Mark's Basilica, Venice.
(b) Pisa cathedral.
(c) Basilica of St. Servatius,
    Maastricht.

are organised. Parts of the buildings such as towers, transepts, and
apsides are clearly articulated and arranged in striking silhouettes.[7]
But within and among these parts, a great variety of detail frequently
occurs.

Many Romanesque inscriptions also display clearly defined elements whose individual treatments can be highly varied. One example, at the abbey of Moissac in southwestern France, demonstrates
this well: a basic set of letterforms is arranged in a direct and unambiguous manner; thereafter, letter variants are distributed irregularly
throughout the text (figure 4, a–b). In places several versions of a
particular letter occur within a single word or line. The inscription
is complex but not confused.

7. Fernie (2010), p. 295.

Figure 4. Inscription, cloister of the abbey at Moissac, France, 1100.
(a) The text gives the cloister's date of construction and the name of the abbot,
    Ansquetil, patron of the work. The text runs: ANNO AB I(N)CARNA / TIONE
    AETERNI / PRINCIPIS MILLESIMO / CENTESIMO FACTV(M) / EST CLAVSTRV(M)
    ISTVD / TEMPORE / DOMINI / ANSQVITILII / ABBATIS / AMEN / V V V / M D M /
    R R R / F F F.
        The sequence of letters V V V / M D M / R R R / F F F may represent: 'Vir
    Vitae Venerabilis / Moyssiacum Domum Melioravit / Restuit, Restauravit,
    Rexit / Fauste, Fortunate, Feliciter', i.e. (Ansquetil) Man of venerable life /
    Improved the house of Moissac / He built it, restored it and ruled it /
    Fortunately, prosperously, fruitfully. (Forsyth, 2008, p. 178)
(b) Detail of figure 4a. Notable letterforms, in addition to the nested small
    capitals and merged and intertwined letters, include square C (in PRINCIPIS
    and CENTESIMO) and a rounded C, uncial E and square E in the same word
    (CENTESIMO), M with straight strokes (CENTESIMO) and in uncial form
    (MILLESIMO), N's of varying width, and O pointed at top and base.

Figure 5. Relief (one of four), Pieterskerk, Utrecht, probably made near Maastricht shortly after 1148. (Den Hartog, 1996, p. 137)

(a) The occurence of variant letterforms is illustrated by the three M's in MULIERUM MENS, the three T's in DEVOTA PUTAT, and the two U's in MULIERUM. The second, reversed, U is a form that is often found in the work of Romanesque letter carvers. Elsewhere the L in MULIERUM is noticeably wide and the N in MENS rather narrow.

(b) Detail of figure 5a.

(c) Detail of figure 5a.

Figure 6. Important characteristics of Romanesque capitals: slight differences between thick and thin parts; gradual transitions from thick to thin parts; straight parts that widen towards their end and have short triangular serifs.

A second example is a series of inscriptions cut into strong, square frames surrounding four panels in the Pieterskerk, Utrecht (figure 5, a–c). Here, numerous alternative letterforms can be seen, which occur irregularly among the words. The inscription shows another characteristic feature shared by most Romanesque capitals: relatively moderate differences between thick and thin parts. This can be seen in the gradual transition of arches and curves, whose thickest parts also tend to occur at their mid-points. Straight parts are shaped similarly, becoming gradually wider towards their ends and typically ending in a wedge shape whose points might equally be described as short, triangular serifs (figure 6).

A third example, a large inscription located on the west façade of the Pisa cathedral, effectively constitutes a catalogue of Romanesque letterforms (figure 7, overleaf). It contains a considerable range of capitals, many variants, and letterforms and spaces that widen and narrow, sometimes arbitrarily it seems, at other times to adjust to the available space.

Figure 7. Inscription, west facade of
Pisa cathedral.

(a) The text of the inscription
describes how in 1063 the inhabit-
ants of Pisa fitted out a fleet that
sailed to Palermo, at that time
occupied by Saracens. There in
the harbour the Pisans captured
six ships containing treasure.
After landing an army, they
destroyed the town and surrounding countryside and killed thou-
sands. The proceeds of the attack
financed the construction of the
cathedral. The text probably dates
to 1118, the year the cathedral was
consecrated by Pope Gelasius II.

(b) Detail. In this inscription, notable
letters include round and angular
versions of C, E, G, H, M, N, T
and U, minuscule N whose height
matches the other capitals, round
and angular spiralling G, M with
diagonals short of the baseline,
O's pointed at top and bottom, R
with an elegantly curved double
leg, S slanting to the left without
exception, and several variants of
U. Among letter combinations,
smaller capitals are nested inside
larger ones, letters have been
merged, and in some cases are
noticeably narrower or wider, both
individually and within a single
line. Throughout the inscription,
variations appear to be irregularly
distributed.

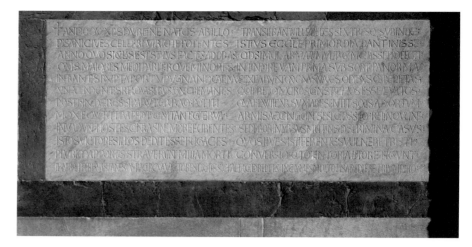

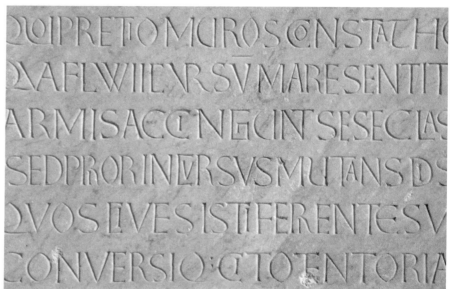

As mentioned, most Romanesque capitals found in inscriptions
are the descendants of Roman imperial square capitals, including A,
B, C, D, E, F, G, H, I, L, M, N, O, P, Q, R, S, T, V, X and Z; K occurs occasionally while W and Y are rare. Among Romanesque letterforms,
widths often differ less than they do among their classical predecessors; individually, letters including E, F, L, P and R are wider, and
others including C, G, M, O and Q are narrower. But all letters show
some variation in width throughout the Romesque period.

Letters also have notable, often recurring, characteristics (figure 8).
K, when found, typically has curved diagonals; the diagonals of M
are usually short; the leg of R is almost always curved (either a single
curve or a double); and S frequently leans to the left or is top-heavy.
Round letters such as C, G and sometimes S also occur as angular
forms, a treatment that extended to O and Q, which were pointed at
their top and base. A, D, E, H, M, Q, T and V occur as uncials and half-
uncials (discussed below) and G is often given a spiralling form. All
of these forms were additionally adapted to each other in proportion
and weight and in their characteristic features and details.

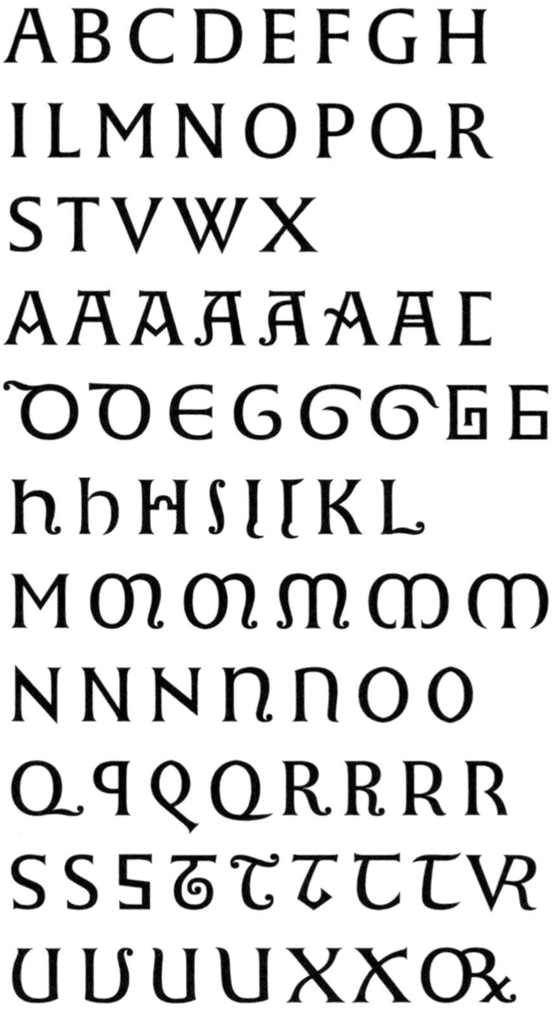

Figure 8. Overview of Romanesque capitals, with alternatives (incomplete). An comprehensive overview of Romanesque capitals is difficult to compile because of the numerous alternatives and variations that exist. An overview may also be misleading since nowhere in Europe nor at any one time in the eleventh or twelfth century were all the letterforms used by or even known to an individual letter carver. While publications such as in 'Die Deutsche Inschriften' series can help to form a more complete picture, it is also the case that many inscriptions (and their particular letterforms) have been lost. Each letter carver probably used a selection of forms, which in all likelihood changed or were supplemented over time through contacts with colleagues and others. Letter carvers probably also passed on letterforms to younger colleagues or apprentices who added their own interpretations in turn.

ABCDEFGH
ILMNOPQR
STVWX
ΛAAAAAAС
ᴅᴅEGGᴳᴳ
ɦbHSⅡKL
Mᴏᴍᴍᴍᴍᴍᴍᴍ
NNNᴨᴨOO
QꟼQᴅRRRR
SSꟅᴛꞆꞆᴛᴠ
ᴜᴜᴜᴜXXᴏ℞

Origins

Although Romanesque capitals begin to appear as an identifiable ensemble in inscriptions sometime before 1000, many of the individual letterforms or their details are found earlier. A page from the Codex Aureus offers an example of antecedents. Made in Canterbury in the middle of the eighth century, it shows many characteristic letters found later in Romanesque inscriptions, notably uncials and angular versions of round letters (figure 9). A second example, the *Royal Bible*, made the following century probably also in Canterbury, shows uncials, angular forms of C and S, spiralling G, and other letterforms descendant from Roman square capitals (figure 10).

Angular versions of round letters belong to insular art, a mixture of mainly Irish-Celtic and Anglo-Saxon elements. Angular letters were influenced by the (Irish-Celtic) ogham and (Anglo-Saxon) runic alphabets; both contain linear and angular characters.[8] Greek letterforms may also have exerted some influence through trading and ecclesiastical contacts.[9] Uncials first appeared in the Mediterranean (probably North Africa) in the fourth century, created after the example of Greek uncials.[10] Uncials were brought to England in 597 by Augustine (of Canterbury), who was sent there from Rome by Pope

8. Gray (1986), p. 61.

9. Gray (1986), p. 49. The first page of the Gospel of St. Matthew in the Lindisfarne Gospels (f. 27ʳ) has Greek letters in the Latin text (Brown, 2011, p. 17).

10. Ullman (1997 [1932]), p. 68.

Figure 9. Page from the Codex
Aureus, probably made in Canterbury,
mid-eighth century. Royal Library,
Stockholm. The vertical parts of letters widen toward their ends, horizontal parts are wedge-shaped, and there
is little difference between thick and
thin parts; the triangular serifs are
very modest or almost non-existent.
There are otherwise many notable
letters. Some A's have horizontal bars
at their apex and broken cross bars.
Spiralling G appears and M's all have
short diagonals. Every R has a double-
curved leg. The majority of S's slant
to the left, while the ends of some are
spiralling; wide and narrow versions
S alternate. There are angular C's and
diamond-shaped O's. (O's in inscriptions, pointed at their top and base,
were possibly derived from diamond-
shaped versions, which rarely occur in
inscriptions.) Forms resembling the
small letters h and q are uncials or
half-uncials and there is also a round
uncial E. N employs a short diagonal
in a low position while its right vertical stroke sometimes stops short of
the baseline.

Figure 10. Capitals from the *Royal
Bible*, 820–850. From Shaw (1853);
original in The British Library.

Gregory I on a Christianizing mission.[11] In the seventh century a
mix of uncials, insular letterforms, and derivations of Roman square
capitals was taken to continental Europe, initially by Irish-Scottish
monks who in the company of Columba founded monasteries such
as Luxeuil and Bobbio. Anglo-Saxon missionaries including Boni-
face and Willibrord also took this mix to the continent where it was
embraced by Gauls, Franks and other groups whose own artistic
cultures used similar forms and patterns. Additionally, uncials were
probably brought to northern Europe by clergy travelling across the
Alps from Rome.

Having reached continental Europe, the use of uncials and angular versions of round letters was uneven. For example, after first
appearing in Carolingian inscriptions in the ninth century (and
especially the latter half[12]), angular C's and G's increase and become
frequent in the eleventh century in combination with other angular
letters such as S shaped like a reversed Z. But over the course of the
twelfth century, angular versions in general lose ground and become
rare.[13] Uncials, on the other hand, introduced into inscriptions more

11. Prior to uncials reaching England,
half-uncials had already arrived in Ireland
(Bischoff, 1993, p. 83) possibly as early as
431, brought there by Bishop Palladius

(Brown, 2011, p. 47).
    12. Koch (2007), p. 108; Debiais *et al*
(2008), p. 113.
    13. Debiais *et al* (2008), p. 119.

Figure 11. Gothic capitals, after the monument of Henry III, Westminster Abbey, c. 1272. From Shaw (1853).

14. Koch (2007), p. 108.
15. This letterform may originate in Ireland. Bischoff (1993), p. 85.
16. Morison (1972), p. 10.
17. Gray (1986), p. 23 and fig. 18.

slowly than angular letters,[14] were used throughout the Romanesque period, eventually evolving into Gothic capitals.

Among uncials and some half-uncials, including A, D, E, H, M, Q, T and U, several shapes of each are found in Romanesque inscriptions, and minuscule N is made the height of other capitals.[15] During the second half of the twelfth century, Romanesque capitals increasingly follow the round uncial and half-uncial forms; their curves swell and their straight parts become heavier and wider at their ends. Letterforms follow a general trend from moderate to considerable differences between thick and thin parts combined with increasing ornamentation. The trend describes the gradual change of Romanesque into Gothic, where in addition capitals such as C, E, F (figure 11) and sometimes S are enclosed by vertical strokes on the right of the letter; others such as M are similarly enclosed by a horizontal stroke.

Some Romanesque letterforms occur considerably earlier than angular insular letterforms and uncials though their precise origins can be difficult to establish. A with a broken cross-bar, for example, can be found in the second half of the first century BC in Greek inscriptions (figure 12); they are later present in Roman mosaics. M with short diagonals is also Greek, occuring as early as 200 BC.[16] These letterforms were possibly transmitted into medieval inscriptions by way of the Romans, though it is equally possible that they were invented anew. Other notable early occurences include spiralling G in second-century Roman inscriptions and flat-topped A in Roman provincial inscriptions of the early fourth century (figure 13).[17] The origin of R with a double-curved leg is also unclear. An early version appears in the Codex Aureus (see figure 9) and it was often used after 800 in Carolingian manuscripts such as the 'Evangeliary of Lorsch'. Left-leaning S can be found much earlier in many early Christian inscriptions (figure 14).

Apart from the construction and details of particular letterforms, combinations of letters found in Romanesque inscriptions also have antecedents. Capital letters nested one inside another, for example,

Figure 12. Gravestone of Zosime, daughter of Herakleon, first century BC. Epigraphical Museum, Athens.

Figure 13. Votive tablet of Lucio Attio Macro al Genio of the seventh Roman legion, AD 127. Provincial Ethnographical Museum of León.

Figure 14. Inscription for Auspicius of Trier, detail, second half of the fifth century, Dom-und Diözesanmuseum, Trier. Notable letters include left-leaning S's, spiralling G's, and A's without a cross bar.

ECIA LITER POSSESSIONONSERVIRE
EANDEMMASSAMQVAEAQVASALVIA
PERTVSA · BIFVRCO·PRIMINIANO
.VCTOINSTRVMENTOQVESVOETC
DEPVTARE ADICIENTESETIAMEIC
NTIBVSAPORTACIVITATISPART
ANI QVODESTANCILLARVMDIPC
AEVOCANTVRFOSSALATRO
:SINISTRA VBINVNCVINEAEFA
OSCOLASTICI ETABALIAPARTEPOS
:SIAEPRAEPOSITOSQVIPERTEMP
(INDEACCESSERITLVMINARIBV:
CIPIMVSVTSVPRASCRIPTAMMAS
RRVLASQVAESVPERIVSCONTINEN

Figure 15. Part of a praeceptum by
Pope Gregory the Great from 604, in
the lapidary of St Paul Outside the
Walls, Rome. Letterforms such as B
and S, which are very wide, deviate
considerably from Roman square capitals. Other notable features include
M with diagonals that do not reach
the baseline, and S that sometimes
leans to the left.

Figure 18. Fragment of a Roman
inscription, south exterior wall, Pisa
cathedral, probably 2nd century AD;
Banti (1996), p. 53.

were already used by the Romans as were letters that overlapped
or whose (vertical) strokes coincided. But the Romans generally
employed such combinations sparingly, at least in contrast to eleventh and twelfth century stone carvers who used them in abundance.
Late Roman inscriptions do show features that seem to prefigure
Romanesque inscriptions more directly (figure 15) and indeed are
probably linked to them – and yet without displaying those variations of letterforms so typical of the Romanesque period. Rome was
certainly visited frequently by clergy on ecclesiastical business and by
many pilgrims. Memories of Roman inscriptions or sketches of them
were quite possibly carried home, though this is conjectural.

Manuscripts and stone carving

The ancestry of Romanesque capitals is not to be found wholly in
inscriptions. Manuscripts also played an important role in their
development. In some instances, interactions between inscriptions
and manuscripts are suggested and indeed seem likely though direct
evidence remains elusive.

The capitals of the Codex Aureus (mid-eighth century; see figure
9), for example, have features typical of letters cut in stone, notably
their small triangular serifs. In the Carolingian period, the Roman
square capital found in ancient inscriptions was copied in manuscripts, as in the Lebuinus Codex (825–50; figure 16, opposite). These
'neo-Roman' square capitals were used together with uncials and
large insular letterforms. More than a century later in the 'Ansfridus
Codex' (950–1000; figure 17), neo-Roman letters and uncials blend
to produce identifiably Romanesque capitals, which among other
things tend toward equal widths (see A, E, N, R).[18] The capitals of
the Ansfridus Codex are no longer classically proportioned.

This sequence of manuscripts suggests that the Carolingian
revival of Roman square capitals disrupted developments toward
Romanesque capitals.[19] Although several letterforms found in the
Codex Aureus (like angular C) also occur in Carolingian manuscripts
and inscriptions, the nostalgia for the era of Roman emperors and
their signature letters was very strong. So while various mixtures of
uncial, insular, and square capital letters can sometimes be found
as early as the first half of the ninth century (see also figure 10), it
would be another 150 years before a similar mixture appeared in
inscriptions.

There is evidence that interactions occurred between scriptoria
and building sites, probably resulting in scribes and letter carvers
taking note of each other's work.[20] Letter carvers in the eleventh and
twelfth centuries would also have been familiar with Roman imperial
square capitals. On the outer wall of the Pisa cathedral, for example,
fragments of ancient inscriptions are conspicuously integrated into
the stonework (figure 18), as are other elements, including the rows
of ancient columns in the nave.[21]

18. This phenomenon has occurred
before, including during Carolingian
period. In the Godescalc-Evangelary,
for example, made in Aix-la-Chapelle
between 781 and 783, capitals that tend

toward equal widths occur next to ones
with more classical (varied) widths.
19. Koch (2007), p. 118.
20. Higgitt (1990), (1999), *passim.*
21. Conant (1973), pp. 232–3.

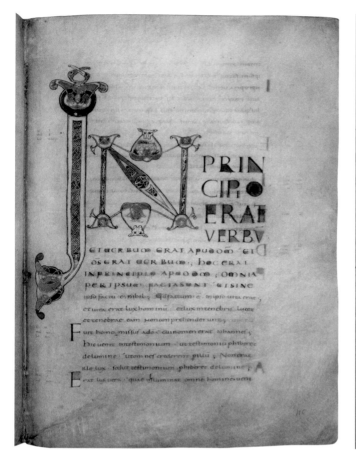

Figure 16. Lebuinus Codex, f. 110, made in north-east France between 825 and 850. Museum Catharijneconvent, Utrecht. The large I and N are insular; the letters of PRINCIPIO ERAT VERBV(M), which imitate Roman square capitals, could be described as 'neo-Roman'. Three lines of uncials follow, after which the text continues in Carolingian minuscules. This ordering demonstrates what has become known as the hierarchy of scripts (Bischoff, 1993, p. 71).

Figure 17. Ansfridus Codex, f. 120, made in St Gallen between 950 and 1000, Museum Catharijneconvent, Utrecht. The capitals of INITIVM . . . GENERATIONIS feature straight and round E's, spiralling G, M with short diagonals, and R with a double-curved leg. Immediately below, DAVID begins with an uncial and ends with a square capital. The large LIBER is insular.

Developments

A gilt copper plate in Essen with plain wide letterforms, made around 970, shows the Romanesque capital fully developed (figure 19, overleaf).[22] Over the next two centuries, between approximately 1000 and 1200, Romanesque capitals change, becoming generally more complex and more ornamented.

Two examples, one early in this period and the other somewhat late, illustrate the change. Both are found on the bronze doors of the Market Portal of Mainz cathedral. The earlier, which dates to 1009, mentions the patron of the doors, Archbishop Willigis, next to Berengerus, the man who cast them (figure 20, a–b). The later example, the 'Adalbert Privilege' put on the doors around 1135, records the rights of the citizens of Mainz (figure 20c). The letters of the first are a mixture of Carolingian and Romanesque features. They vary significantly in width, a feature reminiscent of the Lebuinus Codex; the long serifs are Carolingian. Romanesque features are A with a

22. Date in Hermann (2011), pp. 10–11. These letterforms, whose proportions are also reminiscent of Carolingian capitals, can be described as Ottonian. As mentioned above, Ottonian art was the north European counterpart of the south European, or First Romanesque style and is considered to belong to the Romanesque period.

Figure 19. Gilt copper plate, part of a large gold cross, *c.* 971. Treasury of Essen cathedral. The inscription mentions an abbess Ida (see Fillitz (1993) pp. 392–3). Notable letters include flat-topped A, wide B whose intersecting round strokes do not meet the vertical stroke, uncial E, S slanting to the left, M with short diagonals and R with a double-curved leg. These letterforms are early Romanesque, or, following German terminology, Ottonian.

cross-bar at its apex that extends to the left, square C, spiralling G, uncial H and Q, M with diagonals that do not reach the baseline, R with a double-curved leg, clusters of merged letters, and combinations of small and large capitals. The letters of the Adalbert Privilege, by contrast, are thoroughly Romanesque. The inscription includes a considerable number of variants – there are 16 versions of A – as well as angular C, spiralling G, and many uncials, reversed letters, merged letters, and combinations of small and large capitals, some nested.

    Another important change during this period can be seen in a stained glass window made around 1150 for the abbey church at Arnstein an der Lahn. It shows a self-portrait of the artist Gerlachus

Figure 20. Inscriptions on the bronze doors of the Market Portal, north side of Mainz cathedral.
(a) Detail of inscription on door panel frame, made shortly before 1009. The inscription mentions Charlemagne; like him, the Ottonian Archbishop Willigis probably wanted to associate himself with imperial Rome.
(b) Detail of inscription on door panel frame, made shortly before 1009.
(c) Detail of the 'Adalbert Privilege', positioned on the upper panel of both doors, *c.* 1135.

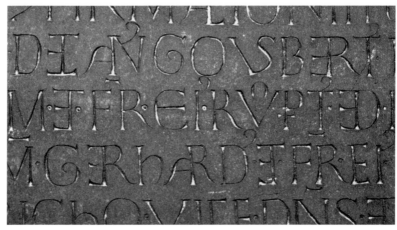

Figure 21. Self-portrait of Gerlachus, detail of a stained glass window from the abbey church of Arnstein an der Lahn, *c.* 1150. Westfälisches Landesmuseum, Münster. Various Romanesque features can be observed: the different A's, uncial and capital E's, spiralling G, the curved horizontal part of L, two forms of R and X with wavy diagonals. Other notable features are the decorative balls positioned at the inside top and base of the two O's and the small arc in the crossbar of H.

holding a brush in one hand and a paint pot in the other (figure 21). He is painting a text that includes his name. While the letterforms are still Romanesque, they display features characteristic of Gothic capitals. The letters are heavier than those in the Adalbert Privilege for example, and have more pronounced differences between thick and thin parts. They are also more ornamented. Such characteristics are found in manuscripts and frescoes, on windows, and in enamel work before they occur in letters cut in stone.

During the second half of the twelfth century, the number of alternative letterforms that occur in inscriptions declines. They are still found among Gothic capitals though the variety is now greatly reduced (see figure 11). This decline in alternative letterforms and in their irregular distribution runs broadly in parallel with larger social and religious changes in the twelfth century. Principal among these changes was the increasing importance of towns and cities, which in turn attracted theological education away from the monasteries. With this relocation, fascination with Romanesque symbolism diminished as interest in the real world and its representation grew.[23]

The positioning and distribution of Romanesque capitals

The positioning and distribution of insular letterforms, uncials, and square capitals in manuscripts and inscriptions, while irregular, was almost certainly done deliberately.

(1) A basis for irregular positioning and distribution was *varietas*, an important idea in early and medieval Christianity.[24] Varietas can be seen, for example, in the arch of Constantine the Great (*c.* 280–337), whose construction from parts of other buildings (*spolia*) resulted in variety though a mixing of established architectural orders. In Romanesque buildings, older architectural parts were often used; and in Romanesque sculpture, varietas occurs in historiated capitals, for example (as at Moissac), partly to counteract boredom among

23. Duby (2002), pp. 346–8; Hagen (2000), p. 9.
24. This item is based on Carruthers (2009); see especially pp. 15, 20–1, 23–4; the quotation is from p. 23. See also Forsyth (2008).

monks. The monotony of monastic life might also be relieved by variety in reading: 'one should read now things new or then old, now obscure, then plain, … now something serious, then something lighthearted' (Peter of Celle). Varietas also played a role in rhetoric by holding an audience captive by, for example, larding one's speech with humour or anecdotes. Augustine of Hippo (354–430), among others, connected varietas and *diversitas*, referring not to the 'fitness' of the elements together as a whole, but to their great differences which are nonetheless brought together, an apt description of the uses of Romanesque capitals, and especially of their continuously changing positions in text.

(2) The variety found in Romanesque letterforms may reflect the various ways texts and images were 'read' and interpreted in the eleventh and twelfth centuries, or conceptions of the universe. People in the Middle Ages were familiar with fables, mysticism, miracles, and relics, with signs from God and the saints, and with magic.[25]

(3) The irregular positioning of letterforms may also be connected with the medieval interest in language games or patterns of several kinds.[26] This interest can be seen, for example, in leonine verse[27] which has a characteristic internal rhyme pattern. The text of many Romanesque inscriptions take this form, including that at Saint-Paul-de-Varax (figure 28). At Moissac (see figure 4), another language game may also be at work in the mysterious stack of letters at the base of the inscription though their combinations have not yet been convincingly explained.

(4) The distribution of the alternative letterforms in texts and play with letterforms, may also be seen as a kind of game. In these instances, such as the relief sculpture at Toulouse (figure 25), the work of pulling apart of text, which is then woven into the sculpture and to which are added mirrored and double letters, has the effect of making the text mysterious.[28] While it has been assumed that this work was merely evidence of illiteracy among stone cutters, it was instead almost certainly a deliberate taking of liberties.[29]

(5) Possibly the irregular positioning of the alternative letterforms functioned as a mnemonic device or served to make the reader pay attention, so that the texts were better remembered.

In general, multiformity appears to have been important to the medieval mind. Artisans almost certainly took pleasure in letterform variety, in the positioning and distribution of existing forms, and in the creation of new ones. Play with letters and with the language they served was part of the larger context of Romanesque art and architecture, which was also characterized by inventiveness and variation in the eleventh and twelfth centuries. This blossoming multiformity was apparently infectious as architects, artists, artisans, and patrons observed each other's work and were inventive in turn.[30] Variation and change thus became the defining features of Romanesque style.

Album

The inscriptions shown on pp. 19–22 are some of the many examples preserved from the eleventh and twelfth centuries that illustrate variety among Romanesque capitals and their uses.

25. Arnold (2009), pp. 1–7.
26. Forsyth (2008), p. 176.
27. In leonine verse (or leonine hexameter) the last word rhymes with the word before the caesura (usually a caesura penthemimeres) in the middle of the line; see *Einführung in die Lateinische literatur des mittelalterliches Europa*, U. Kindermann, Turnhout, 1989, pp. 113, 117–20.
28. In Santiago de Compostela a similar scattering of letters can be seen next to the statue of St. James on the west front (Fachada da Praza do Obradoiro).
29. Forsyth (2008), p. 166.
30. Schapiro (2006), p. 6.

Figure 22. **Sarcophagus of Bernward of Hildesheim.**

This monument made for Bernward, bishop of
Hildesheim, shortly after his death in 1022, shows fully
developed Romanesque capitals. Bernward was councillor
to Emperor Otto II and his Empress Theophanu and tutor
to Otto III. He also commissioned the magnificent bronze
doors of Hildesheim (1015). The letters on the sarcophagus
are not yet as varied as those in later inscriptions though
most features characteristic of Romanesque capitals are
present. A's are flat topped, some C's are angular, and G is
spiralling. M has short diagonals, and O recurs in several
narrow and pointed versions. Q has a short tail, and the leg
of R is only a single curve. The letters show little difference
between thick and thin parts, straight parts widen toward
their ends, and serifs are short and triangular.

Figure 23. **Inscription (and detail) commemorating the
consecration of the church of St. Stephen, Waha.**

The consecreation in 1050 of the church of St. Stephen in
Waha, eastern Belgium, is commemorated by this inscription, which contains numerous notable features. The serifs
are large, cut clearly and are often forked; angular versions
of round letters are lacking. T is half-uncial with a rounded
underside, and many uncials occur as well including M
(top right). K appears (third line from top) with a curled
upper diagonal in K(A)L(ENDIS). A's have top bars extending to the left and most incorporate broken middle (cross)
bars. G is spiralling and several S's lean to the left. In the
third and fourth lines from the base, near the middle, con-
tractions for … RUM occur. L from (L)EODECENSI is missing
(fourth line from top). In the same line the terminal M
has been excised from HONORE(M); the resulting HONORE
is equally acceptable in medieval Latin. In the line below
(fifth from top) VICTORIOSIS has been spelled correctly,
presumably in place of a previous error.

Figure 24. **Sarcophagus of Humbertus.**

Figure 25. **Relief sculpture, Toulouse.**

In 1988 restoration work on the Basilica of St. Servatius in Maastricht brought to light the sarcophagus of Humbertus, builder of this church and provost from around 1063 until his death in 1086.[31] The heavy lid, which is broken and now lies next to the sarcophagus, originally concealed the inscription from view. The inscription's magnificent large letters carved into the rim of the sarcophagus can now be seen through a small opening in the floor on the west side of the church. A lead cross with a lengthy inscription giving information about the construction of the church was also found inside the sarcophagus.

The inscription contains various uncial forms, including E, H and M (in HVMBERTUS). Angular versions of round letters are lacking. Half-uncial T features a winding curl that joins to the contraction VS. A's are flat topped but pointed in the case of Æ. Narrow L's have horizontal parts running obliquely upwards. M has short diagonals. Both apexes of a single N are pointed while the upper left apex of all other N's are flattened. The O of 'obiit' is slightly pointed; all others are fully rounded. R's employ elegantly curved legs. S is narrow and several lean to the left. An ampersand occurs between ECCLESIÆ and LEODINENSIS derived from the Tironian note for 'et'. A number of letters, such as uncial M and H, curled T (and its contraction), and a single R, are all ornamented with a small terminal ball. This group resembles letters found at the Pieterskerk, Utrecht, which were made more than sixty years later.

31. De la Haye (1988), p. 327.

The bold handling of letterforms and texts by Romanesque stone carvers is demonstrated in this relief showing two women, one bearing a lion cub, the other a lamb. The relief dates to around 1120 and was once part of the Basilica of St. Sernin.[32] The text runs (at top): SIGNV(M) LEONIS, SIGNU(M) ARIETIS; and between and below the two women: HOC FUIT FACTUM T TEMPORE IULII CESARIS.

The letters are scattered around and between the women. Two letters among them require additional remarks: the reversed S at the bottom right and the T above TEMPORE. The T has been interpreted either as representing TOLOSÆ (i.e. Toulouse) or is a mistake by the stone carver who instead should have made an I topped by a horizontal bar to produce IN.[33] While the reversed S might also be a mistake, it could equally well provide a symmetrical pairing with the S on the left. Elsewhere in the inscription many familiar Romanesque variants letters appear.

The meaning of the sculpture is not clear. It may be a copy of an earlier sculpture or it may represent an ancient legend associated with Julius Caesar. Contemporary interpretations suggest that it makes reference to medieval zodiacal symbols: the lamb as a precursor of spring, the lion cub, of autumn. Both animals are also representations of Christ.[34]

32. Berne (1999), p. 72.
33. Berne (1999), p. 72.
34. Berne (1999), p. 72.

Figure 26. **The tympanum at Conques (and detail).**

Figure 27. **The Alverata fragment (and detail).**

The tympanum of St. Foy, the pilgrimage church at Conques in southern France, features inscriptions carved into bands between the sculptures; the tympanum itself shows traces of colourful paintwork. The whole is dated to between 1125 and 1130.[35]

The letters are fully developed Romanesque capitals. Notable among them are A's with a small flat top and both straight and broken cross bars, round and angular C and E, and capital D both in its classical form and as an uncial. G occurs in both spiralling and angular versions; the cross bar of H features a small arch at its mid-point. M has short diagonals, and its outer strokes are both straight and oblique; an uncial M also occurs. O's are pointed top and bottom, and Q is uncial. R has a double-curved leg, S usually leans to the left, and T is noticeably wide. The inscription contains some ligatures but no nested letters.

This fragment of a memorial stone is mounted to the wall in the courtyard of Sankt Maria im Kapitol, Cologne. A complete text of the inscription was published in 1645;[36] in the part now lacking, Alverata is mentioned. She was probably a nun in a convent situated at that location who died twenty days after entering the order. Nothing more is known about her.

The letterforms are unusual in that the contrast between thin and thick parts is more pronounced than in most Romanesque inscriptions. The letters are elegant with a number of striking variants. These include a graceful L in the centre of the fragment.[37] To its right an uncial D is given an elegant curl; below and to the right a B is formed from two arcs separated at the middle. Elsewhere three spiralling G's occur; the spiral of one becomes angular as it continues to turn inward. Two different ligatures for VS occur in the second line from bottom, and below at left the R is given a kinked leg. There are no angular versions of round letters.

The inscription is difficult to date. There are no traces of the approaching Gothic period though the graceful L and several other decorative forms including the uncial D and the R (lower left) point to the second half of the twelfth century.

36. Gelenius (1645); Kraus (1894), p. 267.

37. A similar L is also found in an inscription on the tympanum of 'dit du Mystère d'Apollon', dating to around 1170, Grand Curtius Museum, Liège.

35. Salvini (1969), p. 327.

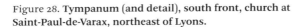

Figure 28. **Tympanum (and detail), south front, church at Saint-Paul-de-Varax, northeast of Lyons.**

Figure 29. **Capital (and detail), Basilica of Our Lady, Maastricht.**

The figure of St. Anthony can be seen on the tympanum being led by a faun to St. Paul the Hermit. The event is described by St. Jerome. The tympanum possibly dates to the middle of the twelfth century.[38]

At the right, an angular C occurs in DOCEB(AT); A is given two different forms. Q, at left, is pointed and has a long straight tail. Opposite, Q recurs but in uncial form; next to it is N with a short diagonal. The diagonals of several A's and V's become abruptly wider halfway along one or other of their strokes.

The tympanum is missing part of its keystone; the loss has halved the P in PAULV(M). The poor joins among the stones suggest that the tympanum was possibly moved at one time, or that the sculpture and the arch (and inscription) were made separately and did not join together satisfactorily when assembled. The A at the far left may belong to DOCEB(AT) (at right) or is the start of an unfinished text.[39]

This capital is in the choir aisle of the Basilica of Our Lady, Maastricht, and has been dated to 1150–60.[40] The scene is of Abraham and a servant bringing food to three men (Genesis 18: 5–8); the text, 'veneratur et orat' (He worships and prays) means that Abraham recognised God in the three men.[41]

The inscription shows a familiar Romanesque combination of square capitals and uncials. Although there are no angular versions of round letters, the second T (from left), derived from an uncial or a half-uncial, incorporates an angular element where, in other inscriptions, a curve is generally found. This T is comparable to the spiralling G in the Alverata fragment whose curve becomes angular as it spirals inward (see figure 27, detail).

38. Favreau (1997), p. 20.
39. Favreau (1997), p. 20.

40. Den Hartog (2002), p. 260.
41. Bosman (1990), p. 72–3.

Revivals

The integration of Gothic characteristics in Romanesque capitals towards the end of the twelfth century led to the latter's gradual disappearance. But in the following centuries, Romanesque capitals reappear at various times in paintings, on sculpture, in architecture, as elements in applied art, and most recently in typeface design.

Among the earliest of those who later adopted Romanesque capitals are painters working in the fourteenth and fifteenth centuries. They include Simone Martini and Lippo Memmi whose *Annunciation* of 1333, for the Siena cathedral (now in the Uffizi Gallery) shows late Romanesque capitals and variants. Later, Romanesque capitals can be found, for example, in Jan van Eyck's *Adoration of the Lamb*, 1432, in Saint Bavo Cathedral, Ghent. Van Eyck's painting includes a flat-topped A, angular C, angular and uncial E's, spiralling G, M with short diagonals and in uncial form, as well as a number of other typical Romanesque letters.[42]

In Italy in the second half of the fourteenth century, early humanists copied the Carolingian minuscule and transformed it into the humanistic minuscule. Early in the following century stone carvers imitated Romanesque capitals in their inscriptions,[43] together with a very limited number of other typical Romanesque ingredients. These capitals are now usually described as early renaissance or humanist. Commonly among the revived Romanesque capitals the slight difference between the thick and thin parts remained, as did the widening of straight parts toward their ends. But the triangular serifs often added to Romanesque capitals were now usually made smaller and sometimes disappeared altogether, while uncials and angular versions of round letters were not revived. The monumental tomb of Cardinal Chiavez in Rome, dated 1447, is exemplary of these developments (figure 30).

42. Gray (1986), p. 133; Smeyers (1996), pp. 403–14.

43. Gray (1986), pp. 122–33.

Figure 30. Tomb of Cardinal Martinez de Chiavez, Basilica of St. John Lateran, Rome, 1447.

Figure 31. Gravestone for the Huguenot Sara le Bachellé, Hameln, Lower Saxony, 1740.

Figure 32. Romanesque capitals cut into the wooden doors of the cathedral at Le Puy-en-Velay. From Day (1902b).

44. Gray (1986), p. 133.
45. Bartram (1986), pp. 20–5.
46. Gray (1986), pp. 146–50.

Discovering why painters, sculptors, and architects revived the Romanesque capitals at this time is difficult. Nicolete Gray assumed that an aversion to the Gothic played a part.[44] A second possible reason was the relative prevalence and visibility of Romanesque inscriptions at that time and up to the seventeenth century, far more so than is the case today following the rebuilding or demolition of many Romanesque buildings in the intervening period.

Although by the early sixteenth century, and over the succeeding decades, Romanesque capitals would be displaced in Rome by the revived square capital of the imperial era, elsewhere in Europe features of Romanesque capitals continued to be used in the sixteenth, seventeenth, and eighteenth centuries as one model among others. The letterforms show familiar characteristics: straight parts that widen towards the ends, often with triangular serifs; A with a broken crossbar; M with short diagonals; and R with a double-curved leg. These characteristics can found in inscriptions in Britain,[45] the Netherlands, Austria, and Germany (figure 31).[46]

In the nineteenth century Romanesque capitals were revived again, this time more accurately than in the three preceding centuries. The earlier revivals had become so varied that in many cases they only vaguely resembled their historical models. Nineteenth-century versions, on the other hand, were more faithful, while accurate reproductions could be found in books such as Henry Shaw's *The handbook of Mediaeval alphabets and devices* (1853; see figures 10, 11) and Lewis F. Day's *Lettering in ornament*, which illustrates, for example, letters on the cathedral doors at Le Puy-en-Velay (figure 32).

Figure 33. Weiss-Lapidar typeface, Emil Rudolf Weiss, *c.* 1931.

A A B C D E E F G H I J K L M
N O P Q R S T U V W X Y Z &
1 2 3 4 5 6 7 8 9 0 O . , - : ; ! ? ´ ·) /

A A B C D E E F G H I J K L M
N O P Q R S T U V W X Y Z &
1 2 3 4 5 6 7 8 9 0 O . , - : ; ! ? ´ ·) /

Figure 34. Typeface design, René Knip, for the Old Church Foundation, Amsterdam, 1999.

Twentieth-century work based on Romanesque letterforms occurs among typeface designers. One example is Weiss-Lapidar, a titling (all-capitals) alphabet in two weights by Emil Rudolf Weiss (figure 33). The letters A, E, and G were provided with Romanesque alternatives while throughout the strokes were nearly monoline, ending in very small serifs. It seems possible that the design was inspired by the nineteenth-century interest in Romanesque letters or by an increasing interest in the Romanesque period among art historians of the early twentieth century. That 'Lapidar' was made part of the typeface name suggests that Weiss had seen examples of original inscriptions though nothing is known about this.[47] A more recent example is a design by René Knip. His alphabet for the Old Church Foundation, Amsterdam, made in 1999, contains numerous references to Romanesque capitals including round and angular C, E, and T; uncial D, H, M, and U; spiralling G; and pointed O (figure 34). Knip's source was the German edition of Day's *Alphabets old & new*, from which he developed this fantasy alphabet.[48]

47. In his recent biography of Weiss, Cinamon (2010), p. 109, remarks on the 'medieval character' of Weiss-Antiqua, a typeface related to Weiss-Lapidar and released by Bauersche Giesserei at the same time (1931). Nothing further has been discovered about the relationship between Weiss's work and medieval sources. Weiss (1875–1942) made frequent use of Romanesque-like letterforms for book covers and title pages, as did other German typographers including Ernst Schneidler; it seems that none of them recorded their reasons for doing so.

48. Rene Knip, e-mail to the author, 26 March 2012. Lewis F. Day, *Alte und neue alphabete*, 1922, revised by Hermann Delitsch, Leipzig: Karl W. Hiersemann Verlag.

Bibliography

Several sources cited below offer substantial overviews of the topic. Nicolete Gray's *A history of lettering* (1986) contains valuable illustrations of Romanesque capitals in their historical context, in manuscripts as well as inscriptions. Her introduction to the subject is helpful though I disagree with her underlying thesis that the Romanesque was a period only of letterform experimentation without stable, durable or fixed models. Walter Koch's *Inschriften-paläographie des abendländischen Mittelalters und der früheren Neuzeit* (2007) shows and discusses Romanesque inscriptions both in historical and geographical contexts though again I am unable to agree with his conclusion that Romanesque letterforms are only transitional between Carolingian and Gothic. The more than one hundred publications in the series 'La nuit des temps' by Zodiaque show work across the whole of Romanesque Europe. Although the series focuses on architecture, many important inscriptions are illustrated and described. Inscriptions in Germany are also illustrated and meticulously documented in the series *Die Deutschen Inschriften* (more than 80 volumes by several publishers). The aim of this long-term project is to cover the whole of Germany. The 'Corpus des Inscriptions de la France médiévale' (CNRS Éditions) has a similar aim for inscriptions in France. Many inscriptions may also be found online at 'The corpus of Romanesque sculpture in Britain and Ireland' (www.crsbi.ac.uk) and 'Deutsche Inschriften online' (www.inschriften.net).

Arens, F. V. (1958). *Die Inschriften der Stadt Mainz von früh-mittelalterlichen Zeit bis 1650*. Stuttgart: A. Druckenmüller Verlag

Arnold, J. H. (2009). *What is medieval history?* Cambridge: Polity Press

Banti, O. (1996). *Le epigrafi e le scritte obituarie del duomo di Pisa*. Pisa: Pacini Editore

Barral i Altet, X. (2000). *La Cathédrale du Puy-en-Velay*. Paris: Skira/Seuil

Barral i Altet, X. (2002). Romanesque art: formation of the style, in: *Sculpture from antiquity to the present day*. Cologne: Taschen

Barral i Altet, X. (2003). *Chronologie de l'art du moyen âge*. Paris: Flammarion

Bartram, A. (1986). *The English lettering tradition*. London: Lund Humphries

Berges, W. (1983). *Die älteren Hildesheimer Inschriften*. Göttingen: Vandenhoeck & Ruprecht

Berne, C. (ed.). (1999). *Romanesque sculpture*. Toulouse: Musée des Augustins

Bischoff, B. (1993). *Latin paleography*. Cambridge: Cambridge University Press

Bosman, A. F. W. (1990). *De Onze Lieve Vrouwekerk te Maastricht*. Zutphen: De Walburg Pers

Brown, M. P. (2011). *The Lindisfarne Gospels*. London: The British Library

Cahn, W. (1974). *The Romanesque wooden doors of Auvergne*. New York: New York University Press

Cahn, W. (1982). *La Bible Romane*. Fribourg: Office du Livre

Carruthers, M. J. (2009). 'Varietas: a word of many colours', *Poetica: Zeitschrift für Sprach- und Literaturwissenschaft*, 41, Band 2009, Heft 1–2, pp. 11–32

Cassanelli, R. (1996). 'La cathédrale de Modène', in F. Aceto (ed.), *Chantiers médiévaux*. Paris: Desclée de Brouwer

Cinamon, G. (2010). *Emil Rudolf Weiss*. Oldham: Incline Press

Coldstream, N. (1991). *Masons and sculptors*. London: The British Museum Press

Conant, K. J. (1973). *Carolingian and Romanesque architecture 800 to 1200*. Middlesex: Penguin Books

Covi, D. A. (1986). *The inscription in fifteenth century Florentine painting*. New York: Garland

Day, L. F. (1902a). *Alphabets old & new*. London: Batsford

Day, L. F. (1902b). *Lettering in ornament*. London: Batsford

Debiais, V., R. Favreau and C. Treffort (2008). 'L'évolution de l'écriture épigraphique en France au Moyen Âge et ses enjeux historiques', in *Bibliothèque de l'École des Chartes*, vol. 165. Paris: Librairie Droz

De la Haye, R. (1988). 'Humbertus' historie herschreven II', in *De Sint Servaas* 41/42. Maastricht: Stichting Historische Reeks Maastricht

Den Hartog, E. (1992). *Romanesque architecture and sculpture in the Meuse valley*. Leeuwarden: Eisma

Den Hartog, E. and E. de Bièvre (eds) (1996). '"… Foderunt manus meas et pedes meos": on the iconography of the twelfth-century reliefs in the Pieterskerk in Utrecht', in *Utrecht: Britain and the Continent*. London: Maney

Den Hartog, E. (2002). *Romanesque sculpture in Maastricht*. Maastricht: Bonnefantenmuseum

Den Hartog, E. (2003). *De weg naar het paradijs*. Maastricht: Stichting Historische Reeks Maastricht

Dercsényi, D. (1975). *Romanesque architecture in Hungary*. Budapest: Corvina

Duby, G. (2002). Introduction to The expansion of Gothic, in: *Sculpture from antiquity to the present day*. Cologne: Taschen,

Du Colombier, P. (1972). *Les chantiers des cathédrales*. Paris: Picard

Favreau, R. and J. Michaud (1982). 'Ville de Toulouse', in *Corpus des Inscriptions de la France médiévale*, vol. 7. Paris: CNRS Éditions

Favreau, R. (1997). *Épigraphie médiévale*. Turnhout: Brepols

Fernie, E. (1996). Introduction to 'Romanesque', in *The dictionary of art*, vol. 26. Oxford: Oxford University Press

Fernie, E. (2010). 'Romanesque architecture', in C. Rudolph (ed.), *A companion to medieval art*. Chichester: Wiley-Blackwell

Fillitz, H. (1993). 'Inschrifttafel eines Gemmenkreuzes', in *Bernward von Hildesheim und das Zeitalter der Ottonen*. Hildesheim: Bernward Verlag

Forsyth, I. H. (2008). 'Word-play in the cloister at Moissac', in C. Hourihane (ed.), *Romanesque art and thought in the twelfth century*. Princeton: Department of Art and Archaeology, Princeton University

Fossi, G. (2005). *Romanesque & gothic*. New York: Sterling

Fuchs, R. (2006). 'Die Inschriften der Stadt Trier (bis 1500)', in *Die deutschen Inschriften*, vol. 70. Wiesbaden: Reichert

Gaborit, J.-R. (ed.). (2005). *L'art Roman au Louvre*. Paris: Fayard

Gaborit, J.-R. (2010). *La sculpture romane*. Paris: Éditions Hazan

Gandolfo, F. (2008). 'La façade sculptée', in P. Piva (ed.), *L'esprit des pierres*. Milan: CNRS Éditions

Gelenius, A. (1645). *De admiranda sacra et civili magnitudine Coloniae …*. Cologne: Kalcovius

Gose, E. (1958). *Katalog der frühchristlichen Inschriften in Trier*. Berlin: Gebr. Mann

Gray, N. (1986). *A history of lettering*. Oxford: Phaidon

Hagen, K. (2000). *Biblical interpretation in the Middle Ages and the Reformation*. Mankato: Bethany Lutheran College

Hamel, C. de. (1994). *A history of illuminated manuscripts*. London: Phaidon

Hermann, S. (2011). 'Die Inschriften der Stadt Essen', in *Die deutschen Inschriften*, vol. 81. Wiesbaden: Reichert

Higgitt, J. (1990). 'The stone-cutter and the scriptorium', in *Epigraphik 1988*. Vienna: Österreichische Akademie der Wissenschaften

Higgitt, J. (1999). 'Epigraphic lettering and book script in the British Isles', in *Inschrift und Material, Inschrift und Buchschrift*. München: Verlag der Bayerischen Akademie der Wissenschaften

Jászai, G. (1986). *Mittelalterliche Glasmalereien*. Münster: Westfälisches Landesmuseum

Kendall, C. B. (1998). *The allegory of the church*. Toronto: University of Toronto Press

Kingsley Porter, A. (1928). *Spanish Romanesque sculpture*. Florence: Pantheon

Koch, W. (2001). 'Insular influences in inscriptions on the continent', in J. Higgitt, K. Forsyth, D. N. Parsons (eds), *Roman, Runes and Ogham*, Donington: Shaun Tyas

Koch, W. (2007). *Inschriftenpaläographie des abendländischen Mittelalters und der früheren Neuzeit*. Vienna and Munich: R. Oldenbourg Verlag

Kraus, F. X. (1894). *Die christlichen Inschriften der Rheinlande*, vol. 2. Freiburg and Leipzig: J. C. B. Mohr

Le Goff, J. (2006). *De cultuur van middeleeuws Europa*. Amsterdam: Wereldbibliotheek

Leisinger, H. (1956). *Romanische Bronzen*. Zürich: Europa Verlag

Mende, U. (1983). *Die Bronzetüren des Mittelalters*. Munich: Hirmer Verlag

Morison, S. (1972). *Politics and script*. Oxford: Oxford University Press

Oakeshott, W. (1959). *Classical inspiration in medieval art*. London: Chapman & Hall

Okasha, E. (1971). *Hand-list of Anglo-Saxon non-Runic inscriptions*. Cambridge: Cambridge University Press

Olson, D. R. (1994). *The world on paper*. Cambridge: Cambridge University Press

Panhuysen, T. (1988). 'Grafmonumenten in de Sint-Servaaskerk (2), De tombe van Humbertus', in *De Sint Servaas* 39–40. Maastricht: Stichting Historische Reeks Maastricht

Petzold, A. (1995). *Romanesque art*. New York: Harry N. Abrams

Piva, P. (ed.). (2008). *L'esprit des pierres*. Paris: CNRS Éditions

Power, D. (2006). *The central Middle Ages*. Oxford: Oxford University Press

Prawer, J. (1970). *Histoire du Royaume Latin de Jérusalem*, vols 1 and 2. Paris: Éditions du Centre National de la Recherche Scientifique

Raguin, V. C. (2003). *The history of stained glass*. London: Thames & Hudson

Reudenbach, B. (2009). *Karolingische und Ottonische Kunst*. Munich: Prestel

Rozenberg, S. (ed.). (1999). *Knights of the Holy Land*. Jerusalem: Israel Museum

Salvini, R. (1969). *Medieval sculpture*. London: Michael Joseph

San Vicente, A. and A. Capellas-Lopez (1971). *Aragon roman*. L'Abbaye Sainte-Marie de la Pierre-Qui-Vire: Zodiaque

Saul, N. (2009). *English church monuments in the Middle Ages*. Oxford: Oxford University Press

Scheller, R. W. (1995). *Exemplum*. Amsterdam: Amsterdam University Press

Schwinn Schürmann, D., H.-R. Meier and E. Schmidt (2006). *Das Basler Münster*. Basel: Schwabe

Shapiro, M. (2006). *Romanesque architectural sculpture*. Chicago: University of Chicago Press

Shaw, H. (1853). *The hand book of mediaeval alphabets and devices*. London: Bernard Quaritch

Silvagni, A. and I. B. de Rossi (1935). *Inscriptiones Christianae Urbis Romae*. Rome: Ex Officina Libraria Doct. Befani

Smeyers, M. (1996). 'Jan van Eyck, archeologist?', in M. Lodewijckx (ed.), *Archeological and historical aspects of West-European societies*, Leuven: Leuven University Press

Spencer, B. (1998). *Pilgrim souvenirs and secular badges*. London: The Stationery Office

Stalley, R. (1999). *Early medieval architecture*. Oxford: Oxford University Press

Stiff, P. (2005). 'Brunelleschi's epitaph and the design of public letters in fifteenth-century Florence', in *Typography papers*, 6. London: Hyphen Press

Stratford, N. (1990). 'Romanesque sculpture in Burgundy', in *Artistes, artisans et production artistique au Moyen Age*, vol. 3. Paris: CNRS Éditions

Stratford, N. (2011). 'Les tombeaux subsistants de la grande église', in *Corpus de la sculpture de Cluny*, vol. 2. Paris: Picard

Swanson, R. N. (1999). *The twelfth-century renaissance*. Manchester: Manchester University Press

Syrett, M. (2002). *The Roman-alphabet inscriptions of medieval Trondheim*. Trondheim: Tapir

Timmers, J. J. (1969). *Handbook of Romanesque art*. New York: Macmillan

Ullman, B. L. (1997 [1932]). *Ancient writing and its influence*. Toronto: University of Toronto Press

Vergnolle, E. (2005). *L'art roman en France*. Paris: Flammarion

Verzar, C. (1992). 'Text and image in North Italian Romanesque sculpture', in D. Kahn (ed.), *The Romanesque frieze and its spectator*. London: H. Miller

Wulf, C. (2003). 'Die Inschriften der Stadt Hildesheim', *Die deutschen Inschriften*, vol. 58. Wiesbaden: Reichert

Zarnecki, G., J. Holt and T. Holland (1984). *English Romanesque art 1066–1200*. London: Arts Council of Great Britain in association with Weidenfeld & Nicolson

Zarnecki, G. (1986). 'Henri of Blois as a patron of sculpture', in *Art and patronage in the English Romanesque*. London: Society of Antiquaries

Images / photography

Berges (1983): figure 22

Gerry Leonidas: figure 12

Musée des Augustins, Toulon: figure 25

Museum Catharijneconvent, Utrecht: figure 17

Alexander Nagel: figure 31

R. Oursel, *La France romane*, pt 1, L'Abbaye de Sainte-Marie de la Pierre-Qui-Vire, 1991: figure 4a

Rijksdienst voor archeologie, cultuurlandschap en monumenten, Zeist: figure 5a–c

Royal Library, Stockholm: figure 9

Silvagni (1935): figure 15

Gerard Unger: figures 1a–c, 2a–b, 3, 4b, 7a–b, 13, 14, 18, 20a–c, 23, 24, 26, 27, 28, 29, 30

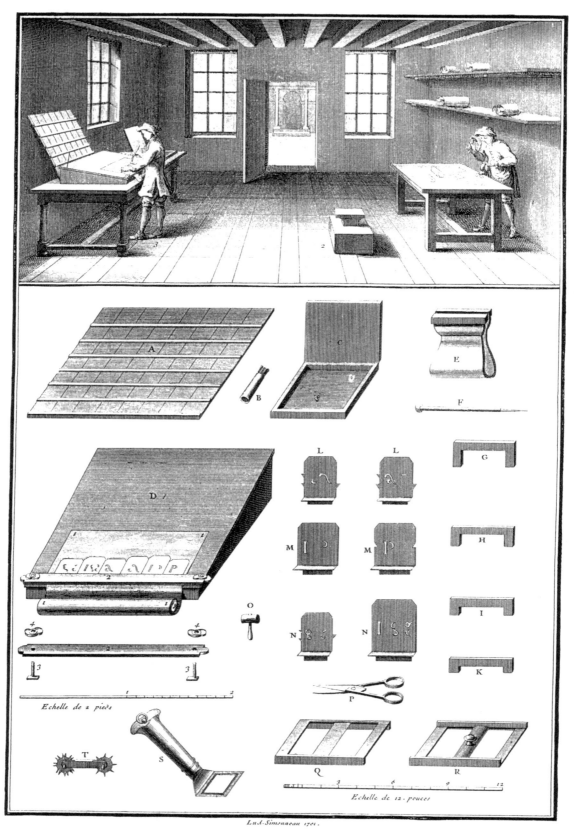

Figure 1. Engraving for Des Billettes's description of stencilling, signed 'Lud. Simonneau 1701.', 268 × 176 mm, from the album 'Les Arts et Métiers de l'Académie des Sciences', St Bride Library and Archives, SB5825 ('Plates relating to printing and kindred arts, principally engraved by L. Simonneau'). See also appendix 3, pp. 52–4 (below).

Eric Kindel
with two appendices
by Fred Smeijers

A reconstruction of stencilling based on the description by Gilles Filleau des Billettes

This essay recounts and illustrates a reconstruction and testing of tools, furniture, and working methods for stencilling texts. The description of stencilling on which the reconstruction is based was written by Gilles Filleau des Billettes as part of work on a 'description of trades' (*Description des arts et métiers*) begun in 1693 and carried out under the direction of the Académie royale des Sciences, Paris. From the reconstruction, observations and conclusions are drawn about the effectiveness of the tools, furniture, and working methods Des Billettes describes, and their likely relationship to stencilling practices of the time. Four appendices address Des Billettes's instructions for designing and spacing letters, the cutting of stencils with chisels, the engraving by Louis Simonneau that accompanies the description, and later stencil materials that incorporate features similar to those described by Des Billettes.

1. Gilles Filleau des Billettes, 'Imprimerie de Livres d'Eglise, Escriteaux ou Sentences &c.', Wing MS oversize Z4029.225, pp.166–89, The Newberry Library, Chicago. For a transcription and translation of this text, see this volume, pp.66–86; for details about the context of its compilation, and for biographical notes on Des Billettes, see this volume, pp.87–90. References to the text in the present essay are given in parentheses, e.g. (166), and correspond to pagination given in the transcription and translation. For examples of stencilled liturgical books, see below (p.47), Kindel (2003), and François (2010).

2. The issue of whether Des Billettes's description is a record of existing practices, or an improvement on them and therefore not wholly representative of contemporary work, is discussed below.

According to Gilles Filleau des Billettes, the use of stencils for marking out texts began around the middle of the seventeenth century. The practice, he says, was employed in the production of 'livres d'église', ornamental liturgical books typically made in only a single copy and customised to a particular secular or monastic church to reflect its preferred liturgical content. Des Billettes also says that stencils were used for setting out scriptural texts or maxims for interior display – on a wall, for example, or above a door.[1] Throughout the eighteenth century and into the nineteenth, in France and elsewhere in Catholic western Europe, texts in liturgical books continued to be stencilled, along with their chant notation and (variously) titles, initials, and decoration. Stencilling in secular contexts is also found during this period: for text and decoration on accounting ledgers, billheads, visiting and trade cards, and for *ex libris* and other marks of ownership in books. While surviving artefacts allow some conclusions to be drawn about how such stencilling was done, at times it is difficult to work out the details of the procedures followed and equipment used. For this reason, Des Billettes's description of stencilling, illustrated with an engraving by Louis Simonneau (figure 1), is of considerable interest.

That the stencilling of texts was well established by the time Des Billettes was writing is suggested by his lengthy treatment of the subject, though he also says so directly, remarking that it 'is currently used quite frequently as having much grace and usefulness'. (166) What is less clear is just how much of what Des Billettes describes is a reflection of contemporary stencilling practices, and how much is an elaboration or extension of them, or indeed newly invented, with the intention of improving on equipment and procedures already used in workshops where stencilling was done. For this reason, it is important to approach his text bearing in mind that it may be a record or a proposal, or both.[2]

This issue is referred to in the account of work on the 'Description des Arts et Métiers' (to which Des Billettes's text was a contribution) given in the *Histoire de l'Académie royale des sciences …* (1699): 'This survey will investigate the smallest detail of each art, difficult though it may often be both to learn from the craftsmen and to explain. It will indicate either by words or figures all the materials and tools used and all the operations of the workman. In this way innumerable techniques, full of wit and invention, but for the most part unknown, will be rescued from their obscurity. Skills will be handed down to posterity, those at least which are practised at this moment, preserved for ever in this compilation, in spite of revolution. […] The ingenious man who cannot take the trouble or has not the leisure to study a trade in the workshop can here take it in almost at a glance and will be encouraged by this to devise improvements. Nor will the Academy omit to indicate the cases where advances might be made, or at least what it considers to be desirable.' Quoted in Jammes (1965), p.73 (translation by Gillian Riley).

In the pages that follow, Des Billettes's method is scrutinized through a reconstruction of the equipment and procedures he describes. The reconstruction is summarised and illustrated with reference to relevant parts of his text. The aim of the reconstruction is to test how the conceptual dimensions of the method translate into actual work, and from this determine what characteristics are specific to it: its visual attributes, speed and order, sources of error and irregularity, physical stresses on equipment and stenciller, and more. The results should in turn offer insights into the usefulness of Des Billettes's method in its own right, and by comparison with surviving artefacts, its relationship to stencilling practices of the time.[3]

Preliminaries

Des Billettes's description, some 10,000 words in length, can be divided into four sections of varying size, according to the content of each. These are proposed only as a convenience, as they are not signalled as such by him. The first section (166) identifies the work of stencilling texts, its possible origins, and its particular nature. A lengthy second section (167–84) describes the items of equipment in detail, the principles of their design, and how they are made; a third section (184 insert) outlines the procedure of work using the ensemble of equipment. The fourth section (184–9) reviews, point by point, the advantages of this method of stencilling over other methods that might be used.

The reconstruction is described and illustrated in an order that best conveys the principles of Des Billettes's method. The order adopted departs from the order of the text in a number of places. Similarly, the narrative of the reconstruction is only a summary, and while Des Billettes's assiduous arguments are quoted in places, the reader is encouraged to turn to his text to take them in more fully. Concerning Des Billettes's technical terms and their English equivalents, these are introduced in the specific contexts where they occur and so their meanings should be generally self-evident. Two instances, though, require advance notice: *caractère*, a term Des Billettes uses to refer to the stencil plate; and *lettre*, which he uses to refer not only to letters but also (often by implication) to numerals and other signs and symbols in the set of characters. To avoid confusion, the (English) word 'character' is avoided as far as possible. Des Billettes's 'caractère' is variously translated as 'plate', 'stencil plate', or 'stencil', depending on the descriptive emphasis required, while 'letter' is used in the same encompassing sense as his 'lettre'.[4] Two other terms, *conduite* and *lumière*, which refer to quite specialized features of the equipment, are generally left untranslated.

3. The reconstruction was carried out between May 2001 and March 2002 as part of a research project funded by the Arts and Humanities Research Board (as was); the project team consisted of Andrew Gillmore (furniture and tools reconstruction), James Mosley (text and linguistic consultant), Fred Smeijers (stencil reconstruction), and Eric Kindel (project direction, stencilling). Aspects of the work were presented by Kindel and Smeijers at the annual congress of the Association Typographique Internationale in Rome (2002), and in subsequent papers; and in Kindel (2003). Elements of the reconstruction were exhibited in 'Fred Smeijers: work so far' (Koninklijke Academie van Beeldende Kunsten, The Hague, 2003; St Bride Printing Library, London, 2004), and 'Fred Smeijers and a new generation of type designers' (Catapult Gallery, Antwerp, 2006). A second phase of reconstruction took place in 2011–13 when a new set of stencils was made. It is important to note that many of the conclusions drawn from the reconstruction, and insights gained, have resulted from the close collaboration of project team members during and after the research project. Particular attention, however, should be drawn to the work of Smeijers, whose extended study of the design and making of the stencil letters proposed by Des Billettes has led to significant advances in their interpretation. These advances are incorporated into the description of the reconstruction at various points, and are discussed in appendices 1 and 2, pp. 48–51, below.

4. It is notable that Des Billettes adopts the term *caractère* rather than *patron*, though the latter was known to him. Indeed he uses 'patron' to denote the stencil employed for adding colour to playing cards in his description of that subject, which among his draft texts follows the section on stencilling. The use of 'caractère' establishes a connection with printing (*imprimerie*), as will be seen below, while at the same time suggests a separation of text stencilling from other kinds of stencil work as found, for example, in wall and furniture decoration, and in the production of playing cards, wallpaper, and *papiers peint*. In these spheres 'patron' is invariably employed; the stencils referred to were made of card (*carton*), or possibly canvas or parchment.

Figure 2. Desk, beech, 15° slope, grooved planks & tongues bonded with animal glue (work surface), dove-tailed planks (supporting box), 850 mm wide × 670 deep × 90 high at front edge of work surface. The desk, as reconstructed, differs from the engraving in its overhanging work surface, introduced to accommodate the nut-and-bolt attachments that fix the conduite. Des Billettes also recommends that the desk be covered with leather, cloth, or vellum (not shown here).

Figure 3. Conduite (details).
(a) Nut-and-bolt attachment.
(b) Raised fore-edge and
     underside.

a

b

Nature of the work
(166)

In this first section of his description, Des Billettes identifies text stencilling as a species of work and proposes a general scenario for how it came about. He then touches on its particular nature. In reference to 'true' printing (*imprimerie*, i.e. with movable type), he states that there are other arts that might also be called printing even though they do not really qualify as such and in fact are only related. One of these is the stencilling of texts. Des Billettes arrives at this conclusion by comparing stencilling with writing and printing, since it appears to share certain features with both. He decides that the relationship with printing is stronger 'owing to the specific affinity which exists between it [text stencilling] and printing, inasmuch as both employ metal characters instead of a pen'.[5] This, however, is immediately qualified 'with this difference among others, that for printing types the letter is in relief and reversed, whereas in this process [stencilling] the letters are the right way round and cut out.'

---

5. While Des Billettes does not elaborate on the affinity of the metal 'caractères' in each sphere of work, it surely extends to their respective configurations that fix and make repeatable the forms of the letters, their spacing, and their consistent baseline location. He notes several further parallels between text stencilling and printing elsewhere in his text.

Desk & conduite
(170–1) | Engraving: D, D2–4

To gain a clear understanding of the method of stencilling Des Billettes sets out, it is best to begin with his description of the desk (figure 2). The desk is comprised of a work surface covered with leather, cloth, or vellum, and sloped at 12–15 degrees. The dimensions of the work surface are left to the maker's discretion; as reconstructed, it can accommodate a maximum page width of 700 mm. (The pages of very large books are stencilled as single leaves, front and back, then bound by stab-stitching along their long edge). The timber is also left unspecified, but in any case should be 'sound, smooth, dry wood that does not twist, bow or warp'; the reconstruction uses beech, a minimally grained utility timber found in much of Europe.

At the base of the desk's work surface is the *conduite* (roughly, a 'ruler'; figure 3). It is 40 mm wide and is fastened to the desk at both ends with bolts and shaped nuts. The nuts can be loosened to allow a sheet of paper or vellum to be slid beneath the conduite, which is then tightened down. A narrower width of 'wool or fabric ribbon' is glued to the lower underside of the conduite (here cotton webbing was used); it makes direct contact with the sheet and holds it in place. Importantly, the ribbon also serves to lift the conduite so the specially configured stencils can be slotted under its fore-edge.

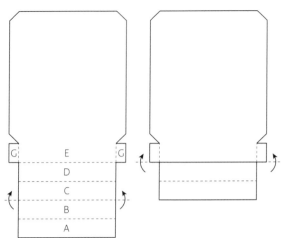
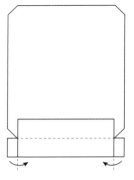
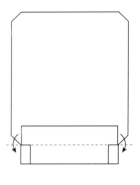
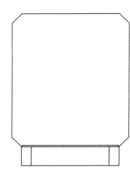

Figure 4. Diagram of plate, unfolded (left); sequence of folds; completed plate (right). Des Billettes supplies sample dimensions (given at right) but recommends making plates of various widths to suit the different letters. Three widths were reconstructed: 20, 28, and 36 *lignes* (45, 63, and 81 mm).

Des Billettes's dimensions (unfolded):
- overall width: 2 *pouces* ('inches') (24 lignes, 54 mm)
- overall height: 4 pouces (108 mm)
- height of bands A–E: 4 lignes (9 mm) each
- width of bands A–E: 20 lignes (45 mm)
- width of lugs G: 2 lignes (4.5 mm) each (1 ligne = *c*. 2.256 mm; metric values, above, are approximate. Reconstructed plates follow these dimensions, apart from the dimensions for overall width and the width of bands A–E.)

Figure 5. Vice extension, brass (jaws) and steel (spring body), 66 mm high × 69 wide × 31 deep. The vice extension is held in a rougher vice; the cut brass sheets for the plates are hammered over its edges to produce sharp, precise folds.

Figure 6. Plate folded, brass, actual size (63 mm width).

Figure 7. Plate under conduite.

Stencil plate configuration | character set
(167–9, 185) | Engraving: E, L, M, N, O, P

The construction of Des Billettes's stencil plate (*caractère*) is relatively complicated, involving more than simply folding a brass plate upward at its base to form a handle. (Stencils of this kind were apparently common or even conventional when Des Billettes was writing and he criticises them towards the end of his text; see (185), also figure A4.3, p. 56, below). The material specified is brass: 'one takes pieces of very thin brass of the kind called "latten" ... as thin as they can be while keeping the strength that will make them last and stand up to the work that must be done with them'.[6] (167) Des Billettes recommends the thickness precisely: a twelfth part of a *ligne*, i.e. a *ligne*

6. See Kindel (2003), p. 70, n. 15, where French terminology associated with brass is discussed in greater detail.

seconde, or just under 0.2 mm. The brass is cut to the rectangular dimensions required, further trimmed to a specific shape (figure 4), then folded (by hammering) in a vice extension (figure 5) using a wood mallet. The result is a plate that is stiff and robust, easy to pick up, and that slots securely and consistently under the conduite (figures 6, 7).

Des Billettes recommends making plates of several widths suited to the various letters. The number of plates needed is determined by the extent of the character set. Des Billettes states that 'around eighty or more characters will be needed' including 'small and big letters, which are to be precise what we call in printing lowercase and capital letters. Then one must have some double letters, punctuation marks, figures etc., and if one wishes to add to that some reference signs, musical notes, and a few others, this can add up to at least a hundred or so characters depending on the purposes of the person who wishes to use them'. (169)

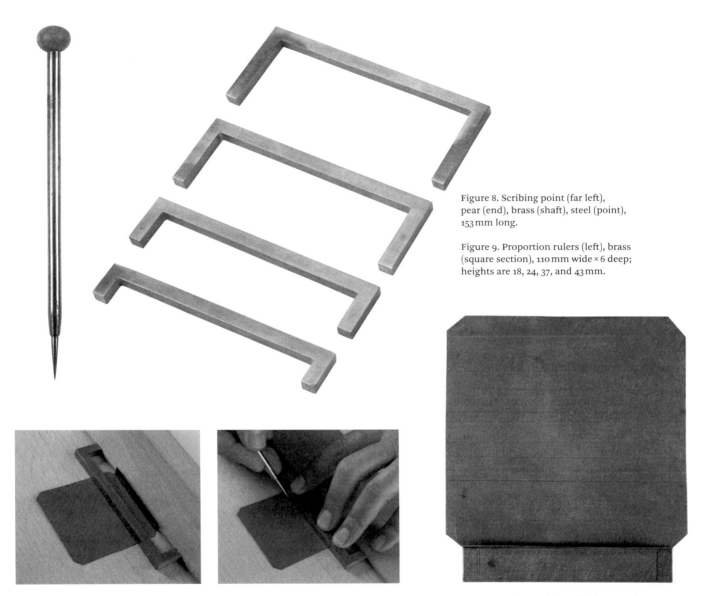

Figure 8. Scribing point (far left),
pear (end), brass (shaft), steel (point),
153 mm long.

Figure 9. Proportion rulers (left), brass
(square section), 110 mm wide × 6 deep;
heights are 18, 24, 37, and 43 mm.

Figure 10. (a) Plate with proportion ruler in position (left);
(b) scribing one of the four proportion lines (right).

Figure 11. Plate, with inscribed proportions.

Inscribing the plate: letter proportions
(170–3) | Engraving: F, G, H, I, K

After the plates have been made in the number and to the several widths required, each is readied to receive the letter that will be cut from it. Des Billettes observes that in printing 'one of the greatest defects (inherent) in it is that the alignment of the letters is not good, but wavers up and down, or is otherwise uneven'. (170) The first steps towards countering similar defects in stencilling have already been described: the conduite, as it holds the substrate and the plates in place, fixes the position of each relative to the other; what remains is to fix the relative position of the letters. This is done with the four specially designed proportion rulers whose height dimensions correspond to the

capital height, x-height, baseline, and descender depth of the letters (figure 9). After a blank plate is slotted securely under the conduite, each ruler is placed successively over the plate and horizontal guidelines inscribed across it with the scribing tool (figures 8, 10). Because the ends of the rulers rest only on the fore-edge of the conduite, the four guidelines on the plate are always in precisely the same position relative to the conduite despite any irregularities in the plate's folded construction (figure 11). The rulers thus establish both consistent proportions among all the letters to be scribed onto the plates, and consistently positioned baselines. When the stencils come to be used, it will not be necessary to align them manually since their configuration, in coordination with the conduite, will ensure this by default.

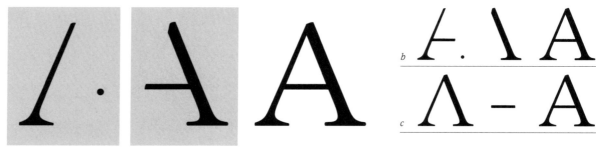

Figure 12, a–c. Composite constructions of 'A'.
(a) As reconstructed, with guiding-mark or dot (*repère*).

(b) Variant 1.
(c) Variant 2.

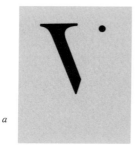

Figure 13, a–c. Composite construction of 'g'.
(a) As reconstructed, with guiding-mark.

(b) Variant 1.
(c) Variant 2.

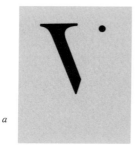

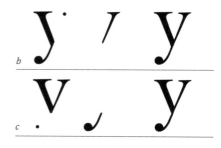

Figure 14, a–c. Composite construction of 'y', which is not
strictly necessary, but is recommended by Des Billettes.
(a) As reconstructed, with guiding-mark.

(b) Variant 1.
(c) Variant 2. This design would suffer from
the weakness in the plate to which Des
Billettes refers, as the counter would be
attached by only a narrow strip of brass.

Principles of composite letters and letter spacing
(173–8, 185–6) | Engraving: L, M, N

Having fixed the relative positions of the conduite, the
paper, and the stencil plates (and their letters), Des Billettes then introduces the principle to be followed for con-
figuring the letters themselves. It arises from his view that
the 'breaks' typical of stencilled letters, formed by 'attachments' (*tenons*, i.e. ties or bridges) in the stencil plate,
mean that when marked out 'the letter has something
missing and is imperfect because its shape is interrupted
by blank space(s)' (174). These blank spaces (breaks)
require the stenciller to 'take the pains to finish off these
shapes with a pen or a brush' (174), something Des Billettes
worried might be done poorly, or not at all (185–6).

To avoid the defect, one which 'greatly disfigures the
beauty of this (kind of) printing', Des Billettes proposes
splitting into two 'halves' those letters that, when cut as
stencils, would normally require attachments. When the
halves are marked out consecutively, they recombine to
form a composite letter that appears complete and unbro-
ken. Des Billettes also recommends a composite design for
letters that do not strictly require it, such as v or y, in order
to avoid weaknesses in the stencil plate where their counters would otherwise be attached by only a narrow strip
of brass (174).

To arrive at a composite configuration, two identical
letters are scribed onto the plate side-by-side. Cut from
each of these are the halves that will together form the
whole. Des Billettes does not specify exactly how each

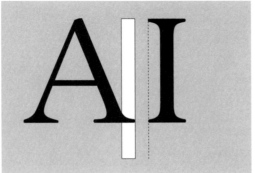

Figure 15. *Lumière* and inter-letter space.
(a) Lumière, is a 'window' through which the previously-stencilled letter is seen. The lumière may extend from the captial height to the baseline, or to the descender depth (as here).
(b) Inter-letter space, is specified as the stem width of capital 'I'. For simplicity, the width for the lumière is made the same as the inter-letter space.

Figure 16. Inter-letter spaces. Des Billettes states that the inter-letter space should be measured between the extremities of adjacent letters, whatever those extremities are (serif, bowl, curve, etc.).

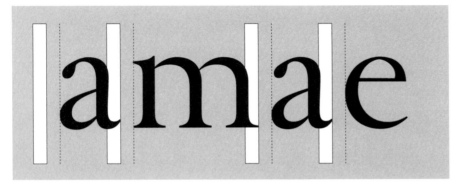

Figure 17. Letter sequence showing the position of (successive) lumières, and the inter-letter spacing that results.

letter is split apart other than advising that whatever the division, the strength of the plate must be preserved and, importantly, where the halves come together, they overlap slightly ('a soldering together') to avoid new, accidental breaks (175, 177). To help the stenciller join the halves of the letter accurately, Des Billettes specifies a guiding-mark or dot (*repère*), which is (usually) positioned to the right of the first half of the letter. The dot is stencilled along with the first half; then, after guiding the placement of the second of the letter, it is covered over when the second half is stencilled (175–7).

The final element to be added is the means of spacing the letters. Des Billettes states that the distance between letters should be the stem width of capital I (177–8). To gauge this distance while stencilling, he specifies a *lumière*

(roughly, a 'window') to be cut from the plate, to the left of the letter. The lumière takes the shape of a tall, narrow rectangle extending from the capital height to the baseline or descender depth (which of the two is not specified). Its right vertical edge is positioned at the recommended distance (stem width of capital 'I') from the leftmost extremity of the letter. If, when stencilling, the rightmost extremity of a just-stencilled letter, as seen through the lumière, touches the lumière's right vertical edge, then the plate is correctly positioned, and the spacing between the two letters, as stencilled, will also be correct (178).

See also appendix 1: Designing and spacing the letters, pp. 48–9, below.

Figure 18. Stencil plate with a pair of identical letters ('A'), lumière, and guiding-mark drawn in position. Actual size.

The letter is assigned to a plate width best able to accommodate it. Once the four proportion guidelines are inscribed on the plate, the letters are set out accordingly. Des Billettes states that for a letter requiring a composite construction, the pair of letters should be drawn, side-by-side, in their entirety. The lumière is also incised in its correct position. Des Billettes offers no guidance on the lateral position of the elements on the plate. In practice, the two element groups (1: lumière + left half of letter + guiding-mark; 2: right half of letter) are best placed equidistant from each other and from the sides of the plate, exploiting a maximum of the plate to shield the stencil brush. Letters that are not composite in design are simply centred on the plate, along with their lumière.

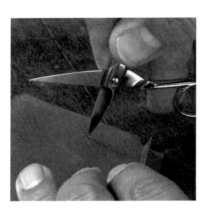
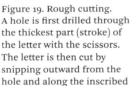

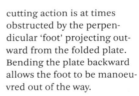

Figure 19. Rough cutting. A hole is first drilled through the thickest part (stroke) of the letter with the scissors. The letter is then cut by snipping outward from the hole and along the inscribed outline. Provided the scissors are very sharp, and there is minimal 'play' between the two arms, they work relatively well, though they are still only able to reach into the larger, wider parts of the letter. Their cutting action is at times obstructed by the perpendicular 'foot' projecting outward from the folded plate. Bending the plate backward allows the foot to be manoeuvred out of the way.

Letters: inscribing on the plate, and cutting
(169, 173, 178, 186) | Engraving: P

In addition to expatiating on the principles of the composite letter, the guiding-mark, and the lumière, Des Billettes describes how they are delineated on the plate and makes several other points about their design. He is surprisingly brief about these matters and the few comments he does offer are scattered throughout his text.

The task begins by drawing the letter (or pair of letters) 'with all the possible accuracy and in the most beautiful proportions' (173). Although Des Billettes does not specify exactly how this is done, his description implies that letters are freely outlined (*dessigner*) but according to the proportional guidelines set by the rulers. This is confirmed in his summary in section four of the text when he asserts that making the letters twice 'is not difficult for someone with a steady hand' and takes little additional time 'if one has the model in front of one' (186). Concerning the style of the letters he is again unspecific, stating only that they should be 'the letters one wants to cut' (169). He offers more guidance on size, advising that it would be 'very difficult or at least quite useless to make any as small as *Gros Parangon* [*c*.22-point Anglo-American], because even if they could be well executed, there would be even more difficulty in marking / printing them out properly' (169). Instead he recommends *Gros Canon* (*c*.44-point) or larger.

After the letters are drawn on the plate, along with the lumière and, if needed, the guiding-mark, the next task is to cut them out. Des Billettes suggests that it is the cutting

Figure 20. Rough cut, and stencilled proof.

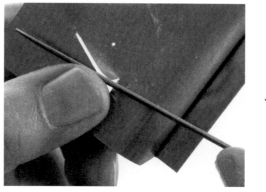

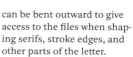

Figure 21. Preliminary filing, and stencilled proof. Much filing is needed to refine the rough cut. Parts of the plate can be bent outward to give access to the files when shaping serifs, stroke edges, and other parts of the letter.

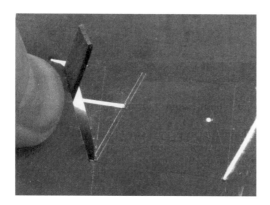

Figure 22. Additional filing. Once the shapes and details of the rough cut are sufficiently well refined, further filing may be needed to add weight to the letter, making it consistent with the weight of others.

Figure 23. Completed letter, and stencilled proof.

wherein 'lies all the skill of this little art' (169), and that its success mostly 'depends on the particular skill of the person who undertakes the task'. (178)

The tools and procedure of work are given: 'the best way to open or to cut them out [i.e. the letters] is to make a hole at one end of the thickest points of the shape with very sharp scissors [*cizeaux*], then continue cutting with the point of the same scissors as close to the outline as possible. And then for the remaining uneven parts or what(ever) remains to be done to finish off the contours, where scissors are not sufficient, one can easily complete the task with small files of a very small gauge, [that are] flat, round, semi-rounded, like a knife, in the form of a sage leaf, and all sorts of other shapes according to the different varieties of letters, such as the small files commonly used by clockmakers'. (178) This description is confirmed by Simonneau's engraving, which shows scissors (P) immediately below several stencil plates (L, M, and N), though no files are illustrated.

Despite the apparent clarity of this description, there remains some ambiguity about the word for scissors, 'cizeaux', as it is also the plural form of 'chisel'. The ambiguity increases in light of a more precise phrasing, 'une paire de cizeaux', that Des Billettes might have used to describe the scissors but does not. While the use of scissors is reasonable on the evidence of the text and the engraving, the production of stencils with chisels was also tested. See appendix 2: Cutting the letters with chisels, pp. 50–1, below.

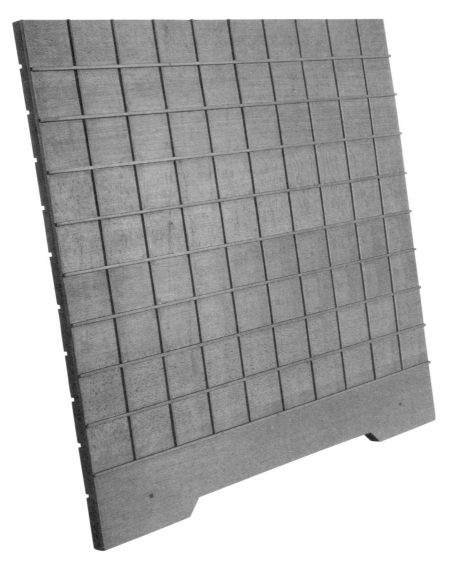

Figure 25. Lettercase (detail), compartments with stencils. The lower ledge of the compartment protrudes sufficiently to provide a secure rest for the stencil, but not so far that it interferes with picking up the stencil by its foot (handle).

Figure 24. Lettercase, beech, grooved planks & tongues bonded with animal glue, 895 mm high × 955 wide. The lettercase, which Des Billettes describes as 'little', must in fact be relatively large to accommodate a set of 80–100 stencils; as reconstructed it has 90 compartments. It is best positioned to the left or right of the stenciller, rather than behind the desk, and low enough for all its compartments to be easily reached.

Figure 26. Lettercase (back), with supports. Such supports, which enable the lettercase to stand on its own, are not described by Des Billettes; the engraving shows the lettercase leaning against a wall.

Auxillary furniture and tools | ink materials
(178–84, 187) | Engraving: A, B, C, Q/R, S, T

To organise and hold the stencils, Des Billettes proposes 'to have behind the desk a little case somewhat similar to that used in printing; that is to say [like] a printer's type case divided into as many little compartments or cells as there are stencils, but with the following difference among others, that each compartment must be very shallow, because only enough space is needed for a single stencil, which must be easy to pick up by its foot. This case must be almost vertical or sloping very slightly backward, but in a word placed in such a way that (every)one can have it within sight and within reach to pick up the stencils easily.' (178) (figures 24–26)

To stencil the parts of a composite letter and at the same time prevent the stencil brush from straying into the lumière, two different masking tools are specified. The more complicated is the *sergent*, roughly a 'sash-clamp' (figure 27). It consists of a frame whose inside vertical dimension is slightly less than that of the stencil plate's upper section. A *curseur* or *coulisse* ('cursor' or 'slide') is set into grooves inside the frame. As the names suggest, the cursor can be slid left or right to make the frame opening(s) wider and narrower. By placing the sash-clamp over a stencil positioned on the conduite and adjusting the size of the frame opening accordingly, those parts of the stencil that should not receive ink can be covered (178–81).

The other masking tool, the *patte*, roughly a 'holdfast', is far simpler: it is a fixed frame (i.e. not adjustable) set

a

b

Figure 27. Sash-clamp (*sergent*), from above (a) and below (b), brass, 110 mm long × 61 wide × 10 high (excluding cursor button).

Figure 29. Ink box, beech, brass (hinges), lead (lining), 300 mm × 300 × 45 (closed). Simonneau illustrates the box with a lid, though Des Billettes makes no mention of it.

Figure 28. Holdfast (*patte*), brass (frame) and oak (handle), 62 mm (width of frame) × 150 (length of handle).

Figure 30. Ink box (detail), showing lead sheet folded into box interior.

Figure 31. Brush, pear (handle), and boar bristle, 85 mm.

into a wood handle (181–2) (figure 28). Its smaller dimensions allow it to be used in confined spaces, for instance near the inner margin of an already bound book (182). In addition to their masking functions, both tools are used to press the stencil plate flat to the substrate.

Several further items are associated with the stencilling ink. A shallow, lead-lined box is specified to contain the ink workings (figures 29–30). To prepare the workings, gum tragacanth or gum arabic (binders) is mixed with soot, or ivory or peach kernel ash, together with a small amount of existing (wet) ink, to form a paste. The paste is then spread onto the lining to form a base, which dries. Drops of wet ink are subsequently added to the base prior to stencilling, into which the brush is rubbed to take up the ink; any surplus is wiped onto the lead lining. Des Billettes gives

recipes for black and red inks (183; neither ink was reconstructed). The size of the ink box is, by implication, large enough to accommodate bases of both colours. To apply the ink, a common brush or paintbrush is recommended, which could be procured 'ready-made from the workers who make whisks and consists simply of a tuft of very stiff pig or boar bristles with cords wrapped tightly around the thick end of the bristle' (184). The latter should be trimmed straight across, a profile that is typical of stencil brushes.

The final tool in the ensemble is a toothed wheel for pricking interlinear increments down the left and right margins, a tool known to scribes (see Johnston, 1908, pp. 99–100). Des Billettes proposes that its teeth be adjustable, to prick out whatever increments are needed by the stenciller (187; this tool was not reconstructed).

Figure 32. Stencilling underway. Prior to stencilling, the
sheet of paper or vellum is
slipped under the loosened
conduite. Prickings already
made along the margins,
which establish inter-linear
spaces, are aligned to the
fore-edge of the conduite,
which is then tightened
down. Simonneau's engraving
shows the lower part of the
sheet rolled around a dowel;
it is not mentioned by Des
Billettes (nor shown here).

Figure 33, a–c. Masking.
(a) Stencil + sash-clamp.
(b) Stencil + holdfast.
(c) Stencil + hand (i.e. no
    masking); this method
    relies entirely on careful
    brush-work.

a   *b*   *c*

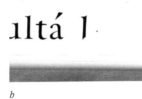

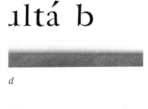

a   *b*   *c*   *d*

Figure 34, a–d (above).
Marking out a letter.
(a) Stencil in position:
    first half of letter.
(b) First half + guiding-mark
    stencilled.
(c) Stencil in position:
    second half of letter.
(d) Letter completed.

Figure 35, a–b (right).
Letter spacing.
(a) Previous 'b' aligned to
    right edge of lumière.
(b) Next letter marked out.

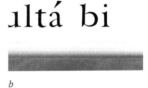

a   *b*

Procedure of stencilling
(183–4, 184 insert, 188)

Stencilling with the ensemble of equipment begins with a
paper or vellum substrate. Des Billettes briefly describes
their preparation at the close of the text's second section
(184), stating simply that the paper should be the whitest, most well-sized and smoothest that can be obtained,
and that it or the vellum should be of the finest quality.
The procedure of stencilling is then described in the third
section. Des Billettes states at the outset that how the
ensemble of equipment is to be used 'is easy to judge …
from what has been said'; and indeed this third section
is evidently an afterthought, as it is written on a separate
loose leaf and inserted into the cahier, using a symbol to
mark its position between the end of the second section
and the beginning of the fourth. Although Des Billettes
rehearses the procedure in full, it will be sufficient to

highlight several points not already mentioned in the second section.

Before the sheet of paper or vellum is slipped under the
loosened conduite, it is pricked along both margins to
establish interlinear increments, using the toothed wheel.
As Des Billettes describes them, the prickings function as
horizontal alignments for the conduite's fore-edge, rather
than as line-ends for the text; the configuration of the
stencil means that the baseline of the text would therefore
sit slightly higher. After a reminder to secure the sheet in
position by tightening down the conduite, the use of the
stencils in combination with the sash-clamp is reviewed.
Letter spacing using the lumière is included in the explanation, though no advice is given on spacing between
words.

Des Billettes advises twice more that excess ink should
be removed from the brush. (Earlier, in the second section,
he recommends the use of a paper cone filled with ink,

Figure 36. Stencilled text, actual size. Expected features of text stencilled according to Des Billettes's method.
(1) Letters without breaks (i.e. composite, where required).
(2) No baseline guide.
(3) Prickings for interlinear spaces positioned below the baseline (not visible here).
(4) Consistent spaces between letters but not words.

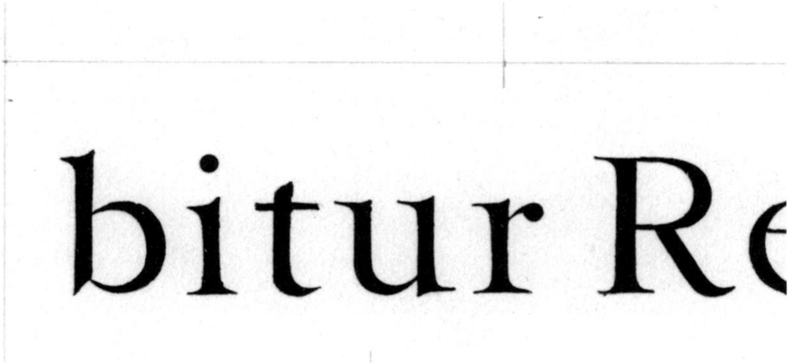

bitur Re

um exultá b

Figure 37. Stencilled letters, actual size. Possible faults generated by Des Billettes's method (left to right).
(1) Mis-aligned halves; guiding-mark visible.
(2) Incomplete inking of second half; guiding-mark visible.
(3) Inked brush strays into lumière, leaving a ghost.
(4) Mis-aligned halves, with (apparent) breaks into the upper interior space only.

b b N &

over which is placed a sponge to moderate the uptake of ink by the brush; if the brush were to become saturated, the excess ink could be wiped onto the lead sheet in the ink box; 183–4.) He also gives an indication of the brush action: '[move] it around several times to the right and to the left until one sees that the letter is clearly marked out' (184 insert), having earlier noted that 'if the letter does not appear deep black at first it will become so subsequently' (183; this change in appearance is characteristic of iron gall ink on exposure to air). To work cleanly, and in particular to prevent ink from seeping under the plate, Des Billettes reiterates the need to press firmly down on the masking tools to flatten out surface deformations in both the stencil plate and the substrate.

The description of the stencilling procedure concludes at this point. It is worth noting that Des Billettes only discusses the stencilling of consecutive lines of text; he offers no comments on procedures for planning and executing

the many other page features typical of stencilled books (see discussion below, p. 46). At (188), in the final lines of section four, brief reference is made to ornamenting the work with 'all sorts of stencils bearing fleurons, vignettes, cartouches, etc., which are used in printing'. These might be left as stencilled, or form the basis for painted colour-work if stencilled first in outline. Des Billettes cuts short this description of ornamenting in anticipation of it being dealt with elsewhere, as 'an art which belongs to illumination or to miniatures and which will be explained in its proper place as the work of painters'. (No such text by him on this subject is known.) Des Billettes also suggests that colour work might be conducted as it is by playing card makers. As noted below, a description of the printing of playing cards follows the text on stencilling in Des Billettes's cahier; there, colour work is described.

The fourth section
(184–9)

The fourth section of Des Billettes's text is different from the previous three in that it is essentially rhetorical, a summary of what has gone before, supplemented by concluding remarks and references. Because it reviews features of Des Billettes's method already discussed, the fourth section is of less immediate interest in this respect. Instead, its importance is in the arguments that accompany and support the summary, in which Des Billettes advances the logic and advantages of his own method while asserting as inferior other methods a stenciller might use. In describing the latter, he incidentally provides valuable clues about the conduct of contemporary stencilling, features of which he clearly did not approve. And by forcefully reiterating the claimed improvements of his own method, Des Billettes also demonstrates the value he ascribed to displacing many of stencilling's irregular features with more regularised alternatives.

Des Billettes begins the fourth section with a list of the equipment used by stencillers unwilling to subject themselves to rules such as those that govern his method. Their equipment includes an ordinary table, a simple ruler, plates folded up once at the base, and letters cut with attachments and without a lumière. Used together, they require the stenciller to have a 'perfectly sure eye and a perfectly steady hand' in order to position each stencil with precision, aided only by triangles (or another shape) cut into the plate at the baseline of the letter, and by baselines ruled on to the substrate for every line of text (184, 1º).

Having summarised the defects of working thus, Des Billettes then reviews the comparative advantages of his method, feature by feature. At (185, 2º): if a stencil plate is simply folded up at the base to make it easy to handle and its configuration has no other purpose, then the effort of positioning it accurately must be 'constantly renewed'; with a more purposefully configured plate and the conduite 'one can work with a vengeance'. At (185, 3º): if the

lumière is dispensed with, then inter-character spacing depends entirely on trial and error guided by eye, or on a spacing dot placed after the letter, to be covered over in most cases, but not all, by the next stencilled letter (see below, figure A4.32); neither can guarantee the even and accurate spacing offered by the lumière. At (185–6, 4º): if composite letters are not used, then attachments are needed; the unpleasant breaks these cause in the stencilled letter need to be filled in with ink using a pen or brush, something the stenciller may be unwilling to do for fear of spoiling the letter, or because the defect is thought imperceptible, or simply out of laziness. Des Billettes continues by arguing for the composite letter: it takes little extra time or effort to draw on the plate, cut out, or stencil; and the letters that result do not have breaks that need filling in. At (186–7, 5º): by dispensing with the conduite, the stenciller must rule in every line, and these may become unevenly spaced or drift out of parallel; with the conduite, only the two line-ends are needed. (It is here that Des Billettes proposes the toothed wheel for pricking line-ends). And at (187, 6º): again, that stencils with triangles cut at baselines and spacing dots to the right of letters are not only more difficult to make, they are 'a very imperfect substitute' for the conduite-lumière combination.

The position Des Billettes arrives at near the end of the fourth section (188) is that while a stenciller may, through practice and concentration, succeed in making good work using only the simplest of means, a similar standard can be reached more easily using his method and equipment (and, he implies, by stencillers of varying skill and experience). Indeed Des Billettes goes on to describe those who use simple tools and procedures as mere economizers, or the associates of people who have 'little refinement' or have bad taste. His lesson (if this is not overstating the matter) is that 'in this [stencilling], as in many other arts, the pains that are taken at first in (making) the equipment or tools of the trade are abundantly rewarded by the sureness, the perfection, and the ease that one subsequently finds in working'.

Discussion

Des Billettes's neat summation just quoted encapsulates a strategy of work that underlies the whole of his text. It is the redirection of effort away from the ad hoc features of the stencilling itself, and toward the earlier stages of its design and planning. Energy otherwise spent (and wasted) marshalling and executing every task uniquely – ruling text lines, aligning stencils, gauging spaces, completing breaks – is instead invested in devising equipment and procedures that more effectively anticipate the stencilling to come. Their integrated design ensures greater regularity, precision, and efficiency in the work. This, he argues, does not simply improve the work, it makes the worker's circumstances less taxing and, by implication, more rewarding.

Theory and practice

The particular way Des Billettes enhanced the regularity of text stencilling represents his principal innovation. His method, as he claimed, is efficient and capable of generating well-composed words and text; the reconstruction confirms as much. But while this is true in general, the reconstruction also reveals features of Des Billettes's method that appear ineffective or superfluous, suggesting that in places Des Billettes was proposing a work concept that does not always hold up in practice. Disjunctures of this kind do not undermine the method's overall effectiveness, though they do raise questions about its relationship to practice.

The question of whether elements of Des Billettes's method were theoretical in origin and remained so, were shaped by testing them, or were borne out of observed practices, can be weighed up by first noting Des Billettes's own remarks on the matter. Near the end of his text (188) he says 'it is always more sure both for the ease of the process and the perfection of the work to follow the methods that we have just described. And we can assure (the readers) that all circumstances being supposed equal we have never seen other simple methods succeed so well'. Referring to existing stencilled books (discussed below), he notes that while they are excellent 'it is nevertheless certain that the[ir] texts never have the accuracy that they would have if produced by our method'. (188) While Des Billettes fails to state categorically that his equipment was made and used, both statements suggest that this was the case.

Support for the suggestion can be sought through an appraisal of the reconstruction. The equipment is mostly realistic in design and relatively easy to construct with the materials, tools, and skills available to metal- and woodworkers of the period. The exception is the stencil plate, which presents some difficulties. While measuring, cutting and folding the plates is straightforward, cutting out the letters with scissors is challenging and time-consuming; as the size of the letter decreases, the cutting becomes increasingly difficult, and below a certain size effectively impossible.[7] And yet Des Billettes does warn that it is difficult to make letters as small as Gros Parangon, and recommends Gros Canon or larger instead. The latter, notably, is roughly the minimum size for which scissors of the kind illustrated in the engraving are not excessively difficult to use. Des Billettes seems to anticipate the challenges involved when he remarks that it is the cutting wherein lies 'all the skill of this little art' (169), and that its success mostly 'depends on the particular skill of the person who undertakes the task'. (178)

Similarly challenging, and also associated with making the stencil plates, is the implementation of Des Billettes's method for consistent letter spacing. His 'normal rule', that all letters should be separated by the stem width of capital I, brings with it implications for the design of letters that are not immediately obvious (see appendix 1). But they can be dealt with, demonstrating that the spacing method is neither impractical nor merely theoretical; indeed its description as a normal rule suggests well-established practice. Nevertheless, Des Billettes's explanation of it is relatively uncomplicated, which may indicate one of two things: that his understanding of such a system was limited, since he takes no notice of its implications; or that he saw no need to provide many details, since it was a skill whose successful execution resided in the know-how of the specialist who would do the work.[8]

7. It is possible that Des Billettes never observed such work directly, or based his description on stencil-making practices employed elsewhere, for example in the production of playing cards where scissors (and knives) were employed, though the material being cut was either card or canvas, and the cut-out shapes comparatively simple.

8. This is also the case with Des Billette's descriptions of the furniture and tool making, where the details of the wood and metal working are left largely unspecified, presumably under the assumption that they would be resolved by the specialists doing the work.

Once made, the use of the equipment gives additional indications of the method's putative relationship to practice. There is much about it, for example, that enables fluent and effective work, and which is again realistic. This is demonstrated by the stencil plate, whose folded configuration is intelligently partnered to the desk and conduite; in use, it is appropriately stiff, robust, and able to resist deformation. The four proportion rulers are equally effective in providing a consistent vertical position for each letter on all the plates, while avoiding each plate's particular irregularities. Consistent positions, together with properly executed letter-lumière combinations, demonstrate that good composition can be readily achieved. Apart from the method itself, there are also some indications that Des Billettes gathered information about the work of stencilling by observing it in action. These are evident in remarks he makes about the ink and brush: he issues several warnings not to overload the brush with ink; he remarks that the uptake of ink can be moderated with a sponge; he notes that the most important feature of the ink, in addition to its blackness, is that it dry quickly; and he calculates that between fifteen and twenty letters can be stencilled with one brush-load of ink. Each of these has a specificity that seems to derive from direct observation; each is confirmed by reconstructed practice.[9]

But if much about Des Billettes's method allows for fluent and realistically effective work, there are also features of it that undermine what he claims for it. One example, which relates to the ink and brush workings, and to the size of the letters, is that small-size letters are difficult to mark out and should therefore be avoided. The claim is doubtful since in practice marking them out is relatively easy if an appropriately sized brush is used whose bristles are the right length and stiffness.[10]

A more significant disjuncture, however, concerns the masking tools, the sergent, and the patte. Initially, they seem to be logical adjuncts to the composite letter and the lumière, since without them the ink-loaded brush would surely stray into various openings in the stencil plate where it would mar the work. But in practice both tools are problematic because their use requires more hands than are available to the stenciller. When stencilling, one hand is needed to pick up, position, and hold the stencil in place against the conduite while the other is occupied with the brush and the sensitive handling it requires to deliver ink fully but not excessively through the stencil. The use of either masking tool in effect requires a third hand: after the stencil is positioned, the masking tool must be picked up with the same hand (the other is holding the brush), adjusted (if using the sergent), and placed on top of the stencil, which almost invariably shifts the stencil out of position. Once the letter is eventually marked out, it must be left to dry completely since removing the masking tool too quickly may again shift the stencil and smear the ink.

Apart from threatening the quality of the work, these various operations are awkward and time consuming. Without a masking tool the stenciller can, with several deft movements, first position the stencil and mark out the letter, then flip the stencil up by its foot and slide it to its next position; or return the stencil to the letter case, pick up another, and set it in position. In either instance, the ink

9. Des Billettes's specifications may suggest that these practices associated with the ink – crucial to good stencilling – were common knowledge.

10. Des Billettes's claim may have been rhetorical, to partner and support his guidance on cutting out the letters with scissors. Certainly as the eighteenth century progresses, letters far smaller than his stated minimum are in evidence, both as stencils and in stencilled books and other applications. They may indicate an increasing frequency in the use of etching for making stencils, which facilitated very small letters, as scissors did not.

(if it is of the correct viscosity) is sufficiently dry before the stencil is repositioned or replaced by another. The increase in speed and ease of working is considerable, far more so than when the sergent or patte is involved. Nor is the masking function of these tools essential: clean and accurate work can still be achieved without their use, so long as the brush retains its shape and is not too broad to begin with, and has no inky fly-away bristles likely to stray into the lumière or those parts of the letter not being marked out.[11]

Contemporary practice

Observations on the reconstruction of Des Billettes's equipment and its use allow one to make statements about its viability as a freestanding proposal. Despite a number of disjunctures between the method as described and as implemented, it remains realistic, efficient, and capable of good quality text composition. But the method's relation to contemporary stencilling practices is less clear. What firm evidence is there that Des Billettes based his method on equipment and procedures already in use, or that he extrapolated the method from less developed practices he observed or was aware of? If neither, and Des Billettes's equipment and procedures were entirely new, is there evidence that his method influenced subsequent text stencilling?

The record of known artefacts suggests that there is some relationship between Des Billettes's method and contemporary practices, though this does not amount to proof of direct influence. The relationship arises through shared features, namely (1) composite letters that are (2) stencilled without visible baseline guides and (3) evenly spaced without evidence of inter-character spacing dots (see appendix 4, figure A4.9, p. 57, below, for examples). Each of these features appear to signal a relationship, though it is not possible to assert a direct connection to Des Billettes's method in the absence of corroborating equipment.[12]

Although little stencilling equipment contemporary to Des Billettes appears to survive, several stencil plates recently recorded and possibly near in date to his text do employ folds in a configuration nearly identical to that which he describes (see appendix 4, figure A4.2, p. 55, below). The stencils also include alignment triangles that extend from the sides of the plate like those illustrated by Simonneau (see appendix 3, figure A3.2, p. 53, below). Despite their inconsistent relationship to Des Billettes's text (as noted, Des Billettes rejected alignment triangles), the stencils are at present the only unambiguous piece of evidence that at least one item of associated equipment was made and used, possibly at or near the time.

One further kind of evidence may be brought to bear on the relationship between Des Billettes's text and contemporary or subsequent practice, though here through its absence. One example already mentioned is very small letters, which have so far not been recorded in early stencilled books. Their absence might suggest that stencil cutting with scissors, as described by Des Billettes, was used at the time since it is not possible to produce small-size letters in this way.[13] Another example is the absence of residual errors of the kind Des Billettes's method generates, such as the ghost of a lumière

11. It is important to note that Des Billettes additionally recommends the use of masking tools to press the stencil plate flat to the substrate and, in turn, the substrate flat to the desk, thereby stopping ink from seeping under the plate. (Here one can discern an echo of the scribe's knife, put to similar use during writing.) But this does not work as planned since the stencil plate's inevitable warps and deformations cannot be completely flattened with either masking tool. The fingers of the hand are in fact more flexibly suited to this purpose, and in any case the likelihood of seeping ink is greatly diminished if the viscosity of the ink, and the length and stiffness of the brush bristles, are correctly gauged at the outset.

12. While one or two of these features occur in some stencilled books of the period, only a few are presently known to exhibit all three features together.

13. The absence of very small letters may, by corollary, indicate that methods other than scissor-cutting, such as etching, were not yet well established. Nevertheless, this absence might be equally well explained by the possibility that small-size letters were simply not needed for large stencilled liturgical books at the time.

left by a wayward brush, or the trace of a repère discernable within or protruding from a letter whose parts it helped to coordinate (see p. 41, above). Such errors have so far not been found in any stencilled text; their absence therefore points away from the use of equipment (and stencil plates, in particular) configured as Des Billettes describes.

Final observations

A summary characterization of Des Billettes's description is that it probably represents several innovations in the stencilling of texts, while in other respects reflects existing practices. Those features of the method he describes at length (the integrated configuration of the stencil plates, the composite letters, and the associated equipment) may be that which is new, since the detail of their description suggests that they were unfamiliar. By contrast, those features he includes, but with little explanation (basic letter design, the rule for spacing letters, scissor cutting), or that he rejects out of hand (conventional stencil letters, alignment triangles, inter-character spacing dots, drawn-in baselines) may be features of stencilling that were already well known.

Given Des Billettes's concentration on the concept, equipment, and procedures for marking out lines of texts, it is worth reiterating the observation that the 'imprimerie' in the title of his description refers only to the work of text stencilling and not to the production of a whole book. Designing, painting, and illuminating decorative matter, or titles and initials, for example, clearly fell into other, related spheres and would presumably be described separately.[14] Equally, the construction of the pages of a book (measuring, pricking, ruling, scoring), or the raking out of staves, or the coordinated composition of text, chant notation, and initials, or the creation of title pages, could also be dealt with elsewhere, though surely some or all of this work falls within (or well within) the stenciller's sphere of operations. Des Billettes's omission of such descriptions indicates that his aims were limited to addressing only that feature of the livre d'église he thought most amenable to improvement: the composition of its text.

A final item, already referred to above, also tantalises: Des Billettes's note near the end of his text where he states '[t]here are two excellent examples of this kind at the Invalides. But it is nevertheless certain that their texts never have the accuracy that they would have if produced by our method'. (188) The remark confirms the observation just made that Des Billettes's principal concern was not the production of an entire book but the improvement of its text element, while also suggesting that 'our method' was both different and had been tested. It additionally indicates the works Des Billettes had in mind, against which his own method could be compared. One of the 'excellent examples' is likely to have been a monumental liturgical book made in 1682 at the Hôtel royal des Invalides, and still to be found there (figure 38, opposite).[15] Des Billettes was clearly confident about his method since this example is among the finest stencilled liturgical books known, complete with well composed

14. See (188). It is important to note that many late seventeenth- and early eighteenth-century liturgical books, for which stencilling was employed for texts and chant notation, otherwise incorporate drawn, painted, and illuminated decorations, initials, and/or titling, the latter usually in the form of large roman capitals. Such work showcased the talents of painters, illuminators, and writing masters, though over the course of the eighteenth century these elements were stencilled with increasing frequency.

15. 'Graduale et antiphonale ad usum S. Ludovici Domus Regiæ Invalidorum pro solemnioribus totius anni festivitatibus', 1682, Paris, Musée de l'Armée, manuscrits et imprimés, 5389 bis, 3251 BIB. Another, similar book made at the Invalides for the royal chapel, Versailles, is now in the Bibliothèque nationale de France (Richelieu): 'Graduale et antiphonale ad usum S.-Ludovici Domus Regiæ Versaliensis pro solemnioribus totius anni festivitatibus', 1686, MS. Lat. 8828. It is not clear whether this is the second of the two examples to which Des Billettes refers. See also following note.

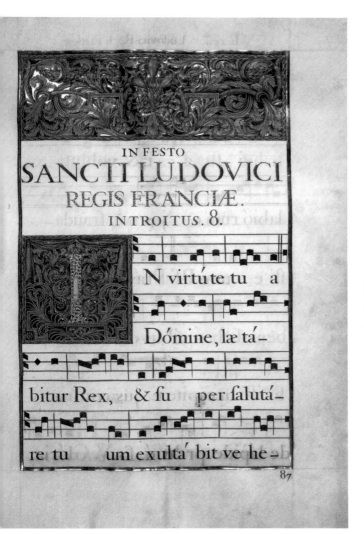

Figure 38. 'Graduale et antiphonale ad usum S. Ludovici
Domus Regiæ Invalidorum …', parchment, 1682. Musée de
l'Armée, Paris.
(left) p. 87, 800 × 570 mm. Stencilled elements include chant
   text and notation.
(above) Detail of p. 87, showing consistent letter spacing, but
   variable syllable and word spacing; cf. appendix 1, note 6,
   p. 49, below.

texts. The reference may also suggest a context in which Des Billettes
envisioned his method being used. The Invalides was a rest home
recently founded by Louis XIV for French ex-soldiers, many of whom
were occupied in artisan workshops on-site.[16] Those employed in
making liturgical books could hardly be expected to have acquired
the expertise of the professional scribe or writing master. In these circumstances, stencilling would have offered precisely the right means
by which 'les manchots'[17] could contribute to the work by producing
texts capable of outshining even the best of those made with a pen.

16. The Hôtel royal des Invalides was
founded in 1674. Thomas Povey, emis-
sary of Charles II, made a detailed record
of the Invalides in 1682 to inform the
planning of the Royal Hospital Chelsea;
see Povey, 'The hostel of the Invalides',
transcribed in Ritchie (1966). Povey's
list of workshops does not include one
devoted to liturgical book production.
The first official account of the Invalides

was written by Le Jeune de Boullencourt
the following year (*La description générale
de l'Hôtel royal des Invalides …*, Paris,
1683). Boullencourt does indicate that
by 1683 such books were being made at
the Invalides, and that on a recent visit
Louis XIV had expressed his wish to have
one for the royal chapel at Versailles:
'[L]a dernière fois qu'elle [Sa Majesté]
y est venue, on luy fit voir des livres

d'Église travaillez par des Invalides manchots. Elle les trouva si beaux qu'elle vou-
lut qu'ils en fissent de semblables pour sa
chapelle de Versailles'. Quoted in Maral
(2001), p. 26, where additional accounts
relating to liturgical book production are
given. See also the original research of
Vanuxem (1974).
   17. 'The one-armed'; in zoology,
'penguins'.

Fred Smeijers

Appendix 1: Designing and spacing the letters

When designing and making letters by whatever means, two basic problems present themselves: how the letters should look, and how they should be spaced. The first problem is connected to the second: how letters look influences how they are spaced, though it is also possible to state the inverse: how letters are spaced influences how they look.

Shapes and spaces

Des Billettes gives no clear instruction in his text about how letters used for stencilling should look. He only remarks that they should be 'the letters one wants to cut' (169), and further on, that they should be drawn 'with all the possible accuracy and in the most beautiful proportions'. (173) (To get an idea of the letters he may have had in mind, see figure 38, above; also p. 86, below.) But if Des Billettes is vague about how letters should look, he does provide a relatively clear rule for how they should be spaced: in short, that the distance between the rightmost extremity of one letter and the leftmost extremity of the next should be the stem width of capital I.[1]

The rule thus stated, however, seems too simple and on its own an insufficient guide to the work of making the stencil letters. Some additional understanding is needed about how letters are devised, though Des Billettes only alludes to this in his assumption that the letters will be made with accuracy and beautiful proportions. In the absence of any further remarks, one can do little more than speculate on exactly how the work was carried out, or on what basis letter shape and letter space were coordinated.[2]

If one asserts (as above) that the space between letters partly determines how the letters themselves look, then one might test Des Billettes's spacing method by devising the accompanying letter shapes on the same basis, that is to say, from units of stem width. Some treatises dealing with inscriptional capitals establish the proportions of the letters in this way, and among writing masters the stem (or stroke) width would have been one of several factors influencing decisions about letter height, width, and counter size. To adopt units of stem width to determine both shape *and* spacing does not, therefore, seem wholly anachronistic, though admittedly no source (known to the author) before or contemporary to Des Billettes proposes this explicitly.[3]

quodim

The sequence of illustrations (figure A1.1, opposite) incorporates this approach to test the effectiveness of Des Billettes's rule for letter spacing. The purpose of the test is to demonstrate the relationship between letter shape and letter spacing, and show how the spacing rule works in practice.

1. While this is a fair summary of the rule, Des Billettes's explanation is considerably longer; cf. (177–8), p. 77, below.

2. As discussed above (p. 43), Des Billettes's omission of detailed guidance on letter shape might be understood as an assumption by him that the person devising the stencil letters already possessed such knowledge, and that an exposition on the matter was not therefore needed.

3. Des Billettes is an early source supplying a rule for spacing letters on the basis of stem width, though by describing it as 'the normal rule' (177), he implies that it was generally known. Crucially, the Commission Bignon, which undertook the making of the *romain du roi*, and of which Des Billettes was a member, based its roman (and italic) designs on modules that equated to stem width; the work apparently did not, however, extend to the specification of spaces between letters. See Mosley (1997), pp. 12–13. Later, the Dutch writing master Jan Pas, in *Mathematische of wiskundige Behandeling der Schryfkonst* (1737), illustrates alphabets proportioned in units of stem width and promises that in a subsequent work he will demonstrate how to space letters; no such work by him is known.

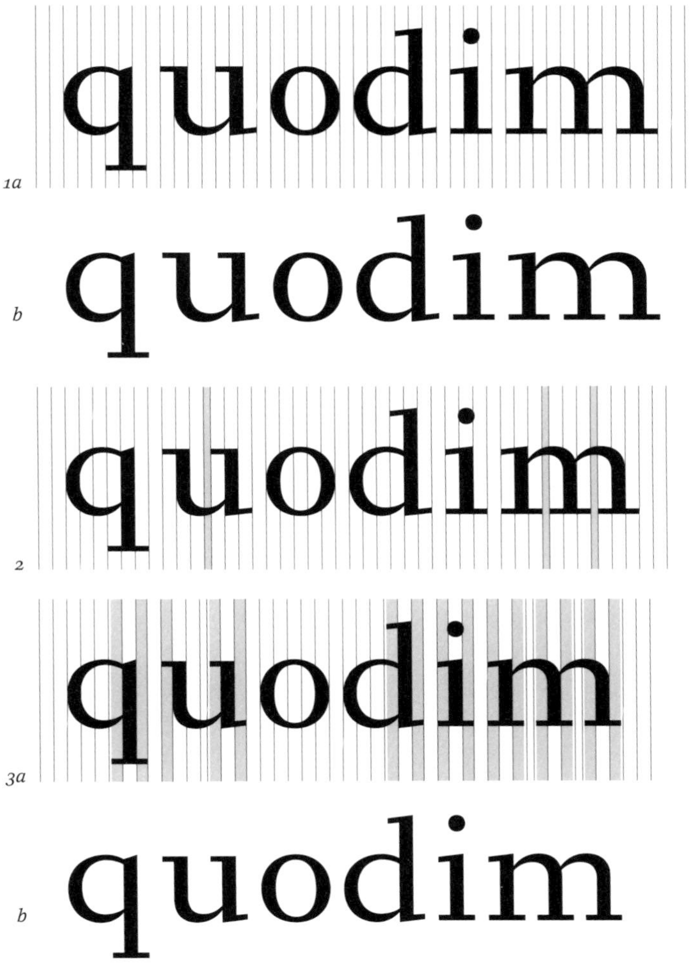

quodim

1a

quodim

b

quodim

2

quodim

3a

quodim

b

Figure A1.1. Letter shape and spacing based on stem width.

quodim (1). The letters of the made-up word 'quodim' are initially proportioned on units of stem width: the x-height is 5; the counters are 3; the serif lengths are 1.[4] The word includes the principal letter and stem/stroke combinations a spacing system needs to resolve: a straight followed by a straight (qu, dim); a straight followed by a round (uo) or vice-versa; and a round followed by a round (od). Applying Des Billettes's spacing rule to the sequence of letters results in (1a, b). The spacing produces a relatively cohesive word shape. Problems of both letter shape and spacing, however, do occur: u and m appear too wide, while the space between q and u is excessive, and between o and d is insufficient; overall the word appears too loosely spaced.

quodim (2). The problems of quodim (1) can be addressed by reducing the counter widths of u and m by half a stem width (indicated by the grey tints). But problems remain: the word still appears too loosely spaced (except between o and d), while the internal serifs of m are now nearly touching.

quodim (3). The problems in quodim (2) can be mostly resolved by shortening the serifs (again, indicated by grey tints). This improves the m and reduces the space between the straight strokes throughout (the stem width unit is retained between the shortened serifs of adjacent letters). The result is quite acceptable (3a, b). One or two problems remain, in particular the space between q and u, which is still too large. While these problems would need to be resolved with further refinements, Des Billettes's rule, combined with basic alterations to counters and serifs, proves generally effective and able to be extended to the complete set of small letters.[5] The result would be relatively evenly spaced letters and coherent word shapes.[6]

Capital letters

In his text, Des Billettes only draws on sample combinations of small letters when explaining his spacing rule. The spacing of capital letters is not mentioned, either in all-capital situations (titles) or in combination with small letters. In (reconstructed) practice, the spacing rule continues to work for capitals as long as adjustments are similarly allowed to their serif lengths and counters, and the stem widths of the capitals and small letters are taken as roughly equivalent. Des Billettes's instruction to use the same four proportion rulers for devising both capital and small letters implies that their designs should be coordinated in other respects, too.[7]

4. For this demonstration, the stem width of capital I is taken as equivalent to the (vertical) stem width of the small letters (it is normally wider). The letters roughly emulate those found in contemporary (French) stencilled books, where round shapes (b, d, o, p, q) are based on a circle. To achieve this, and to (again, roughly) emulate letter weight, the 'o' is assigned horizontal and vertical dimensions of 5 stem widths. This produces a counter of 3 stem widths (horizontal dimension), which is then initially adopted for the counters of the other letters, as shown in the 'quodim' sequence.

5. While Des Billettes's rule works well for most small letter combinations, some letters present difficulties, including those that do not have straight or curved strokes on one or both sides (e.g. f, r, t, v/y). In general, his rule works best for the letters he probably had in mind, i.e. romans with relatively conventional proportions. Using the rule with letters based

on more extreme or unconventional proportions, especially counter size and serif length, would be unlikely to produce good results, though such letters were not used for stencilled texts at the time.

6. Consistent spacing in the chant text is relatively unusual in stencilled liturgical books. This arises from the dynamic relationship that exists between the text and the chant notation, where the phrasing and duration of notes, syllables, and complete words require variable spacing to ensure their correct correlation. The generally preferred result, it appears, was

text composition that produced consistent letter spacing to preserve syllable and word identity, but which was otherwise regulated by varying spaces between syllables and words. This might explain why Des Billettes offers no guidance on word spaces, since they would be context dependant (see figure 38, above).

7. A review of stencilled books contemporary to Des Billettes, however, shows that this coordination did not always occur in practice. Instead, stencil capitals are often taller than the ascenders of small letters, and bolder.

Fred Smeijers

Appendix 2: Cutting the letters with chisels

As described above (p. 37), Des Billettes uses the term 'cizeaux' to describe the tool employed for cutting the letters from the plate. Although it seems relatively certain that Des Billettes is referring to scissors (a supposition supported by Simonneau's engraving), there remains sufficient ambiguity for the meaning of the term to be taken as 'chisels' instead. For this reason, chisel cutting was also tested as part of the reconstruction. A 'chisels' reading is worth considering for two reasons: first, while reconstructed practice shows that cutting letters with scissors can be done, the work is nevertheless difficult and relatively time-consuming; second, the design of the scissors (shown by Simonneau) makes it impossible to cut out letters below a certain size.

The use of chisels, by contrast, is easier and quicker, though they, too, can only cut letters of a certain minimum size (albeit somewhat smaller than scissors). The work requires several chisels whose cutting edges range in length.[1] Once the letter and the other elements (guiding-mark, lumière) have been drawn onto the plate, a chisel with a longer cutting edge is used both for straight parts (stems and other strokes) and interior curves (roughly shaped using overlapping long cuts). A chisel with a short cutting edge is used to shape exterior curves, again roughly at first. Thereafter, files are used to refine all shapes and edges. Unlike cutting with scissors, it is not necessary to bend the foot of the plate out of the way when using chisels; this is because chisel strikes are (for the most part) perpendicular to the plate. The plate only requires a solid (wood) support. Smaller parts of the plate must still, however, be bent outwards to facilitate filing.

In general, chisels are sharper than scissors and therefore cut more readily. More cutting can be done with them initially because they can reach into smaller parts of the letter. Overall, cutting a letter with chisels takes about half the time needed to cut the same letter with scissors.

1. The lengths will vary depending on the size of the letter being cut; for the present reconstruction, five chisels were used; the shortest cutting edge was approximately 1 mm in length, the longest approximately 7 mm.

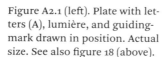

Figure A2.1 (left). Plate with letters (A), lumière, and guiding-mark drawn in position. Actual size. See also figure 18 (above).

Figure A2.2, a–b (above left, and above). Initial chisel cuts, made with the longest chisel edge (7 mm).

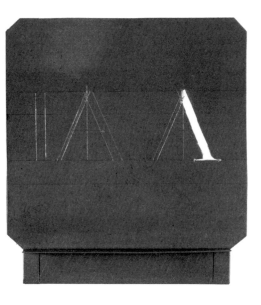

Figure A2.3 (left). Partially complete rough cut.

Figure A2.4, a–b. Cuts with long chisel edge (above, left); a short chisel is used for the serif bracket (above, right).

Figure A2.5.
(a) Rough cut complete (left).
(b) Proof of rough cut (above).

Figure A2.6, a–b (above).
Initial refinements to rough cut.

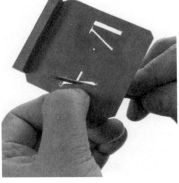

Figure A2.7 (above, left).
Proof of initial refinements.

Figure A2.8 (above, right).
Further refinements.

Figure A2.9.
(a) Finished stencil (right).
(b) Final proof (far right).

Appendix 3: The engraving by Louis Simonneau

Figure A3.1. Engraving to accompany Des Billettes's description of stencilling, signed 'Lud. Simonneau 1701.', 268 × 176 mm, from the album 'Les Arts et Métiers de l'Académie des Sciences', St Bride Library and Archives, SB5825 ('Plates relating to printing and kindred arts, principally engraved by L. Simonneau').

Upper section:
(1) worker probably folding brass sheets into stencil plates (right)
(2) anvil (middle)
(3) worker stencilling (left)

Lower section:
(A) lettercase
(B) brush
(C) ink box
(D) desk, with (D1) substrate, rolled around dowel, (D2) ruler (*conduite*), (D3) bolts, (D4) nuts
(E) vice extension
(F) scribing tool
(G, H, I, K) letter proportion rulers
(L, M, N) stencil plates (*caractères*)
(O) wood mallet
(P) scissors
(Q, R) sash-clamp (*sergent*)
(S) holdfast (*patte*)
(T) toothed wheels

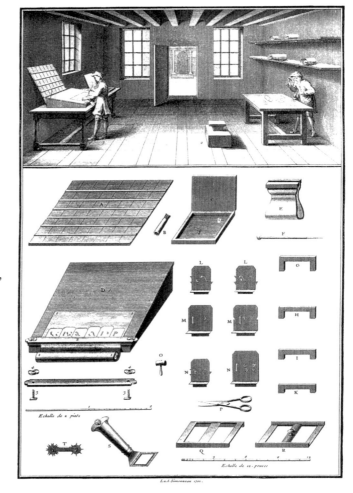

1. Other engravings associated with the Description des Arts et Métiers are compiled in the album 'Les Arts et Métiers de l'Académie des Sciences', St Bride Library and Archives, SB5825. See also sources given in James Mosley, 'A note on Gilles Filleau des Billettes', this volume, pp. 87–90.
2. These reference letters and numbers were no doubt introduced to the engraving in anticipation of its publication alongside the text, into which such references would have also been inserted. They are not present in Des Billettes's draft.

Des Billettes's description of stencilling is paired with an engraving signed by Louis Simonneau, dated 1701 (figure A3.1). The engraving is divided into an upper section that presents a scene of workers engaged in stencil-making and stencilling, and a lower section that illustrates their equipment.[1]

The items of equipment in the lower section are assigned reference letters (A–T); elements that are attached to the desk (D) are assigned secondary reference numbers (1–4).[2] The lower section is divided notionally in half vertically, with items in the left half shown at half the relative size of items in the right half, according to the accompanying scales. The ink box (C) appears to be out of position; its size seems better determined by the left scale. The hammer (O) is equivocally positioned, and may be incorrectly sized relative to either scale. The holdfast (S) and toothed wheels are better referred to the right scale. The sash-clamp is shown twice, once from above (R), and again from below (Q) to make clear its flush underside. The engraving also includes one item of equipment Des Billettes does not mention: a dowel of some kind around which the paper/vellum

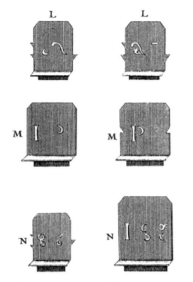

Figure A3.2. Stencil plates, variant configurations, detail of engraving by Simonneau.

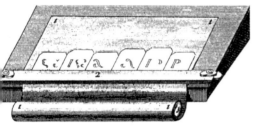

Figure A3.3. Stencil plates positioned on conduite, detail of engraving by Simonneau.

Figure A3.4. Worker probably folding brass sheets into stencil plates, detail of engraving by Simonneau.

on the desk is rolled to protect it from denting or creasing during stencilling, given its vulnerable position between the desk and the stenciller's hips.

Reviewing the illustrations of the equipment (and leaving aside issues of scale), they are mostly accurate in relation to Des Billettes's text, except the six stencil plates, about which there appears to have been some confusion (figure A3.2; cf. marginal figures 7–10, p. 75, below). The basic folded shapes of all the plates are correct, more or less, though they are inaccurate where the flat 'face' of the plate meets the 'foot' (cf. figure 6, p. 32, which is correct to the text). The various configurations of letter and lumière on each plate are again inaccurate, in different ways. The right plate of the 'N' pair is nearly correct, and is defective only in the distance shown between the lumière and the left part of the letter (it should be the stem width of capital 'I'); each of the other plates omits the lumière. The plates 'L' (left) and 'M' (left) both show an accurate composite letter, while their paired plates (right) show a conventional letter with attachments of the kind that Des Billettes explicitly rejects. The letter of N (left), shown both complete and incomplete, is probably an error; L (right) includes a superfluous horizontal bar.[3] Only two of the plates, M (left) and N (right), correctly omit the conventional side alignment triangles that Des Billettes also rejects. The latter do occur in plate M (right) where they are cut into the plate, and in the L pair and N (left) where they are protruding.[4] The six plates are also shown on the desk in the left half of the engraving, set in a row above conduite (figure A3.3). The letter configurations are largely the same, though the letter of N (left) is now shown correctly as simply a composite letter (g), while the letter-lumiere combination on the plate second from left matches Des Billettes's description in every respect. Alignment triangles are correctly omitted from the all plates; the perpendicular 'feet' of the plates, which should protrude above the fore-edge of the conduite, are not shown.

Turning to the scene of work in the upper section of the engraving (figure A3.4), the first observation to be made is simply that the scene itself provides some understanding of the scale of the equipment relative to the workers. The activities of the workers, to the right and left, are each given a reference number (1 and 3, respectively), while located between them is an anvil, also numbered (2). On the right, the worker is very probably folding brass sheets into the plate configuration specified by Des Billettes, with the aid of the vice extension (E) and the wood mallet (O). The brass is shown as small flat pieces on the table, and in larger curled sheets on the shelves above. It is otherwise difficult to draw secure inferences from the activity illustrated. Notably, the sheet brass is shown curled up, suggesting that it was supplied this way, or curled naturally, but in any case needed to be beaten flat. The anvil (2) may have been for this purpose, though

3. The horizontal bar is in fact the cross bar of 'A', and should be part of a plate carrying a composite A, not 'a'; cf. (174) (pp. 74–5, below), where the composite A is described and illustrated.

4. Both kinds of alignment triangles are found among historical artefacts. Those cut into the plate are far more common and have become conventional; those protruding from the plate are rare and may only have been used at around the time Des Billettes was writing. See appendix 4, figures A4.2, A4.3, and A4.32, pp. 55, 56, and 63, below.

Figure A3.5. Worker stencilling,
detail of engraving by Simonneau.

Des Billettes does not mention it in his text. Instead he recommends that the brass be worked with the wood mallet on a smooth wood surface, after it has been annealed to make it more pliable (169). This working with the mallet may have involved both flattening the sheet brass (and pounding it to the desired thinness) as well as folding the brass into plates (with the help of the vice extension). Any or all of these activities might be part of what is illustrated on the right.

On the left of the scene, it is notable that the stenciller is working in a standing position, with the desk surface at about waist height or slightly higher (figure A3.5). This would appear to be somewhat too low for stencilling comfortably for an extended period. The location of the lettercase behind the desk seems similarly inconvenient, requiring the stenciller to reach repeatedly across the desk to pick up and replace the stencils – as shown in the engraving, it would be very difficult to do this. There is also a discrepancy between the number of compartments in the lettercase: in the scene of work only 35 are visible, while in the lower section of the engraving the lettercase has 56. In each instance, the number falls short of what is needed if the compartments are intended to match the number of stencils Des Billettes's specifies for a complete set (80–100; see 169). A final observation of the scene of work concerns the workers' attire: it is secular and not ecclesiastical. This is notable, given that stencil work was also conducted in monastic workshops. That is clearly not the context shown here.

Reviewing the engraving of Simonneau more generally in the context of Des Billettes's text, it is possible to state that while the procedures of work described by Des Billettes are shown in only a very general and limited way, the equipment is illustrated with a considerable degree of fidelity, though in places discrepancies occur, some significant. It may be telling that these discrepancies are mainly found in relation to the stencil plates and their composite letters and lumière, elements that in Des Billettes's text are ironically described at great length. How and why these discrepancies arose is difficult to ascertain. They are perhaps surprising if one accepts that Des Billettes's equipment was constructed at the time or was based on existing equipment. In either case, this would have provided Simonneau with actual objects to refer to. It is similarly unclear whether the sketches Des Billettes added to his handwritten text played any role in the design of the engraving. One can at least say that the letters 'a' and 'g' sketched by Des Billettes to explain the composite letter principle do reappear in the engraving, incorporated into the stencils. Two other sketches in the cahier are also translated to the engraving: one of the rulers that delineate the proportions of the letters, and the toothed wheels for pricking line increments.[5]

Assuming that Simonneau's engraving post-dates Des Billettes's text, the engraving's date of 1701 appears to provide a *terminus ante quem* for the text's compilation.[6]

5. See also Pinault (1987), pp. 79–80, where two preparatory drawings by Simonneau for other engravings associated with the Description des Arts et Métiers are shown; and pp. 83–5, where an account of surviving drawings is given. No preparatory drawing for the engraving of stencilling is listed.

6. It may be worth noting that Des Billettes's description of the printing of playing cards, which occurs after the description of stencilling in his cahier, is also paired with an engraving by Simonneau, dated 1697.

Appendix 4: Examples of practice

This appendix groups together examples of stencils and stencilling that in one or several respects can be related to Des Billettes through their principle of design, method of work, or other conceptual features. The examples mostly occur after Des Billettes compiled his text and are found in a variety of circumstances, artefacts, and texts. Unless stated, there is no intention to assert any direct connection between Des Billettes and the examples tallied here. Instead the appendix mainly enumerates principles, methods, and features whose recurrence is evidence of their durability over time, whether continuously so, or as a result of periodic rediscovery or reinvention.

Plate configuration

Stencil plates have been recorded in a variety of configurations. For some time, the folded configuration described by Des Billettes was thought to be specific to his equipment. Recently, however, several similar plates have been recorded, though the configuration may, in general, be relatively uncommon. Far more common and indeed conventional is the simpler unfolded plate, with or without an upturned 'foot' (forming a handle) – which was criticised by Des Billettes as less effective than his own. A number of other configurations are included below, for comparison. Of these, plates with groups of characters (from 2 up to 14 or more) arranged vertically or in a matrix, were apparently made principally in the eighteenth and nineteenth centuries, while plates with groups of characters arranged horizontally occur mainly in the nineteenth and twentieth centuries. 'Settable unit' plates, configured for 'adjustable' or 'interlocking' composition, enable an unlimited number of characters to be assembled laterally.

Figure A4.1. Stencil plate, folded brass, scissor-cut and filed, 72 × 63 mm. Reconstructed according to the description of Des Billettes.

Figure A4.2. Stencil plates, maker not known, French, *c.* late 17th or early 18th century, brass, 45 × 43 mm (left), 77 × 73 mm (right, shown unfolded). Abbey of Bellafontaine (near Nantes).

Figure A4.3. Stencil plate, maker not known, French, late 18th or early 19th century, brass, etched, and filed, 71 × 54 mm. Stencil plates with four angled corners, an upturned base forming a handle, and alignment triangles cut into the sides, were apparently common when Des Billettes was writing and possibly conventional. He criticises them towards the end of his text (185). Notable in this example is the '12' punched into the upper left corner of the plate; it gives the size of the letter (capital height) in *lignes* (1 ligne = *c*. 2.256 mm). In France, size designations of this kind later became generic set numbers (i.e. 'No. 12') accompanied by a metric size (i.e. '27 m/m').

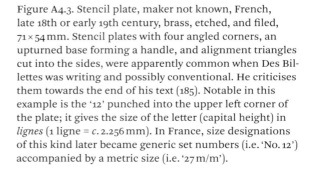

Figure A4.4. Stencil plate, maker not known, British, 20th century, zinc, routed, 114 × 95 mm. Plates with four angled corners and no upturned handle at the base are typical of (but not exclusive to) British manufacture.

Figure A4.5. Stencil plates, makers not known, French, *c*. first half of the 19th century, brass, etched; 108 × 47 mm (left), 88 × 97 mm (right). Example at right: Abbey of Bellafontaine.

Figure A4.6. Stencil plate with complete character set, maker not known, probably French, *c*. first half of the 19th century, brass, etched, 50 × 195 mm. Stencil alphabets and numerals used by architects, engineers, and surveyors were also typically arranged horizontally on several plates. See Kindel (2010).

Figure A4.7. Stencil plate, configured for 'settable units' (i.e. adjustable or interlocking) composition, Reese's Adjustable Stencil Plates, made by S. W. Reese & Co., United States, based on US Letters Patent no. 148,087 (1874) and no. 173,058 (1876), die-stamped and folded, spring brass, 57 × 30 mm. See also figure A4.36, below.

Composite letters

Des Billettes's method is based on composite letters, which are closely allied to the configuration of the stencil plate, and thereafter to the desk, conduite, and masking tools. Relatively few examples of composite small letters have been found in liturgical books (composite capitals are more common); where they are found, it is unclear if the stencils used were part of specially configured apparatus.

Composite letters in stencilled texts seem to disappear after about 1730 (very roughly), though they were regularly and continuously employed for titles and initials. They are found in several US patents of the 19th century, and in ticket- and signwriting 'outfits' of the 1920s. Composite letters also occur in lettering based on a 'kit-of-parts' assembly, and in stencils used to assist typeface design.

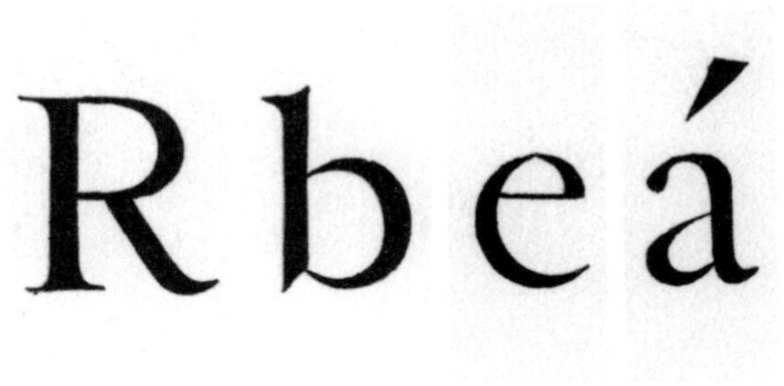

Figure A4.8. Composite letters, as marked out with stencil plates reconstructed according to the description of Des Billettes.

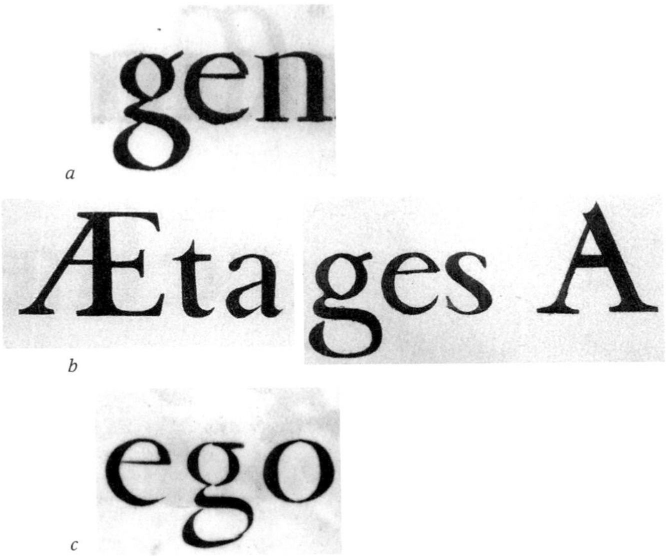

Figure A4.9. Composite letters, from stencilled liturgical books roughly contemporary to Des Billettes's text. Each of these examples exhibit the three features (composite letters, no visible baseline guides, even spacing without evidence of inter-character spacing dots) whose combination suggests a relationship with Des Billettes's method, at least through similar results. See discussion above (p. 45).

(a) from 'In coena domini [suivi de:] Canon missae', no date (17th century); x-height: 14 mm. Bibliothèque municipale de Besançon, Arch.G.II.152.

(b) from 'Graduale et Antiphonale, ad usum regalis monasterii Sancti Nicasii Remensis, pro festis primi ordinis', 1685. Bibliothèque de Reims, MS 267.

(c) from 'Graduale pro missis solemnibus, seu canonicalibus celebrandis in ecclesia cathedrali Sanctæ Mariæ, Ruthenensis', 1693; x-height: 14 mm. Archives départmentales de l'Aveyron, Rodez. The design and spacing of letters in the texts of this book resemble the specifications given by Des Billettes.

Figure A4.10. 'Stencillor Signwriter', made by Display Material Co, St. Paul, Minnesota, introduced February 1926. A stencil-based signwriting outfit employing composite characters. Alphabets were cut from shellac-reinforced card to form long stencils (177 × 467 mm). The stencils were used in combination with a desk-like apparatus that incorporated a fixed straight-edge across its width, against which the stencil was positioned (and slid laterally) to facilitate the alignment of baselines and the sequential stencilling of composite letter parts. The straight-edge could be raised to admit the paper or card being stencilled, then lowered to secure it in place. Thus despite some differences in configuration, the Stencillor is conceptually similar to Des Billettes's desk-conduite-stencil configuration. Among other signwriting outfits based on composite stencil letters were the 'Showcarder' (Showcarder, Inc, introduced March 1926, also of St. Paul, Minnesota), the 'Signmaster' (National Display Specialties, c. 1950s), and the 'Econosign' (1922/27; see figure A4.11, overleaf).

Figure A4.11. The 'Econosign', made by The 'Econosign' Co. Ltd, London, based on British patents 176,525 (1922) and 282,895 (1927). The Econosign outfit is similar to the 'Stencillor' (figure A4.10), but simpler and more compact. It was packaged in a box or small case that contained a portfolio of alphabets, each cut from one or several celluloid sheets. Outfits additionally included a grooved straight-edge, drawing pins, and brushes and inks. Characters were either composite in design, or 'natural' (e.g. a Gill Shadow equivalent; see also figure A4.23, below). Celluloid sheets were slid along and below the grooved straight-edge, which at its ends was fixed over the substrate with the pins. Composite parts were stencilled consecutively to form a complete character; the alignment of parts, and letter- and word-spacing, was aided by the celluloid's transparency. Econosign also sold a ready-made desk with evident similarities to the one described by Des Billettes.

Figure A4.12. Alfred Hunter, *Professional ticket-writing*, 2nd edn, London: Blanford Press, 1946. Characters are divided into two parts; these are stencilled consecutively with an apparatus comprised of two hinged frames, to create complete characters without breaks.

Figure A4.13. Specification drawing, Ezekiel B. Foster, US Letters Patent no. 4045 (1845). 'The nature of my invention consists in forming all the letters of the alphabet in stencil painting and printing by means of nine characters by changing, reversing and combining the said characters. Thus making nine characters to answer the place of twenty seven letters, in the operation of which the letters are made more perfect – leaving no spaces or interstices to be filled up after the brush has passed over the stencil as in the present mode, or mode now in use.' Foster included instructions for how each letter should be made, for example: 'X is formed by no. 5 as represented and a reversed impression annexed.'

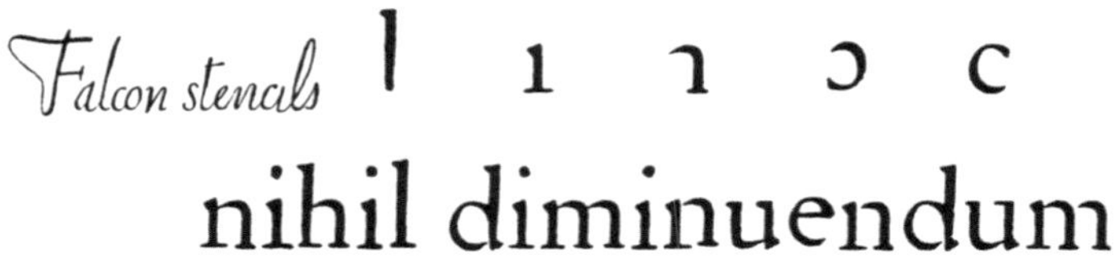

Figure A4.14. 'Falcon' stencils, W. A. Dwiggins, from *WAD to RR: a letter about designing type*, Cambridge, Mass: Harvard College Library, 1940. 'In making the Falcon I tried another scheme for arriving at the characteristics of the first-run experimental letters. I cut stencils in celluloid – a long and a short stem, the n arch, and a loop – *twice* the size of 12 point – pretty small! – and constructed letters from these elements by stencilling.' (p. [6])

Breaks completed

The practice of filling in the breaks of stencil characters with ink and a pen or brush appears to be longstanding. The earliest known individual stencilled letters, made by Johann Neudörffer, *d. Ä.*, around 1550, were completed in this way. Des Billettes refers to the practice to emphasize its likely faults and thereby encourage the take-up of his method, which avoided them. Stencilled texts in liturgical books show considerable variability: in some, breaks are filled in exactingly, while in others the work is done indifferently, poorly, or not at all. Generally, but with notable

exceptions, the filling-in of breaks appears to diminish over the course of the eighteenth century and into the nineteenth, while characters with breaks become increasingly prevalent and possibly even valued for their graphic effect. Some nineteenth- and twentieth-century texts dealing with stencil lettering in architecture, engineering, and surveying, including Wilme (1845), Stanley (1866), and Lineham (1915), recommend filling in breaks, though the evidence of surviving technical drawings indicates that this was often not done.

Figure A4.15. Johann Neudörffer, *d. Ä.*, 'Gründlicher Bericht der alten lateinischen Buchstaben', *c*. 1550. Museum für angewandte Kunst (MAK), Vienna, S 10 (Inv. Nr. B. I. 5697), f. 16ʳ (digitally altered to emphasize breaks). Neudörffer's manuscript contains a geometrically constructed alphabet of large roman capitals, outlined with ink and filled with wash. Consecutive letters of the alphabet are drawn on every other leaf of the manuscript; on the leaf that follows each drawn letter, the same identically-sized letter has been reproduced using a stencil, probably made of card or parchment. Each stencil letter has been marked out with thick black ink. The breaks, created by bridges apparently glued across the stencil's voids, were initially left intact. A thinner ink wash was then used to fill in the breaks and complete the letter. See also Doede (1957), pp. 54, 60; and Linke & Sauer (2007), pp. 108–11.

Figure A4.16. Letters with breaks filled in with pen and ink, from stencilled liturgical books.
(a) 'Gradualis de tempore ecclesiæ Parisiensis', 1669, with later additions. Musée de Notre-Dame de Paris.
(b) 'Antiphonarium pro solemnitatibus majoribus iuxta ritum santæ Autissiodorensis ecclesiæ', 1730.

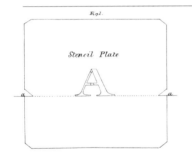

Figure A4.17. B[enjamin]. P[ickever]. Wilme, *A manual of writing and printing characters, both ancient and modern: for the use of architects, engineers and surveyors, engravers, printers, decorators, and draughtsmen; also, for use in schools and private families* ..., London: printed for the author by John Weale, 1845. 'The white spaces which are seen in the impression from the stencil-plate are caused by the small pieces of brass in these places stopping out the ink. These pieces of brass are necessarily left to keep together those parts bordering on the perforated spaces. The white spaces must be made good with a pen and ink.' (p. 10)

SPECIMEN

Figure A4.18. Block letters, from W. F. Stanley, company catalogue, 1912, p. 85. '[T]he *block letter* ... having all the strokes of equal thickness, is one of the most imperfect stencil letters, there being so many breaks which have to be left in the metal to give support to interior portions, as the centre part of O's, etc., thus to make block letters look sightly, it is necessary to fill up the breaks with the colour employed in stencilling.' William Ford Stanley, *A descriptive treatise on mathematical drawing instruments* ..., London: n.p., 1900 (1866). (p. 227)

ABC2345
ABC2345

Figure A4.19. Wilfred J. Lineham, *A treatise on hand lettering for engineers, architects, surveyors and students of mechanical drawing*, London: Chapman and Hall, 1915. 'Now supposing the lettering is completely stencilled, do not let the result be marred by leaving the bars, now white, unfilled with ink, for the lettering is immensely improved by filling-in with black, and the labour is but small.' (p. 239)

Breaks avoided

To avoid the obvious imposition of breaks on otherwise conventional characters, strategies have been devised to disguise the breaks. These include 'composite' characters (discussed above); 'natural' characters, whose design integrates breaks seamlessly; and 'bridge' characters, marked out from stencils whose bridges do not leave breaks in the characters as stencilled.

Natural form. Breaks can be disguised by making them integral to the design of characters from conception, rather than imposing breaks on to already designed characters at a later stage. Des Billettes makes no mention of letters designed in this way, probably because at the time he was writing decorated letters (which are very amenable to such treatment) were painted and illuminated rather than stencilled. Stencilled examples begin appearing in liturgical books in the middle decades of the eighteenth century, sometimes partnered with other kinds of decoration (borders, head- and tail pieces) conceived on the same basis; they are in evidence throughout the remainder of the century. They appear to have been used less frequently in liturgical books made in the early decades of the nineteenth century, then re-appear with greater frequency in a wide variety of styles. They are also illustrated by Stanley (1866), and in catalogues offering stencils for architects, engineers, surveyors, and the legal profession. For Scott-Mitchell (1906), natural stencil letters were an extension of stencilling in general, in which 'natural' breaks were fundamental to the idiom. Throughout the twentieth century, and up to the present day, natural stencil letters have appeared with regularity and often with considerable invention.

Figure A4.20. Titling letters from 'Graduale Romanum de Tempore & Sanctus' Abbey of Loo (Flanders), 1755. Gilmore Music Library, Yale University.

Figure A4.21. Stencil plate, Jean Gabriel Bery, Paris, 1781, brass, etched and filed, 78 × 54 mm. American Philosophical Society Museum, Philadelphia.

Figure A4.22. Sample stencil letters, from William Ford Stanley, *A descriptive treatise on mathematical drawing instruments . . .*, London: n. p., 1900 (1866), p. 348. 'The [stencil] letters which appear most perfect are shaded outline, old English, and ornamental. Although there are breaks in these, by the style or ornamentation they can scarcely be noticed.' (p. 349)

Figure A4.23. Specification drawing, Albert J. McCauley, US Letters Patent no. 1,098,745 (1914). 'My improved stencil is formed by slotting a sheet of material to represent shadows of complete alphabetical or numerical characters, and leaving portions of the material between some slots to represent faces of the characters. The material between the slots is an integral part of the stencil sheet so that the stencil has ample strength, and the characters formed by painting through the stencil do not have the mutilated appearance of the ordinary stencil characters.'

FIG. 101.—STENCILLED LETTERS FROM JOHN M. CLARK'S ALPHABET BOOK.

Figure A4.24. 'Stencilled letters', Frederick Scott-Mitchell, *Practical stencil work*, London: The Trade Papers Publishing Co, 1906, p. 166. 'Some fancy types make better stencils than the styles now in vogue, and the ties then may become part of the lettering as necessary to the letter as to the stencil plate. Curves, scrolls, and other embellishments become then the beauty and the strength of the letter'. (p. 165) Scott-Mitchell devoted an entire section of his text to ties (i.e. bridges, or attachments), which he described as the 'keynote' of the stencil. Ties integrated seamlessly into a design are termed 'natural' and compared favourably to those imposed irrespective of the design. 'There are good and bad kinds of these ties. The old fashioned stencil cutter would appear to have drawn his design independently of ties and then put them in promiscuously before cutting. Afterwards he would go over his work again "filling in" these blanks with a sable or camel hair pencil [i.e. a fine brush], freehand, or would in some cases cut a separate stencil plate to cover those ties and thereby obliterate all trace of ties if he could do so, apparently to hide the fact that he had used stencils at all. All that is now reversed. The kind of ties that require "filling in" are the wrong kind. The majority of stencilled work now remains untouched after the stencil plate is removed from the work.' (p. 26)

Bridges. Breaks have also been avoided by the use of stencils whose bridges are constructed in a way that allows the brush (with ink) to pass underneath the bridge, resulting in characters without breaks. In some instances, these bridges actually rise up from the stencil plate as they span the plate's voids.

Figure A4.25. Stencil plate, maker not known, copper and wire, United States, late 19th or first half 20th century, 316 × 260 mm. The wires holding in place the counters of the B are sufficiently thin to allow an ink-filled brush to sweep beneath them, producing a letter without breaks.

Figure A4.26. Specification drawing, J. A. Jordan, UK patent 11,491 (1892). 'In order to avoid the necessity of using two stencils for letters &c., the loose centres … of the letters are hung from beams … which are supported on pillars … on the plate.'

Figure A4.27. Illustration from G. Charrière, *Le pochoir, un outil merveilleux … mal connu* (The stencil, a wonderful tool … not well known), Paris: G. Charrière, 1935, p. 20. This manual addresses many aspects of stencilling, including the use of *ponts* (bridges) fastened to a stencil plate to secure its separate parts in position.

Inter-character spacing

A number of methods have been devised over the centuries to regulate the spaces between stencil characters. Des Billettes's *lumière* is an early example, though there is no direct evidence of its use in stencilled liturgical books. Instead, and despite his warnings, another early method, the inter-character spacing dot, was commonly employed and may have been conventional. It remained in continuous use and was still a feature of French-made stencils well into the twentieth century. Variations are also found, mainly incremental markings set out above or below letters to regulate their spacing. Several uses of a similar

kind of opening, or 'window', are found in the nineteenth century, both in the patent record and in manufactured stencilling devices. Devices that achieve inter-character spacing through the composition of individual plates ('settable units') were also introduced in the nineteenth century, most enduringly as the 'Adjustable Stencil'. Accurate spacing of letters and words was also achieved through the use of transparent celluloid stencils. Celluloid easily improved on the various mechanical solutions that were necessitated by brass and other opaque materials.

Figure A4.28. Lumière, reconstructed according to the description of Des Billettes. Complete stencil shown in figure A4.1.

Figure A4.29. Stencil disk, made by New York Stencil Works, based on US Letters Patent no. 81,032 (1868) and reissue no. 4402 (1871), 250 mm dia. 'The orifices through the plate … adjoining the figures serve as windows to see how to place the figures in marking. … The space between the orifices and the figures is used for spacing the figures …, the same as the marginal space of the plate [i.e. at the edge of the plate] is used for spacing the latter [*sic*; letters]'; (from reissue). See also US Letters Patent nos. 257,423 (1882) and 1,345,653 (1920).

Figure A4.30. Specification drawing, Leo Wallenstein, US Letters Patent no. 1,413,246 (1922). This invention assured the aligned fitting of successive plates by means of their shape, and by abutting the plate to the vertical flanges to the left and below the character. The window to the left of the character alternatively assisted alignment, especially when marking out on other than a straight line.

Figure A4.31. Specification drawings, Thomas C. Hough, US Letters Patent no. 931,309 (1909). An unusual vertical stacking of characters. To their left are 'gauge perforations' through which the right-most parts of the previously stencilled character could be seen and thus accurately spaced. Hough devised a separate, adjustable strip that could be positioned over these perforations to mask them from the inked brush. Examples of this invention survive. Other alphabet or numeral stencils configured as vertical strips simply position the characters a consistent distance in from the left edge of the plate; this distance then determines the space between consecutively stencilled characters, similar to the stencil disk, above (figure A4.29).

Figure A4.32. Stencil with inter-character spacing dot, maker not known, France, probably 18th century, brass. The inter-character spacing dot is the small hole cut through the plate to the right of the letter. When stencilled, the resulting dot indicates the position of the next letter. In theory, the dot is covered over by the left part of the next letter stencilled, but in practice this is not always possible while maintaining even spacing (e.g. with f, t, or z; or with x, v, or y). The vertical position of the dot may be as low as ½ the x-height (as here), or as high as ⅘, but is usually around ⅔ to ¾, to maximise the likelihood of it being covered by the following letter. The spacing that results from inter-character spacing dots is fairly consistent, and most stencil makers observe the need to place dots closer to round strokes (of b, c, e, o, p, æ) to lessen the distance to the next letter and maintain even spacing. There is some indication that average letter spacing decreases in more recent (19th-century) sets of stencils.

Figure A4.33. Stencil plate, made by Johann Merkenthaler, Nuremberg, late 19th or first half of the 20th century, etched zinc, 53 × 42 mm. Two spacing lines are cut from the plate, above the letter ('a'); the letter and its righthand spacing line are then marked out together. The next stencil is positioned such that its lefthand spacing line aligns with the already marked out righthand spacing line from the 'a' plate.

Figure A4.34. Stencil plate, made by Huntington Stencil Co., United States, mid 20th century, 'oiled cured' card, 114 × 380 mm. After a numeral is marked out, a line is made (with a pencil) down the left vertical edge of the cut-out rectangle positioned below and to the right of the numeral. The pencil line is then aligned with the right vertical edge of the rectangle positioned below and to the left of the next numeral to be marked out. Other vertical edges may be used to increase letter spacing.

Figure A4.35. Stencil plate, made by Cia. de Canetas Compactor, Brazil, early 21st century, plastic, 59 × 38 mm. After the letter is marked out, additional (pencil) marks are made through either pair of vertically aligned holes to the right of the letter, depending on the amount of letter spacing desired. The pencil marks are then aligned with either pair of vertically aligned holes to the left of the next letter to be marked out.

Figure A4.36. Reese's Adjustable Stencil Plates, made by S. W. Reese & Co., United States, based on US Letters Patent no. 148,087 (1874) and no. 173,058 (1876), die-stamped and folded, spring brass, 57 × 30 mm (R plate). The earliest patent for a 'settable-units' stencil was issued in 1840, in the US. A succession of related patents followed, culminating in the Reese patents of 1874 and 1876 (definitive). This invention, unchanged but now known as 'interlocking stencils', is still in production by the original manufacturer (Hanson). See Kindel (2006).

Masking

Des Billettes describes two masking tools, the sash-clamp (*sergent*) and the holdfast (*patte*). Neither are attached to the stencil plate but are instead placed separately, on top of it, after the plate has been set in position. Des Billettes's are the only such masking tools presently known.

In the nineteenth century, in the United States, at least two stencilling devices incorporated a mask or shield, as did at least one French device, which is later in date. In these instances, the mask/shield is physically attached to the stencil plate.

Figure A4.37. Stencil disk, made by New York Stencil Works, based on US Letters Patent no. 81,032 (1868) and reissue no. 4402 (1871), 250 mm dia. 'The shield has orifices through it which correspond in position with the circles of letters and figures on the plate. This shield is broad enough to cover a portion of the plate and protect the latter from the stencil-brush while the letter or figure which it is desired to use is exposed through the orifices …. The shield allows the letter … and the figure … to be used without interfering with any other letters or figures'.

Figure A4.38. Number/date stencil, maker not known, United States, probably 2nd half 19th century, brass (number strips), copper (plate), wood (handle), 192 mm (width). The plate through which the number strips are threaded doubles as a shield against the ink-filled brush. This specific device, while apparently not patented, is similar to devices specified in US Letters Patent no. 37,648 (1863), no. 56,674 (1866), and no. 80,711 (1868). See Kindel (2006), p. 71.

Figure A4.39. Alphabet plates (1 of 3 in the set) with sliding shield, maker not known, France, 20th century, etched brass (plate), zinc (shield), 35 × 167 mm.

Ink

In his description of the stencilling ink, Des Billettes recommends the use of a (paper) cone filled with ink, over which is placed a sponge to moderate the uptake of ink by the brush. While this specific advice has not (yet) been found elsewhere, use of a sponge together with stencil ink is found in alphabet sets made in the US in the nineteenth and twentieth centuries. Here, however, the sponge serves either to draw ink out of the brush if at first an excessive amount has been taken up, or it moderates the uptake of water by the brush before it is rubbed on a dry ink cake.

Figure A4.40. Ink cake and sponge in tin holder, from Reese's Adjustable Stencil Plates, boxed set, *c*. 1880s, 92 mm (length).

References

Des Billettes, Gilles Filleau. 'Imprimerie de Livres d'Eglise, Escriteaux ou Sentences &c.', Wing MS oversize Z4029.225. The Newberry Library, Chicago

Doede, Werner (1957). *Schön schreiben, eine Kunst: Johann Neudörffer und seine Schule im 16. und 17. Jahrhundert.* München: Prestel Verlag

François, Claude-Laurent (2010). 'Les écritures réalisées au pochoir', in Yves Perrousseaux, *Histoire de l'écriture typographique: le XVIIIᵉ siècle*, vol. 1 of 2. Yves Perrousseaux éditeur, pp. 48–77

Jammes, André (1961). *La réforme de la typographie royale sous Louis XIV: Le Grandjean*, Paris: Librairie Paul Jammes

Jammes, André (1965). 'Académisme et typographie: the making of the romain du roi', *Journal of the Printing Historical Society*, no. 1, pp. 71–95

Johnston, Edward (1908). *Writing & illuminating, & lettering* (2nd edn). London: John Hogg

Kindel, Eric (2003). 'Recollecting stencil letters', *Typography papers*, 5. Reading: Department of Typography & Graphic Communication, University of Reading, pp. 65–101

Kindel, Eric (2006). 'Patents progress: the Adjustable Stencil', *Journal of the Printing Historical Society*, new series, no. 9, Spring 2006, pp. 65–92

Kindel, Eric (2009). 'Delight of men and gods: Christiaan Huygens's new method of printing', *Journal of the Printing Historical Society*, new series, no. 14, Autumn 2009, pp. 5–40

Kindel, Eric (2010). 'Fit to be seen: stencils for architects, engineers and surveyors', *AA Files*, 61, pp. 100–9

Linke, Oliver and Christine Sauer (2007). *Zierlich schreiben: Der Schreibmeister Johann Neudörffer d. Ä und seine Nachfolger in Nürnberg*. München: Typographische Gesellschaft München

Maral, Alexandre (2001). 'L'étonnante destinée d'un édifice provisoire: la chapelle royale de Versailles entre 1682 et 1710', *In Situ, revue des patrimoines*, no. 1, 2001. http://www.insitu.culture.fr/index.xsp

Mosley, James (ed.) (1995). *The Manuel typographique of Pierre-Simon Fournier le jeune, with Fournier on typefounding, an English translation of the text by Harry Carter, facsimile edition in three volumes*. Darmstadt: Technische Hochschule

Mosley, James (1997). 'French academicians and modern typography: designing new types in the 1690s', *Typography papers*, 2. Reading: Department of Typography & Graphic Communication, University of Reading, pp. 5–29

Mosley, James (2002). 'Les caractères de l'imprimerie royale', in *Le Romain du Roi: la typographie au service de l'État, 1702–2002*. Lyon: Musée de l'Imprimerie de Lyon, pp. 32–78

Pinault, Madeleine (1987). 'Dessins pour un Art de l'Imprimerie', 112ᵉ Congrès national des Sociétés savantes, Lyon, *Histoire des Sciences*, vol. 2, pp. 73–85

Ritchie, Carson I. A. (ed.) (1966). 'The hostel of the Invalides by Thomas Povey (1682) (Lambeth Palace Library MS. 745)', *Medical History*, vol. 10, no. 1, January 1966 (part 1), pp. 1–22; and vol. 10, no. 2, April 1966 (part 2), pp. 177–97.

Vanuxem, Jacques (1974). 'Un exemple de trésor perdu pour Les Invalides: les manuscrits enluminés de la fin du XVIIᵉ siècle', in René Baillargeat (ed.), *Les Invalides: trois siècles d'histoire*. Paris: Musée de l'Armée, Hôtel National des Invalides, pp. 105–12

Acknowledgements

I owe a deep debt of gratitude to my colleague James Mosley, who by making available copies of Des Billettes's description and Simonneau's engraving in 1999, as my interest in stencilling was just getting underway, provided me with research material of fundamental importance, which has, in turn, led to enriching collaborations and not a few adventures. I would like to thank James and my other collaborators, Andrew Gillmore and Fred Smeijers, for their careful, sensitive, and questioning work on the reconstruction documented here, and additionally, James and Fred for their contributions and partnership in the present publication.

For funding the original project of reconstruction (2001–2) I gratefully acknowledge the support of the Arts & Humanities Research Board (as was), and thank Nicolas Barker and Michael Turner for serving as referees for the grant proposal. During the course of the project, and subsequently, I have enjoyed the kindness and unstinting support of Paul F. Gehl at the Newberry Library, Chicago, to whom I extend my sincere thanks.

I would additionally like to thank Veronica Heath for her valuable English translation of Des Billettes's text, which guided the reconstruction; Claude-Laurent François, who since our first meeting in 2003 has generously shared his own discoveries in France, which have provided context for the reconstruction and, in places, corroboration; David M. Riches, Lia Monica Rossi and José Marconi Bezerra de Souza, Michael Twyman, and Gerard Unger for supplying several of the examples shown in appendix 4; Sue Walker, who as head of the Department of Typography & Graphic Communication at Reading during the original project, fostered a congenial research environment for it; and my department colleagues, who have taken a welcome and productive interest in the research described here.

Finally, I would like to thank the organisers of the annual congress of the Association Typographique Internationale in Rome (2002) for providing Fred Smeijers and myself with a first opportunity to present the work of reconstruction to colleagues and peers.

Reconstructions

Andrew Gillmore: figures 2, 3, 5, 8, 9, 24–31
Eric Kindel: figures 4, 6, 32–37, A4.8
Fred Smeijers: figures 7, 10, 11, 12–17 (glyphs), 18–23, A1.1, A2.1–2.9, A4.1, A4.28

The reconstructed equipment is presently located in the Department of Typography & Graphic Communication, University of Reading, and may be consulted there. Unless noted, other artefacts are in the author's collection.

Photography & imaging

Figures 2, 3, 5, 8, 9, 24–31, 32–35; A4.3–4.7, 4.25, 4.29, 4.32–4.40: Laura Bennetto (D&PS, University of Reading)
Figures A4.2, 4.9, 4.16: Claude-Laurent François
Figures 4, 6, 7, 10, 11, 18–23; A2.1–2.9; A4.1, 4.21: Eric Kindel
Figure 38: (C) Paris – Musée de l'Armée, dist. RMN – © Photo Musée de l'Armée
Figures 1, A3.1: St Bride Library, London
Figure A4.15: Museum für angewandte Kunst, Vienna
Figure A4.21: American Philosophical Society, Philadelphia

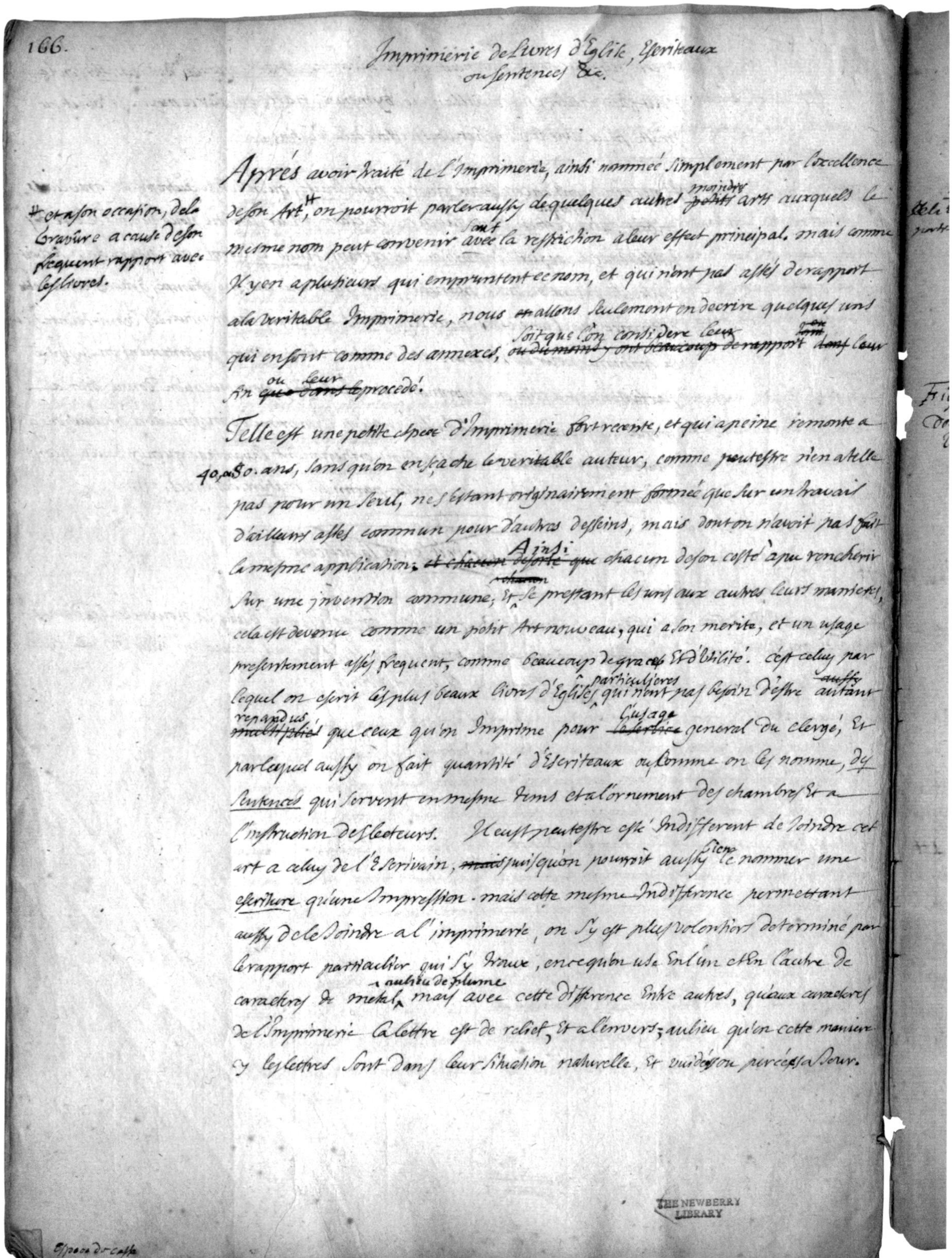

Imprimerie de Livres d'Eglise, Escriteaux
ou Sentences &c.

Aprés avoir traité de l'Imprimerie, ainsi nommée simplement par l'excellence
de son Art, on pourroit parler aussi de quelques autres petits arts auxquels le
mesme nom peut convenir avec la restriction a leur effet principal. mais comme
il y en a plusieurs qui empruntent ce nom, et qui n'ont pas assés de rapport
a la veritable Imprimerie, nous allons seulement en decrire quelques uns
qui en sont comme des annexes, ou du moins ont beaucoup de rapport dans leur
fin ou leur.

Telle est une petite espece d'Imprimerie fort recente, et qui a peine remonte a
40, 50. ans, sans qu'on en sçache le veritable auteur, comme peut estre rien a elle
pas pour un seul, ne s'estant originairement formée que sur un travail
d'ailleurs assés commun pour d'autres desseins, mais dont on n'avoit pas fait
la mesme application. Ainsi chacun de son costé a pu rencherir
sur une invention commune, et se prestant les uns aux autres leurs manieres,
cela est devenu comme un petit Art nouveau, qui a son merite, et un usage
presentement assés frequent, comme beaucoup de grace et d'utilité. c'est celuy par
lequel on escrit les plus beaux Livres d'Eglise particulieres qui n'ont pas besoin d'estre aussi autant
repandus que ceux qu'on Imprime pour l'usage general du clergé, Et
par lequel aussi on fait quantité d'Escriteaux ou comme on les nomme, de
Sentences qui servent en mesme tems et a l'ornement des chambres et a
l'instruction des lecteurs. Il eust peut estre esté Indifferent de Ioindre cet
art a celuy de l'Escrivain, puisqu'on pourroit aussi bien le nommer une
escriture qu'une Impression. mais cette mesme Indifference permettant
aussi de le Ioindre a l'imprimerie, on s'y est plus volontiers determiné par
le rapport particulier qui s'y trouve, en ce qu'on use l'un et l'autre de
caracteres de metal au lieu de plume, mais avec cette difference entre autres, qu'aux caracteres
de l'Imprimerie la lettre est de relief, et a l'envers; aulieu qu'en cette maniere
cy les lettres sont dans leur situation naturelle, et uuides ou percées a Iour.

[marginal note:] et a son occasion, de la
Gravure a cause de son
frequent rapport avec
les livres.

Figure 1. Cahier of Gilles Filleau des Billettes, showing the first page of the text
'Imprimerie de Livres d'Eglise, Escriteaux ou Sentences &c.', Wing MS oversize
Z4029.225, p.166, The Newberry Library, Chicago.

edited by
Eric Kindel

The description of stencilling by Gilles Filleau des Billettes: transcription and translation

This article presents the description of stencilling by Gilles Filleau des Billettes. The French text, approximately 10,000 words in length, is here transcribed and accompanied by a parallel English translation. Introductory notes on the preparation of both texts are provided; images of stencil letters found among the papers of Sébastien Truchet, Des Billettes's colleague, are shown in an appendix.

Permission to publish this transcription and its supplementary images has been given by the Newberry Library, Chicago, and is gratefully acknowledged.

The description of stencilling by Gilles Filleau des Billettes sets out a method for stencilling letters, words, and texts, and specifies equipment for doing the work. (For a reconstruction of the equipment and the method, see this volume, pp. 28–65.) Des Billettes's description is one of a number of texts drafted by him that deal with methods of printing, and which together contributed to work on a 'description of trades' (*Description des arts et métiers*), a project begun in 1693 under the direction of the Académie royale des Sciences, Paris. (For further information about this project, and Des Billettes, see James Mosley, 'A note on Gilles Filleau des Billettes', this volume, pp. 87–90.) Des Billettes's handwritten text on stencilling occupies 24 pages of a folio *cahier* (figure 1), plus two sides of a loosely inserted leaf; and is supplemented by marginal and intratextual drawings.

A transcription and translation of Des Billettes's text are presented in the pages that follow, together with images of his drawings.

A note on the texts

The transcription follows guidelines established by James Mosley, based on his own work on Des Billettes's draft texts.

The orthography and punctuation of the original is followed as exactly as possible, including inconsistencies in spelling, in the use of diacritics (acute and grave accents, diaëresis and cedilla), and in the inclusion or omission of commas or points separating characters in a sequence (e.g. 'A, B,' or 'A. B.' or 'A B'). Points that sometimes follow figures have not been transcribed.

Capitalization in the original is generally followed in the transcription. Sentences that follow a full point are made to begin with a capital. Where it is unclear if a majuscule or a minuscule is intended (other than at the start of a sentence), a lowercase letter is used. I and J, which are invariably capitalized at the start of a word, are also rendered in lowercase. Initial E is sometimes used in simple words like *et*; here it is transcribed as lowercase, though in other instances a capital is retained.

Terms that are underlined in the original are rendered in italic. Where an alternative word or phrase occurs, usually written above the original word or phrase (which is not cancelled), both are supplied; in these instances, the original is followed by the alternative, which is placed between angle brackets, as in 'seule ⟨simple⟩'. A space between curly brackets { } indicates an illegible word; two en-dashes -- indicate a missing figure.

Marginal notes in the original that are clearly a continuation of the main text, and whose insertion point is indicated, have been silently taken into the transcription;

otherwise they are placed in a footnote. Individual words and short passages that have been decisively cancelled have not been transcribed, except where they seemed to be worth keeping; in these instances they are also placed in a footnote.

Because Des Billettes's text is a draft, various phrases and passages lack clarity or are unresolved. Throughout, minor clarifications have been added to the translation; these are placed in parentheses (by the translator) or square brackets [by the editor]. More significant ambiguities in the French are retained in the translation, but explained in footnotes where possible. The translation of key French terms is also explained in the footnotes. Footnotes are by the editor, unless signed (JM). The transcription and translation are presented on facing pages. Drawings are reproduced adjacent to the text that refers to them, and are numbered in square brackets.

A draft transcription of Des Billettes's text was made in late 1999 and early 2000 by Eric Kindel, with consultation from James Mosley. The transcription was made using photocopies supplied by JM from his working materials, having been captured from microfilms supplied by the Newberry Library. In spring 2000, a draft translation was made by Veronica Heath; it guided the project of reconstruction undertaken in 2001–2. In 2011, EK photographed Des Billettes's cahier at the Newberry Library, and using these images he and JM made revisions to the transcription in the latter months of 2012. From this transcription, VH in turn made revisions to the translation in early 2013. EK and JM supplemented this work with clarifications to passages containing technical and other special terms or descriptions.

166

Imprimerie de Livres d'Eglise, Escriteaux
ou sentences &c.

Aprés avoir traité de l'imprimerie, ainsi nommée simplement par l'excellence de son Art et a son occasion, de la
Gravure a cause de son frequent rapport avec les livres,
on pourroit parler aussy de quelques autres moindres
arts auxquels le mesme nom peut convenir avec ⟨sont⟩
la restriction a leur effect principal. Mais comme il y en a
plusieurs qui empruntent ce nom, et qui n'ont pas assés de
rapport a la veritable Imprimerie, nous allons seulement
en decrire quelques uns qui en sont comme des annexes,
soit que l'on considere leur fin ou leur procedé.

Telle est une petite espece d'imprimerie fort recente, et
qui a peine remonte a 40, a 50 ans,[1] sans qu'on en sçache le
veritable auteur, comme peutestre n'en a telle pas pour un
seul, ne s'estant originairement formée que sur un travail
d'ailleur asses commun pour d'autres dessins, mais dont
on n'avoit pas fait la mesme application. Ainsi chacun de
son costé a pû rencherir sur une inversion commune, et se
prestant les uns aux autres leurs manieres, cela est devenu
comme un petit Art nouveau, qui a son merite, et un usage
presentement asses frequent, comme beaucoup de grace
et d'utilité. C'est celuy par lequel on escrit les plus beaux
livres d'Eglises particulieres qui n'ont pas besoin d'estre
autant repandus que ceux qu'on imprime pour l'usage
general du clergé, et par lequel aussy on fait quantité
d'Escriteaux ou, comme on les nomme, *des sentences* qui
servent en mesme tems et a l'ornement des chambres et a
l'instruction des lecteurs. Il eust peutestre esté indifferent
de joindre cet art a celuy de l'Escrivain, puisqu'on pourroit
aussy bien le nommer une *escriture* qu'une impression.
Mais ceste mesme indifference permettant aussy de le
joindre a l'imprimerie; on s'y est plus volontiers determiné
par le rapport particulier qui s'y trouve, en ce qu'on use en
l'un et en l'autre de caracteres de metal au lieu de plume
mais avec cette difference entre autres, qu'aux caracteres
de l'imprimerie la lettre est de relief, et a l'envers; au lieu
qu'en cette maniere cy les lettres sont dans leur situation
naturelle, et vuidées ou percées a jour.

167

[p. 167] Voicy comment cela se fait dans la plus grande
perfection, supposant une mesure certaine de lettre pour
la facilité de la description, sauf a y mettre du plus ou du
moins selon les diverses grosseurs de lettre dont on se
voudra servir. On prend des plaques ou des lames de cuivre
c'est a dire du laton bien minces, cela va peutestre a la 12e.
parte d'une ligne. Voir.[2] Et autant qu'elles peuvent l'estre
en gardant quelque consistence pour la durée et qui puisse
soustenir le travail qu'on y doit faire, et celuy de leur usage.
On les taille de 4 pouces de long (par exemple) sur 2 de

large, et quarrèment a angles droits. A 4 lignes c'est a dire
a un tiers de pouce audessus du bout dessiné pour le bas
on trace une ligne parallele au bord; et audessus encore 4
autres paralleles toutes en pareilles distances d'un tiers de
pouce. Ces 5 lignes forment ensemble dans une hauteur
d'un pouce deux tiers cinq bandes chacune de 4 lignes de
large sur 2 p. de long que nous nommerons A B C D E.[3]

Sur chaque bout des bandes A.B.C.D. on retranche la
longeur de 2 lignes et ainsy il ne leur reste plus que 20
lignes de long, pendant que la bande E en a 24 au dessus
de chaque bout de laquelle on fait une tranche ou coupure
de 2 lignes de long pour degager ces deux bouts d'avec
le dessus ou haut de la piece. Et pour le mieux il est bon
mesme de retrancher de ce dessus un petit triangle aigu
pour degager encore davantage ces 2 bouts. Et par ce
moyen la bande E outre la longeur de 20 lignes qui luy est
commune avec les 4 autres a de plus a chaque bout un
petit parallelogramme de 2 lignes de long sur 4 de haut
que nous nommerons des *orillons*, et que sont marqués
par GG[.]

On plie des bandes A. B. prises ensemble sur celles de
C. D. et on les applanit a coup de marteau en sorte qu'elles
ne font plus toutes quatre que comme une seule bande
de deux epaisseurs de laton sur 8 lignes de large. On plie
encore une fois cette double bande en montant du mesme
sens que la premiere fois, puis ayant encore bien applani
ce pli, il se trouve trois Epaisseurs de laton ensemble sur
une largeur de 8 lignes. Alors on rabat les 2 orillons – G, G,
sur les extremités de cette triple bande qui se trouve ainsi
liée sans les pouvoir déprendre l'espace de 4 lignes de haut
qui est la hauteur [p. 168] des orillons. Mais comme il reste
encore 4 autres lignes c'est a dire la moitié d'en haut de
cette bande qui ne sont retenues d'aucun lien, on ramene
cette moitié en dehors par un autre pli jusqu'a ce qu'elle
soit recoudée a angle droit ou à plomb sur l'autre moitié.
Et cela fait, la construction de la piece se trouve telle qu'au
lieu qu'elle avoit d'abord 4 pouces de haut en bas, elle n'a
plus en tout que 2 pou. 8 lig. dont le bas que nous nommons la queuë est une bandes [*sic*] de 3 Epaisseurs a l'endroit des orillons il y a 4 Epaisseurs de laton sur 20 lignes
de long et 4 large; le haut que nous nommons le corps de
la piece ou du caractere est d'une seule ⟨simple⟩ Epaisseur
sur 2 pouces 4 lignes de haut ⟨long⟩ et 2 pouces de large;
et la bande perpendiculaire, ou le rebord ⟨recoude⟩ elevé
a plomb, que nous nommons *le pied* de 2 Epaisseurs du 20
lignes de long et 4 de haut.

Il n'est pas necessaire de s'attacher scrupuleusement
a une egalité precise ces mesures; car un peu plus ou
moins de hauteur du corps ou du pied, et de la largeur de
la queuë ne fait point d'inconvenient. Et l'on peut aussy

168

---

1. In the cahier, '40, a 50' is overwritten on '30'; see figure 1,
above. This transcription, resolved after magnified examination
of Des Billettes's emendation, corrects mis-transcriptions given
in Kindel (2003, n. 14) and (2009, n. 58); see references above, p. 65.
2. 'Voir' (see) apparently represents an incomplete reference to
information elsewhere.

---

3. A marginal note occurs next to this paragraph: 'Fig. en
bois ou taille douce. Videbitur.' The words 'en bois' have been
cancelled (throughout, cancelled passages are generally struck
through with a line or similarly crossed out).

166

Printing of church books, scriptural texts
or maxims etc.

After having discussed printing, thus called simply by
virtue of the excellence of its art, and, in its proper place,
engraving because it is frequently related to books, one
could also talk of other lesser arts to which the same
name could apply considered solely with respect to their
principal purpose. But as there are several which adopt
this name, and which do not have a sufficiently close
relationship to true printing, we shall merely describe
some of these (lesser arts), which are as it were subsidiary,
related arts, whether one considers their end result or their
procedure.

One such is a minor kind of printing which is very
recent, and indeed scarcely dates back forty to fifty years,
without us knowing who was the real inventor of it, as it
may be that it was not the invention of any single person,
merely being modelled on a way of working which was
quite common for other purposes, but which had not (previously) been used for this same application. Thus each
(workman) on his own account was able to take further
a shared invention, and by sharing and exchanging their
practices, this practice became as it were a new minor art,
which has its merits, and is currently used quite frequently
as having much grace and usefulness. This is the means
used to produce the most handsome books for the specific
uses of particular churches, and which do not have to be
as widely distributed as those which are printed for the
general use of the clergy;[1] and it is by this means also that
a good number of scriptural texts are printed, and what
are called maxims, which serve the double purpose of
ornamenting rooms and instructing their readers. Perhaps
one might equally well affiliate the art to that of the writer,
as one could as aptly call it a writing process as a printing
process; but by the same token one could equally well affiliate it to printing. We decided rather more readily to do the
latter owing to the specific affinity which exists between
it and printing, inasmuch as both employ metal letters
instead of a pen, but with this difference among others,
that for printing types the letter is in relief and reversed,
whereas in this process the letters are the right way round
and cut out.[2]

167　This is how this is done with the greatest degree of
perfection, supposing a fixed size for the letter for ease
of description, except inasmuch as this must be varied
according to the different sizes of letter that one wishes
to employ. One takes pieces of very thin brass of the kind
called 'latten' (this can be made a 12th part of a *ligne* thick.
See.[3]) as thin as they can be while keeping the strength
that will make them last and stand up to the work that

must be done with them. They are trimmed to four inches
long (for example) by two wide, and squared off to right
angles. At four lignes, that is to say at a third of an inch,
above the end designated as the bottom one draws a line
parallel to the edge, and above it four more parallel lines,
all at the same distance of a third of an inch from each
other. These five lines together form five bands of a height
of one inch and two-thirds overall, each band of four lignes
wide by two inches long, which we will call A, B, C, D, E.[4]

At each end of the bands A, B, C, D, you remove a length
of two lignes and thus only a length of twenty lignes
remains, while band E has twenty-four, above each end of
which one makes a depression or cut of two lignes long to
separate these two ends from the upper part of the piece.
And to do this in the best possible fashion it is even a good
idea to take out from this upper part a small sharp triangle
to separate these two ends still further. And by this means
band E, in addition to the twenty lignes which it has in
common with the [four] other bands, also has at each end
a little parallelogram of two lignes long by four high, that
we call lugs and which are labelled G, G.

One folds bands A, B taken together over bands C, D
and flattens them with a hammer in such a way that all
four constitute a kind of single band of two thicknesses of
brass and eight lignes wide. One again folds that double
band in the same direction as for the first (operation), then
having yet again thoroughly flattened the fold, this gives
three thicknesses of brass pressed together over a width
of eight lignes. One then turns back the lugs G, G so that
they are folded over the ends of this triple band, which is
thus secured firmly and is unable to come undone over the
space of four lignes high (which is the height of the lugs). 168
But as this still leaves four other lignes, that is, half the
height of that [triple] band, which are not secured by any
fastening, one brings this half back out[wards] by means
of another fold until it is at a right angle or perpendicular
to the other half. And when that is done, the construction of the piece is such that whereas initially it was four
inches from top to bottom, it is now in total two inches
eight lignes, of which the lower part which we call the tail
is a band of three thicknesses (at the lugs there are four
thicknesses) of brass of twenty lignes long by four wide,
the upper part which we call the body of the piece or the
caractère[5] is a single ply of one thickness of two inches four
lignes long and two inches wide, and the perpendicular
band, or the perpendicular raised edge, which we call the
foot of two thicknesses of twenty lignes long by four high.

It is not necessary to adhere scrupulously to a precise
conformity with these measurements, as variations more
or less in the height of the body or the foot, and of the
width of the tail, do not matter. And one can also assign to

---

1. See this volume, p. 29, for additional remarks on the specific
uses these books served.

2. Des Billettes uses the word *lettre* to include (often by implication) letters, numerals, and other symbols, i.e. the set of characters. Here and below, 'letter' is used in this same encompassing
sense. See n. 5, below, for additional remarks on the translation
of *caractère*.

3. This phrase, here rendered parenthetically, is given as a
marginal note in Des Billettes's text, but with its insertion point
indicated. 'See' apparently represents an incomplete reference
to information elsewhere. A 'ligne' is approximately 2.256 mm;
1 ligne = 1/12 *pouce* ('inch') = 1/144 *pied de roi*. Here and below,
ligne is left untranslated.

---

4. A marginal note occurs next to this paragraph: 'Woodcut or
copperplate engraving. Videbitur.' The word for 'woodcut' has
been cancelled (throughout, cancelled passages are generally
struck through with a line or similarly crossed out). 'Woodcut'
may be read as a 'cut' (obsolete), that is to say, an illustration.

5. Des Billettes here uses the word 'caractère' to describe
the (upper) part of the stencil plate where the letter is located;
elsewhere, however, and throughout his text this word usually
describes (or implies) the stencil plate in general. Below,
caractère is variously translated as 'plate', 'stencil plate',
or 'stencil', depending on the emphasis required.

donner a quelques caracteres jusqu'a prés de la moitié moins de largeur partout selon que les lettres qu'ils
portent en occupent par leur construction, comme un i
par Example, ou une r qui ne renferment pas beaucoup
de place en largeur, et n'ont besoin d'estre percées qu'une
fois dans leurs caracteres, comme on l'entendra assés dans
la suite. Le plus important est seulement de bien plier et
applanir ce laton tant au maillet de bois, qu'au marteau
d'acier poly; et on peut mesme avoir pour
cela et pour le pli une maniere de tenaille
ou presse [1] d'un morceau d'acier applati
premierement sur une largeur d'environ
2 pouces, puis replié en sorte qu'il se
fasse ressort quand on le presse, et qu'il

porte par les bouts couppes quamn{ }t et tres uniment
un[e] maniere de rebord Epais d'environ 3 a 4 lignes de
large de mesme sur 2 a 3 pouces de long, ce qui fait a peu
pres la mesme figure que les machoires d'un Estau sin{ }
qu'elles vont un peu en rond ou en bizeau en montant,
au lieu que celles de cett presse sont couppees tout ras et
plat et se joignant de mesme le uniment estant presses
qu'elles ne donneroient pas outres a un brin de soye bien
fine ou a un cheveu. Par ce moyen on rend aisement les
plis fort unis et egaux, mieux qu'on ne pourroit faire dans
les machoires d'un Etau ordinaire, a cause qu'elles sont
dentées comme une lime, et qu'a la continue le travail en
corrompt bientost l'egalité outre qu'ordinairement elles ne
sont pas assés plates par dessus ⟨le haut⟩ pour faire ce pli
assés proprement. Il est bon aussy de conserver a peu pres
la mesme hauteur a tous les caracteres depuis leur pied
jusqu'au haut de la teste comme on le jugera aisement
par la suite de ce discours.[4]

[p. 169] On peut distinguer les Alphabets par *sortes*
comme dans l'imprimerie, mais qui sont icy en petite
quantité parce qu'on ne peut pas faire de ces caracteres en
petit, et qu'il seroit mesme tres difficile ou du moins fort
inutile d'en faire d'aussy petits qu'un gros Parangon, car
quand on pourroit le bien executer, il seroit encore plus
difficile de le bien marquer/imprimer. Ainsy on se trouve-
roit assés bien fourni de *sortes* en cet art en ayant seulement 4 ou 5 depuis la grosseur du gros canon en montant.
Quoy qu'il en soit il faut environ pour chaque *sorte* environ
80 caracteres et plus, chacun devant avoir sa *courante* et
sa *majuscule*, qui est precisement/justement ce que nous
avons nommé dans l'imprimerie le *bas de casse*, et les *capi-
tales*. Puis il faut quelques lettres doubles, des ponctua-
tions, des chiffres &c. et sy l'on y veut ajouter des renvois
des notes de musique et quelques autres, ce tout pourra
bien aller du moins jusqu'a une centaine de caracteres suivant l'intention de celuy qui s'en veut servir.

Pour les mettre dans l'estat que nous avons dit on prend
d'ordinaire un certain laton battu dont les marchands
de fer ou les chinquailliers sont communement fournis
de diverses Epaisseurs, et dont il faut choisir le plus Egal
et le plus sain, et mesme du plus mince, principalement
pour les plus petits caracteres. On le fait recuire douce-
ment au feu jusqu'a commencer a rougir un peu et on le
dresse aisément avec un maillet de bois dur sur quelque
table unie. Ensuite on le couppe tout par morocaux[5] de la

grandeur qu'on a besoin, puis on les trace et plie comme
nous avons dit; et alors ils sont en estat d'estre uuidés ou
percés a jour selon les lettres qu'on y veut tailler, apres les
avoir tracés comme on va dire, et c'est en quoy consiste
presque toute l'adresse de ce petit Art.[6]

[p. 170] Comme nous avons remarqué parlant de l'imprimerie qu'un des plus grands defauts qui s'y trouvent
est lors que l'alignement des lettres n'en est pas bon, mais
on de, haut et bas, ou autrement inegal; c'est aussy la
première chose a quoy il faut se precautionner icy dans la
traceure des lettres; et cela demande assés de sujection,
comme on va voir, quand on veut faire les choses avec
toute l'exactitude et la delicatesse dont elles ont besoin
pour plaire aux bons connoisseurs/personnes de bon
goust.

Il faut donc commencer par preparer le pulpitre sur
lequel on voudra mettre le papier ou veslin dessiné a cette
impression. On le fera d'une Elevation a discretion aussi
bien que sa grandeur mais le plus commode ce semble
est de luy donner un plan incliné seulement de 12 ou 15
degrés ou Environ. Il doit estre d'un bois bien sain, uni et
sec qui ne se tourmente point en se cambrant ou en voi-
lant, et il faut le couvrir d'un cuir qui paroisse par le costé
de la chair, ou d'un drap fort uni et egal, ou d'un veslin
bien bandé dessus. Un drap fin bien tendu semble estre le
meilleur pour cela parce que la feuille y sera mieux arrestée et ferme que sur quelque chose de plus doux et plus
glissant. Sur le bord d'en bas on appliquera tout du long
de droit a gauche une regle de bois d'environ un pouce et
demi de large sur 3 a 4 lignes d'Epais attachée a chaque
bout par une vis dont la teste sera noyée dans le dessous
du pulpitre, et sortant au travers du pulpitre et de la regle,
y sera bridée par une [sic] escroux qui pressera dessus; ou
si l'on veut, la teste de la vis se pourra mettre au dessus
de la regle et les filets avoir leur escroux dans le bois du
pulpitre. De l'une ou de l'autre maniere, dont la 1ere. est
plus commode, la regle se trouve assujetie et ferme sur
le pulpitre sans pouvoir varier de part ni d'autre, a quoy il
faut aussy observer de la placer Ensorte qu'elle fasse des
angles droits, ou a Esquerre avec les 2 costes du pulpitre, et
soit parallele au bas. Pour faciliter l'explication du procedé
nous la nommerons cette regle *la conduite*. Mais parce qu
il faut que les queuës des caracteres entrent sous cette
conduite jusqu'a leur pied, et que par consequent elle ne
doit pas [p. 171] estre entierement appliquée de toute sa largeur immediatement sur le pulpitre; on trouve moyen de
la rehausser environ de l'Epaisseur d'une carte a jouer ou
moins en y collant tout du long par dessous un ruband de
laine ou de fil de 4 a 5 lignes moins large; afin que la partie de la conduite ou il manque du ruband laisse un petit
vuide tout du long sur le pulpitre pour placer les queuës
des caracteres qui doivent glisser ⟨s'enfoncer⟩ dessous
jusqu'a ce qu'ils se trouvent arrestes par leur pied qui ne
permet pas d'enfoncer plus avant. A moins que de cela il

---

4. A marginal note, written as a list, occurs next to this para-
graph: 'Fig. en bois | tenaille | pincette | presse a ressort'; [1]
occurs immediately below the list.

5. This word is clearly written 'morocaux', but is almost
certainly a mis-writing of 'morceaux'.

---

6. Three marginal notes occur near the bottom of p. 169:
'Nª. ces 10 ou 12 lignes se doivent peutestre mettre cy devant';
'J'ay transporté tout cet article vers le commencement du
discours, en mettant ce cy au n[e]t';
'Nª. qu'en tous metiers ou il y a plusieurs pieces a manier
souvent, il faut toujours faire tout de suite un mesme travail a
chaque piece plustost que d'en mettre une a fin ⟨bout⟩ avant que
de passer aux autres. Autrement on perd beaucoup de tems.'

some stencil plates up to almost half less width through-out depending on the width that the letters that they represent will occupy by virtue of their shape, like an i for example or an r which does not take up much width and only needs to be cut out as a single shape on the plate, as we shall subsequently detail. The most important thing is to flatten the brass thoroughly, whether with a wooden

mallet or with a smooth steel hammer; and one can even have (at hand) for this operation and for the folding [of the plates] a pair of pincers or a press [1] made with a piece of steel first flattened for a width of around two inches, then folded back in such a way that it springs up when pressed, and bearing on the cut edges { } and very even, a kind of raised edge of around three to four lignes thick, the same (measurement) wide [i.e. high], by two to three inches long, [two of] which [together] make much the same shape as the jaws of a vice, except { } that they [the jaws of a vice] are slightly rounded or bevelled as they go upwards, whereas those of this press are cut level and flat, and join equally flat and with a closeness of fit such that they would not let through a very fine silk thread or a hair. By this means one can easily make very smooth and even folds, better than one can in the jaws of an ordinary vice because they are serrated like a file, and because the continued use of a vice distorts the evenness (of the metal), in addition to the fact that ordinarily they [the jaws] are not flat enough on top to make a fold cleanly enough. It is also advisable to keep the stencil plates to the same height from their foot to the top of the head, as will easily be judged by what will follow later in this description.[6]

169   One can distinguish the alphabets by sizes as in print-ing, but these will be few in number as one cannot make the stencil letters [very] small, and it would be very difficult or at least quite useless to make any as small as *Gros Paran-gon*, because even if they could be well executed, there would be even more difficulty in marking/printing them out properly. Thus one will find that one is sufficiently sup-plied with sizes if one has four or five only, of *Gros Canon* and upwards. In any case for each size around eighty or more characters will be needed, as each has to have small and big letters, which are to be precise/exact what we call in printing lowercase and capital letters. Then one must have some double letters, punctuation marks, figures etc., and if one wishes to add to that some reference signs,[7] musical notes, and a few others, this can add up to at least a hundred or so characters depending on the purposes of the person who wishes to use them.

To bring them to the state we have described above normally takes a certain kind of beaten brass which iron merchants or ironmongers usually stock in different thick-nesses, of which one must select the most even and the best quality, and even the thinnest, mainly for the smallest stencil plates. One reheats it over the fire until it begins to redden a little and then one moulds it easily with a wooden mallet on a smooth wooden table. Next one cuts it into pieces of the requisite size, then one delineates and folds them as we have already described, and then they are

in a state to be cut out with the letters one wants to cut, after having drawn them in the way we shall describe, and therein lies all the skill of this little art.[8]

As we have observed in connection with printing, one of   170 the greatest defects (inherent) in it is that the alignment of the letters is not good, but wavers up and down, or is otherwise uneven; this is also the first thing over which careful precautions must be taken when drawing the letters; and this demands a high degree of mastery and observance of rules, as will be seen, when one wishes to do things with all the accuracy and delicacy which is required if one wishes to please the real connoisseurs/people of good taste.

It is therefore necessary to begin by preparing the desk on which one wishes to lay the paper or vellum designed for printing. One can make it of a height as well of a size of one's choosing, but the most convenient would seem to be to give it a slope of twelve to fifteen degrees or so. It must be of a sound, smooth, dry wood that does not twist, bow or warp, and it must be covered with a piece of leather flesh side out, or with a very smooth and even cloth, or with a piece of vellum tightly stretched over it. A fine cloth tightly stretched over it would seem to be the best because the sheet (of paper or vellum) will be more firm and secure on it than on something softer and more slippery. All along the lower edge from right to left should be fixed a wooden ruler of around an inch and a half wide by three to four lignes thick, fastened at each end by a screw the head of which should be sunk into the underside of the desk and protrude out of the desk and the ruler, secured by a nut or bolt pressing on top of it; or if desired, the head of the screw can be put into the topside of the ruler and the threads screwed into the wood of the desk. Using one or other of the above methods of which the first is the most convenient, the ruler is firmly fastened on without it being able to move. It is also necessary to take care to place it so that it makes a right angle or is square with the two sides of the desk, and that it should be parallel to the bottom of it. To facilitate the explanation of this procedure we will call this ruler the *conduite*.[9] Because the tails of the stencil plates must go under this conduite as far as their foot, and consequently it [the conduite] must not be flush with   171 the desk for the whole of its length, one therefore finds a means of lifting it up by about the thickness of a playing card or less by sticking all along the underside of it a wool or fabric ribbon four to five lignes narrower, so that in the part of the conduite where there is no ribbon a little gap is left running across the width of the desk, into which are placed the tails of the plates which should slide ⟨slot⟩ in until they are brought to a stop by their foot, which does not allow them to go in any further; otherwise it would

---

6. A marginal note, written as a list, occurs next to this para-graph: 'Woodcut: | pincers | tweezers | spring press'; [1] occurs immediately below the list.

7. i.e. asterisks, crosses, and so on.

8. Three marginal notes occur near the bottom of p. 169: 'Note that these ten or twelve lines must perhaps be placed before this.'
'I have moved this whole article towards the beginning of the description, revising this.'
'Note that in all trades where there are several tools to be used, it is best to use each tool in order, on every item where it is needed, rather than to complete all the work on one item before moving on to the others. Otherwise one wastes a lot of time.'

9. There is no obvious English equivalent to this specially con-figured part of the desk; 'conduite' is therefore left untranslated here and below.

faudroit a tout-heure lascher les vis de la regle pour enfoncer les queuës des caracteres dessous; et il faudroit mesme les lascher tantost plus tantost moins selon les differentes Epaisseurs de ces queuës, de sorte qu'on ne pourroit s'assurer qu'elle fust asses stable pour ne varier d'aucun costé comme lors qu'elle est presque toujours ferme dans une mesme situation; et l'on ne travailleroit ni si promptement, ni si juste.

Cela estant ainsi disposé il est certain qu'en garnissant toute la longueur de la conduite de caracteres coste a coste enfoncés Exactement dessous jusqu'a leur pied; et appliquant une autre regle le long de l'autre surface du pied de ces caracteres qui les pressast tous contre la conduite, il est certain dis-je que supposant la largeur de cette regle bien egale, et tirant tout contre une ligne sur ces caracteres pour en faire le haut on le bas des lettres qu'on veut percer a jour, toutes ces lettres se trouveroient dans un parfait alignement, lors qu'elles seroient precisement enfoncées sous la conduite comme la première fois qu'on les auroit tracées. Mais comme toutes les lames de laton ne sont pas de mesme Epaisseur, et qu'il faut revenir a plusieurs fois pour presenter toutes les caracteres [*sic*] sous la conduite afin de les tracer; puisqu'il n'y en rangera pas quelquefois une douzaine tout d'un coup; il se trouve que le pied des uns estant plus on moins Epais que celuy des autres il arriveroit souvent que la mesme regle dont on auroit alligné une partie des caracteres ne feroit pas le mesme effet sur d'autres, Parce que sy leur pied estoit par Exemple moins Epais cette regle feroit monter plus haut la traceure. Ainsi pour le plus seur il ne faut pas faire cette traceure avec une regle ordinaire et le compas, mais avoir d'autres regles faites Exprés comme nous allons dire.

[p. 172] Avant que de donner la description de ces regles il est bon de faire ressouvenir le lecteur qu'en parlant de l'imprimerie nous avons dit que pour bien former des lettres il faut tirer quatre par[alleles dont la longueur soit de droite a gauche; que les 2 du milieu marquent la hauteur precise ou l'oeil des lettres courantes sans queuë comme a, m, o, &c; que la plus haute marque les Extremités des lettres dont la queuë est en haut comme b. d, &c. et la plus basse l'extremité des queuës qui vont en bas comme au p. q. &c.

Pour avoir donc ces quatre parall[eles bien exactement espacées sur chaque caractere il faut quatre petites regles

un peu entaillees entre les deux bouts [2] et que cette entaille soit un peu plus longue que la largeur des caracteres; et elles doivent estre aussy chaqu'unes de largeurs differentes en sorte que la plus Etroite A soit precisement de la largeur qui il faut pour tracer le bas des queuës, celle d'après B pour tracer le bas de l'oeil des lettres, la troisieme C pour le haut du

mesme oeil, et la derniere ou plus haute D pour tracer l'extremité des queuës d'en haut. Tellement que pour chaque *sorte* il faut les quatre petites regles qui luy conviennent. Et si l'on objecte qu'il semble y avoir bien de la sujection de cette multiplicité, pouvant tout faire d'une mesme regle avec l'usage de compas, il est aisé de faire voir par l'experience qu'on regagne avec un tres grand avantage le tems qu'il faut a disposer toutes ces regles dans leurs justes proportions, par la facilite et la justesse qu'on trouve dans leur usage, n'y restant jamais rien a compasser de nouveau.[7]

Ayant ces regles bien exactement mesurées, il n'y a qu'a placer l'un apres l'autre tels et tant de caracteres qu'on voudra sous la conduite, et les y enfoncer jusqu'a ce qu'ils la touchent de leur pied; puis appliquant a la conduite la regle A, c'est a dire en sorte qu'elle y touche de ses deux pieds ⟨bouts⟩ Entre les quels se trouve le caractere sans qu'elle les touche, on trace la premiere ligne sur ce caractere pour le bas des queuës des g. p. q. et de quelques autres quand c'est de la penchée ⟨l'italique⟩. En suite par la regle B on tracera le bas de l'oeil de toutes les lettres courantes, avec la regle C. le haut de l'oeil, et avec D le haut des b. d. f h &c. Et par ce moyen on aura toujours les 4 parall[eles dans la derniere precision d'allignement independamment de toute difference d'epaisseur du pied des caracteres car il est aisé de voir que quelle que soit cette difference d'Epaisseurs elle ne [p. 173] peut faire hausser ni baisser plus ni moins aucune des parall[eles a quoy qu'on trace tous les caracteres un a un separement si l'on veut; puisque c'est chaque regle mesme qui porte toujours sa hauteur egale des qu'elle touche par ⟨pose⟩ de ses bouts a ⟨contre⟩ la conduite et que toute la largeur des caracteres se trouvant placée entre les bouts des regles, il est indifferent que le pied de chaquun soit egal a l'autre ou dix fois plus Epais.

Il n'est donc rien si aisé que d'avoir tres promptement et exactement 4 lignes parall[eles par le moyen de ces 4 regles sur chaque caractere et de choisir Ensuite indifferemment le premier venu pour y tracer telle lettre qu'on voudra; bien entendu que si c'est pour une majuscule la ligne d'en bas ne servira de rien parce que toute la hauteur de la majuscule est comprise entre le bas de l'oeil des courantes, et le bout d'en haut des queuës de celles qui en ont; et si ce n'est que pour des courantes sans queuë haute ni basse les deux parall[eles d'en haut et d'en bas n'auront point non plus d'usage. Ce qui n'empeche pas au peu de tems qu'il faut pour tirer ces 4 lignes qu'il ne soit toujours plus a propos de les tirer toutes quatre sur chaque caractere, parce que dans la suite on a souvent besoin de faire une lettre d'une certaine facon sur un caractere qu'on n'auroit pas preveu devoir y estre employé.

172

2

173

---

7. A marginal note occurs next to this paragraph: 'Fig. en bois'. A sketch of one of the four rulers, [2], occurs above the note.

be necessary to constantly loosen the screws of the ruler to push the tails of the plates in, and it would even be necessary to loosen them [the screws] to varying degrees according to the various thicknesses of these tails, so that one could not be certain that they were stable enough not to slip to one side or the other (while [using the other method] they are always secure in the same position), and so one would not be able to work so quickly nor so accurately.

This [equipment] being set up in this way, it is certain that by filling the entire length of the conduite with stencil plates arranged side by side and pushed in exactly up to their foot, and by applying another ruler all along the other [opposite] surface of the foot of these plates, so as to press them all against the conduite, it is as I say certain, supposing that the width of that ruler is quite even, and by drawing a line on all these plates to mark the top and bottom of the letters one wishes to cut out, [that] all these letters would be in [as] perfect an alignment when they [the plates] are precisely pushed in under the conduite [subsequently], as (they would be) the first time they [the lines] were drawn. But since all the strips of brass are not of the same thickness, and as it will be necessary to go back several times to position (all) the plates under the conduite in order to draw [lines on] them, [and] since sometimes one will scarcely fit in a dozen or so [plates] all at once, the foot of some being thicker or thinner than others, it will often happen that the same ruler with which one aligned some of the plates will not have the same effect on others, because if, for example, their foot was thinner the ruler would make the drawing [of the lines] at a higher point. So the safest thing is not to do this drawing with an ordinary ruler and a compass, but with other rulers expressly made for the purpose, as we will describe.[10]

172   Before giving a description of these rulers, it is necessary to remind the reader that when talking of printing we said that to form the letters it is necessary to draw four parallel lines running along from right to left; that the two middle lines mark out the precise height of the letter or *oeil*[11] of the small letters with no ascenders or descenders, such as a, m, o, etc; that the uppermost [line] marks the highest part of the letters with an ascender, such as b, d, etc; and the lowest line [marks] the lowest part of those with a descender, such as p, q, etc.

To have these four parallel lines absolutely evenly spaced on every stencil plate, four rulers slightly notched

2

between the two ends are necessary [2], and let that notch be slightly longer than the width of the plates; and they (the rulers) must also each be of different widths [heights] so that the narrowest [shortest] (A) should be exactly the right width [height] to trace the (lowest point of the) descenders, the next (B) to trace the bottom of the oeil of the letters, the

third (C) for the top of this oeil, and the last or tallest (D) to trace the upper point of the ascender.[12] So that for each size [of letter] one must have the four little rulers which are appropriate to it. And if the objection is raised that there seems to be a great deal of constraint and imposition (on the workmen) in this use of a multiplicity of rulers when everything can be done with a single ruler with the help of a compass, it is easy to demonstrate by experience that you get back with substantial interest far more than the time required to devise these rulers in their correct proportions, through the ease and accuracy which can be found in their use, since nothing further needs to be measured.[13]

Once these rulers are measured out exactly, it only remains to place one after another such and such stencil plates as one desires (to use) under the conduite, and to slot them in until their foot touches it; then applying ruler (A) to the conduite, that is to say in such a way that it touches it [the conduite] with its two tips, between which the plate sits, but without it (the plate) touching them [the tips], one draws the first line on this plate to (position) the lowest point of the descenders of g, p, q, etc. and of certain other letters when sloping/italic script is being used. Next with ruler (B), one should draw the bottom of the oeil of all the small letters, with the ruler (C) the top point of the oeil, and with (D) the highest point of the ascenders of b, d, f, h, etc. And by this means you will always have the four parallel lines placed to the last degree of precision of alignment independent of any variation in the thickness of the foot of the plate, for it is easy to see that whatever the difference in thickness it can not raise or lower by a greater or lesser degree any of the parallel lines which one draws on all the plates separately one by one if one so desires, since each ruler always has its correct height when its tips are resting against the conduite, and as the entire width of the plate is positioned between the two tips of the rulers, it is of no consequence whether the foot of each (plate) is equal thickness or ten times the thickness.

173

There is therefore nothing so easy as to have to hand very quickly and accurately four parallel lines by means of these four rulers, and then to choose randomly the first [plate] that comes to hand to draw such and such a letter that one wishes to do; of course if it is for a big letter the lowest line will be redundant, as all the height of a big letter fits between the bottom of the oeil of the small letters and the top point of the ascender in those letters which have them; and if it is being used for the small letters which do not have an ascender or a descender the two parallel lines which are highest and lowest respectively will not be needed either. Nonetheless this does not mean that with so little time being required to draw these four lines, it is not always more appropriate to draw all four of them for each plate, because subsequently one often needs to draw a letter of a certain kind on a plate when one would not have foreseen having to do so.

---

10. Here and below, Des Billettes seems to suggest that the use of a compass (i.e. its spike, or if a dividing compass, then one of its two spikes) for drawing lines on the brass gives an inferior result. See this volume, p. 33 (figure 8) and p. 52 (Simonneau engraving) for illustrations of a tool intended for this work but not mentioned by Des Billettes.

11. The part of a letter between the baseline and the x-height; there is no exact English equivalent.

12. While the French text refers to the different widths of these rulers, it is perhaps better to describe these as their heights, since their varying sizes correspond to the several height dimensions of the letters; see this volume, p. 33 (figure 9), where the rulers are shown.

13. A marginal note occurs next to this paragraph: 'Woodcut'. A sketch of one of the four rulers, [2], occurs above the note.

Tous les caracteres ainsi marqués de leurs 4 lignes il s'agit de former sur chaquun la lettre qu'on y veut vuider, on percer a jour. Et il faut pour cela dessigner cette lettre avec toute la justesse possible et dans la plus belle proportion. Mais parce que s'il falloit vuider par Exemple un A, ou un a, on ne pourroit pas le faire entierement a cause du petit triangle du premier qui se trouve isolé de trois lignes, comme la petite espece d'ovale qui se trouve aussi isolée de la panse de l'autre, puisque si l'on trenchoit entierement les trois lignes de A, ou sa panse de l'a, le triangle et l'ovale tomberoient n'ayant aucun lien ni support; on est ordinairement obligè de laisser de [p. 174] laisser [sic] au laton de petits endroits solides sans les atteindre. Comme par Exemple pour l'A, il faudroit seulement le percer ⟨vuider⟩ a peu pres ainsi [3], et pour l'a aussi de cette maniere [4] de sorte que ces deux lettres ne viendroient pas entierement imprimées parce que ces deux petits endroits solides du laton ne permettroient pas au papier de recevoir l'encre. Ce sont ces petits endroits qu'on nomme *tenons* par ce qu'ils servent a *tenir* ou lier la lettre; et comme il manque cela a la lettre qu'elle ne soit parfaite son trait se trouvant ainsi interrompu par du blanc. Il faut avoir la peine ensuite d'achever tous ces traits avec une plume ou un pinceau.[8]

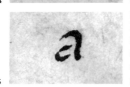

Pour eviter cet inconvenient qui a beaucoup d'incommodité a cause du grand nombre de tenons qu'il faut dans un alphabet de cette maniere, et qui defigure aussy grandement la beauté de cette impression, lors qu'on n'a pas eu le soin de remplir tous les blancs que les tenons ont laissés; on a trouvé qu'il est plus a propos de dessigner deux fois la mesme lettre sur chaque caractere quand la figure de la lettre oblige a y laisser des tenons, en ne la vuidant qu'une fois car il y en a quelques unes ou il n'en est pas besoin, comme il y en a d'autres aussy ou quoy qu'il n'en faille pas pour conserver des parties isolées, il y en faut neanmoins pour la conservation de la lettre entiere quand elle a tant d'ouverture et si peu de force au solide du laton qui la borne, que la brosse en passant et repassant peut aisement rompre, ou corrompre la piece, comme on voit en ces deux lettres Y. V. [6] [9]

Supposé donc par Exemple qu'on veuille faire un a, il faut en dessigner deux l'un a costé de l'autre dans une parfaite egalité. Puis on en vuidera l'un jusqu'a une certaine mesure seulement, et l'autre dans la portion qui manque pour achever le premier, et quelque peu davantage, comme

par exemple ainsi [7]. De mesme pour un A on pourra faire ainsi [8], ou ainsi [9]. Et pareillement pour un g on peut le vuider de cette maniere[10] [p. 175] [10]. Et enfin pour toutes les autres lettres qu'il sera besoin de faire a deux fois, c'est a l'ouvrier a s'imaginer la maniere la plus commode pour en partager les vuidures ⟨ouvertures⟩ en sorte que les lettres achevent de se marquer parfaitement justes et entieres a la seconde fois qu'on passe la brosse on pinceau sur le caractere. Car dailleurs la maniere de partager les vuidures de la lettre est fort arbitraire pourveu qu'elle ait cet effet de faire une impression nette ou il ne soit plus besoin de retoucher et que le caractere n'ait pas trop a souffrir du frottement de la brosse ⟨du pinceau⟩. Il faut neanmoins avertir en general que pour bien parvenir au raport ou rencontre d'une moitié a l'autre on doit premierement avoir soin que chaquune ne soit pas trop precisement bornée a l'impression d'une moitie de la lettre, mais donner tant soit peu plus d'extension, c'est a dire prolonger un peu le trait aux endroits ou les moities se doivent joindre, a fin que l'extremité de l'une anticipe quelque peu sur celle de l'autre. Car il ne peut arriver de la d'autre accident que celuy de couvrir deux fois d'encre un tres petit endroit de la jonction (qui est pour ainsi dire comme une soudure de ces deux moities) et cela ne peut causer aucune imperfection, cette petite recharge d'encre estant imperceptible.

Aprés avoir dessigné deux fois la lettre il faut faire un repére, c'est a dire vuider, ou percer a jour quelque endroit a costé de la premiere moitié qu'on voudra vuider, qui fasse partie de l'autre moitié qu'on veut rapporter et qui fasse connoitre ou doit estre placé le caractere pour passer le pinceau la 2e fois. Si par Exemple on avoit dessinè la lettre a a deux fois en cette maniere [11] pour vuider seulement ainsi chaque moitié [12], ou ce qui est noir represente la vuidure; il faut avoir soin de marquer dans la panse de la premiere lettre un point de mesme Epaisseur ⟨module⟩ ou diametre que le trait et le percer a jour en cette maniere [13] d'ou il est aisé de comprendre que[11] [p. 176] comme a la seconde lettre on ne vuide a jour qui la panse il arrivera qu'ayant imprimé du premier coup de pinceau le jambage de la premiere et un point de la panse ce jambage avec la panse de la seconde lettre qui se formera du second coup de pinceau feront la

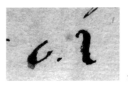

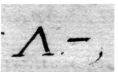

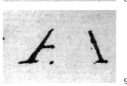

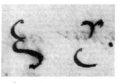

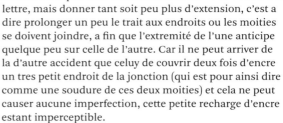

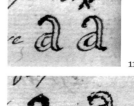

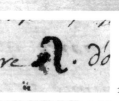

---

8. A marginal note occurs next to this paragraph: 'Fig. en bois'; it is accompanied by the small sketch of 'a' [5].

9. Marginal sketches of 'y' and 'v' [6] occur next to this paragraph.

10. A marginal note occurs next to this paragraph on p. 174: 'Fig. en bois', possibly referring to [6] or [7–10].

11. A marginal note occurs next to this paragraph on p. 175: 'Fig. en bois', probably referring to [14].

When all of the plates have been marked with their four lines, the next task is to form on each (plate) the letter one wishes to cut out. And to do this it is necessary to draw this letter with all the possible accuracy and in the most beautiful proportions. But if you have to cut out for example a [big] A, or a [small] a, it cannot be cut out entirely because of the little triangular shape of the former [i.e. of A] which is isolated by the three strokes (which make up the letter), like the little oval shape that is isolated in the bowl of the other [i.e. the a]; because if one cuts out the three

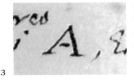

strokes of the A entirely, or the bowl of the a, the triangle and the oval would fall out because they would not be attached or supported. Normally [therefore] one is obliged to leave small solid areas in the brass uncut. So for example for A, it would be necessary to cut out only almost all (of it) thus [3], and for the a thus [4]

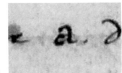

also, so that in this way the two letters will not be printed out in their entirety because these two little solid areas in the brass will not allow the paper to receive the ink. These are the points which we call ties because they serve to tie or hold the letter together; and as this means that the letter has something missing and is imperfect because its shape is interrupted by blank space(s), this necessarily

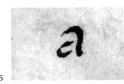

means having to take the pains to finish off these shapes with a pen or a brush.[14]

To avoid this difficulty which is very inconvenient owing to the large number of ties which are required in an alphabet of this kind, and which moreover greatly disfigures the beauty of this (kind of) printing, when one has not taken care to fill in all the blanks that the ties have left, it has been found that it is better to draw the same letter twice on each stencil plate in which the configuration of the letter makes it necessary to leave ties, only cutting it [the letter] out once when this is unnecessary; likewise there are also other letters [which are better to draw twice] where, although it is not necessary to preserve isolated parts of the letter, it is nonetheless necessary to preserve the shape of the whole letter where it has such a wide opening and so

little strength in the solid portion of the brass that bounds it, that the brush rubbing over it repeatedly can easily break or deform this piece [of the stencil], as one sees (for example) in these two letters Y and V [6].[15]

Let us suppose for example that one wants to make an a, one must draw two of them side by side exactly equal (in size and shape). Then one should cut one out to a certain extent only, and (cut from) the other the portion which is missing to complete it, and even a little more,

as for example thus [7]. Similarly for A one can do thus [8] or thus [9]. And likewise for g one could cut it out in this way [10].[16] And in fact for all the other letters that will need to be done twice, it is up to the worker to devise the most convenient fashion to apportion the divisions in such a way [that] the letters are completed and marked perfectly accurately in their entirety at the second time of passing the brush (or paintbrush) over the stencil plate. In any case the apportioning of divisions of the letter is a matter of choice provided that it has the effect of making a clear imprint where there is no longer any need to go over it and retouch it, so that the letter does not have to endure too much friction from the brush. We must nevertheless warn in general that in order to successfully manage the joining or meeting of one half with the other, one must first take care that each part is not too precisely limited to the printing of each half only, but rather one should extend each half a (very) little, that is to say slightly add to the shape at the places where the two halves have to join, so that the furthest part of one slightly overlaps that of the other, so that no other (worse) accident can result from this than that of covering a very small portion of the junction between the two with ink twice over (which) is, so to speak, a soldering together of these two halves. And this will not cause any imperfection, as this little double load of ink is imperceptible.

After having drawn the letter twice, a guiding-mark must be made, that is to say cutting out a small hole beside the first [half of the] letter one wants to cut out, which forms part of the (overlap with) the other half that one wishes to join up with it and which identifies (the spot) where the stencil plate must be placed to (pass the) brush over it a second time. If for example one had drawn the letter a twice in this way [11] to cut out each half (thus) [12], where what is black represents the cut out part, care must be taken to mark out in the bowl of the first letter a dot of the same thickness ⟨module⟩ or diameter as the stroke and cut it out in this way [13], whence it is easy to understand that,[17] since from the second letter one cuts out the bowl, what will happen is that having with the first application of the brush printed out the vertical stroke of the first letter and a dot of the bowl,

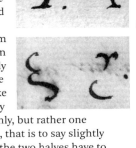

7

8

9

10

175

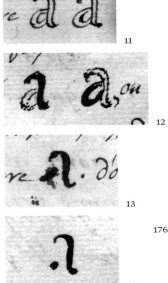

11

12

13

14

176

---

14. A marginal note occurs next to this paragraph: 'Woodcut'; it is accompanied by the small sketch of 'a' [5].

15. Marginal sketches of 'y' and 'v' [6] occur next to this paragraph.

16. A marginal note occurs next to this paragraph on p. 174: 'Woodcut', possibly referring to [6] or [7–10].

17. A marginal note occurs next to this paragraph on p. 175: 'Woodcut', probably referring to [14].

lettre entiere et parfaite, et que ce point marqué la premiere fois se confondra dans la panse qu'on marque a la seconde, sans qu'on puisse remarquer ⟨connoitre⟩ qu'il eust deja esté imprimé. Et il n'y a pour cela qu'a prendre garde apres avoir imprimé la premiere moitié, a placer le caractere en sorte que ce point ou repère paroisse entier par l'ouverture faite au second dessein de la lettre. Car alors si l'on a esté bien exact, comme on doit l'estre, dans la construction, le caractere ne peut manquer d'estre dans sa juste situation pour achever de former la lettre entière. Ce point rond ouvert est sans doute la maniere de toutes la plus commode pour bien faire venir *de rencontre* les deux moitiés de la lettre; et il n'y a point a cela d'autre sujection que de la placer en tel endroit qu'on voudra de la partie du trait qu'on n'entame point en vuidant le premier dessein, pourveu qu'on observe de n'exceder pas la largeur du trait, mais plutost faire mesme ce repère tant soit peu plus etroit. Car Estant plus large il gasteroit le trait de la seconde partie de la lettre qui ne seroit pas net et Egal en cet endroit la, mais paroitroit *baveux*; au lieu que quand le repere est quelque peu plus estroit il n'en peut arriver aucun inconvenient pourveu qu'on place bien le caractere, puisqu'en marquant la seconde partie de la lettre le trait imprimé sera toujours conforme a l'ouverture qu'on y aura faite. Ainsi il est arbitraire de faire ce repère en tel endroit qu'on voudra pourveu qu'il soit aisé d'observer quand il se presentera juste a l'ouverture de l'autre partie de la lettre. Mais on jugera pourtant facilement que le plus seur est toujours de le placer a quelquun des plus gros endroits du trait parce qu'on se trompera moins a travailler en grand qu'en petit, comme a remarquer la situation precise du caractere. Il faut [p. 177] estre averti qui quoy que nous ayons toujours parlé jusqu'icy d'une premiere et seconde moitié de la lettre, cela n'est encore d'aucune sujection et qu'il ne depend que celuy qui fait ces caracteres de partager comme il voudra les ouvertures qu'il doit donner au double dessein de la lettre estant indifferent d'en donner plus ou moins a l'un qu'a l'autre ou les prendre haut ou bas, ou de costé, ou en travers pourveu qu'il fasse en sorte de menager la force du caractere, et la rencontre des deux parties qui doivent former la lettre entiere. Nous nous sommes un peu Estendus la dessus quoy que la chose semblast asses claire d'elle mesme pour estre entendu en peu de mots. Mais on a creu ne devoir rien negliger pour l'aplication d'un procedé d'ou depend presque toute la perfection de ce petit art.

Apres avoir Establi l'usage de ce repère, d'ou s'ensuit certainement la juste rencontre des deux parties qui forment la lettre entiere; et estant aussi certain dailleurs que par le moyen de la conduite et du pied des caracteres qu'on y applique toutes les lettres se trouvent dans une juste

177

hauteur ou allignement; il ne reste qu'a s'assurer aussi de les faire venir dans une juste distance entre elles. La regle commune pour cette distance est de donner entre chaques lettres l'espace du trait d'un I qui est comme le module de tous les plus gros traits des lettres. Mais cet Espace ne s'entend pas seulement entre les jambages des deux lettres qui se joignent, car elles se trouveroient souvent trop proches et anticiperoient sur les potences qui se trouvent au bout de ces jambages; et il faut donc prendre cette distances [*sic*] entre les potences[12] mesmes des jambages quand les 2 lettres en ont un, ou en general entre la plus grande avance du corps ou oeil de chaque lettre. De sorte que si par exemple une [*sic*] m suit un a, il faudra laisser l'espace d'un I entre la potence ou crochet d'en bas de l'a, et la potence de la premiere jambe de l'm; ou si l'a suit l'm, il faudra aussi l'espace d'un I entre la potence de la troisieme jambe [p. 178] de l'm, et l'exterieur de la panse de l'a, et sur cela on peut se regler pour tout le reste. Or pour disposer ⟨faire⟩ la construction des caracteres en sorte qu'on n'ait aucune peine a trouver promptement cette distance de quelque suite de lettres dont il s'agisse, il n'y a qu'a faire a chacun une autre ouverture, comme celle du trait d'un I sans potences a costé gauche de la premiere moitié de la lettre, en laissant encore un pareil Espace solide entre cette ouverture et le trait de la lettre. Et par ce moyen après avoir imprimé une lettre il faut en prenant le caractere suivant appliquer cette ouverture, que nous nommerons *lumiere*, sur le trait d'a main droite de la lettre imprimée et alors celle qu'on veut imprimer se trouve dans la distance precise qu'il luy faut. Desorte qu'en couvrant cette lumiere par le moyen d'un *sergent*, ou d'une *patte* dont nous parlerons ⟨allons parler⟩ bien tost il n'y a qu'a passer hardiment le pinceau sur ce qui paroist a decouvert du caractere.

Nous n'avons point dit de quelle maniere on couppe ces lettres après qu'on les a eu dessignées, parce que cela depend du genie particulier de celuy qui l'entreprend. Mais on peut neanmoins s'assurer que quand tous ces traits doubles ou simples des lettres, les repères, et les lumieres sont parfaitement dessinés la meilleure maniere de les ouvrir, ou percer a jour, est de faire un trou en quelquun des plus gros endroits du trait avec des cizeaux fort aigus, puis suivre toujours en coupant de la pointe des mesmes cizeaux le plus approchant qu'on peut du trait. Et ensuite pour ce qui reste d'inegalités ou qui manque pour achever les contours ou les cizeaux ne peuvent suffire, on en vient aisement a bout avec de petits limes d'une taille tres fines, plates rondes demi rondes, a couteau, a feuille de sauge, et de toutes sortes d'autres figures differentes selon la diversité des lettres, telles qui sont les petites limes ordinaires des horlogers; et c'est ainsi qu'on finit parfaitement les lettres avec toute la propreté necessaire, a quoy l'on ne

178

---

12. A marginal note is marked for insertion at this location in the paragraph: 'Hic revoir au juste le mesure'.

this vertical stroke [together] with the bowl of the second [half of the] letter, which will [be] formed at the second application of the brush, will make up a complete, perfect letter, and this dot marked out on the first occasion will blend into the bowl of the letter which is marked out the second time around without it being possible to see ⟨know⟩ that it [the dot] had been printed beforehand. And to achieve this one only has to take care, after having printed the first half, to place the stencil in such a way that the dot or guiding-mark appears in its entirety through the opening made from the second drawing of the letter. Then, if one has been strictly accurate in the construction of the stencil, as one has to be, it can not fail to be in its proper position to complete the formation of the whole letter. This open[ed] round dot is without doubt the most convenient of all possible methods to bring about the exact joining up of the two halves of the letter; and to achieve this nothing more is required than to position (it) where one desires within that part of the letter which is not going to be removed when cutting out the first part of the letter, providing that one observes (the rule of) not exceeding the width of the stroke, but rather to make this guiding-mark ever so slightly smaller. If it was wider, it would spoil the second part of the letter, which would not be sharp and smooth at that point, but would appear smudged; whereas when the guiding-mark is somewhat narrower no problem can result, provided that one positions the stencil properly, since in marking in the second part of the letter, the shape imprinted will always correspond to the opening [i.e. the dot] that has previously been left. Thus it is a matter of individual choice to make this guiding-mark in whatever place one wishes, provided that it is easy to see when it appears accurately in the opening of the second part of the letter. But it can easily be judged that the safest method is always to position it in one of the thickest parts of the letter, because one will make fewer mistakes working on a large scale than on a small scale when determining the precise position of the stencil plate. It is necessary to be aware that although we have always talked until now of the first and the second part of the letter, this still does not impose any constraints, and it depends entirely upon (the discretion) of the person who is making the stencils to apportion as he wishes the divisions that he must put into the double drawing of the letter; it is of no consequence whether he makes more or less in one or the other, or positions them high or low, on the side or crosswise, as long as he manages it in such a way as to conserve to the maximum the strength of the stencil plate and the joining of the two parts which must form the letter as a whole. We have spoken at length thereupon, although the matter would seem to be sufficiently clear to be understood in few words, but we judge it right to neglect nothing concerning the application of this procedure on which depends almost all the perfection of this little art.

After having established what the use of this guiding-mark is, on which the accurate joining-up of the two parts which form the letter as a whole depends, and since it is certain, moreover, that by means of the conduite and the foot of the stencil being employed (as described) the letter

177

will be at the correct height or alignment, it only remains to ensure that they [the letters] are placed at the correct distance from one another. The normal rule for this distance is to leave between each letter the width of the stroke of an I, which is like the module for all the thick strokes of the letters. But this is not merely the space between the vertical (or sloping) strokes of two letters which are adjacent, because they would often be too close and would encroach upon the crosswise strokes [i.e. serifs] which are situated at the ends of these vertical (or sloping) strokes; therefore it is necessary to take the measure of this distance as between the crosswise strokes[18] of the vertical or sloping strokes (when the two letters have these), or in general between the furthest point of the body or oeil of each letter. So that if, for example, an m follows an a, it would be necessary also to leave the space of an I between the crosswise stroke or hook at the bottom of the a, and the crosswise stroke of the first vertical stroke of the m; or if the a follows the m, one must also leave the space of an I between the crosswise stroke of the third vertical stroke of the m and the outer edge of the bowl of the a; and from this one can use this as a guide for all the rest. Now, to arrange ⟨devise⟩ the construction of the stencil plates in such a way that there is no difficulty in quickly finding this distance for whatever sequence of letters is involved, one has only to make another opening in each plate, like that of the line of an I without crosswise strokes, on the left side of the first half of the letter, leaving another similar solid space between this opening and the edge [i.e. nearest point] of the letter. And by this means, having printed out a letter, one must, when taking the next stencil, position [the right hand edge of] this opening, which we will call the lumière,[19] on the right hand edge of the printed letter, and then the letter which one wants to print will be positioned at the precise distance required. [And] in such a way that by covering this lumière by means of a sash-clamp or hold-fast, of which we will speak presently, one then has only to brush over the exposed part of the stencil, which one can do without fear.

178

We have not described how one cuts out these letters after having drawn them, because that depends on the particular skill of the person who undertakes the task. But one can nonetheless be certain that when all these single or double outlines of letters, guiding-marks and lumières are perfectly drawn, the best way to open or to cut them out is to make a hole at one end of the thickest points of the shape with very sharp scissors, then continue cutting with the point of the same scissors as close to the outline as possible. And then for the remaining uneven parts or what(ever) remains to be done to finish off the contours, where scissors are not sufficient, one can easily complete the task with small files of a very small gauge, [that are] flat, round, semi-rounded, like a knife, in the form of a sage leaf, and all sorts of other shapes according to the different varieties of letters, such as the small files commonly used by clockmakers; and by such means one finishes off the letters with the requisite sharpness, in which

18. A marginal note is marked for insertion at this position in the paragraph: 'Here check the accuracy of the measure'.

19. Because the meaning of 'lumière' is sufficiently clear, and the word itself is usefully evocative, it is left untranslated here and below.

peut estre trop exact si l'on veut avoir une impression fort agreable.[13] Les caracteres estant parfaitement finis, et en estat de faire un beau travail, il est bon d'avoir derriere le pupitre une petit espece de casse a peu pres comme celle de l'imprimerie; c'est a dire une caisse divisée en autant de cassetins ou cellules qu'on a de caracteres, mais il y a cette difference entre autres, que chaque cassetin doit estre fort peu profond, parce qu'il n'est besoin de mettre en chacun quun seul caractere qui doit estre aisé a prendre par son pied. Cette casse doit aussy estre presque a plomb ou fort peu inclinée en arriere, mais en un mot tellement située que chacun la trouve plus a la veuë et a la main pour manier facilement les caracteres.

Il est maintenant question de voir comment on couvre la [p. 179] lumiere dont on vient de parler, aussy bien que chaque moitié de la lettre, quand on ne veut imprimer que la premier ou la seconde, comme on ne le peut faire que l'une apres l'autre, mais estant aussi fort indifferent par laquelle on commence quoyque pour la commodite du discours nous ayons coutume de nommer *premiere* celle qui est prise sur le dessein tracé a main gauche du caractere, et celle de l'autre dessein la *seconde*. Cela se fait par le moyen d'un outil qu'on nomme un *sergent*, ou un autre nomme *patte*, dont chacun peut avoir quelquefois son usage particulier. Le premier est pourtant le plus commode en ce qu'il fait ordinairement toutes les fonctions du second, ce qui n'est pas de mesme au contraire.

Ce sergent donc est une maniere de petit chassis de fer ou de cuivre, et qui se peut faire aussy d'autre metal, ou mesme de bois ou d'yvoire, mais il y faut chercher en mesme tems la durée, le menage et la solidité. Sa figure est en parallelograme ou quarré oblong plus ou moins grand en tout sens, selon la grosseur des caracteres qu'on veut imprimer; de sorte qu'il est bon d'en avoir plusieurs, comme deux ou trois pour la commodité du travail. On peut communement luy donner — pouces de long sur — de large.[14] Et avec cette mesure il servira pour beaucoup de divers caracteres. Sa construction consiste proprement en une simple plaque, ou lame ouverte de la mesure qu'on vient de dire et portant par les deux costés de sa longeur un rebord d'environ 3 a 4 lignes de haut, aux bouts de laquelle on Epargne seulement une largeur solide d'environ — lignes et seulement autant qu'il en faut pour luy donner de la consistence et de la force pour ne corrompre pas trop aisement sa figure a l'usage et telle aussy qu'il y ait de quoy promener le pinceau sans maculer le caractere ou papier. Toute l'Epaisseur tant du plat que des rebords peut estre de moins d'un ligne, et cela est assés arbitraire,

mais la moindre est la meilleure pourveu qu'il y ait de la fermeté. On concevra peutestre mieux cette construction en la considerant comme un assemblage de quatre [p. 180] pieces, lames ou tringles chacune de — lignes de large, dont deux longues de — pouces posées sur le chant sont soudées ou attachees par les bouts sur deux autres de — pouces de long couchées sur le plat. Les deux longs costés doivent avoir par le bas en dedans une petite resnure dans la quelle s'ajuste et coule aisement tout du long un *curseur* ou *coulisse* pour l'avancer ou reculer autant qu'on veut vers les deux bouts. La hauteur du reste du rebord au dessus de la resnure est asses indifferente, et ne sert proprement qu'a pouvoir prendre et tenir aisement le sergent et le remuër de costé et d'autre, ce qui ne seroit pas facile s'il estoit trop plat comme il est aux deux bouts. Cette coulisse ou curseur mobile est une petite platine de metal qui doit par le dessous affleurer parfaitement juste le dessous des deux bouts en sorte que cela fasse un plan fort uni. Elle doit avoir en son milieu un petit bouton relevé par le quel on la fait aller et venir, et sur lequel on appuye le doit quand on encre les caracteres. C'est pourquoy il est bon que ce bouton ait une largeur considerable comme de 4 a 5 lignes de diametre et mesme qu'il soit un peu concave en haut, car tout cela soulage beaucoup le doit de celuy qui imprime. Il faut aussy que les deux autres costés de cette coulisse par ou elle va et vient parallelement vers les bouts du sergent soient rabattus ou amoindris en bizeau, ou comme on dit en cousteau et venant a rien; et pareillement ces deux bouts du sergent doivent estre taillés de mesme en dedans c'est a dire par ou ils regardent parallement [*sic*] la coulisse. Autrement le pinceau ou brosse qui porte l'encre ne joueroit pas bien à laise, et ne manqueroit pas de laisser ⟨d'amasser⟩ toujours beaucoup d'ordure d'encre contre les Extremités interieures de ces deux bouts, et entre ceux du curseur s'ils se trouvoient Elevés de quelque Epaisseur sur le papier qu'on [p. 181] imprime, au lieu que venant comme on a dit a rien, c'est a dire n'ayant aucune Epaisseur en cet endroit la, le pinceau glisse aisement dessus et ramasse ou pour ainsi dire balaye toute l'encre qui s'y pourroit arrester.

Par ce moyen quand un caractere est placé par sa queuë sous la conduite du pupitre, il n'y a qu'a mettre le sergent sur ce caractere l'appliquant ferme de plat sur le papier ou autre maniere qu'on imprime (qu'on doit pour cela coucher sur le pupitre – et faire passer sous la conduite) et en mesme tems aussi de costé c'est a dire pressant le pied du caractere contre la conduite; puis en menant comme on veut le curseur on cache ou decouvre tel endroit qu'on voudra de caractere, et passant le pinceau chargé d'encre sur ce qui est a decouvert on imprime toutes les figures qui s'y trouvent percées a jour; d'ou il est aisé de comprendre comment il est facile d'imprimer separément chaque moitié des lettres qui sont dessinées a deux fois, et cacher l'ouverture qu'on nomme *Lumiere* sans qui l'encre puisse rien gaster.[15]

L'autre outil qu'on nomme *patte* est plus simple et ne consiste qu'en une simple plaque percée d'un trou quarré, ou oblong a discretion, ayant les quatre costés interieurs

---

13. A reference to a marginal note, '# v. en haut', occurs here. The reference, in fact, is to two notes in the margin. The lines of first note, preceded by a '#', have been cancelled; the note reads: 'ce renvoy estoit fait pour mettre icy quelque addition. Mais il ne m'en souvient plus. C'est peutestre pour faire icy une figure de la lumiere ou quelque invention a vuider ou a unir le trait de la vuidure'. The second marginal note, also preceded by a '#' but not cancelled, follows this footnote's reference in the text above and runs to the end of the paragraph (i.e. from 'Les caracteres estant …' to '… facilement les caracteres.')

14. A marginal note occurs next to these two blank spaces: 'N^a. un seul fort Elevé pourroit servir a tout, mais il faudroit pour cela que les plus petits caracteres fussent aussy haut en cuivre que les plus grands ce qui seroit une perte inutile du cuivre.' Immediately below, a second note occurs: 'Fig. en bois'.

15. A marginal note occurs next to this paragraph: 'donner peu d'encre de peur de maculer'.

matter one can not be too accurate if one wishes to make a very pleasing impression.[20] When the stencil plates are perfectly finished off, and in a fit condition to produce fine work, it is useful to have behind the desk a little case somewhat similar to that used in printing; that is to say [like] a printer's type case divided into as many little compartments or cells as there are stencils, but with the following difference among others, that each compartment must be very shallow, because only enough space is needed for a single stencil, which must be easy to pick up by its foot. This case must be almost vertical or sloping very slightly backward, but in a word placed in such a way that (every) one can have it within sight and within reach to pick up the stencils easily.

179 We shall now look at how one covers the lumière, of which we have spoken a little earlier, as well as each half of the letter, when the situation arises where one desires to print out the first or the second (half), which one can do one after the other, though it is of no importance which (half) one does first, although for the sake of convenience of description we have named the first that which is drawn on the left side of the plate, and that drawn on the other [i.e. the right side of the plate] the second. This [covering] is effected by means of a tool which is called a sash-clamp, or of another called a holdfast, each of which can have on different occasions its own particular use. The former is nonetheless the most useful, inasmuch as it performs (ordinarily) all the functions of the latter, which is not the same vice-versa.

This sash-clamp, then, is a kind of small frame made of iron or brass, but which can also be made of other metals, and even wood or ivory, but the main object is that it is necessary to look for a material which combines durability, ease of handling and strength. Its shape is that of a parallelogram or rectangle which varies in its dimensions, according to the size of the letters that one wishes to print; so that it is useful to have several, such as two or three, for ease of working. Ordinarily one can make it -- inches long by -- inches wide.[21] And with these dimensions it will serve for many different stencil plates. Its construction consists of a simple plate or open strip of the dimensions that we have just described, having on its two lengthwise sides a raised edge around three to four lignes in height, at the ends of which one leaves a solid width of -- lignes, only the minimum that is required to give it enough thickness and strength not to bend too easily and go out of shape with use and also enough room so that one can run the brush along it without blotching the

letter or the paper. The total thickness of the flat section as well as of the raised edges can be less than a ligne, and the width can be determined at will, but the least possible thickness is best, provided that it is also rigid. One will perhaps be better able to conceive this structure if it is considered as an assembly of four parts, strips or rods each of -- lignes wide, two of them -- inches long, placed edgewise, and which are joined or fastened at the ends to the other two, which are -- long and laid flat. The two longest sides must have at their base, at the inside lower edge, a small groove along which a cursor or slide can run easily and be adjusted so as to advance or draw it back as desired towards either end. The height of the rest of the raised edge above the groove is of no consequence, and only really serves to enable the sash-clamp to be picked up and held easily, and to enable it to be moved from side to side, which would not be easy were it too flat as it is at the two ends. This slide or moving cursor is a small metal plate the underside of which must be exactly flush with the underside of the two ends in such a way that the whole forms a very smooth plane. It [the slide or cursor] should have a small raised button set in the middle of it, to enable it to be pushed backwards and forwards, and on which one presses down with one's finger while inking the stencils. This is why it is useful for this button to have a considerable width, such as four to five lignes in diameter, and it should ideally be slightly concave at the top, as this is more comfortable on the finger of the person printing. It is necessary also that the two other sides of this slide that move back and forth in parallel should be flattened down or reduced with a bevel, or filed down and ground to nothing; and likewise the two ends of the sash-clamp must also be bevelled inside, that is to say, where they face (in parallel) the slide. Otherwise the paintbrush or [other kind of] brush containing the ink will not run along (them) smoothly and will not fail to leave ⟨deposit⟩ a lot of surplus ink on the inner extremities of these two ends, and those of the cursor, if they are raised by some degree of thickness above the paper that is being printed, whereas if it is filed down to nothing, that is to say has no thickness at that point, the brush will slide easily over it and will pick up and sweep away, so to speak, all the ink which could become clogged up there.

By means of this sash-clamp, when a stencil plate is put in place by [slotting] its tail under the conduite of the desk, one only has to put the sash-clamp on the stencil, pressing it firmly flat on the paper or other material that one is printing (that one must for this purpose lie flat on the desk and secure under the conduite) and at the same time applying firm pressure to the side, that is to say, pressing the foot of the stencil plate against the conduite, then positioning the cursor as one desires, one covers up or exposes whatever part of the stencil plate one desires, and passing the brush loaded with ink over the exposed part one prints out all the shapes which are cut out; whence it is easy to understand how easy it is to print each of the letters which are drawn twice, and hide the opening called the lumière, without the ink being able to spoil the print in any way.[22]

The other tool, which is called a holdfast, is more simple, consisting only of a simple plate with either a square or a rectangular hole cut out of it, according to your own

180

181

---

20. A reference to a marginal note, '# see above', occurs here. The reference, in fact, is to two notes in the margin. The lines of first note, preceded by a '#', have been cancelled; the note reads: 'this reference sign was to put some addition here, but I no longer remember what it was – perhaps to put here an illustration of the lumière, or perhaps some invention to cut out or to smooth out the outline of the cut-out piece'. The second marginal note, also preceded by a '#' but not cancelled, follows this footnote's reference in the text above and runs to the end of the paragraph (i.e. from 'When the stencil plates are …' to '… pick up the stencils easily.')

21. A marginal note occurs next to these two blank spaces: 'Nota. A very tall one can serve for every purpose, but for that the plates for the smallest letters must be as tall as (the plates for) the larger ones, which would be a waste of brass.' Immediately below, a second note occurs: 'Woodcut'.

22. A marginal note occurs next to this paragraph: 'apply a small amount of ink for fear of spattering'.

de ce trou abattus en couteau comme on vient de dire, et portant une queuë retroussée et emmenchée pour pouvoir tenir cela debout a la main, et appliquer cette ouverture sur les endroits du caractere ou l'on veut passer le pinceau. Il manque la deux grandes commodités du sergent, l'une en ce que la coulisse du sergent fait ou cacher ou decouvrir tant et si peu qu'on veut des parties du caractere; l'autre que par son rebord relevé appliqué contre le pied de caractere qui joint va le long de la conduite, on tient ce caractere ferme en sorte qu'on est bien assuré qu'il ne peut varier ni faire manquer la justesse de l'impression; et qu'ainsi l'on a en mesme tems la promptitude et la regularité. Mais de plus le [p. 182] sergent peut servir a autant de differentes grosseurs de lettres que pourroient faire plusieurs pattes a cause de leur ouverture determinée au lieu que celle du sergent se diversifie comme on veut en largeur; et en un mot on peut le faire servir partout ou peut servir la patte. Et il est bon neanmoins davoir aussi quelques pattes de differentes grandeurs d'ouverture, parce que s'il est besoin d'escrire en quelque livre proche d'une marge de fond ou en tels autres endroits soit de livres, ou autres, ou la longueur du sergent pourroit nuire par ce qu'il ne seroit pas aisé de l'y placer, alors la patte y seroit plus de commode parce qu'occupant beaucoup moins de place, on luy peut donner telle situation qu'on a besoin.

A l'egard de l'encre et de la maniere de s'en servir cela demande encore la description particuliere. Il faut avoir une boiste ou cassete de grandeur arbitraire, comme par exemple environ d'un pied, ou de 8 a 10 pouces delong sur 7 ou 8 de large; et en un mot il vaut mieux qu'elle soit grande que petite sy l'on a de la place libre sans incommodité. Il suffit d'un pouce ou beaucoup moins de profondeur. On couvre le dedans d'une plaque de plomb avec des rebords un peu relevés ajustés a ceux de la caisse. Puis prenant de la gomme adragant ⟨tragagant⟩, ou simplement de l'Arabique delayée assès Epais, on broye dedans du noir de fumée, ou pour mieux du noir d'yvoire brulée ou de noyaux de pesche y meslant un peu d'encre en broyant. De tout cela on fait un lit ou couche forte Epaisse sur tout le fond de cette caisse de plomb, et on la laisse secher a l'ombre; et c'est sur cela qu'on passe ou frotte la brosse ou pinceau quand on veut imprimer. C'est a dire qu'ayant mis la dessus quelques goutes d'encre on l'estend avec la brosse on la passant et repassant diverses fois ou de long, ou en rond pour le faire degorger et ressuyer de son superflu, c'est a dire afin qu'elle ne se charge pas tant d'encre qu'il y ait danger de maculer ou barbouiller le papier. Car avec ce peu que la brosse en retient on ne laisse pas d'imprimer quelque fois des 15, et 20 lettres sans reprendre d'encre nouvelle.[16]

La perfection de cette encre, outre celle de secher promptement consiste [p. 183] principalement a estre extrèmement noire. La meilleure maniere d'y parvenir est de la faire deux fois; c'est a dire qu'ayant deja fait de bonne encre commune, on s'en sert tout de nouveau au lieu de vin, d'eau, ou de biere pour la recomposer avec le mesmes ingrediens qu'a la premiere fois. Voicy une des plus excellentes manieres de la premiere composition.

Sur 4 pintes d'eau de pluye mettès une livre de bonnes Galles concassées, et demie livre de couperose verde sechée sur une pelle de feu. Laissés infuser cela dans une cruche de Grez bien nette pendant 8 jours, remuant chaque jour plusieus fois avec un baston de figuier fendu en quatre par un bout et entre ouvert avec ⟨par⟩ d'autres petits bastons du mesme bois. Au bout des 8 jours mettès y une once d'ecorse de grenade sechée et concassée et environ 5 a 6 de gomme Arabique en poudre. La cruche estant bien bouchée laissès le tout infuser pendant 2 ou 3 mois le baston demeurant dedans avec le quel on remuera quelque fois sans déboucher la cruche, qu'il ne faut aussy exposer ny au feu ny au soleil. Au bout de ce tems coulés le tout par un tamis et conservés l'encre en des vaisseaux bien bouchez. S'il y vient du moisy il faut l'y laisser car il en reviendroit toujours d'autre. Et sy elle se trouve deja aussy noire qu'on la veut on n'a que faire d'y la recomposer une seconde fois.[17]

Pour s'en servir bien proprement aux caracteres de laton dont nous venons de parler il faut la mettre dans un cornet avec une Eponge fine, puis en passer comme on vient de dire sur la couche de gomme adragant. Quand la lettre ne paroistroit pas d'abord fort noire le deviendra dans la suite.

Sy l'on veut Escrire en rouge, ayant une autre brosse, qui ne sert qu'a cela, on met l'eau[18] de six blancs d'oeufs frais bien fouettés, avec ⟨dans⟩ une cuillerée du vinaigre blanc, et ayant laisse reposer cela un quart d'heure on le met dans une bouteille. Pour s'en servir on en prend avec un peu de beau vermillon le detrempant du bout du doigt dans un godet de fayence ou autre; puis on use de la brosse, comme on a dit de celle du noir en la passant et repassant sur une plaque de plomb pour la faire degorger.

Il seroit bon tant pour le rouge que pour le noir de tenir toujours l'encre dans [p. 184] une Eponge mouillée, et ne tremper jamais la brosse dans l'encre seule, de peur qu'elle ne s'en charge tant qu'on ne puisse assès bien la ressuyer sur le plomb.

La brosse ou pinceau est une chose trop commune pour avoir besoin d'explication. Cela se trouve tout prest chez les ouvriers qui font des vergettes, et ce n'est qu'un amas de soye de cochon ou de sanglier lié bien ferme avec des cordes prés a pres par le gros bout de la soye, et pour s'en bien servir au metier dont nous parlons il faut rogner un peu ou ebarber tout ras le menu bout de cette soye, au contraire des pinceaux destinés a peindre aux quels on laisse ce bout un peu plus long par le milieu afin de le pouvoir amenuiser en pointe selon les traits qu'on veut faire.

Pour la preparation du papier il suffit de dire icy qu'il doit estre le plus blanc, fort de colle, et le mieux uni qu'on peut avoir, et de mesme du veslin qu'il soit aussy de la meilleure qualité. Car du reste nous reservons les

---

16. A marginal note occurs next to this paragraph: '[l]a gomme adragant fait mieux que tout autre.'

17. A marginal note occurs next to this paragraph: 'mon manuscrit dit 7 ou 8 onces ce qui me paroist trop.' A second note occurs below it: 'ajoutons icy la nouvelle encre de bois d'inde'.

18. A marginal query that has been cancelled is marked for insertion at this location in the paragraph; it reads: 'le nom de cette eau d'oeufs separée de l'erume?'

discretion, with the four inner sides of this hole filed down [i.e. bevelled] with a knife-file as just described above, and equipped with an upturned tail section with a handle fitted so that it can be held upright in the hand and its opening positioned over the parts of the stencil plate one wishes to brush over. It [the holdfast] lacks the two convenient features of the sash-clamp: one, that the slide of the sash-clamp can cover up and expose however little (and however much) of the stencil one chooses; and the other, that by means of its raised edge pressed against the foot of the stencil plate, which is [in turn] pressed against the conduite, one is able to hold this stencil firm so that one is guaranteed that it cannot move out of position or spoil the exactness of the printing; and thus one has at the same time both quickness and regularity. But what is more the sash-clamp can be used for as many different sizes of the letters as would require several holdfasts, owing to their fixed aperture, whereas for that of the sash-clamp one can vary the width as one wishes; and in a word one can use it wherever one can use the holdfast. And yet it is useful nevertheless to have some holdfasts of different aperture sizes, because it is necessary to write [i.e. mark out letters] in some books close to an inner margin or in other such places, be it in books or in other (types of) texts, where the length of the sash-clamp could be disadvantageous because it would not be easy to position it there, whereas the holdfast would be more convenient because, as it takes up less space, it can be positioned wherever it is needed.

With regard to the ink and the manner of using it, a particular description is required. One needs to have a box or tray of whatever size one wishes, such as for example a foot, or eight to ten inches long by seven or eight wide; and in a word it is better that it should be bigger rather than smaller if space can be found for it without inconvenience. It need only to be an inch or even considerably less in depth. The inside must be lined with a sheet of lead with the edges slightly raised and adjusted to fit those of the box. Then taking some gum tragacanth or simply some gum Arabic diluted to quite a thick paste, one grinds into it some lampblack or ideally the (ash of) burnt ivory or peach kernels, mixing in a little ink while grinding. With the whole mixture, one makes a thick bed or layer (spread) over the bottom of this lead (lined) box or tray and lets it dry in a cool dark place, and it is over this mixture that the brush is passed or rubbed when printing; thus having sprinkled on it a few drops of ink, one spreads it with the brush by passing it [the brush] back and forth or round in circles several times to clear or wipe off from it the surplus ink, so that it does not take up so much ink that there is a risk of spattering or smearing the paper. Then, with the small amount of ink that one retains, one is sometimes able to print up to fifteen or twenty or so letters without replenishing the brush with ink.[23]

The perfection of this ink, apart from that of drying quickly, is that it is extremely black. The best way to make it successfully is to make it in a two stage process: that is to say, having already made a good ordinary ink, one uses it again instead of wine, water or beer, to reconstitute it using the same ingredients as those used for the first making-up

(process). Below is one of the best ways to make up the ink for the first stage of the process.

To four pints of rainwater add a pound of oak galls and half a pound of green vitriol dried on a fire shovel. Leave it to infuse in a clean stoneware jug for eight days, stirring several times each day with a twig from a fig tree cut in four at one end and splayed out by means of other small sticks of the same wood inserted into the (four) splits. After eight days, add an ounce of dried and crushed pomegranate peel and around five or six (ounces) of powdered gum Arabic. Corking the jug tightly, let the mixture infuse for two or three months leaving the twig inside to enable it to be stirred occasionally without uncorking the jug, which should not be exposed either to fire or to sunlight. At the end of this time, pour the whole mixture through a sieve and keep the ink in tightly corked bottles. If mould grows on it, it should be left there because if removed it will always grow back. And if it is already of the blackness required, one can dispense with making it up a second time.[24]

To use it correctly with the brass stencils which we have spoken of above, one must put it [the ink] into a cone with a fine sponge, then spread some as described above on the layer of gum tragacanth. If the letter does not appear deep black at first it will become so subsequently.

If one wants to write [i.e. print] in red, using another brush which is kept solely for this purpose, one puts the liquid[25] from six whites of egg which have been well beaten, with ⟨in⟩ a spoonful of white vinegar, and having let this mixture stand for a quarter of an hour, put it in a bottle. To use it one takes a little (good quality) vermilion, diluting it with a fingertip in an earthenware pot or (a pot of) some other material; then one uses the brush as described for the black (ink) by passing it repeatedly over a sheet of lead to clean off the surplus.

Ideally, it is best for both the red and the black to always hold the ink in a damp sponge, and never dip the brush into the ink alone, for fear that it will become so filled (with an overload of ink) that one will not be able to wipe off enough of it on the lead (sheet).

The brush or paintbrush is a common enough tool to need no explanation. It can be procured ready-made from the workers who make whisks and consists simply of a tuft of very stiff pig or boar bristles with cords wrapped tightly around the thick end of the bristle; and to use it properly in the work we are describing, one must slightly trim or shave level the narrow end of the bristles, in contrast to (paint) brushes designed for painting in which the slightly longer hairs in the middle are left so as to enable the brush to be tapered to a point depending on the shapes one wishes to paint.

As far as the preparation of the paper is concerned suffice it to say here that it must be the whitest one can obtain, well sized, and the smoothest that one can obtain, and similarly with vellum that it should be of the finest quality. In any case, we will leave (the description of) the

23. A marginal note occurs next to this paragraph: 'gum tragacanth works better than any other.'

24. A marginal note occurs next to this paragraph: 'my manuscript specifies seven or eight ounces, which seems to me to be too much.' A second note occurs below it: 'add here the new ink of Indian wood'.

25. A marginal query that has been cancelled is marked for insertion at this position in the paragraph: 'the name of that liquid of white of egg separated from the viscous part?'

preparations particulieres de l'un et de l'autre au traité de l'escriture ⟨escrivain⟩.[19]

Voy a la fin de la minute de la description de la presse d'imprimerie[20]

[p. 184 insert, front] Enfin pour la maniere de se servir de tout ce petit equipage, il est aisé d'en juger par tout ce qui vient d'estre dit. Mais en un mot, aprés qu'on a marqué au veslin ou au papier des points de haut en bas a droite et a gauche selon la distance qu'on veut avoir entre les lignes, il n'y a qu'a Etendre la feuille sur le pupitre, et la faire passer sous la conduite, en laschant un peu les vis, jusqu'a ce qu'on voye les deux points de la premiere ligne d'en haut se presenter au bord d'en haut de la conduite. Puis resserrer les vis afin que la feuille demeure arrestée ferme dessous. En suite prenant le caractere de la premiere lettre de cette ligne, et en enfonçant la queüe jusqu'au pied sous la conduite, on la presse tout contre par le sergent qu'on couche de plat sur le caractere. Puis mettant le caractere en telle situation qu'il laisse a decouvert quelque peu plus que l'ouverture de la lettre, sy elle est toute entiere en un seul dessein, on passe sur cette ouverture le pinceau bien degorgé, comme nous avons dit, en le promenant on rond diverses fois a droite et a gauche jusqu'a ce qu'on trouve que toute la lettre soit bien marqué. Aprés cela on prend le caractere de la lettre suivante, et on pose sa lumiere en sorte qu'elle decouvre le trait d'a main droite de la precedente; puis avec le sergent couvrant cette ouverture et ne laissant paroitre qu'un peu plus que la lettre, on fait comme a l'autre fois, et toujours ainsy jusqu'a la fin, en remontant la feuille a mesure qu'on a achevé les lignes, pour les ecrire tout de suitte chacune en son rang. Que sy les lettres qu'on veut imprimer sont dessinées a deux fois,

alors on fait [p. 184 insert, back] alors on fait [*sic*] marquer seulement par la premiere operation la premiere moitié de la lettre et le point qu'on a fait a costé; puis on avance le caractere jusqu'a ce qu'on decouvre ce point justement dans ⟨par⟩ un endroit de l'ouverture de la seconde moitié, et couvrant de curseur la premiere, on passe de mesme le pinceau sur la seconde, et par consequent sur ce point qui en fait partie, et s'y trouve confondu. Et tout cela se fait sans aucun danger de maculer sy l'encre est bien faite et degorgée au pinceau; pourveu que d'ailleurs on sache travailler proprement et ne laisser pas salir le dessous du caractere; comme il pourroit arriver sur tout sy le sergent ne l'appliquoit pas asses uniment sur la feuille, mais qu'il se trouvast des boursoufflures ou autres inegalités qui fissent du jour entre la feuille et la caractere. [insert ends]

[p. 184 continues] Quoy que tout ce que nous venons de dire de la figure du pupitre, du pliement des caracteres, des 4 regles pour les tracer, de la maniere d'y dessiner quelques lettres deux fois, de la construction du sergent &c. soit assurément ce qu'il y a de plus seur pour reussir facilement et correctement en cette espece d'impression; il faut neanmoins avoüer que la grande adresse d'un ouvrier pourroit suppléer en quelque maniere a toutes ces sujections, se contentant d'une simple table et d'une regle commune avec des caracteres aussi d'un simple pli, et d'une seule ouverture de lettres, et sans cette lumiere que nous mettons au devant. Mais en ce cas il faut 1º que l'ouvrier soit assuré d'avoir l'oeil parfaitement droit, et la main trés assurée ⟨seure⟩, pour placer bien precisement ses caracteres dans leur juste situation. Et pour cet effet il luy faut aussi une autre sujection bien plus incommode, qui est de tracer au compas et a la regle sur son papier toutes les lignes qu'il veut escrire, et que chacun de ses caracteres ait une ligne tracée le long du bas des lettres courantes sans queüe, et qu'a chaque bout de cette ligne a droit et a gauche [p. 185] il y ait une petite echancrure en triangle, ou autre figure qui luy laisse voir la ligne tracée sur son papier, pour y ajuster celle du caractere [15].[21]

2º. Si d'un costé il se contente de donner un pli tout simple au pied de son caractere sans autre façon, pour former ce pied, que de relever un peu le bord d'en bas ni se mettre en peine qu'il soit droit, ni a Equierre, ni parallele a la ligne du bas des lettres, mais seulement tel qu'il puisse aisement le manier; il a besoin aussi d'une plus grande assurance de la veüe et de la main pour la bien placer d'allignement, et cette sujection recommence a tout moment, au lieu que de nostre maniere, on travaille pour ainsi dire a tour de bras.

3º. S'il s'epargne le soing de faire une lumiere au devant de la lettre de chaque caractere pour le faire quadrer dans un juste Eloignement de celle qui la precede, il a besoin aussi de tastonner un peu plus pour donner aux lettres ce juste Eloignement dont il n'a que sa veüe pour guide par ou il est tres difficile de faire quelque ouvrage bien regulier, ou bien il faut qu'au lieu de cette lumiere que nous mettons au devant de chaque lettre, il mette du moins un petit trou après en cette maniere a• par Exemple, auquel cas ce petit trou qui doit marquer un point, doit estre placé en sorte qu'il se trouve justement dans le corps ou oeil de la lettre suivante, ce qui n'est pas a beaucoup pres si certainement juste que nostre lumiere, parce que toutes sortes lettres ne conviendront pas Egalement a la distance de ce point.

4º. S'il Epargne aussi cette precision d'egalité dont nous avons besoin pour dessiner deux fois exactement certaines lettres, ou sans ce la il seroit necessaire de laisser des tenons; il a aussi en échange la peine de repasser en suite ou la plume ou le pinceau par tout ou ces tenons ont empesché que le trait de la lettre ne fust entierement marqué, et ou il se trouve interrompu du blanc du papier; mais il arrive le plus souvent qu'il laisse ces blancs sans y repasser, soit qu'il ne puisse le faire asses proprement pour ne pas defigurer le trait de la lettre, soit que la paresse le luy fasse negliger sous [p. 186] { } que c'est accumuler dautant du travail, ou qu'il juge ce defaut imperceptible.

---

19. A marginal query occurs next to this paragraph: 'Sçavoir si l'on veut icy anticiper les diverses manieres de preparer le papier pour escrire?' The reference to a planned 'traité de l'escriture' (a treatise on formal writing) is the only reference to such a topic, which does not appear to be included in the other drafts by Des Billettes. (JM)

20. This phrase, which is cancelled, suggests that Des Billettes planned to include a note on paper after his descriptions of the printing presses, which appear on pp. 1–27 and pp. 29–35 of his drafts. A note on paper does appear in the section paginated [77]–108, which deals with imposition, printing ink, and presswork. Between the latter two topics, on pp. 84–6, is the note 'Preparation du papier pr. l'Impression' (The preparation of paper for printing). It deals mostly with the damping of paper. (JM)

21. A marginal note occurs next to this paragraph: 'Fig. en bois', immediately above [15].

particular methods of preparation for both these materials to the treatise on writing ⟨the writer⟩.[26]

See at the end of the note of the description of the printing press.[27]

4 INSERT
FRONT

Finally (concerning) the way in which one uses the (little assemblage of) equipment, it is easy to judge (how to do so) from what has been said. But in a word, after one has marked out on the paper or the vellum dots from top to bottom, right and left, according the distance that one wishes to leave between the lines, it only remains to spread the sheet [of paper or vellum] out on the desk, and slip it under the conduite, loosening the screws a little until one sees the dots marking the first line at the top align with the upper edge of the conduite. Then tighten up the screws so that the sheet is firmly secured underneath. Next, taking the stencil for the first letter of that line and pushing the tail of it under the conduite up to the foot, one presses the whole of it (firmly) against it [the conduite] by (means of) the sash-clamp, which one lies flat on the stencil plate. Then placing the stencil in such a way that it [the sash-clamp] leaves exposed slightly more than the opening of the letter, if the whole letter is [to be] done as a single shape, one passes over the opening [with] the brush, which has been properly cleaned of surplus ink, moving it around several times to the right and to the left until one sees that the letter is clearly marked out. After which one takes the stencil for the next letter and places the lumière so that it reveals the right hand side of the preceding letter and then with the sash-clamp covering this opening [i.e. the lumière] and only exposing a little more than the space taken up by the letter, one does as described above, and so on, repeating the process until it is finished, moving the sheet up as one finishes (each of) the lines, printing out each letter in its proper place, one immediately after the other. Whereas if the letter that one wishes to print out is

4 INSERT
BACK

made up of two parts, then in the first part of the operation one only marks out the first half of the letter and the dot one has made beside it; then one shifts the stencil sideways until one reveals this dot in the opening in ⟨of⟩ the second half, and covering the first half with the cursor, one brushes (ink) over the second (half) and consequently over the dot which forms part of it and thus is blended into it. And all this can be done without the risk of spattering if the ink is properly made and the excess is cleaned off the brush, provided moreover that one knows how to work cleanly and not let the underside of the stencil plate get dirtied, as can happen in particular if the sash-clamp is not applied evenly enough to the sheet, but where there are lumps or other irregularities which create a space between the sheet and the stencil plate.

26. A marginal query occurs next to this paragraph: 'work out if one wants to make some introductory remarks on the different methods of preparing paper for writing?' The reference to a planned 'treatise on [formal] writing' is the only reference to such a topic, which does not appear to be included in the other drafts by Des Billettes. (JM)

27. This phrase, which is cancelled, suggests that Des Billettes planned to include a note on paper after his descriptions of the printing presses, which appear on pp. 1–27 and pp. 29–35 of his drafts. A note on paper does appear in the section paginated [77]–108, which deals with imposition, printing ink, and presswork. Between the latter two topics, on pp. 84–6, is the note 'Preparation du papier pr. l'Impression' (The preparation of paper for printing). It deals mostly with the damping of paper. (JM)

Although what we have just said regarding the configuration of the desk, the folding of the stencil plates, the four rulers to trace them, the method of drawing some letters twice, on how to construct the sash-clamp etc., is assuredly the most certain method to succeed in performing this kind of printing in the easiest and most accurate fashion, it must nevertheless be admitted that the great address of the worker can in some way form a substitute for subjecting himself to all these rules, the worker sufficing himself with a simple table and an ordinary ruler, as well as stencils with a simple fold and with a single opening in the letters, without that lumière which we highlight. But in this case it is necessary, (1) that the worker should be sure of having a perfectly sure eye and a perfectly steady hand to enable him to place the stencils in their correct position with perfect precision. And for this purpose he will be subject to a yet more inconvenient constraint, that of drawing with a compass and a ruler onto his paper all the lines that he wishes to print on, and each of his stencil plates will have to have a line drawn along the base of the small letters without descenders, and at each end of this line, right and left, he must put a little triangular indentation or another shape which allows him to see the line drawn on his paper to align his stencil to it [15].[28]

185

15

(2) If on the one hand he satisfies himself with making a very simple fold in the foot of his stencil plate, without any ceremony in forming this foot other than to slightly raise the lower edge, nor taking pains that it should be straight or square or parallel to the line beneath the letters, but only devises it so that he can handle it easily, he also needs a great steadiness of hand and eye to position and line it up properly, and this effort has to be constantly renewed, whereas with our methods one can work with a vengeance, so to speak.

(3) If he dispenses with the effort of making a lumière in front of the letter of each stencil to space it out at the correct distance from the previous one, he then also needs to use trial and error a little more to give the letters this correct spacing for which he has only his eye to guide him whereby it is difficult to produce evenly spaced work; or else instead of that lumière he must at least put a little hole after (the letter) in this fashion, a•, for instance, in which case this little hole, which has to mark a point, must be positioned in such a way that it fits into the body or oeil of the following letter, which is by no means of such guaranteed accuracy as our lumière because not every kind of letter will be equally well suited to the spacing of this dot.

(4) If he also dispenses with that precision and evenness which we need to draw certain letters twice with accuracy, where without this (technique) he will have to leave ties, then he also has in exchange to take the pains to go back over and ink with a pen or brush all those places where the ties have prevented the letter being marked out fully and where the shape is interrupted by blank spaces on the paper; but what most often happens is that he leaves these blanks without going back over them, whether it is because he cannot do this properly without spoiling the shape of the letter, or whether it is laziness that makes him neglect it on the grounds that it is merely creating work, or that he thinks that this defect is imperceptible. But although

186

28. A marginal note occurs next to this paragraph: 'Woodcut'; it is written immediately above [15].

Mais comme il est vray que ce travail sera aussi long qu'im-
portun, il ne faut pas croire pourtant que le defaut en soit
imperceptible. Car outre que quelque petit qu'il pust estre
il n'eschaperoit pas aux yeux de tout le monde, mais tout
au plus a quelques uns quand la chose ne se verroit que de
fort loin, il est certain que cela est fort desagreable de prés
c'est a dire de la distance ordinaire dont on regarde ces
sortes d'Escritures.

  Que si l'on objecte qu'en faisant seulement chaque lettre
a une fois on la travaille ⟨vuide⟩ plus correctement selon
l'oeil qu'elle doit avoir, et qu'outre cela on a beaucoup
plutost fait les Alphabets et plutost imprimé; il est aisé de
reprendre 1º· quant au menage du tems qu'on n'en perd
tout au plus en faisant les Alphabets que ce qu'il en faut
pour dessiner une seconde fois les lettres, ce qui va a tres
peu de chose en ayant un modele devant soy, car pour ce
qui est de percer et vuider parfaitement le trait, c'est tout
un de vuider deux moities de lettre ensemble ou separè-
ment. Et quant a l'impression on y en gagne beaucoup
plus qu'on n'en perd. Car il en faut incomparablement
davantage a retoucher ⟨finir⟩ les blancs laissès par les
tenons qu'a passer deux fois le pinceau sur le mesme
caractere. 2º· a l'egard de la correction du trait, pourveu
que chaque dessin de la lettre soit parfaitement egal la
correction sera tout aussi seure et bonne que celle des
lettres qui s'impriment a une seule fois. Or il n'est pas difficile a une bonne main de faire ces deux traits ou dessins
de lettre parfaitement egaux et rapportans, les voyant si
proches l'un de l'autre, et en ayant deja le haut et le bas
si bien reglés entre deux paralleles qu'on ne sçauroit se
tromper a cet egard et qu'il n'y a plus qu'a bien observer
les Epaisseurs ⟨pleins et les deliés⟩. 3º· il s'en faut de
beaucoup qu'il n'y ait tant de peine a dessiner et vuider
correctement ces traits qu'a bien finir ceux qui restent a
faire quand les caracteres ont des tenons.

  5º· L'Epargne du pupitre ou du moins de la regle, ou
conduite qu'il [p. 187] porte n'est pas a beaucoup près si
considerable que la peine qu'on se donne autrement a
regler tout du long toutes les lignes sur le papier; joint
que pour le faire il faut une telle application qu'on peut
aisément s'y tromper en plusieurs manieres soit pour le
parallelisme soit pour l'uniformité des interlignes &c,
au lieu qu'avec la regle immobile que nous nommons
conduite on n'a qu'a marquer simplement les distances
d'une ligne a l'autre par le moyen d'un seul point a chaque
bout sans y tracer de ligne, parce que des que chacun de
ces deux points affleurent ou paroissent au bord de cette
conduite on est assuré que le papier est en sa juste situation. Et cette petite sujection de diviser ces entrelignes de
haut en bas est commune aux deux manieres d'operer. Elle
est mesme si peu considerable que rien n'est si facile que
de l'abreger. Car sans se servir de compas il n'y a qu'a marquer une fois les 2 points qui doivent terminer la premiere
ligne, puis mener de chacun de ces points
de petites roulettes dentées [**16**], dont on
aura compassé les dents justement selon
l'intervalle des lignes et l'oeil des lettres
de sorte qu'en les faisant rouler de haut
en bas ou de bas en haut de la feuille
qu'on veut imprimer on marque en un moment tous ces
entrelignes a droit et a gauche dans une parfaite precision.
Sur quoy nous pouvons remarquer davance un usage de
ces roulettes pour un Escrivain, en ce qu'on peut en ajuster les dents de telle manieres que de deux en deux elles

187

16

marquent tout d'un coup la hauteur du corps des lettres,
et ces Entrelignes[.]²²

  6º· Au reste les deux petites Echancrures a droit et a
gauche du caractere, pour assurer l'allignement, et le point
a costé de chaque lettre pour marquer les Eloignements
ne suppleant que très imparfaitement a l'usage de ce
que nous avons ⟨l'effet de ce que nous avons⟩ nommé la
conduite, et *la lumiere*, et sont d'une beaucoup plus grande
peine et sujection pour la construction des caracteres,
sans epargner celles de tracer les quatre paralleles qui sont
necessaires pour faire tout un alphabet d'un bon allignement, et d'une parfaite uniformité.

  [p. 188] En un mot s'il est vray que quelque ouvriers
reussissent asses ⟨passablement⟩ bien en ce petit Art a
fabriquer et mettre un usage leurs Alphabets, sans toutes
les façons et outils dont nous avons parlé, on doit unique-
ment l'attribuer a leur pure adresse et a une longue
habitude qui reussit quelque fois mieux que les meilleurs
outils maniés d'une mechante main. Mais cela n'empeche
pas qu'il ne soit toujours plus seur et pour la facilité du
procedé et pour la perfection de l'ouvrage de suivre la
maniere que nous venons d'expliquer. Et nous pouvons
assurer que toutes circonstances supposées d'ailleurs
egales nous n'avons jamais veu si bien reussir par ces
autres voyes simples, qui ne conviennent ordinairement
qu'a des gens qui n'ont d'autre veuë que l'Epargne, ou
n'ont affaire qu'a des personnes peu delicates ou de mau-
vais goust; outre qu'en cecy, comme en beaucoup d'autres
Arts, la premiere peine qu'on se donne pour l'Equipage
ou appareil du metier est abondamment récompensée par
l'assurance, la perfection, et la facilité qu'on trouve dans
la suite en travaillant, sans avoir besoin d'avoir toujours
une application fort bandée, et souvent au dessous de
l'ouvrage.²³

  Pour l'ornement de cette maniere d'impression, on
peut faire aussi de toutes sortes de caracteres de fleurons,
vignettes, cartouches &c dont on se sert dans l'imprimerie
soit pour les marquer tout d'un coup d'une seule couleur;
soit pour en avoir le trait seul, et l'enluminer ensuite de
diverses couleurs au pinceau, ce qui appartient a l'enlumi-
nure ou la miniature dont l'Art sera expliqué en son lieu
comme faisant partie de celuy des Peintres; soit pour tirer
plusieurs traits pour plusieurs couleurs comme aux cartes
a jouër qui sont aussi l'effet d'une autre petite espece
d'imprimerie. Cela nous donne occasion de passer a sa
description. Car quoyque l'usage qu'on en fait d'ordinaire
ne meritast pas de la mettre au nombre des Arts, si elle ne
pouvoit aussi en avoir un plus innocent, il est pourtant
certain qu'originairement l'invention en pouvoit estre
[p. 189] de quelque merite, aussi bien que cela de beaucoup
d'autres jeux dont on ne laisse pas d'abuser tous les jours
quoyque peut estre plus rarement que de celuy cy.²⁴

188

189

22. A marginal note occurs next to this paragraph: 'Fig. en
bois'. Below, a sketch of the device for marking out line-ends
[**16**] is added; below that a second note occurs: 'Je me suis servi
fort utilement de cette petite invention pour escrire tout un livre
dans une parfaite egalité'.

23. A marginal note occurs next to this paragraph: 'Il y en a
deux excellens en ce genre aux Invalides. Mais il est pourtant
certain que leurs ouvrages n'ont jamais l'exacte perfection qu'on
leur donneroit selon nostre methode.'

24. The description, 'Imprimerie des cartes a Jeux', follows
in Des Billettes's cahier.

it is true that this task will be as long as it is tiresome and unwelcome, one must not imagine for all that that the defect can not be seen, because in addition to the fact that however small it might be it will not escape the eye of everyone, but at most will escape some people's eyes when viewed from a distance, it is (also) certainly very unpleasant close to, that is to say [as seen] from the ordinary distance at which one usually looks at these kinds of texts.

If it is objected that by only doing each letter once, one cuts it out more accurately in accordance with the shape that the letter should have and that moreover one would make alphabets and print them more rapidly, it is easy to reply. First, that as far as the economy of time is concerned, at most one does not spend any more time in making the alphabets than what is required to draw the letters a second time, which comes to little if one has the model in front of one, because as far as cutting out the letter is concerned it is all the same whether one cuts out the two halves of the letter together or separately. And as far as the printing itself is concerned, one gains far more time than one loses because it needs incomparably more (time) to touch up ⟨finish off⟩ the blanks left by the ties than to pass the brush over the same stencil twice. Second, in regard to the accuracy of the shape of the letter, provided that each drawing of the letter is exactly the same, the accuracy will be as certain and as good as for those letters printed out in one go. And it is not difficult for someone with a steady hand to draw the shapes of the letter perfectly equal and matching seeing them close to each other, and having the top and bottom (of them) so well measured out between the two parallel lines that one cannot make any mistakes in that respect and it only remains to take proper care with the thicknesses ⟨thick and thin parts⟩ of the strokes. Third, there is very far from being as many pains required to draw and cut out these shapes correctly than [there are] to properly finish off the shapes which remain to be done when the stencils have ties.

(5) Dispensing with the desk, or at least with the ruler or conduite which is attached to it, is not anything like as considerable (a saving of time and trouble) as the trouble one otherwise makes for oneself in ruling the lines all along the length of the (sheet of) paper; added to which (the fact that) to do it requires such application that one can easily go wrong in several ways, be it for keeping the lines in parallel and evenly spaced etc., whereas with a fixed ruler which we call the conduite one only has to mark the differences between one line and another by means of a single dot at each end without drawing in the line, because as soon as the two dots [at each end] touch or appear at the edge of the conduite, one is guaranteed that the paper is in its correct position. And that little effort of dividing up the spaces between the lines from top to bottom is common to the two methods. It is even so slight that nothing is easier than to do it without resorting to a compass. One only has to mark the two dots where the first line should terminate, then make each of [the remaining of] these points [with] little toothed wheels [**16**], the intervals between the teeth of which have been set to correspond to the spacing of the lines and the oeil of the letters, so that by rolling them up or down the sheet that one wishes to print on one can in a moment mark all the spaces between the lines to [the] right and [the] left with perfect accuracy.

16

Upon which we can foresee a use (that) these toothed wheels (could have) for the writer, in that one could adjust the teeth in such a way that (when) used in pairs they simultaneously mark out the height of the body of the letters, and these spaces between the lines.[29]

(6) Moreover, the small indentations to the right and left of the stencil plate to guarantee that they are aligned, and the dot beside each letter to mark the distances (between them), are only a very imperfect substitute for the use of what we have ⟨the effect achieved by what we have⟩ called the conduite and the lumière, and cause much more trouble and constraint in constructing the stencils, without avoiding that of drawing the four parallel lines which are necessary to make an entire alphabet with the proper alignment and of a perfect uniformity.

In a word, if it is true that some workers succeed quite well in this little art of manufacturing and making use of their alphabets without all the methods and tools which we have described, this should be attributed to their sheer address and long practice, which sometimes succeeds better than the best tools handled by unskilful hands. But nevertheless the fact remains that it is always more sure both for the ease of the process and the perfection of the work to follow the methods that we have just described. And we can assure (the readers) that all circumstances being supposed equal we have never seen other simple methods succeed so well; these normally only suit people who have no other object than economising or who only have to do with people who have little refinement or have bad taste; besides which in this, as in many other arts, the pains that are taken at first in (making) the equipment or tools of the trade are abundantly rewarded by the sureness, the perfection, and the ease that one subsequently finds in working, without needing to have one's concentration stretched to its limit and yet still below that which is normally required for the work.[30]

In order to ornament this kind of printing one can also make all sorts of stencils bearing fleurons, vignettes, cartouches, etc., which are used in printing, whether to mark them out in one go in one colour alone, or else to make the outline only and then illuminate it in different colours with a paintbrush (an art which belongs to illumination or to miniatures and which will be explained in its proper place as the work of painters); or to draw several shapes (for each of) several colours as for playing cards, which are also the product of another minor kind of printing. This lets us move to its description ... although, given its use, it [the printing of playing cards] does not deserve to be counted among the Arts – though they [playing cards] can be used innocently, and we can be sure that it [the printing technique] was of some use, like that of other games which are often misused, though less than this one.[31]

187

188

189

---

29. A marginal note occurs next to this paragraph: 'Woodcut'. Below, a sketch of the device for marking out line-ends [**16**] is added; below that a second note occurs: 'I used this little invention to write out an entire book perfectly evenly'.

30. A marginal note occurs next to this paragraph: 'There are two excellent examples of this kind at the Invalides. But it is nevertheless certain that their texts never have the accuracy that they would have if produced by our method.' One of these examples is probably that shown in this volume, p. 47 (figure 38).

31. The description, 'The printing of playing cards', follows in Des Billettes's cahier.

Appendix: Stencilled letters, papers of Sébastien Truchet

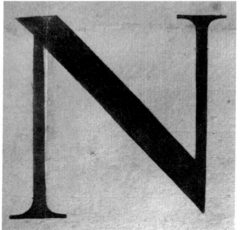

These stencilled letters are found among the papers of Sébastien Truchet, a colleague of Gilles Filleau des Billettes, and a contributor to the 'description of trades', of which Des Billettes's description of stencilling was a part.

The full sheet (top) is 195 × 343 mm; B and N (above) are reproduced at actual size (56 mm capital height); a (at left, and lower right on the full sheet) is 13 mm in height. Note that A, B, g, o, and the four a's are made as composite forms.

Archives nationales, Paris; M850, dossier 8, liasse 5; photographs by James Mosley.

James Mosley

A note on Gilles Filleau des Billettes

This note provides biographical details of Gilles Filleau des Billettes (1634–1720), one of a group of 'technicians' recruited to work on the project for an encyclopedic 'description of trades' (*Description des arts et métiers*), carried out under the direction of the Académie royale des Sciences in Paris. A brief account of this work, and Des Billettes's part in it, is also given, which includes references to his text on stencilling that is transcribed and translated elsewhere in this volume (see pp. 66–86). Additional remarks describe the fate of the project in the later eighteenth century.

Gilles Filleau des Billettes, the compiler of the text on stencilling that is transcribed and translated in this volume of *Typography papers* (see pp. 66–86), was born at Poitiers in 1634, the youngest of the three sons of Nicolas Filleau of Orleans and Françoise Belliard from a family of the region of Poitou. As catholics, the family of Nicolas Filleau had moved to Poitou from Orleans in order to evade what they perceived as its prevailing Calvinist tendency. The title 'Des Billettes' derived from an estate in Poitou of which Gilles Filleau became the proprietor in 1659. In 1660 he married Françoise Sicard, the daughter of a landowner.[1]

Gilles Filleau des Billettes was devoutly catholic. He was also influenced by the contemporary spirit of scientific enquiry and he counted Pascal, and later Leibniz, among his acquaintances and correspondents. In 1657 Cyrano de Bergerac is reported to have said of the young man, 'Monsieur des Billettes at twenty-three knows everything that others boast of knowing at fifty'.[2]

An account of the local family of Roannez[3] contains this appreciation of Des Billettes:

> His natural cheerfulness, conversation that was as pleasant as it was informative, gained him the respect and affection of many friends, notably that of Leibniz, who often saw him during his stay in Paris from 1672 to 1676. And yet his letters show a figure who seems embarrassed by the admiration of which he felt himself unworthy. The frankness and honesty with which he expresses his incompetence led Leibniz to reproach him with neglecting much invaluable information which might have been of value to the public.[4]

In his obituary *éloge* of Des Billettes, written for the Academy of Sciences, Fontenelle has this passage:

1. 'Le 31 janvier 1659 il est à Poitiers. Il se qualifie d'écuyer, sieur des Billettes de Ribouard, nom d'une métairie située dans la paroisse de Cissé, au nord-ouest de Poitiers, où les Filleau possédaient quelques terres, outre leurs principaux domaines de la région de Saint-Martin-la-Rivière. Par cet acte du 31 janvier, il achète, dans la paroisse même de Saint-Martin, une métairie appelée Le Censif. Les 23 et 27 mars suivants, il demeure encore à Poitiers et continue certainement à y résider jusqu'à son mariage, dont le contrat fut passé le 19 avril 1660. Il se disait alors seigneur des Billettes et de Bois-Clerbault: le fief de Bois-Clerbault,

situé dans la paroisse de Saint-Pierre-les-Églises, appartenait à l'ensemble des domaines de la famille dans la vallée de la Vienne. Des Billettes épousait Françoise Sicard, fille de Claude, écuyer, sieur de Laudraire.' Mesnard (1965), p. 682.

2. 'Monsieur des Billettes qui n'ignore rien à 23 ans de ce que les autres font gloire de sçavoir à cinquante.' *Histoire comique … contenant les Estats et Empires de la Lune* (1657), cited by Mesnard (1965), p. 682.

3. Artus Gouffier, Duc de Roannez (1627–1696) was Governor of Poitou during the ministry of Mazarin, and a close friend of Blaise Pascal.

4. 'Plein de gaîté naturelle, d'une conversation aussi agréable qu'instructive, Des Billettes avait gagné l'estime et l'affection de nombreux amis: notamment de Leibniz, qui le vit souvent pendant son séjour à Paris de 1672 à 1676. Pourtant ses lettres le montrent comme embarrassé d'une admiration dont il se sentait profondément indigne. C'est avec naturel et saveur qu'il affirme constamment une incompétence dont il était si bien convaincu que Leibniz put lui reprocher de laisser perdre par un excès de modestie … une infinité de belles connaissances, qui pourroient être utiles au Public.' Mesnard (1965), p. 686.

5. 'Surtout il possédait le détail des arts, ce prodigieux nombre d'industries singulières inconnues à tous ceux qui ne les exercent pas, nullement observées par ceux qui les exercent, négligées par les savans les plus universels, qui ne savent pas même qu'il y ait là à apprendre pour eux, et cependant merveilleuses et ravissantes, dès qu'elles sont vues avec des yeux éclairés.' Fontenelle (1720).

6. Jérôme Phélypeaux de Pontchartrain (1643–1727), Comte de Pontchartrain, Chancellor of France 1699–1714. Jean-Paul Bignon, son of a favourite sister, became responsible for the Royal Academies, and later for the Royal Library. His advancement within the church was hindered by the worldly characteristics recorded by the Duc de Saint-Simon: 'C'était ce qui, véritablement et en bonne part, se pouvait appeler un bon esprit, très savant, et qui avait prêché avec beaucoup d'applaudissements; mais sa vie avait si peu répondu à sa doctrine, qu'il n'osait plus se montrer en chaire, et que le Roi se repentait des bénéfices qu'il lui avait donnés. Que faire donc d'un prêtre à qui ses mœurs ont ôté toute espérance de l'épiscopat? Cette place de conseiller d'État d'Église parut tout propre à l'en consoler et à le réhabiliter dans le monde en lui donnant un état. ... Son oncle le mit dans des bureaux en attendant qu'il lui en pût donner, et à la tête de toutes les Académies.' Saint-Simon (1983), vol.1, p.817.

7. Académie royale des Sciences, 'séance du 19 juin 1675 où Claude Perrault lit, de la part de Colbert, un ordre du Roy, enjoignant d'examiner les moyens de faire un traité de mécanique, avec une description exacte de toutes les machines utiles à tous les arts et métiers dont on se sert à présent en France et dans toute l'Europe.' Salomon-Bayet (1969), p.234, n.1.

8. 'Monsieur Jaugeon ... a donné la Description d'un Mortier de bronze qu'il a imaginé, qu'un homme peut porter avec son affust et sa charge, qui peut être pointé sans aucun instrument de Mathématique, qui jette à la fois une douzaine de Grenades à quatre cens pas, et auquel on ne met le feu qu'en un temps. L'épreuve en a été faite, il y a déjà plusieurs années, par ordre du Roy, et en présence de feu M. de Louvois, et ce Mortier fut mis dans le Magazine de Brest.' *Histoire de l'Académie royale des Sciences*, 1699.

9. The pioneering study is Jammes (1961). See also Mosley (1997), (2002) and (2008).

10. A manuscript list, cited by Jammes (1961), is in the Bibliothèque nationale de France, Paris, MS nouv. acq. fr. 5148, ff.19–86. There are printed accounts in the published volumes of the *Histoire de l'Académie royale des Sciences*, and a summary appears in Lalande's preface to his text *L'art du tanneur* (1764).

11. MS 2741. 'Description et Perfection Des Arts-et-Mestiers. Des Arts. De Construire Les Caracteres. De Grauer Les Poinçons de Lettres. D'Imprimer Les Lettres. et De Relier Les Livres. Tome Premier. Par Monsieur Jaugeon De L'Accademie Royale Des Sciences. M.V.CC.IIII.', a small folio of 424 pages. A later handwritten text in two volumes, containing a larger number of the original plates engraved for the 'Description des Arts et Métiers', is MS fr. 9157 and 9158 of the Bibliothèque nationale de France. It appears to be copied from the earlier text, the orthography of which it partially modernizes but the text is defective in some places. It is also less legible. There is a preliminary draft manuscript of the section on typefounding at the Newberry Library, Chicago. I have transcribed the parts of this text relating to punchcutting and typefounding, with a view to preparing a text for publication.

Above all, he was perfectly informed about the details of the innumerable trades that are unknown to those who do not practise them, are never described by those who do, and are ignored by the learned, who do not realise that they offer a field of study that is extraordinary and fascinating when it is approached with open eyes.[5]

In 1692 Des Billettes was one of the group of 'technicians' (*technologues*) who were recruited to work under the chairmanship of Jean-Paul Bignon (1662–1743), nephew of the Comte de Pontchartrain,[6] to realise the project for an encyclopedic 'description of trades' (*Description des arts et métiers*) that had originated in 1675 during the administration of Colbert.[7] The others were Sébastien Truchet (1657–1729), born in Lyon, a member of the Carmelite order who was a mathematician and a hydraulic engineer, and Jacques Jaugeon (*c*.1655–1724), who had been responsible for the design and making of several things, including a portable launching device for mortar bombs.[8]

The 'commission Bignon' (a term suggested by André Jammes in 1961 as more appropriate than the 'commission Jaugeon' that had been more commonly used) began its work in 1693, first examining printing and the alphabet, as 'the art which preserves the arts'. In 1694 a decision was taken by Pontchartrain to initiate another project of which the idea dated from the time of Colbert, namely the making of a printed volume recording the series of medals that had been struck in order to commemorate events that had taken place during the reign of Louis XIV, including naval and terrestrial battles and conquests, but also civil events, such as the founding in Paris in 1666 of the Académie royale des Sciences. The current work of the commission was interrupted in order for it to concentrate on a practical task, namely the design of a new alphabet and the making of a new printing type based on it for use at the Imprimerie royale. The new type, which became known as the *romain du roi* (in distinction from the *grec du roi*, the Greek type that had been made by Claude Garamont for François I in 1540), was begun in 1696 and it was used for the first time in the folio volume, *Médailles sur les principaux événements du règne de Louis le Grand* (1702).[9]

Des Billettes and Jaugeon are named among those who gave addresses during the first years of the eighteenth century to members of the Academy of Sciences in Paris.[10] Jaugeon compiled a volume giving an account of alphabets for many scripts, schemes for the geometrical design of letters, and an account of the cutting of punches and the casting of type, and of typographical printing and bookbinding. His manuscript, dated 1704, is in the library of the Institut de France.[11] Series of plates were engraved, beginning in 1694, relating to the topics discussed by the technicians, many of them by Louis Simonneau, who was also responsible for the decorative engraved borders to the designs of Berain that are on each page of the *Médailles*.[12]

Meanwhile Des Billettes began to draft his own account of typographical printing, a text which is incomplete and of which the exact date of writing is not known. It is fuller than the account given by Jaugeon, and quite independent in its composition. He added a description of other methods of printing: etching and engraving with the burin on copper, and also mezzotint, and printing from plates, wood engraving.[13] In 1704 he is recorded as addressing the Academy of Sciences on stencilling.[14] Much of the extensive theoretical work of Des Billettes remains unpublished among the records of the Academy of Sciences, and it is chiefly known from summaries published by Claire Salomon-Bayet. It includes some measured sketches of printing presses, and some wide-ranging general overviews of different fields of technology. In the words of Des Billettes himself, cited by Salomon-Bayet, 'Un traité des arts très exacts [*sic*] serait presque une espèce d'Encyclopédie'.[15] More plates were engraved, some of those for the text on typefounding being signed by Rochefort in 1719, and editorial reponsibility for the project passed to Réaumur,[16] but the work appears to have lost momentum as he became more concerned with natural history.

> The descriptions were not printed, but kept in order to make a collection in a methodical order, and they remained as manuscripts in the store of the Academy [of Sciences] until M. de Réaumur took on the task of continuing the work, which he did for the rest of his life. … On 15 July 1758, the manuscripts that had been found among the papers of M. de Réaumur, having been placed in order, were handed to twenty Academicians who undertook to revise whatever was fit to publish, to make additions to trades which had been improved, and to investigate new developments in the trades that were not covered among those in the Academy's manuscripts.[17]

After the publication began of the *Encyclopédie* of Diderot and D'Alembert in the 1750s, some of the texts and plates that had been assembled for the Description des arts et métiers were revised and published under the direction of Henri Louis Duhamel du Monceau. They include the account of papermaking by Lalande (undated, but about 1761), and Dudin's text on bookbinding (1772), both of which made use of some of the plates engraved by Simonneau in the 1690s. The material on printing and typefounding was entrusted to the Parisian printer Philippe-Denis Pierres, who is known to have asked contemporary makers of type for information and specimens of their work in an attempt to bring the work up to date, but he did not complete a revised text.[18]

Duhamel du Monceau died in 1789, and the project lapsed for a second time. Thereafter it was largely forgotten until the publication of the study of A. H. Cole and G. B. Watts in 1952.[19] In 1961 André Jammes published his edition of the plates of alphabets which had survived at the Imprimerie Nationale, and which are related to the making of the romain du roi, drawing for his extensive text on the archives of the Académie des Sciences and other related materials

12. For an introductory note on the plates relating to printing, see Pinault (1987).

13. Newberry Library, Chicago, Wing MS oversize Z4029 .225. These are the chief headings: Description de la Presse d'imprimerie, Imposition, encre, etc. Le graveur, Le Graveur à l'eau forte, Graveure au burin, Description de la Presse du graveur, La maniere d'imprimer les estampes, Graveure en bois, Imprimerie de livres d'église, Imprimerie des cartes à jouer. I have made transcriptions of all these texts.

14. *Histoire de l'Académie des Sciences*, année 1704: 'Monsieur des Billettes continuant l'Art de l'Impression, a fait une Description de la Presse, & ensuite de l'impression particuliere des livres d'Eglise, Escriteaux, Sentences, &c. De là il a passé à l'Art de graver en Tailledouce.'

15. Salomon-Bayet (1969), p. 238, n. 1.

16. René Antoine Ferchault de Réaumur (1683–1757).

17. 'Ces différentes descriptions ne furent point imprimées, parce qu'on les réservoit pour former ensuite une collection qui devoit être rangée dans un ordre méthodique; elles restèrent manuscrites dans le dépôt de l'Académie jusqu'au temps ou M. de Réaumur se chargea seul de continuer ce travail, auquel il a véritablement donné ses soins pendant toute sa vie. [...] Le 15 Juillet 1758, les papiers trouvés chez M. de Réaumur, & qui venoient d'être remis en ordre, furent distribués à vingt Académiciens qui se chargerent de revoir & de publier ce qui seroit en état de paroître, de faire des additions aux Arts qui auroient été perfectionnés, d'employer les matériaux qui n'auroient pas une forme convenable, de faire enfin des recherches nouvelles pour les Arts qui ne se trouvoient pas traités dans les papiers que possédoit l'Académie.' Lalande, *L'Art du tanneur*, 1764.

18. P. X. Leschevin, *Notice biographique sur P.-D. Pierres*, 1808, p. 4.

19. A. H. Cole and G. B. Watts, *The handicrafts of France, as recorded in the Description des arts et métiers, 1761–1788*, Cambridge, MA: Baker Library, Harvard Graduate School of Business Administration, 1952.

at the Bibliothèque nationale de France and the Archives nationales, Paris. Dudin's account of bookbinding (1772) was published in an Italian translation, *L'Arte del legatore e doratore di libri, introduzione e note di Jean Toulet* (1964). Lalande's text on papermaking and some others which described related trades, including Dudin's French text on bookbinding, were published in facsimile in one volume under the title *Les arts du papier* (1994).[20]

Sustained by a moderate, even an austere, style of living, wrote Fontenelle, Des Billettes maintained his health. It declined gradually with age, but without leading to serious illness, and he retained his reason. On 10 August 1720, he predicted correctly that he would die on the 15th day of the month. He was 86.

20. *L'Arte del legatore e doratore di libri, introduzione e note di Jean Toulet*, Milano: Il Polifilo, 1964; *Les arts du papier*, Geneva: Slatkine Reprints, 1994.

Sources

Bomstein-Erb, Erwan (2001–02). 'Leibnitz et Pascal: l'infini comme principe de réforme', Mémoire de Maîtrise, Université de Paris IV, Sorbonne, année 2001–2002, www.erwan.net/Memoire.pdf

Fontenelle, Bernard le Bouvier de (1720). 'Eloge de M. Des Billettes', *Histoire de l'Académie Royale*, année 1720, pp. 122–4.

Jammes, André (1961). *La réforme de la typographie royale sous Louis XIV: le Grandjean*, Paris: Librarie Paul Jammes; reprinted in a smaller format, Paris: Promodis, 1985. There is an English translation of the larger part of the text under the title 'Académisme et typographie: the making of the romain du roi', with reproductions of the plates on a reduced scale, in *Journal of the Printing Historical Society*, no. 1, 1965, pp. 71–95

Mesnard, Jean (1965). *Pascal et les Roannez*. Paris: Desclée de Brouwer

Mosley, James (1997). 'French academicians and modern typography: designing new types in the 1690s', *Typography papers*, 2. Reading: Department of Typography & Graphic Communication, pp. 5–29

Mosley, James (2002). 'Les caractères de l'Imprimerie royale', in *Le romain du roi: la typographie au service de l'état*. Lyon: Musée de l'imprimerie, pp. 33–80

Mosley, James (2008). 'Médailles sur les principaux événements du règne de Louis le Grand, 1702: the making of the book', *Bulletin du bibliophile*, 2, pp. 296–350

Pinault, Madeleine (1987). 'Dessins pour un Art de l'Imprimerie', 112ᵉ Congrès national des Sociétés savantes, Lyon, *Histoire des Sciences*, vol. 2, pp. 73–85

Saint-Simon, Louis de Rouvroy, duc de (1983). *Mémoires, additions au journal de Dangeau; édition établie par Yves Coirault*, vol. 1. Paris: Gallimard (Bibliothèque de la Pléiade)

Salomon-Bayet, Claire (1969). 'Une préambule théorique à une Académie des Arts: Académie royale des Sciences, 1693–1696, présentation et textes', *Revue d'histoire des sciences*, pp. 229–50

Sauvy, Anne (1973). 'L'illustration d'un règne: le Cabinet du Roi et les projets encyclopédiques de Colbert', in *L'Art du livre à l'Imprimerie nationale*. Paris: Imprimerie nationale, pp. 103–27

Maurice Göldner

The Brüder Butter typefoundry

This essay seeks to construct a history of the Brüder Butter typefoundry from the few archival sources that remain following the destruction of Dresden in 1945, and from the rich collection of type specimens that the foundry issued from the turn of the twentieth century. The specimens – well designed and printed – illustrate not only the foundry's range of typefaces, but also trace its business expansion through export, the incorporation of type designs from the USA and other sources into its repertoire, and the development of modular ornaments and type systems.

In the early years of the twentieth century, the typefounding trade in Germany turned oligopolistic, while also expanding through the increased export of advertising and jobbing types to Scandinavia, South America, and the USA. Because competition was tough, merely producing the types was no longer good enough. Type had to be promoted vigorously and selling points explained; it had to be marketed across frontiers, not least because samples of metal type were heavy and expensive to send abroad. Type specimen booklets, regularly published, were an indispensable and important prerequisite for successful sales overseas. In the design and production of the specimen booklets, great importance was attached not only to the content, but also to formal and technical excellence. When one compares these booklets today, the specimens of the Dresden typefoundry Brüder Butter (later 'Schriftguß A.-G. vormals [formerly] Brüder Butter') immediately catch the eye. The company not only emphasized quality of design and manufacturing, but their specimens also communicate a relaxed and humorous attitude in the advertising of type, sometimes taken to the point of self-mockery.

The strength of Brüder Butter's catalogue lay in its striking, highly creative display types, and by 1920 a large body of specimen booklets had accumulated. About the company itself however – its origins, its functioning, its economic strategies – hardly any sources can be found, apart from a few contemporary reports. Brüder Butter is neither mentioned in recent essays on German typefounding nor has a company history of this once-eminent business ever been published.

The change of the political system in Germany after the Second World War caused radical changes in the agenda and catalogue of Brüder Butter's successor company, Typoart – the national typefoundry in the former German Democratic Republic. The collapse of Typoart following German reunification in 1989, and the problems of unsettled structures of ownership that followed the collapse, makes a search for documentation difficult. Only a few secondary sources can be found, but these are sometimes inconsistent or demonstrably incorrect. Friedrich Bauer's *Chronik der Schriftgießereien in Deutschland und den deutschsprachigen Nachbarländern* of 1928 – an important standard work for the period – is an example of this. Here, Brüder Butter's founding year is given as 1890, two years before the actual date, which can be shown by checking the entries in the trades register of the Dresden magistrate's court. Furthermore, Bauer's prehistory of the firm is very brief.

Primary sources for the present essay are the entries that still exist in the trade register of the magistrate's court and the trade files of

Figure 1. Type specimen issued by
the Brüder Butter printing works,
Komotau, *c.*1873. 300 × 210 mm.

For references to archival sources,
see p. 115

1. *Komotauer Jahrbuch* (1998) p. 38,
Komotauer Jahrbuch (2007) p. 107.
2. Bürger- und Gewerbeakte, Carl
Heinrich Butter, 1889, Stadtarchiv.
3. Bürger- und Gewerbeakte, Otto
Ludwig Bechert, 1889, Stadtarchiv;
Handelsregister.
4. Letter of 25 November 1889, Bürger-
und Gewerbeakte, Otto Ludwig Bechert,
1889, Stadtarchiv.
5. Handelsregister.
6. Letter from Franz Sysel to the
Dresden city council, 30 January 1892:
Bürger- und Gewerbeakte, Franz Sysel,
1890, Stadtarchiv.
7. Handelsregister.
8. Bürger- und Gewerbeakte,
Fürchtegott Hermann Butter, 1892,
Stadtarchiv.
9. Handelsregister.
10. Letter of 2 February 1892, Bürger-
und Gewerbeakte, Fürchtegott Hermann
Butter, 1892, Stadtarchiv.
11. Patent 'Verbesserung an Drucktypen
mit überhängenden Schrifttheilen'
by F. H. Butter, Patent Nr. 2964,
Schweizerische Eidgenossenschaft,
24 November 1890.
12. Receipt 19 January 1920, cease of
trading notice, Bürger- und Gewerbeakte,
Franz Sysel, 1892, Stadtarchiv.

the Dresden city archive. Otherwise the published specimens represent the sole direct source of information from Brüder Butter that sheds light on the working methods of the company. Through their words, and also through their design, we can see something of the company's spirit and that of the period.

The Butter family and the origins of the company

The Brüder Butter typefoundry originated in a printing works, also named Brüder Butter, which offered book printing, art printing, and lithography (figure 1).[1] From this family business, which from 1863 had been carried on in the Bohemian (now Czech) city of Komotau, three brothers seem to have sprung: Carl Heinrich Butter, Fürchtegott Hermann Butter, and Ernst Julius Butter. All three were significantly involved in the creation of the Dresden foundry.

In August 1889 Carl Heinrich Butter established a business in the city of Dresden by purchasing a printing shop there.[2] The other two brothers followed later. In the meantime, Otto Ludwig Bechert, a typefounder from Danzig, appeared in Dresden and established a typefoundry in November 1889, located at Schäferstraße 4.[3] He initially set up his business with two small hand-casting machines, a melting pot, a lathe, and a circular saw.[4] The existence of a lathe and a circular saw may indicate that Bechert, apart from casting type, also produced a range of printer's paraphernalia. On 5 March 1890 Bechert officially launched a typefoundry named Bechert & Co. together with his partner Franz Sysel, a mechanic from Klado near Prague.[5] At this point, the company was already employing four hand-typecasting machines.[6] On 22 May 1890, shortly after the company was established, Otto Ludwig Bechert quit, leaving Franz Sysel in sole charge of the business.[7] Less than two years later, on 29 January 1892, Fürchtegott Hermann Butter, the second of the Butter brothers, a trained typefounder, was now a co-owner of Franz Sysel's company.[8] On 19 February 1892, the company's name was changed to Butter & Sysel.[9] The typefoundry, at that time located on the first floor of a wing of Schäferstraße 11, in Dresden, was still operating four hand-typecasting machines.[10] Fürchtegott Hermann Butter cannot have been unknown in the typefounding trade. A patent from 1890, entitled 'Verbesserung an Buchdrucktypen mit überhängenden Schrifttheilen' (Improvement to type with overhanging parts), suggests that he was already working as a typefounder in Komotau. The invention, which would later be labelled 'Fundamental-Schreibschrift-System' (Fundamental system for scripts) in the printing trade, was an attempt to 'correct a deficiency in type with overhanging letterforms that can be found in English [i.e. script], Latin, or cursive type, and lend them a durability comparable to that of other kinds of type.'[11] The breaking off of overhanging parts when printing cursive type, common in those days, was averted through strengthening the supporting part of the letter. An illustration from the patent specification shows the letters from different angles and demonstrates the idea (figure 2, opposite).

In July 1892, Franz Sysel left the company to run his own business in the related trades of stereotyping and electrotyping.[12] His place was taken by the youngest of the three brothers, Julius Butter, also

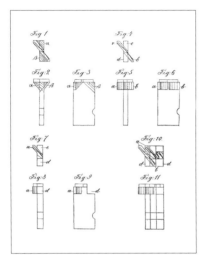

Figure 2. Details of Swiss patent issued to Hermann Butter for an 'improvement to type with overhanging parts', 1890.

13. Letter of 26 July 1892, Bürger- und Gewerbeakte, Ernst Julius Butter, 1892, Stadtarchiv.

14. Entry for 18 July 1892, Handelsregister.

15. Letter of 17 November 1898, Bürger- und Gewerbeakte, Fürchtegott Hermann Butter, Stadtarchiv.

16. Entry for 2 July 1901, Handelsregister.

17. Letter of 27 December 1909, Bürger- und Gewerbeakte, Fürchtegott Hermann Butter, 1892, Stadtarchiv.

18. Bauer (1928), p. 47.

19. Eule (1935), p. 156.

a trained typefounder. Julius Butter remained a resident of Komotau and conducted business from the Brüder Butter printing office there.[13] On 18 July 1892, the typefoundry was renamed Schriftgießerei Brüder Butter (Butter Brothers' Typefoundry).[14]

Early years

There are few sources documenting internal developments at the Brüder Butter typefoundry during its first two decades. In November 1898, the company filed an application for an extension and asked for permission to install a gas engine to operate two typecasting machines.[15] The foundry had reorganized its production from hand operation to machine operation. The business was slowly increasing in size. Perhaps this was also the reason for a relocation in Dresden in 1899. In July 1901, Ernst Julius Butter left and from then on his brother Fürchtegott Hermann Butter was in charge. In the same year, Fürchtegott installed his son Hermann Butter in the business, with power of attorney.[16] Eight years later, in December 1909, the company increased the power of its gas engine to 4 hp, quadrupling its performance so that eight typecasting machines could be operated at the same time.[17]

The centre of both the printing and type industry in central Germany was the city of Leipzig. Dresden, 100 km away, was the political centre and capital of Saxony. What was the shape of the printing industry there? Up to 1906, a number of the firms listed in the Dresden trade directory worked in the fields of stereotyping and electrotyping. The only competitor to Brüder Butter in the field of type production was the Müller & Hölemann typefoundry, which was in business from 1887 to 1910.[18] A photograph from 1897, showing the tenth anniversary of the company Müller & Hölemann, gives an insight into the typefounder's trade at the time (figure 3, overleaf). At first glance, it seems that type is still being cast by hand. The presence both of large ladles and force pumps suggest that the handcasting process was merely being accelerated by the use of force pumps. The job of the women and children in the picture was to clean casting residue from the individual types and sort them. But a closer look reveals that also Müller & Hölemann must also have been using automatic casting machines. Two founders in the upper part of the picture hold wooden composing sticks, which were used to collect the letters from the automatic casting machines. Unfortunately, no type specimens have been discovered that reveal more about the material being produced. But one can suppose that the company could not compete with the working methods and the increasingly industrialized type production of Brüder Butter, which from 1909 had more than eight typecasting machines. Müller & Hölemann was forced to declare bankruptcy in 1910, and from 1911 on, Brüder Butter had no competition in the city of Dresden. One can assume that the company supplied the whole of eastern Saxony with its type, blocking Leipzig from trading eastwards. The prominence gained by Brüder Butter in the following years is illustrated by a quotation from 1935: 'In Saxony, apart from Leipzig, the typefounding trade is only practised in Dresden.'[19] At that time, Dresden was represented in the trade solely by Schriftguß A.-G. formerly Brüder Butter.

Figure 3. Workers at the Müller & Hölemann typefoundry, Dresden 1897.

Figure 4. Advertising stamp, 1912.

20. 'Fünf praktische Garnituren zu Spezialguß-Preisen' (specimen collection, summer 1913).

21. Bürger- und Gewerbeakte, Fürchtegott Hermann Butter, 1892, with company notepaper from 1914, Stadtarchiv.

22. Entry for 2 May 1914, Handels-register.

Growth and recognition

In 1912 the foundry moved yet again to a larger building at Großen-hainer Straße 92. This change of address had become necessary as the company grew. On an advertising stamp from 1912 an illustration of the building can be seen. A man in old-fashioned dress with a large ladle steps through the picture. In his left hand, he holds a type with the letter B (for Butter; figure 4). This illustration, in red and green, is also one of the first uses of the figure of a typefounder to characterize Brüder Butter in advertising, and who was to appear repeatedly in modified forms. From the illustration it appears that the business occupied a three-storey industrial building, but this is an exaggeration. In reality, it only occupied the the first floor.

By 1913, the company had 80 employees and was equipped with 30 automatic casting machines.[20] In only four years, the number of machines had nearly quadrupled – from 8 to 30. How this was made possible is indicated by a specimen booklet dating from November 1913. About half of its 96 pages are dedicated to the types on offer, some of which were newly released. Additional emphasis was put on the ornaments and rules. For the first time, a small catalogue of printer's paraphernalia was included, in which tools such as bodkins, metal quoins, galleys, composing sticks, and typecases were listed. Apart from offering such products, the company was also the general agent for a brand of American numbering machines in Germany.

In May 1914, the company's owner Fürchtegott Hermann Butter stepped down at the age of 68: 'I hereby announce my retirement from the business (typefounding), which I have managed for 20 years. Most humbly, Fürchtegott Hermann Butter'.[21] These lines were written on a Brüder Butter letterheading with an unusual illustration that demonstrated the self-confidence with which the foundry represented itself (figure 5, opposite). This variant of a typefounder is depicted as a jester with a casting ladle. He plays his flute and so tempts letters out of the city of Dresden, seen in the background. The pictured letters, running from city gates in the form of a large hollow-bodied display type ('Sparguß-Type', see p. 102), closely resemble the patterns from the ornaments 'Die Dresdner Linie' (see figure 16). This motif, clearly referring to the story of the Pied Piper of Hamelin, sym-bolized the self-confident air and self-mockery of the Butter brothers. Like the Pied Piper, they had special powers – over metal type, and the typefounding trade in the city, in which they had a monopoly. After the retirement of Fürchtegott Hermann Butter in 1914, his son Hermann Butter junior, a trained chemist, and the merchant Ernst Otto Hensel, took over the management of the company.[22]

In May 1914, the Internationale Ausstellung für Buchgewerbe und Graphik (the international exhibition of the book trade and graphic arts, known as BUGRA) opened in Leipzig. In the main hall, devoted to the German book trade, the country's most important type-foundries presented themselves to the public. Heinrich Hoffmeister described the exhibition in detail: 'The walls of the corridors were covered with golden fabric, embellished with an ornamental black edge at the top and at the bottom ... on the floor, coconut mats in

Figure 5. Brüder Butter company
notepaper, 1914, 297 × 210 mm.

a grey hue were laid out.'[23] The German typefounders association
exhibited collectively, while Brüder Butter, not yet a member, was
present in an individual booth. There 'the main attraction was three
huge types of different sizes (the largest weighing about 400 kilos)
representing the growth in business; also on display were samples of
casting, leads, etc., and numbering machines.'[24] Although this is only
a brief description of Brüder Butter's exhibit, it is in clear contrast
to all the other stands described. Brüder Butter presented itself at
the BUGRA in an unaffected, contemporary, and unorthodox fashion,
with three big letters – presumably BBD (i.e. Brüder Butter Dresden).

A public limited company

In September 1922 the company was converted to a public limited
company (Schriftguß A.-G. vormals Brüder Butter) and it also joined
the German typefounder's association.[25] In spite of the change of
name the foundry maintained its link to the family name with the
suffix 'formerly Brüder Butter' as a link to their past. Alongside
Hermann Butter and Ernst Otto Hensel, the new partners were Curt
Albert, a factory owner; Max Schaarschmidt, a private investor from
Dresden; and Georg Seiring, a member of the city council and later
director of the Deutsches Hygiene-Museum in Dresden. The management of the firm was taken over by Butter junior and Hensel, while
the board of directors was represented by Albrecht, Schaarschmidt,
and Seiring.[26] The declared purpose of the conversion was the 'acquisition and continuation of the foundry business until now run by
the firm of Brüder Butter, Dresden ... operation of the typefoundry
and the trades connected with it, incorporation of lines of production and administration of commercial transactions ... [eligibility]
to establish branches inland and abroad ...'.[27] The total capital of
the company at this point had increased to 16.6 million Reichsmark.
On the balance sheet, a net profit of 11.8 million Reichsmark was
indicated.[28]

The need for increased production capacity had made it necessary
to move to a self-contained factory in the form of a square courtyard
building. The move to this new building at Großenhainer Straße 9,
very near the railway station at Dresden-Neustadt, was completed in
1923. Up to 1926, the former headquarters at Großenhainer Straße 92
was also used as a branch.[29] The company had at its disposal over
4,000 square metres of work space with a capacity of 50 casting
machines. In addition to the cast types, machines and equipment
for letterpress printing were sold. Beyond that, it had its own railway
siding for shipping type or machine equipment. In an advertisement in *Klimschs Jahrbuch* of 1923, Schriftguß A.-G. defined its three
most important product ranges: ornaments, types, and vignettes.
The focus in its typeface design on 'modern types for promotional
and display use' was publicly advertised. The company reinforced its
publicity with further advertisements in various trade journals and
began to figure more prominently in reviews of new typeface
releases.

23. Hoffmeister (1914), p. 268.
24. Hoffmeister (1914), p. 275.
25. *Handbuch der Deutschen
Aktiengesellschaften* (1923/4), p. 1268.
26. Handelregister; *Handbuch der
Deutschen Aktiengesellschaften* (1923/4).
27. *Handbuch der Deutschen
Aktiengesellschaften* (1923/4), p. 1268.
28. *Handbuch der Deutschen
Aktiengesellschaften* (1923/4), p. 1268.
29. *Dresdner Adressbuch* (1922–7).

Figure 6. View of the courtyard at Großhainer Straße 9, Dresden. The overprinting describes the dispatch of 14,000 kg of printing materials to a Brazilian state printing house. Specimen, c. 1926.

Figure 7. Graph showing sales growth in Portuguese and Spanish. Specimen, c. 1926.

Figure 8. Marggraff Kursiv. Specimen no. 52, 1928, set in nine languages. 297 × 210 mm.

30. Eule (1927/8), p. 538.

Schriftguß A.-G. and the international market

There are several clues suggesting that a large proportion of the types sold by Schriftguß A.-G. must have been gone abroad. There was the factory's railway siding and its proximity to the Neustadt railway station, which could be used to ship its products long distances. The various specimen catalogues indicate foreign markets too. One of these catalogues is a specimen collection issued around 1926, in Portuguese and Spanish, with the title 'Fundição de Typos, Schriftguß A.-G. vorm. Brüder Butter Dresden (Alemanha)'. In it are photographs of the headquarters and several interior views of the shop floors. There are pictures of the two halls where the founders worked, as well as views of the punchcutters' shop, the drilling shop, the brass rule department, the type warehouse, and the in-house printing office, which produced the specimen booklets (figures 6 and 9). A graph (versions of which appear repeatedly in following years) illustrates the rise of the company and the accompanying text declares: 'Uma argumentação eloquente para a boa qualidade de seus productos' ('An eloquent argument for the quality of their goods') (figure 7). Another example shows that Schriftguß A.-G. had a Latin American distribution partner in Rio de Janeiro. Gaston Meinert & Cia., together with Schriftguß A.-G., published the catalogue *Typos alemãos,* which provides, in Portuguese, a complete overview of all the types available. Many single specimens refer to international sales as well. In a specimen of the typeface Marggraff Kursiv, an original release of 1928, designed by Gerhard Marggraff from Berlin, the type is advertised in a total of nine languages (figure 8).

The year 1928 was important for the growing recognition of the Dresden firm. In its April number of that year, the trade journal *Deutscher Drucker* turned its attention to Schriftguß A.-G. under the heading 'Homes of the graphic industry'. The description of the company building is especially interesting:

A printer … visiting Dresden, cannot feel more at home in this beautiful city than by visiting the green building at Großenhainer Straße 9, not far from the Neustadt railway station. Here, in this spaciously designed factory complex, whose façade is graced with a coat of green paint, the Schriftguß A.-G. has … its home … and one may recognize the green colour of the paintwork as a symbol of the vitality and vigorous spirit dwelling in this enterprise.[30]

Figure 9. The works at Großhainer
Straße 9, Dresden. Specimen, c. 1926.
(a) general view
(b) casting hall
(c) punchcutters' shop
(d) drilling shop
(e) brass rule department
(f) type warehouse
(g) in-house printing office

a

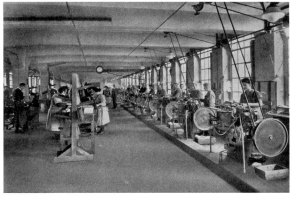

b

c

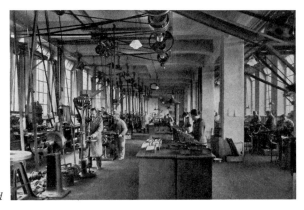

d

e

f

g

This green colour, which was already conspicuously used in other specimens and in the 1912 advertising stamp already mentioned, was developed as the identifying colour of Schriftguß A.-G. According to the author of the article, the company was by now employing 55 casting machines. The inventory comprised 300,000 kg of type and ornament material, and a yearly production rate of 450,000 kg of typographic material is specified. It had developed into a large-scale firm capable of producing considerable output.

National Socialism, war, and expropriation

With the seizure of power by the National Socialists in January 1933, a new period began for Schriftguß A.-G. This is particularly apparent in the replacement of the management. Some four months before the change of political regime, the last member of the founding family, Hermann Butter, resigned from the board.[31] Why Hermann Butter left the company at this time, and whether there is a connection with the coming to power of the Nazis, remain open questions. At that point, the Schaarschmidt family took over the greater part of the shares and the obligations of management. Four years later, in 1937, the company became a limited partnership under the law for the conversion of public limited companies and was re-titled 'Schriftguß K.-G., vorm. Brüder Butter'. The associates were the two directors Oskar Max Schaarschmidt and Otto Schaarschmidt, the lawyer Dr Fritz Schaarschmidt, Edith Wacker (née Schaarschmidt), and her husband Hermann Wacker.[32]

Scarcely any documentary sources for the company's internal procedures survive for the period up to 1945. Only a trial of 1950, which concerned the denunciation by and subsequent suicide of a supervisor in the year 1936, sheds some light on the National-Socialist era. The supervisor had passed on internal company information to the authorites: 'You wouldn't believe how the office for the inspection of metal stocks … [is being duped], we've got a thousand kilos of lead in our basement under a canvas which the office doesn't know about.'[33] To safeguard the firm's assets from bombing attacks, some of the machines and factory equipment, and a part of the stock and other material, were evacuated. These items were freighted to the areas of Lusatia, Saxon Switzerland (*Sächsische Schweiz*), and the Erz Mountains.[34]

Near the end of the war, another change in the management took place. 'We hereby announce that due to his death during the air attack of 13 February 1945 the partner and managing director Otto Schaarschmidt is no longer a member of the limited partnership and that Dr Friedrich Schaarschmidt has taken his place as a partner.'[35] Allied air attacks in April 1945 destroyed all the company files. At that time the company reported the value of its business to be 700,000 Reichsmark.[36] In July 1945 the new Soviet Military Administration (SMAD) granted a permit for the resumption of production by the company, after the shutdown due to the war, and for the sale of type from stock.[37] In August 1945 the SMAD concluded: 'As a contribution to the reparations to the Soviet Union, the Schriftguß A.-G. is to be

31. Entry for 20 May 1933, Handelsregister.
32. Entry for 1937, Handelsregister.
33. *DDR-Justiz und NS-Verbrechen* (2005), p. 95.
34. *Zehn Jahre VEB Typoart* (1958), p. 4.
35. Letter of 22 July 1945 from Schriftguß K.-G. to the Amtsgericht in Dresden, Hauptstaatsarchiv.
36. Letter of 12 April 1945 to the Amtsgericht Dresden, Handelsregisterakte.
37. *Zehn Jahre VEB Typoart* (1958), p. 6.

dismantled. The capitalist proprietor Schaarschmidt, like others, had put his business at the service of armaments.' It was probably only after the dismantling that the evacuated machines and materials were brought back, in December 1945, to resume production.[38] In April 1947 the 'committee for de-Nazification of the city of Dresden … unanimously decided, that with immediate effect the general partner Max Schaarschmidt may no longer preside over his company and is to be discharged.'[39]

On 5 January 1948, after the replacement of the directorate by caretaker manager Matthias Alois Hansen and the former attorney Fritz Hans Lorenz, the 'former proprietor, Mr Schaarschmidt, has been arrested by order of the public prosecuter's office on suspicion of intending to sell the company to western corporations. … Mr Schaarschmidt [had] tried on several occasions to sell or lease the company. By command … of the SMAD the company has been seized and on 17 February (1948) has been placed in sequestration.'[40] The federal government of Saxony declared the foundry 'federal property' in March of the same year. Two months later, in May 1948, the former factory manager Schaarschmidt and his assistant Harms were convicted: 'Concluding the legal proceedings against Mr Schaarschmidt and Mr Harms for crimes against humanity on 21 May 1948, Schaarschmidt has been sentenced to one year and nine months in a detention centre and to confiscation of his assets, and Harms has been sentenced to two and a half years in a detention centre. Both men had reported foreign workers to the Deutsche Arbeitsfront [the Nazi trade union organization] and the Gestapo.[41]

Due to the unsettled ownership structure, the company passed into 'ownership by the people' through a resolution of the SMAD and thereby officially expropriated. From July 1948, Matthias Alois Hansen resumed direction of the company under the new name VEB Schriftguß Dresden. The former Leipzig foundry Schelter & Giesecke was also incorporated into VEB Schriftguß Dresden. Two workplaces were formed at the existing company locations in Dresden and Leipzig.

After the foundation of the German Democratic Republic, a final change of name took place in October 1951: 'VEB Schriftguß' was changed to 'VEB Typoart – Drucktypen, Matrizen, Messinglinien' ('VEB Typoart – printing types, matrices, brass rules'). 'In this way, the physical "memory" of the previous capitalist era [was] disposed of as well.'[42] The change of political system was followed by a change in the typographic agenda. First of all, the greater part of the display and advertisement types disappeared from the type specimen books of VEB Typoart. Only a few typefaces were retained, for instance Super-Grotesk, which sold well up to 1989. The change of name, the clear differentiation in the range of types sold, as well as the changed methods of production due to the state-directed economy, mark the start of the era of VEB Typoart and the end of the separate identity of the Brüder Butter typefoundry.

38. *Die Entwicklung des Betriebes Typoart in Fakten und Daten, 1945–1985,* p. 11 ff.

39. Letter of 14 April 1947, council of the city of Dresden, Handelsregisterakte.

40. *Die Entwicklung …,* p. 18 ff.

41. *Die Entwicklung …,* p. 20.

42. *Die Entwicklung …,* p. 28.

Figure 10. Early poster specimen issued by Brüder Butter, c. 1900. 530 × 720 mm.

Figure 11. Details from the poster specimen, *c.* 1900.

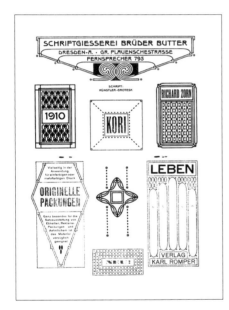

Figure 12. Jugendstil borders, specimen, *c.* 1910. 297 × 210 mm.

43. The specimen does not carry a date. However, the spelling of the word 'Brod' in the title may be a clue to the date of production. The spelling of this word as 'Brot' was officially established only in 1900. See Hermann Paul, *Deutsches Wörterbuch,* Tübingen: Niemeyer, 9th edn 1999, p. 190.

Types and specimens

Typefoundries market their typefaces through advertisements in trade journals, single type specimen booklets, and comprehensive catalogues. Questions about the Brüder Butter typefoundry and the typefaces it offered in the years immediately after its founding in 1892 are hard to answer, because of the lack of specimens from this period. In later years most of the published specimen booklets are numbered, but the numbering appears to start at 51. If this number is based on the specimens already published, it can be assumed that copies of many specimen booklets no longer exist (see list of specimens, pp. 114–15).

In an early poster specimen from about 1900 titled 'Billige Brod-, Auszeichnungs- und Accidenz-Schriften' (Fonts for body, display and jobbing text at fair prices) (figures 10 and 11), the foundry presented itself with the following words: 'Brüder Butter typefoundry, Dresden: stereotyping and electrotyping, xylographic services, vignettes, printer's paraphernalia … comprehensive sample sheets of borders, contemporary ornaments, vignettes for merchants and newspapers, etc., as well as price tables for all our products at your disposal. New creations of any size in the shortest amount of time, small-scale creations available straight away at all times. Numerous letters of appreciation and references from major companies'.[43] This indicates that, in its early years, the firm was a typefoundry with production branches in stereotyping, electrotyping, and xylography. The firm offered a full range of artwork for commercial printing, not just the making of type. The offer of 'comprehensive sample sheets' suggests that at that time the foundry advertised the material they produced in the form of single sheets. The types shown in this poster specimen are typical of the period. Furthermore, they carry straightforward, generic names such as 'Fraktur', 'Gothic', 'Schwabacher', 'Roman', and so on. It gives the impression that these types had not been cut in-house, but that single sets of matrices had been purchased. With respect to the constraints of hand-composition at the time, the perforated 'advertising initials' are interesting (figure 11). They made it possible for the compositor to fill the interior space of a capital letter with small letters to create word marks or logotypes.

Another specimen, of about 1910, titled 'Dresdner Schriften, Einfassungen, Vignetten, Ausschluß-Material' (Types, borders, vignettes, and spacing material from Dresden), shows a clear Jugendstil influence, both in its design and in the types offered (figure 12). The decorative and floral style of the ornaments is most apparent in the borders, vignettes, and the reproduced ornaments. As well as two Jugendstil types and a Gothic, a widely spaced Grotesk and different kinds of typewriter-types were offered. A notable type from this specimen is the Dresdner Amtsfraktur (Dresden administrative blackletter). This restrained typeface is showcased on a whole seven pages.

Yet another and more extensive specimen that gives insight into the foundry's programme of the time, is a green collection of specimens of about 1911–13, labelled 'Schriftgießerei Brüder Butter, Dresden-N.' The cover design demonstrates a considerable change from the advertising material produced before. A two-colour

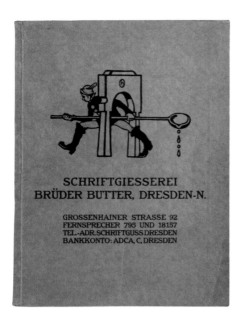

Figure 13. Cover of the *c.* 1913 specimen. 280 × 200 mm.

illustration, in black and red, depicts a foundryman, again with a big, dripping ladle. He walks swiftly through a monumental letter (figure 13). It is a so-called 'Sparguß-Type' (casting economy type) with the stubs still sticking out. These types were cast in bigger sizes – from 72 to 96 point, for example – a suggestion of the large display sizes being produced at the time. The typeface used on the cover was the newly issued Wellington, shown on the first three pages of the booklet as a preliminary specimen (figure 14). This somewhat unconventional type, available in two weights, normal and bold. It is a low-contrast slab serif design whose proportions are not based on historical precedents. The capital letters show a trace of Jugendstil, evident in the high waistline of the R.

This unorthodox albeit interesting design reflects a way of thinking at the start of the twentieth century, in which foundries tried to meet the demand for display type through an increasing range of variants. The evident faults and unbalanced character of Wellington are symptomatic of a deterioration of quality in letterforms due to increasing mass production. The capitals are too heavy and not well proportioned. The contrast in the bold weight of the type is too low, which results in a very clumsy appearance. The double-storey g, present only in some sizes of the bold weight, is an inconsistent detail. An understanding of the relations within a type family did not exist in the way it does today. Type designs would often only be extended some years after the first forms were made, with these additions executed by different people. In this case there are also other reasons. The normal and bold weights are not properly matched to each other because the bold weight of Wellington is based on the typeface Foster, which was issued about 1905 by the American Inland Type Foundry, while the normal weight of Wellington (Wellington Gewöhnlich) was probably an addition by Brüder Butter. But who designed this typeface? If we look further at the shapes

Figure 14. A preliminary display of the Wellington-Schrift (specimen, *c.* 1913). The bold weight is based on Foster, issued in 1905 by the Inland Type Foundry of St Louis, Missouri.

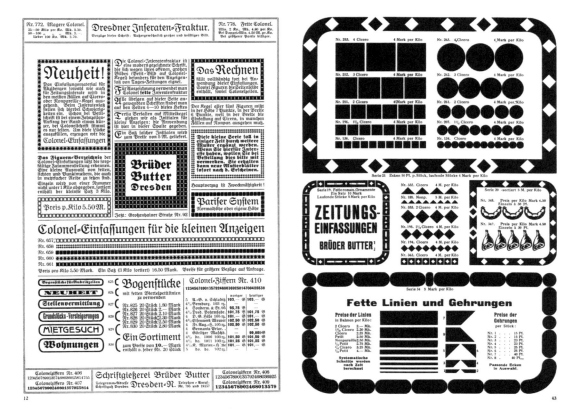

Figure 15. Dresdner Inseraten-Fraktur and modular border elements, specimen, c. 1913. 280 × 200 mm.

and proportions of Wellington, especially in a few of the lowercase characters, it seems likely that this design is the work of commercial artists, whose expertise would have been in designing single word images for posters. The Wellington type, although not original, signalled a new period of increased prominence for the company.[44]

A further ten pages of this green specimen show the Dresdner Amtsfraktur in use in various examples. This blackletter, originally designed for setting body text, was supplemented with light and bold weights, and also a display version. The latter, called Dresdner Inseraten-Fraktur (Dresden advertisement blackletter) was described as 'a type particularly suitable for setting advertisements in newspapers because of its open, large appearance'.[45] The display version appears very large in relation to the body, which makes for very effective composition with no linespacing needed (figure 15, above left). Furthermore, the character set contains additional capitals with no side bearings. These were designed as initials.

At the same time, Brüder Butter expanded their catalogue with material for jobbing printing and advertising. Here, the first modular systems for the composition of borders and line ornaments can be found. The rounded sections for borders are worth noting; judging by their size they had been cast for setting poster-sized advertisements (figure 15, above right). The predominance of this kind of typographic material in a catalogue is not uncommon. The introduction of composing machines in Germany around 1895 forced typefoundries to reduce their dependence on text types, which could be more economically set by machine, and instead offer a wider range of typographic materials, such as ornaments and display type, which still

44. The Otto Weisert typefoundry of Stuttgart marketed bold and bold outline versions of this typeface under the name Moderne Egyptienne from c. 1908, which featured in the *Klimschs Jahrbuch* of 1912.

45. 'Schriftgießerei Brüder Butter, Dresden-N.', specimen collection, c. 1913, p. 12.

Figure 16. (left and centre) Border and ornament elements from the 'Dresdner Linie' series, (right) specimen of the Fette Otfried type, using the word 'Komotau'. Specimen, c. 1913.

had to be set by hand. Moreover, the increasing complexity of printed information called for typographic devices to structure it hierarchically. Accentuation devices such as borders, line ornaments, or patterns were increasingly used. Accordingly, the foundry produced its collection of line ornaments and patterns, called 'Die Dresdner Linie' (the Dresden line), as an original product, as part of the green specimen collection (figure 16, left and centre). The specimen collection was rounded off with a 16-page overview of all types on offer, with some sanserifs added to complement the existing catalogue. One can observe that many of the words used to show the types relate directly to the Butter brothers' background; for example, the city of Komotau (figure 16, right), or the city of Olbernhau in the Erz Mountains, from where the founder of the Brüder Butter printing shop in Komotau originated.[46]

Through this expanded range of products, the company was able to react to economic developments more flexibly, and it could also capitalize on its international business connections for the home market. In the domain of type, this is illustrated by the typeface Ohio, which was also an American import. Through this type, the wider printing trade became aware of the Dresden typefoundry. 'The foundry Brüder Butter from Dresden makes quite a refreshing and modern impression. It publishes a number of typographically accomplished sheets that show off the Ohio types brilliantly.'[47] The first separate specimen of Ohio was published in 1913 in the booklet *Die Ohio-Schrift, Ohio-Kursiv: eine Rasse-Schrift für eigenartige Druckausstattung* (Ohio, Ohio Italic: a quality type for distinctive typography) (figure 17). The typeface, labelled here as a 'work-horse with personality' quite clearly shows its origins in American-influenced typography and 'old-style' types. Ohio was not an original design but a typeface licensed by American Type Founders (ATF). It is based on lettering by Frederic W. Goudy for the American Pabst Brewing Company in 1902. From this design, Goudy later developed a complete

46. *Komotauer Jahrbuch* (1998), p. 38.
47. Windisch (1920), p. 275 ff.

Figure 17. 'A quality type for distinctive typography': Ohio-Schrift, Ohio-Kursiv. Specimen, 1913. 295 × 215 mm.

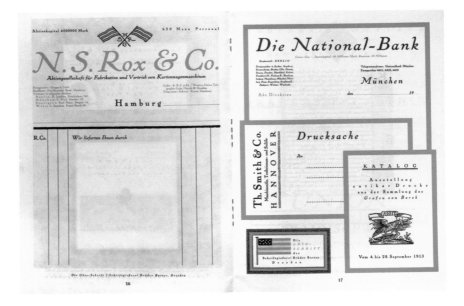

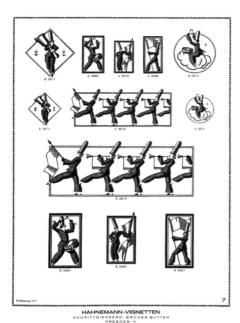

Figure 18. Ornaments designed
by Hahnemann, Schütze, and
Sigrist. 'Buchschmuck' specimen,
1920. 290×205 mm.

typeface including an italic, which was sold under the name Pabst
Old Style around 1907.[48]

In 1920 Brüder Butter published a specimen catalogue of 132
pages, comprised entirely of vignettes, ornaments, and other decorative elements.

> This catalogue contains our complete range of ornaments, omitting
> all the superseded material. The new expressionist ornaments are a
> selection of the most mature designs of Germany's most eminent com-
> mercial artists ... We offer a versatile and thoroughly usable selection
> of material, entirely our own creation, which can impart the spirit of
> the times to any kind of printed matter.[49]

The catalogue, printed in nine colours, demonstrates the kind of
effort the foundry put into the production of specimen booklets.
It includes the information that machine capacity had increased
to 40 automatic casting machines – a sign of continuing growth.
Accordingly, the foundry was by now reviewed in trade journals
more frequently. An article in the *Archiv für Buchgewerbe und Graphik*
reported: 'The Brüder Butter seem to put special value on the creation of contemporary book ornaments, and it cannot be denied that
in Sigrist, Osang, Mönkemeyer-Corty, and others, they have found
artists with a feeling for effective advertising ... with whom they have
boldly taken the path of progress.'[50] The foundry signed local commercial artists (Sigrist and Mönkemeyer-Corty) who were particularly
influential designers in Dresden in that period (figure 18).[51]

In the following years the type catalogue was expanded with a
multitude of new designs. Two typefaces from that time which make
clear the intensified development of eye-catching display types are
Lehmann Fraktur and Ohio Kraft. The light weight of Lehman Fraktur is another example of the blending of styles of that period and an
uncommon approach to the fraktur form. This letterform does not
have any contrast, as formal consistency would normally dictate for
letterforms based on writing with a broad-nibbed pen. The principle

48. McGrew (1993), p. 243.
49. 'Buchschmuck' specimen collection,
1920.
50. Windisch (1920), p. 275 ff.
51. The exhibition 'Dresden plakativ!
Kunst, Kommerz und Propaganda im
Dresdner Plakat 1865–1990' (Stadtmuseum
Dresden, 2011) and its catalogue provided
evidence for this.

Figure 19. Lehmann Fraktur (1920), designed by K. Lehmann, showing light and heavy weights (*Klimschs Jahrbuch 1921–1922*). Each image 90 × 120 mm.

52. *Klimschs Jahrbuch* (1923), p. 170 ff.

of this 'monolinear Fraktur' or 'Fraktur-Grotesk with serifs' was not applied to the heavier weights (figure 19). Such monolinear typefaces were called 'Skelettschriften' (skeleton typefaces).

The second type, Ohio Kraft, was designed as a complementary display style to the Ohio type, which had been released some ten years earlier. The character set contains alternative swash capitals and alternative lowercase characters for word endings, designed for the effective setting of headlines and advertisements. Ohio Kraft is an 'immensely rugged commercial type, undoubtedly of striking effect especially in large sizes … The typeface, despite its seemingly crude design, has a pleasing character, revealing an able hand and lending a certain artistic effect to it.'[52] This able hand belonged to the little known commercial artist Eduard Lauterbach from Berlin, as recorded in a specimen from 1922. Ohio Kraft was further evidence that the foundry was expanding its catalogue with an emphasis on commercial and display types.

A specimen booklet for Ohio Kraft from 1924 documents the kind of quality with which specimens could by then be produced. This is evident in the precision of the printing and the treatment of the material. The cover of the Ohio specimen, printed in silver and blazing red, has a very dynamic and striking effect through its diagonal layout (figure 20). In the two-colour inner section, this dynamism increases. One of the vignettes, a manikin from the Sigrist series, had in the meantime become a logotype for the foundry, replacing the typefounder figure used before. Cheerfully greeting the reader, the

Figure 20. Ohio Kraft, designed by Eduard Lautenbach. Specimen, 1924. 320 × 235 mm.

Figure 21. Super-Grotesk was issued in ten variants between 1930 and 1938 (from Schaefer-Versalien specimen no. 76, 1931; first line is Schaefer-Versalien).

manikin is a self-deprecating capitalist, printed in red and standing in front of the new company building, printed in yellow.

Sanserifs constituted another important part of the foundry's repertoire. The Grotesk types, released in the mid-1920s, were also issued by other foundries under different names: Handels-grotesk (Stempel), Aurora (C. E. Weber), and Edel Grotesk (Wagner & Schmidt). These designs consisted of a wide variety of styles differing in weight, width, and slope. In the 1930s the Super-Grotesk family was introduced (figure 21). Unlike Grotesk, Super-Grotesk was designed from the outset with the concept of a type family in mind. Designed by Arno Drescher from Dresden, it was further expanded in the following years. In addition to the three weights – regular, semi-bold, and bold (and associated obliques) – condensed versions, and several capital and display styles were released. Super-Grotesk is one of few typefaces that survived the change in the political system after the Second World War, becoming a very successful typeface for VEB Typoart.

One typeface that was shown to advantage, especially in the design of its specimens, was Schaefer-Versalien, an all-capitals type. Designed by Karl Hermann Schaefer from Hagen and released in 1927, Schaefer-Versalien carried the spirit of New Typography. An outstanding feature of the design is its use of colour (figure 22). A character index included in the specimen booklet also explains the concept of a reversed-out typeface that is defined by negative spaces. The characters are designed on a background grid of vertical stripes. The character widths are the result of the addition or subtraction of these stripes. By inserting separate intermediate pieces, words can be spaced out. With the extensions included in the range, compositors could make words into banners and panels.

Similar reversed-out typefaces can be found in the catalogues of other foundries. Examples are Lucina, an all-capital variant of Erbar-Grotesk from Ludwig & Mayer, and Baustein Grotesk published in 1929 by Schelter & Giesecke. Lucina contains variations for extensions as well, which appear quite historicized compared to those of the Schaefer Versalien. The Baustein Grotesk, which features a similar approach, has unsatisfying character shapes that appear clumsy and unbalanced. The Schaefer Versalien is superior to these two types not only because of its idiosyncratic forms, but also because of its concept of matching the characters to the background grid.

Specimen booklet number 92, released in July 1932, presents another original release – the display type Zeus (figure 22). This 'bold roman for modern typography' was designed by Jan Tschichold.[53] It has been described as an 'elegant and inventive twist within typographic tradition', and it became the most lucrative of Tschichold's early type designs.[54] The cover of the specimen is striking: a brilliant metal coating is printed in two colours. The pages inside show examples of the type used in different languages. An advertisement for the Deutsches Hygiene-Museum in Czech suggests the influence of Georg Seiring, one of the co-owners of Brüder Butter and also director of the museum.

53. 'Zeus', specimen no. 92, 1932.
54. Burke (2007), p. 175.

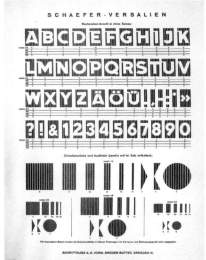

Figure 22. Schaefer-Versalien (specimen no. 76, 1931, 280 × 215 mm), compared with Lucina from Ludwig & Mayer (right, top; 'STEINWAY') and Baustein Grotesk from Schelter & Giesecke (right, bottom; 'ROLAND').

Figure 23. Zeus, specimen no. 92, 1932. 290 × 215 mm.

Figure 24. 'The focal point of the display': Blickfang-Schmuck. Specimen, 1927.

55. 'Messingschmuck Reflex', specimen no. 78, 1931.

Modular ornaments and type systems

Among the types that were mainly intended for display purposes, several were based on the principle of assembling modules. Some of these modular systems were developed from line ornaments that had already been released. From its beginnings, the company had emphasized the design of line ornaments. This category was now expanded by modular systems for type and the illustration of advertisements. With a small number of combinable elements and a restricted number of options for designing, abstract letterforms and illustrations with an eye-catching quality could be made. The specimen booklets published by the company clearly show the use of these systems. The creativity and variety of forms permitted by the reduction to basic elements is remarkable. The specimen booklets were produced by the in-house printing office. Regrettably, in most cases nothing can be said about who designed these booklets, because no information is given about them.

One of the first specimens of this kind is that of the Blickfang-Schmuck ('eye-catching ornaments') of 1927 (figures 24 and 25). Similar collections of ornaments of the same period from other German foundries are Elementare Schmuckformen from D. Stempel (also 1927), Werbeklötze from Ludwig & Mayer, and Futura Schmuck from Bauersche Giesserei. The influences of New Typography and constructivism are clear, evident both in the adoption of basic elements like circle, square, and triangle, and in the use of stark contrasting colours – the inside pages are printed in red and green, blue and yellow, as well as black. The modular system itself is composed of basic geometric shapes, allowing for the assembly of new shapes. In addition, the foundry offered specially made 'Blickfänger' ('eye-catchers'), designed as visual focal points for advertisements and posters. The designs go back to the work of the commercial artist K. H. Schaefer. These visual 'noisemakers' were labelled 'siren', 'horn', or 'gong' depending on their respective size, which again suggests how informal and associative the firm was in promoting the material it issued.

The Dekora-Schmuck set of 1930 demonstrates how modular systems could be used not only for illustrations and symbols, but also for the composition of letters. The character index gives information about the individual components of the modular system. These silhouette ornaments were offered in two weights of dot that provide tonal contrast. The weights contained respectively twenty-four and twelve elements that were made with matching widths so that they could be combined with each other. The ornaments, whose preferred use was for attention-grabbing illustrations, were employed by the foundry itself for the composition of type in their specimen booklets (figure 26). A similar modular typeface of the same time from another German typefoundry is Kombi (or Kombinette) from Ludwig & Mayer (1932). Another system of this kind from Brüder Butter was Reflex ('contemporary brass ornaments'; figure 27).[55] Analysis of a piece of lettering from a specimen published in 1931 shows that the characters were composed of only three basic elements and five rule sections. This ornament set was expanded to a small family of two alternative styles.

Figure 25. Blickfang-Schmuck, 'eye-catching ornaments'. Specimen, 1927. 280 × 210 mm.

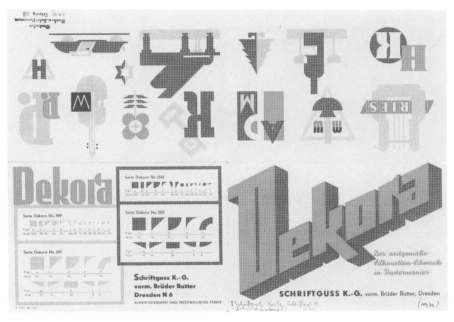

Figure 26. Dekora, the 'contemporary grid-style silhouette ornaments'. Specimen, 1930, 280 × 210 mm; single sheet, 1939, 210 × 300 mm.

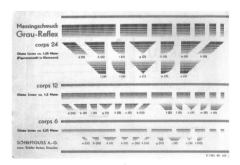

Figure 27. Reflex brass ornaments used to construct letters. Synopsis sheet, 105 × 150 mm, and specimen no. 78, 1931, 280 × 210 mm. The diagram shows how the word Reflex was constructed from three basic elements and five straight rule sections.

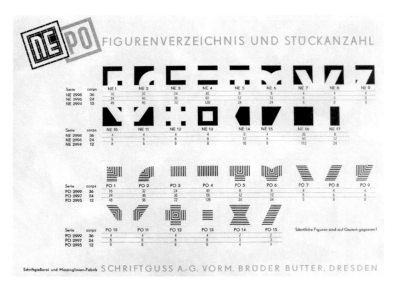

Figure 28. NePo leaflet, 105 × 180 mm, and sample card, 1934,
105 × 205 mm. Seventeen negative and fifteen positive elements
can be used in single or multiple colours.

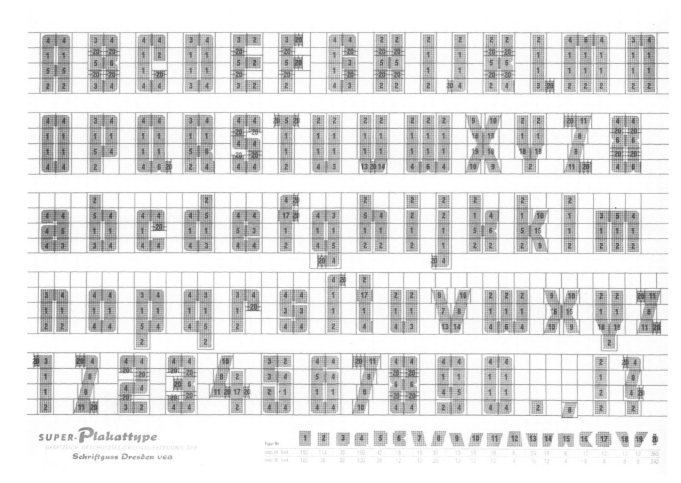

Figure 29. Explanatory scheme for Super-Plakat. Single sheet, 1949,
280 × 370 mm. Twenty elements allow for the construction of any
letter or numeral.

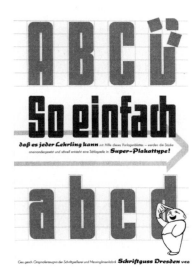

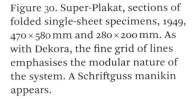

Figure 30. Super-Plakat, sections of folded single-sheet specimens, 1949, 470 × 580 mm and 280 × 200 mm. As with Dekora, the fine grid of lines emphasises the modular nature of the system. A Schriftguss manikin appears.

56. 'Super-Plakattype', folded single-sheet specimen, 1949.

In the field of display types, one of Brüder Butter's decisive achievements lay in their modular type systems. Here knowledge of the production and use of line ornaments was combined with constructivist principles. While the modules of Dekora-Schmuck and Reflex could be used to construct illustrations and backgrounds as well as letters, NePo (negative positive) consisted of modules that were primarily intended to make up letters, although backgrounds could also be constructed. The pieces were cast on a square em body, and therefore could be freely rotated and combined. NePo was offered in two versions, negative and positive, which could be combined to print together in multiple colours as well as in one colour. The specimen pages and the examples show clearly the zest with which the in-house printing office used this system (figure 28).

Interestingly, in its post-war period of change before its absorption into VEB Typoart in 1951, the foundry issued one final display type system that shared the character of its modular predecessors. A specimen from 1949 describes the Super-Plakat type (figures 29 and 30) as follows: 'So simple, every apprentice can do it – with the guideline sheet as an aid, the parts are placed together and swiftly a headline is formed …'.[56] Presumably the idea for the typeface had been there for some time, because the type harks back to the decorative elements of Dekora. With such systems for type and illustration, VEB Typoart (and other foundries, too) could offer handy kits for the construction of modern-looking decorative letterforms. The compositor was free to create his own letters using the given basic elements. The specimens were meant to stimulate experiment and explain the character set, as well as function as effective pieces of marketing.

List of specimens issued by Brüder Butter, 1900–1949. An asterisk indicates a specimen illustrated in this essay.

Year	No.	Typefaces/format	Year	No.	Typefaces/format
c.1900		*Billige Brod-, Auszeichnungs- und Accidenz-Schriften *poster specimen*	1927		Schriften Auszug *specimen collection*
			1927		Unsere Schlager *single sheet*
c.1910		*Dresdner Schriften, Einfassungen, Vignetten, Auschluß-Material *specimen collection*	1927		Weihnachts Schmuck *specimen collection*
			1927		Wieynck Gotisch
1913		*Schriftgießerei Brüder Butter, Dresden-N *specimen collection*	1928	51	Grotesk Musterbuch *specimen collection*
1913		*Die Ohio-Schrift Ohio-Kursiv	1928	52	*Marggraff-Kursiv
1913		*Fünf praktische Garnituren *specimen collection*	1928	55	Weihnachts Schmuck *specimen collection*
1913		Schriftgießerei Brüder Butter, Nov 1913 *specimen collection*	1928	57	Jasmin
			1928	58	Arpre
1919		Ohio *leaflet*	c.1928		Butterfly
1920*		Buchschmuck *specimen collection*	1928		Kress Versalien
1921		Mendelsson	c.1928		Unger Fraktur
1921		Schriften 1921 *specimen collection*	1928		Schmuck, Buchschmuck Katalog
1921		Buchschmuck 1921 *specimen collection*	1929		Kennen sie unsere Neuheiten
1922		Ohio-Kraft Vorprobe *leaflet*	1928	59	Copra
1922		Die Gebrauchs-Vignette in neuem Gewand *specimen collection*	1928	60	Schmuck *specimen collection*
1923		Neues Schmuckmaterial *specimen collection*	1929	61	Die Minister Antiqua, Minister Kursiv
			1929	63	Zarte Marggraff Kursiv
1923		Jean-Paul Fraktur	1929	64	Schaefer-Versalien
1924		Härtel Antiqua	1929	65	Plakat Holzschriften *specimen collection*
c.1924		Die Grotesk Familie *specimen collection*			
c.1924		Hamburger Römisch	1929	66	Stadion Grotesk
1924		Kartenschriften *specimen collection*	1929	68	Zarte Marggraff-Kursiv
1924		*Ohio	1929	69	Marggraff-Kursiv
1924		Mirabelle	1929	70	Thannhaeuser
1924		Vignetten dritter Teil *specimen collection*	1929	71	Butterfly
			c.1929		Einfassungen *specimen collection*
1924		Die Aktie! *specimen collection*	1929		Stadion Grotesk
1924		Lichte Hollendisch	1930	72	Divina
1924		Die Bänder *specimen collection*	1930	73	Cooper
1924		Die Zacken *specimen collection*	1930	74	Cito
1924		Der Meyer Schmuck	1930	75	Super-Grotesk
1925		Dresdner Amtsfraktur	1930		Dekora
c.1925		Graue Hahnemann Linie *single sheet*	1930		Dekora *single sheet*
c.1925		Hollendisch	1931	76	*Schaefer-Versalien
1925		Schriften Katalog *specimen collection*	1931	77	Messing Linien *specimen collection*
c.1925		Suevia Fraktur	1931	78	*Reflex
1925		Ziffer Probe *specimen collection*	1931	79	Die fette Super-Grotesk
1925		Neuheiten Vorprobe	1931	80	Bodoni
1925		Klinger Type	1931	81	Cooper-Halbfett
1925		Klassische Frakturschriften *specimen collection*	1931	86	Super-Grotesk
			1931	87	Dekora
1925		Pallas	1932	88	Capitol
1925		Saxonia Kursiv	1932	92	*Zeus
c.1926		Antiqua Schriften *specimen collection*	1932	93	Supremo
1926		Elisabeth Schmuck	1932		Energos
1926		*Buchschmuck *specimen collection*	1932		Super Blickfang
1926		Kress Versalien	1933	94	Hansa Fraktur
1926		Cooper	1933	95	Minister Antiqua
1926		Messing Linien *specimen collection*	1933	97	Deutsche Schriften *specimen collectionn*
1926		Die graue Linie *specimen collection*			
1926		Vignetten Neuheiten *specimen collection*	1933	99	Fatima
			1933	100	Symbol
1927		*Blick Fang Schmuck	1934	101	Armin Gotisch
c.1927		Drescher Versalien	1934	102	National
1927		Schaefer-Versalien	1934	105	Miami
			1934	106	National

Year	No.	Typefaces/format	Year	No.	Typefaces/format
1934	107	Thannhaeuser Kursiv	1938	130	Kursachsen
1934	108	Schreibedeutsch	1938	132	Faro
1934		*NePo *leaflet*	1938		Eichenlaub Vignetten *single sheet*
1934		Super-Grotesk	1938		Patricio
1935	109	Druckhaus Antiqua	1938		Antiqua Schriften *specimen collection*
1935	110	Thannhaeuser	1938		Apell
1935	111	Ondina	1938		Alte Zeichen *specimen collection*
1935	112	Römisch	1938		Jubileums Schmuck *specimen collection*
1935	113	Aktuell	1939	133	Echo
1935	114	Orginell	1939	134	Gilden Fraktur
1935		Handwerker Vignetten *single sheet*	1939	135	Marggraff-Deutsch
1936	115	Helion	1939	136	Ambassador
1936	116	Luxor	1939	137	Burgund
1936	117	Ultra	1939	138	Jasmin
1936	118	Edelweiß	1939	139	Marggraff-Deutsch Fett
1936	119	Golf	1939	140	Ramona
1936	120	Regatta	1939		*Dekora *single sheet*
1936	122	Lido	1939		Hermes Grotesk
c. 1936		Aktuell *single sheet*	1939		Parlaments-Antiqua
c. 1936		Diva *single sheet*	1939		Patria
c. 1936		Diva	1939		Pfeil Antiqua
1936		Intermezzo	1939		Piccadilly
c. 1936		National, Schräg	c. 1939		Stafette
1936		Prominent	1939		Trumpf
c. 1936		Unger Fraktur	1939		Walhalla
1936		Wieynck Gotisch	1940	141	Marggraff-Deutsch Leicht
1937	123	Trio	1940	142	Maximum
1937		Messing Kreise	c. 1940		Mimosa
1937		Ultra *single sheet*	1941	143	Milo
1938	124	Klinger-Type	1941	144	Splendor, kräftig
1938	125	Splendor	1941	145	Gladiator
1938	126	Orchidea	1941	146	Minister Antiqua
1938	127	Duplex	1941	147	Zahlen uns Zeichen *specimen collection*
1938	128	Diamant	1941		Patria Kursiv
1938	129	Schreibedeutsch	1949		*Super-Plakat *single sheets*

Archives referenced

Handelsregister	Handelsregister Amtsgericht Dresden, Hauptstaatsarchiv Dresden
Handelsregisterakte	Handelsregisterakte Sächsisches Staatsarchiv Dresden
Hauptstaatsarchiv	Hauptstaatsarchiv Dresden (Sächsisches Staatsarchiv)
Stadtarchiv	Stadtarchiv Dresden

Other archives consulted

Archiv des Deutschen Museums, München
Deutsches Buch- und Schriftmuseum, Leipzig
Klingspor Museum, Offenbach am Main
Stiftung Werkstattmuseum für Druckkunst Leipzig

Image sources: Deutsches Buch- und Schriftmuseum, Leipzig; Manfred Richter; Maurice Göldner

Bibliography: works cited

Archiv für Buchdruckerkunst und verwandte Geschäftszweige (1864–99); *Archiv für Buchgewerbe* (1900–19); *Archiv für Buchgewerbe und Graphik* (1920–1); *Archiv für Buchgewerbe und Gebrauchsgraphik* (1922–43). Leipzig: Verlag des Deutschen Buchgewerbevereins

Dr B. (1928). 'Aus der Geschichte der Schriftgußtechnik', *Klimschs Druckerei-Anzeiger*, 55, pp. 541–2

Bauer, Friedrich (1928). *Chronik der Schriftgießereien in Deutschland und den deutschsprachigen Nachbarländern* (2nd rev. edn). Offenbach am Main: Verlag des Verein Deutscher Schriftgießereien

Bauer, Friedrich (1922). *Das Gießinstrument des Schriftgießers*. Hamburg: Schriftgießerei Genzsch und Heyse

Bauer, Konrad Friedrich (1937). 'Das deutsche Schriftgießereigewerbe und das Ausland', *Graphische Nachrichten*, 16, pp. 118–20; 129–31

Biedermann, Lothar von (bearb. von) and Oscar Jolles (hrsg. von) (1923). *Die deutsche Schriftgießerei: eine gewerbliche Bibliographie*. Berlin: Berthold

Böckel, Hans (1914). *Das Schriftgießer-Gewerbe in Deutschland*. Schmölln S.-A.

Burke, Christopher (2007). *Active literature: Jan Tschichold and New Typography*. London: Hyphen Press

Chronik der Schriftgießerei Genzsch & Heyse in Hamburg 1833–1908 (1908). Hamburg: Genzsch & Heyse

DDR-Justiz und NS-Verbrechen (2005), Band 7. Amsterdam: Amsterdam University Press

Die beruflichen und organisatorischen Verhältnisse im deutschen Buchdruckgewerbe und im deutschen Schriftgießereigewerbe (1930). Berlin: Verb. d. Dt. Buchdrucker

Die Entwicklung des Betriebes Typoart in Fakten und Daten: 1945–1985 (1986). Dresden: VEB Typoart

Eule, Wilhelm (1935). 'Das Schriftgießereigewerbe in Sachsen', *Archiv für Buchgewerbe und Gebrauchsgraphik*, Heft 72/3-4, pp. 156–7

Eule, Wilhelm (1927/8). 'Stätten der graphischen Großindustrie 7. Im Reich der Schrift. Schriftguß A.-G. vormals Brüder Butter, Schriftgießerei u. Messinglinien-Fabrik, Dresden', *Deutscher Drucker*, Band 34, pp. 537–42

Fritsch, Rudolf (1913). 'Zur Entwicklung des Schriftgießereigewerbes', *Typographische Mitteilungen*, 10, pp. 92–4

Genzmer, Fritz and Walter Großmann (1936). *Das Buch des Setzers*. Berlin: Gutenberg Druckerei und Verlag

Goebel, Theodor (1892/3). 'Ein Kapitel vom Schriftguß', *Buchgewerbeblatt*, 1, pp. 59–68

Handbuch der deutschen Aktiengesellschaften (1923/4). Darmstadt

Handbuch der Schriftarten (1927). 1. Nachtr. Leipzig: Albrecht Seemann Verlag

Hoffmann, Hermann (1927). *Der Schriftgießer; Ein Lehrbuch f. d. Gewerbe*, Leipzig: Verlag des Verein Deutscher Schriftgießereien

Hoffmeister, Heinrich (1914). 'Die Schriftgießerei auf der Weltausstellung für Buchgewerbe und Grafik Leipzig 1914', *Archiv für Buchgewerbe und Graphik*, Band 51

Hörning, Hans (1923). *Das Schriftgießereigewerbe der Gegenwart*. Inaugural-Dissertation (doctoral thesis), Heidelberg

Klimschs Jahrbuch (1900–40). Frankfurt am Main: Klimsch

Komotauer Jahrbuch (1998). Folge 3. Nürnberg: Preußler

Komotauer Jahrbuch (2007). Folge 12. Nürnberg: Preußler

McGrew, Mac (1993). *American metal typefaces of the twentieth century* (2nd rev. edn). New Castle, Delaware: Oak Knoll Books

Mori, Gustav (1921). *Das deutsche Schriftgießgewerbe in Vergangenheit und Gegenwart*. Frankfurt am Main: D. Stempel

Mori, Gustav (1928). 'Der Schriftguß und seine Entwicklung zum selbständigen Gewerbe', *Klimschs Druckerei-Anzeiger*, 55, pp. 542–3

Muzika, František (1965). *Die schöne Schrift: in der Entwicklung des lateinischen Alphabets*, Band 2. Hanau/Main: Verlag Werner Dausien

Otto, Mathias (1996). 'Die Rolle der Zeitungsverleger bei der Einführung der Setzmaschine am Ende des 19. Jahrhunderts: Ein Vergleich von Innovationsprozessen in Deutschland und den USA', *Leipziger Jahrbuch für Buchgeschichte*, Jahrgang 6, pp. 341–52

Rodenberg, Julius (1926). 'Neuschöpfungen führender Schriftgießereien', *Gutenberg-Jahrbuch*, pp. 181–95.

Rodenberg, Julius (1927). 'Neues aus den Werkstätten der Schriftgießereien', *Gutenberg-Jahrbuch*, pp. 215–51

Schäfer, Roland (1991). 'Leipzig als Zentrum des deutschen Verlagswesens im 19. Jahrhundert', *Leipziger Jahrbuch für Buchgeschichte*, 1, pp. 249–61

Wilkes, Walter (1990). *Das Schriftgießen: von Stempelschnitt, Matrizenfertigung und Letternguß*. Stuttgart: Hauswedell

Windisch, Albert (1920). 'Betrachtungen über das Schriftschaffen der letzten Jahre', *Archiv für Buchgewerbe und Graphik*, 57, pp. 275 f

Zehn Jahre VEB Typoart [1948–58] (1958). Dresden: VEB Typoart

William Berkson &
Peter Enneson

Readability: discovery and disputation

This essay recovers the breakthrough work on readability done by Matthew Luckiesh in collaboration with the Mergenthaler Linotype company. In the late 1930s, Luckiesh developed the concept of readability as ease of reading continuous text; he also discovered that he could measure readability by studying blink rate during reading. After describing how Luckiesh began research in typography, his collaboration with Linotype is explained. The views of, and reaction to, this work by the type-face designer W. A. Dwiggins is also presented. The validity of Luckiesh's work was attacked by psychologist Miles Tinker. Tinker's own back-ground and work are presented, along with the several dimensions of his dispute with Luckiesh. An argument is put forward that, in the light of methodological standards then and now, Tinker's case against the work of Luckiesh is not sound. The essay con-cludes with reflections on the recep-tion and value of both Tinker and Luckiesh today, and on the insights Luckiesh's work in particular may bring to the practice of typography and research into reading.

Between the research scientist and the technician in the graphic arts there has been a degree of common interest in readability, but a colossal absence of mutual understanding.[1] – Harry L. Gage (1942)

Since the late 1920s, when psychologists began systematically study-ing the impact of typography on reading, there has been a divide in understanding between them and practising typographers. Psychologists have generally been wary of typographers' expert craft knowledge, regarding their practices as the product of introspec-tion, conditioning, and preference that lacked scientific validation or objective measures. Typographers, for their part, have often regarded psychologists as naïve about type, and their experimental results consequently weak, obvious, or misleading.

An important indicator of these differing perspectives is the term 'readability'. Many books on typography written in the last fifty years have defined the term as the ease of reading extended text. 'Legi-bility', also referred to in books on typography, is generally defined as how quickly readers can accurately identify individual letters. Authors generally explain the distinction at the outset, then describe how both contribute to good typography. In psychology, by contrast, a distinction between readability and legibility is not made. Instead, the concept of legibility alone – not defined, but as a rule measured by reading speed – is used to assess and describe readers' experience of type in print and on screen.

How did the concept of 'readability' come about, and why was it separated from 'legibility'? And, if the distinction is valid, as many typographers believe, why has it not been adopted by psychologists? The concept of readability of type, defined as the ease of reading extended text, was developed in the late 1930s, during a collaboration between Matthew Luckiesh, a prominent researcher for the General Electric Company, and Harry L. Gage, a vice president at the Mer-genthaler Linotype Company.[2] Luckiesh found that reading strain and fatigue caused by factors such as length of time reading, low

1. Luckiesh and Moss (1942), p. ix.
2. Berkson came across the work of Matthew Luckiesh while investigating the distinction between readability and legi-bility made by Lieberman (1967) and oth-ers; see Berkson (2011). The subsequent narrative has been assembled by Berkson and Enneson collaboratively. We would like to thank: Kent Lew for providing documents relating to Luckiesh, which he uncovered in the Chauncey Hawley

Griffith papers, Special Collections, University of Kentucky; Ann Sindelar, Research Center, Western Reserve Historical Society, Cleveland, Ohio, where the Luckiesh archive is located; Peggy Luckiesh Kundtz and John Kundtz for sharing recollections of their father and grandfather, respectively, and for help with the Luckiesh archive; and Terry McGowan for information on Luckiesh and Nela Park, Cleveland.

lighting, and small type size could be measured by increases in blink rate while reading. He proposed using the term 'readable' for text that is easier (or requires less effort) to read, and so generates less strain or fatigue.

Though simple in outline, the story of the origins of readability is a fascinating one in detail, involving an ambitious research program, a remarkable collaboration, an important discovery, an acrimonious dispute, and fundamental differences over research methods. The story also includes a penetrating appraisal of Luckiesh's work by the type designer W.A.Dwiggins. Despite recognition of Luckiesh's work on readability at the time, it subsequently fell from view, in large part the result of a dispute with a fellow researcher, Miles Tinker. So while readability as a concept has endured among typographers, there is little if any awareness of its origins in Luckiesh's work. Nor did psychologists continue his work on readability. But in recent decades, researchers interested in fatigue have returned to Luckiesh's research and confirmed its general validity. This has been especially true of blink rate as an indicator of fatigue, currently of interest to neuroscientists studying brain function.

In this essay, we will argue that a mostly one-dimensional notion of 'legibility' used by Miles Tinker against Luckiesh's readability has contributed to the divide between typographers and psychologists. Good typography can enhance the reading experience in many ways, and Luckiesh's focus on ease of reading was a promising step towards revealing the numerous dimensions of reader experience. For this reason, renewed engagement with Luckiesh's research is of value both as a recovery of an important historical episode in typography and psychology, and in the insights it may bring to issues that concern typographers, psychologists, and other scientists seeking to understand how we read.

Matthew Luckiesh

Matthew Luckiesh (1883–1967; figure 1) rose to distinction from modest beginnings.[3] His father, orphaned in Austria, emigrated to the small town of Maquoketa, Iowa, where he worked as a school janitor. Luckiesh taught himself to play trombone in high school, and afterwards performed in one of the last touring minstrel shows in the United States, earning enough money to pay his tuition at Purdue University, where he studied electrical engineering. In 1910 he was hired by the National Electric Lamp Association (NELA) in Cleveland, Ohio, which became part of Thomas Edison's General Electric Company (GE) the following year.[4] Electric lighting was at this time a new, exciting, and socially transformative technology, and initially Luckiesh invented specialty light bulbs. But he soon turned to questions concerning the optimal conditions of electric lighting for visual tasks, part of what is now the field of human factors.

Figure 1. Matthew Luckiesh lecturing, probably 1940s.

3. 'Luckiesh' is pronounced LOO-kish (rhymes with 'dish'). Unless otherwise indicated, personal information about Luckiesh is taken from Covington (1992).

4. The National Electric Lamp Association was formed in 1901 to rival General Electric. In 1913, after its

acquisition by General Electric, NELA moved to its present location, Nela Park, Cleveland, Ohio. Nela Park was the first industrial research park in the world and remains the headquarters of GE Lighting. See Covington (1992), ch. 7.

Luckiesh's career at GE proved highly successful. Outgoing, confident and energetic, indeed something of a showman, Luckiesh was exceptionally industrious. By 1924 he was head of the Lighting Research Laboratory at Nela Park, a position he held until his retirement in 1949. Colleagues were apparently awestruck by his brilliance, take-charge manner, and powers of persuasion.[5] Luckiesh was well supported by GE and given almost everything he asked for, including facilities designed to his specifications. He also wrote and published extensively: over the course of his career, some 28 books and more than 600 articles dealing with subjects relating to light and lighting, ranging from color and optical illusions to camouflage and reading.[6] One likely reason GE supported Luckiesh so fully was his ability to promote light bulbs, in particular by recommending high illumination levels for tasks such as reading. General Electric's 'Better Light – Better Sight' campaign, for example, which lasted from 1933 until 1979, was based on research work at Nela Park. By showing customers how to light their homes and offices, the campaign helped to sell a lot of light bulbs.

Early work and first dispute

Matthew Luckiesh began his career when the first and second generations of experimental psychologists were active in the USA. Luckiesh did not, however, learn about methods of human factors research from psychologists, but from a physician, Percy Wells Cobb. Cobb had studied mechanical engineering before training as a medical doctor. Soon after receiving his medical qualification, he began teaching and doing research in experimental psychology, first at Western Reserve University, and then at Nela Park where he was head of the Lighting Research Laboratory during the early years of Luckiesh's career. Cobb adhered to the research methodology pioneered by Claude Bernard, the French founder of experimental medicine. In his *Introduction to the study of experimental medicine* (1865), Bernard described an approach to research that encouraged the search for the 'immediate causes' of any phenomenon. Bernard also emphasized the need to avoid being bound by past theories; one should instead constantly attempt to refute them, as well as one's own hypotheses, to discover the truth. Bernard's view of scientific method was prevalent in experimental medicine and, probably via Cobb, became a decisive influence on Luckiesh.

When Luckiesh succeeded Cobb as head of GE's Lighting Research Laboratory, his principal task was to study the effect of different lighting conditions on the eye. Two important developments in the study of illumination would lead him towards research in typography and reading. The first development was an insight that Cobb had arrived at while investigating appropriate illumination levels for various tasks. Cobb realized that Fechner's Law, one of the earliest hypotheses in experimental psychology, was inadequate as a description of the eye's response to illumination. Fechner had proposed a simple logarithmic relationship between the level of a stimulus, such as brightness, and a 'just noticeable difference' from that level. Working together with Frank K. Moss,[7] Cobb showed that the immediate causes of the eye's response to illumination were more complex.

5. This characterization of Luckiesh is based in part on the personal recollections of Terry McGowan, who worked at Nela Park, from 1961 to 1998 and met the retired Luckiesh. John Kundtz, Luckiesh's grandson, recalls playing under his grandfather's desk as a boy while Luckiesh worked furiously above him. Personal communications from Terry McGowan (June 2011) and John Kundtz (June 2011 and October 2012).

6. A further indicator of Luckiesh's stature and reputation was the commission to design the lighting for the White House during the Franklin D. Roosevelt administration.

7. For remarks on Frank K. Moss, see n. 15.

Not only was the brightness of an object involved, but also the its size, the amount of time the object was looked at, and the contrast between the object and its background. This approach of looking at multiple causal factors would later be decisive in Luckiesh's work.[8]

The second development that provided a major impetus for Luckiesh involved the work of two other researchers on illumination, Clarence Ferree and Gertrude Rand.[9] In 1911, at a joint meeting of the American Medical Association and the Illuminating Engineering Society, a physician had issued a challenge: find a way of accurately measuring the effect of various lighting conditions on the eye. The normal test for visual acuity, the optometrist's eye chart, was insufficiently sensitive to discriminate the effects of glare, low light, and other lighting conditions that accompanied the new technology of electric light. A new measure was needed.

In taking up the challenge, Ferree and Rand supposed that time – and specifically the power of the eye to sustain clear vision over time – would be a key test factor. Looking at an object for a much longer time than normal might increase the sensitivity of visual acuity tests. One test they developed and used extensively required subjects to stare continuously at the letters 'li' for three minutes under various illumination levels; the subject pressed a lever to indicate when the i became blurred and confused with the l, or when the dot of the i fused with its stem. Ferree and Rand used the length of time the eye could sustain clear vision (acuity) as an indication of its efficiency under specific lighting conditions. The test was repeated before and after periods of fixed duration, during which visual work was done continuously under varying lighting conditions. They also compared the ratio of blurred to unblurred time before and after extended work at different lighting configurations and levels, to see how 'time-on-task' and lighting affected visual acuity. The effects of time-on-task were then attributed to fatigue and reading comfort.

Cobb, on the other hand, had begun to place great importance on the fact that normally the eye is constantly in motion, with short fixation times. Following this idea, he studied the impact of contrast, size, and brightness on how *quickly* objects are recognized. He was sceptical that Ferree and Rand's 'li' test of fixed, staring eyes indicated anything important or valuable about sight; commenting on a paper published by Ferree and Rand in 1915, he pointed out that their data derived from subjective reporting by participants who were carefully chosen, trained, and aware of the goal of the experiments. Cobb was therefore unable to trust the results as an accurate measure of the eye's loss of efficiency. Some years later, in 1927, Cobb, now with Luckiesh and Moss, proposed a way to check the validity of the 'li' test.[10] They repeated the test but without any rest interval between the three-minute periods when subjects stared at the letters. Over the course of successive three-minute periods, they were unable to establish a consistent baseline value for, or drop-off in, visual acuity. From this they concluded that the test was in fact useless as an indicator of suitable illumination levels for visual tasks.

In a lengthy reply appended to the 1927 article by Luckiesh, Cobb, and Moss, Ferree and Rand objected that their tests had not been repeated with the same controls. They dismissed the critique as

8. See Cobb and Moss (1928). Cobb's insight was also the foundation of what Luckiesh called 'the science of seeing'; see Luckiesh and Moss (1937a).

9. Clarence Ferree and Gertrude Rand, husband and wife, were researchers at Bryn Mawr College and from 1928 at Johns Hopkins University. Rand is noted as one of the early, outstanding women of twentieth-century science.

based on a 'lack of understanding', 'confusion', and a 'lack of knowledge', and declared the results of the repeated experiment 'irrelevant'. Ferree and Rand also put forward additional data to support their objections. In a concluding note, Luckiesh, Cobb, and Moss replied, in turn, that they remained unimpressed by the additional data collected using the same questionable methods they were criticizing.

Aside from what had proved a heated exchange, it is notable that Luckiesh, Cobb, and Moss nevertheless agreed with Ferree and Rand's original supposition: that testing the effect periods of continuous work had on vision offered a viable way to measure the impact of lighting, from which good lighting standards could be established. Indeed, Luckiesh and and his colleagues had singled out at the outset of the exchange the idea that 'a test which would give a reliable measure of fatigue or other temporary impairment of vision after a period of work would be of immense value in lighting practice'.[11] Finding such a reliable measure, or measures, of fatigue would soon became the focus of Luckiesh's research.

Visual effort, fatigue, and ease

After the critique of Ferree and Rand's work, Luckiesh became convinced that measures of visual *performance*, such as that for acuity, were not sensitive enough to adequately understand the interaction of light and seeing. The human body's ability to compensate for the effects of low light and thereby sustain performance confused matters. The ability to accommodate for various effects did take a physiological and psychological toll on the body in the form of strain and fatigue, and it was these *costs of performance* that Luckeish thought might be the key to a better understanding of seeing. In order to measure the impact of lighting on seeing, Luckiesh would now look not only at the performance of visual work, but also at its costs.[12]

In 1929, Luckiesh published a chart that would form the conceptual basis of his research for the next twenty years (figure 2).[13] The chart distinguishes *effectiveness* in performing a visual task from the *efficiency* of that performance. Efficiency involves not only the level of performance, such as the ability to sustain clear-seeing or to sustain reading speed, but also the *resources* or *effort* needed to achieve that level of performance. While the body may sustain high performance throughout periods of sustained work, the fatigued performance requires increased effort. That greater effort correlates with changes in the body, such as increased muscular tension or weakness, indicating an increased demand on resources. The premise of Luckiesh's ongoing work was that the fatigue from periods of continuous work,

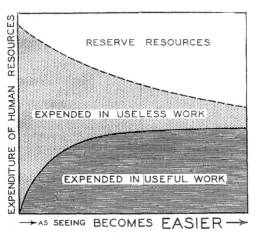

Figure 2. Graph showing the relation of any aid to seeing to the expenditure of human resources in the performance of any task of seeing. Luckiesh (1948), p. 403.

10. Luckiesh, Cobb, and Moss (1927); Cobb's critical remarks of 1915 were first published in this article.

11. Luckiesh, Cobb, and Moss (1927), p. 77.

12. Luckiesh (1930). This paragraph draws on the terminology of David DiLaura to describe Luckiesh's concept. To define the efficiency of doing a task, DiLaura, an illuminating engineer and historian, distinguishes between

performance and the *psycho-physical cost* of performance. For example, an office worker might be able to perform a job equally well in a good office chair or a bad one, but the cost in aches and pains would be much lower in the good one. See DiLaura (2005).

13. Luckiesh (1948), p. 403. The earliest version of the chart occurs in Luckiesh (1929), p. 39; modified versions appear in subsequent publications by Luckiesh.

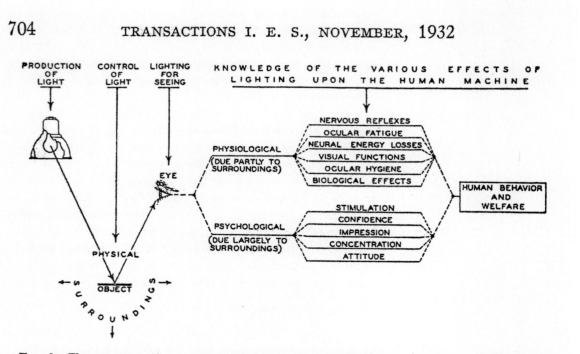

704   TRANSACTIONS I. E. S., NOVEMBER, 1932

Fɪɢ. 2—The sequence of external and internal factors, influencing the human seeing-machine, from light-source to the efficiency, behavior and welfare of human beings.

Figure 3. Factors involved in visual performance. Luckiesh (1932), p. 704.

and its inverse, ease, were as important for assessing lighting or typography as the level of performance. His experimental approach was to systematically identify and employ better, objective, measures of effort. He called his research program 'humanistic' because he focused not just on output, but also on the human costs of effort and work.

From the outset, Luckiesh saw that many physiological and psychological factors were involved in visual performance (figure 3), and so he sought out good ways to measure how these different factors were affected by fatigue in the 'human seeing-machine'. Like Cobb, Luckiesh wanted to identify underlying causes. He studied how physiological and psychological resources were used in vision, and conducted experiments to determine how time-on-task and adverse visual conditions affected the use of these resources. Luckiesh also followed Cobb's example by introducing new variables to the study of reading. Where Cobb had added speed, contrast, and time to the variable of illumination level, Luckiesh added the consideration of effort, and the use of resources involved in visual tasks. Luckiesh introduced three measures in particular: general muscular tension, heart rate, and the strength of eye muscles used to maintain binocular vision. He found that each was affected by time-on-task and low illumination levels. Based on this new research, Luckiesh made his own recommendations for illumination levels for reading and for other demanding visual tasks, levels that were significantly higher than those implied by the research of Ferree and Rand.[14]

14. See, for example Luckiesh and Moss (1937a), p. 303 ff.

Figure 4: 'Visibility and ease of seeing', plate from *The science of seeing* (1937) by Matthew Luckiesh and Frank K. Moss.

15. Frank K. Moss worked as an assistant to Luckiesh from 1929 until his death in 1943, aged 45. Moss never published solely under his own name, making it difficult to judge his contribution to works co-authored with Luckiesh. Based on later comments by Luckiesh, it seems that Moss was a very helpful lieutenant but not an innovator.

16. Luckiesh (1935).

17. G. A. Litinsky, 'Recording of winking as a method of study of ocular fatigue in children resulting from reading', *Sovietskii Viestnik Opht.*, 4 (1934), p. 275; cited in Luckiesh and Moss (1937), and Luckiesh and Moss (1939). See also Ponder and Kennedy (1927).

18. It is worth noting that Ferree and Rand had already been aware that visual fatigue was related to 'ocular discomfort' and that this discomfort was relieved by blinking. But they regarded blinking only as a possible confounding factor whose influence on their test of visual acuity under stress needed to be eliminated.

In 1935 and 1936, Luckiesh, now working solely with Moss,[15] made two further advances in this research. The first was the invention of the Luckiesh-Moss visibility meter, which measured the visibility of objects.[16] It consisted of spectacles fitted with two filters that rotated over each eye to decrease contrast and brightness until an object could no longer be identified (figure 4). The second advance was the adoption of blink rate as a measure of fatigue in seeing. It appears that Luckiesh recognized the potential of blink rate as a measure in the mid 1930s, having encountered the idea in a 1934 article in a Russian journal; he probably then became aware of an article on blinking by Eric Ponder and W. P. Kennedy published some years earlier.[17] Ponder and Kennedy drew on a number of tests and observations to argue that spontaneous blinking was neither a reflex action nor solely a means to cleanse and moisten the eye, since blinks were too frequent for that alone; instead, blinking served to relieve 'mental tension'.

Luckiesh and Moss, with their new interest in 'non-performance' impacts of periods of continuous work, began testing how blink rate was affected by different conditions, including visibility.[18] For their tests, they turned to one of the most demanding visual tasks: reading. They found that blink rate, which is normally considerably slower during reading, in fact increased the longer a subject was reading. Similarly, they found that under conditions normally considered adverse for reading, such as the use of very small type or low levels of illumination, blink rate increased as well. Luckiesh and Moss also used their new visibility meter to determine which typefaces were more and less visible. They evidently hoped that their meter's ability to measure visibility quantitatively would prove crucial in understanding the impact of the physical conditions of reading on reader experience. But they were not able to find a simple rule characterizing the relationships of visibility and reader experience.

Luckiesh was convinced that typographic factors were only weakly discriminated by existing performance tests that involved speed and accuracy of reading. He also dismissed introspective reports of 'esthetic comfort' by readers, or indeed by expert typographers, as 'of little value' as a measure since 'this attribute is not one which yields to standardization'. The only clear correlation he had discovered between the physical conditions of reading (size of type, lighting, and so on) and the experience of effort, or ease, was the relationship of blink rate to illumination. But he and Moss remained hopeful that 'refinements in technique' might yet establish clearer relationships between quantitatively measured visibility and ease of reading.[19]

Luckiesh and Moss published the results of their research in scientific journals,[20] printing trade journals, and more widely in magazines and newspapers with a general readership.[21] It was probably through some element of this publicity that their work came to the attention of the Mergenthaler Linotype Company, at that time the largest manufacturer of typesetting machinery in the world.

Breakthrough

In 1937, Mergenthaler Linotype appointed Matthew Luckiesh and Frank K. Moss as 'consulting research staff' who would undertake research on typographic factors in reading.[22] Their collaborator throughout this project, and probably the project's initiator, was Harry L. Gage, a vice president at Linotype.[23] Gage, who was also a painter (figure 5), had already served as president of the American Institute of Graphic Arts and had written a manual of typographic design for apprentices in the printing trade. He had also recruited the book designer and illustrator William Addison Dwiggins to design typefaces for Linotype. Gage's knowledge of typography was thus extensive.

In an article in *Linotype News* announcing the collaboration, Gage described the research Luckiesh and Moss would do for Linotype.

Figure 5. Harry L. Gage as a young painter, probably 1920s.

19. Luckiesh and Moss (1937a), p. 455.
20. Luckiesh and Moss (1935) and (1937).
21. 'Measuring type visibility', *The Trade Compositor*, December 1936. Public relations staff at Nela Park were apparently able to secure notice of Luckiesh's work in magazines and newspapers, which were then clipped out and collected in scrap books. These scrap books, containing many hundreds of clippings, are preserved in the Luckiesh archive, Research Center, Western Reserve Historical Society.
22. *American Printer and Lithographer*, vol. 105, 1937. 'Mergenthaler Linotype Co. announces that Dr. Matthew Luckiesh

and Frank K. Moss, scientists, will be associated as consultants with the company's present research and development department, to specialize in research projects in type legibility. Dr. Luckiesh and Dr. Moss are widely-known for their work in the science of seeing.' The appointments were also announced in an article praising Luckiesh's work in *Linotype News,* May–June, 1937. Below, for convenience, the Mergenthaler Linotype Company will be referred to simply as 'Linotype'.
23. Harry L. Gage, foreword to Luckiesh and Moss (1942), p. ix.

In general, they would seek answers to practical questions about typography that concerned printers and publishers. This would be done by bringing typography and science together to resolve long-standing typographic issues.[24] Gage was impressed by the number and variety of techniques Luckiesh and Moss had already used to study seeing, and that these techniques had proven scientifically robust. He was cautiously hopeful about where the research might lead:

> Whether this research may open a new approach to further developments in legibility remains to be seen. Such progress would be welcome. But we shall feel well rewarded if our work clarifies and defines the many beliefs, hazy traditions and mere habits of type image which characterize modern practice in the graphic arts.[25]

Luckiesh and Moss would apply scientific method to the study of common typographic matters, such as the ideal line length and leading for a given size of type. Gage also wanted them to test the 'speed of fatigue' experienced by subjects when reading texts typeset in different ways: in uppercase only, lowercase only, in a range of type sizes and styles, as white type reversed out of black, and as printed on various coloured papers. Gage named a number of factors that Luckiesh and Moss would consider, including visibility, as measured by the Luckiesh-Moss visibility meter, and degree of muscular fatigue, as measured by temporarily weakened eye muscles.

Although Gage did not mention blink rate in his article about the new collaboration, six months later, in a first progress report in *Linotype News*, he stated that Luckiesh and Moss believed that blink rate was 'the most important factor yet appraised in these studies.'[26] According to Gage, Luckiesh regarded blink rate as the best indicator of readability, though Luckiesh still felt that visibility (as measured by the Luckiesh-Moss visibility meter) was a good indicator, too. At this point Luckiesh was also still including both performance (speed and accuracy) and cost-of-performance (ease) measures in the concept of 'readability'.[27]

The fourth of Gage's progress reports, in July 1938, documents a turning point in the collaboration. Luckiesh and Moss had compared Caslon Old Face, Textype, and Memphis Medium[28] (figure 7, overleaf) using three tests: *visibility,* a measure of contrast thresholds for reading printed type, as ascertained by the Luckiesh-Moss visibility meter; *readability,* ease of reading, as measured by blink rate in

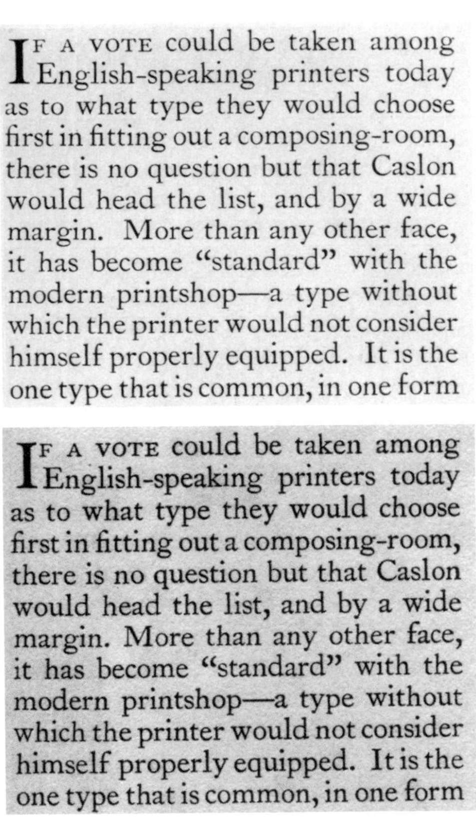

IF A VOTE could be taken among English-speaking printers today as to what type they would choose first in fitting out a composing-room, there is no question but that Caslon would head the list, and by a wide margin. More than any other face, it has become "standard" with the modern printshop—a type without which the printer would not consider himself properly equipped. It is the one type that is common, in one form

IF A VOTE could be taken among English-speaking printers today as to what type they would choose first in fitting out a composing-room, there is no question but that Caslon would head the list, and by a wide margin. More than any other face, it has become "standard" with the modern printshop—a type without which the printer would not consider himself properly equipped. It is the one type that is common, in one form

Figure 6. Comparison of Linotype Caslon Old Face on smooth (top) and rough paper. Linotype specimen booklet (1928). (See n. 28, at right.)

24. Gage (1937).

25. Gage (1937); cf. n. 27, below, for subsequent remarks by Gage on 'legibility'.

26. Gage (1938), a. These and subsequent progress reports published in *Linotype News* were principally distributed to the printing trade.

27. Gage (1938), b. 'We prefer the term readability, rather than legibility since, (1) it is descriptive of the act of reading and (2) it is not so likely to be confused with visibility. Obviously, readability is a function of visibility and, in specific cases, the two may be synonymous for empirical reasons. In general, the readability of printed or written material may

be defined as that characteristic which determines the speed, accuracy and ease with which it may be read.' The identical passage occurs in Luckiesh (1937a), p. 455.

28. Textype was designed 'primarily for printing textbooks and related works requiring intensive study and prolonged reading'. In figure 6, and in the Luckiesh and Moss test material, Caslon Old Face was printed on smooth paper, which produces a weaker, thinner type 'image' than when the typeface is (letterpress) printed on rough paper – its traditional use – where ink gain (or squash) produces a stronger, sturdier image.

CASLON OLD FACE, 11-point, 3 points leaded

This type represents a faithful reproduction of the original type of William Caslon of 1734. In selecting seven type-faces for a research, this 11-point Caslon Old Face was estimated to be approximately equal in face-size to the other 10-point faces of the series. The length of the lower-case alphabet is 122 points and the average number of characters per pica is 2.75. The visibility of 11-point Caslon Old Face is 91 percent of that of 10-point Textype.

TEXTYPE, 10-point, 3 points leaded

Readability of this size of type for a line-length of 21 picas increases markedly as the leading is increased from solid-set to 3 points. Apparently there is some gain from a further increase in leading but the increase is so little compared with the unsatisfactory appearance of the page that no further increase in leading appears to be desirable for 10-point type. It is particularly interesting to compare this paragraph with the preceding one.

MEMPHIS MEDIUM, 10-point, 3 points leaded

This type is the second of four weights or degrees of boldness of the square-serif family. The average length of the lower-case alphabet is 135 points and the average number of characters per pica is 2.5. The visibility of 10-point Memphis Medium is 106 percent of that of 10-point Textype.

Figure 7. Specimens of Caslon Old Face, Textype, and Memphis Medium, printed on coated paper. Luckiesh and Moss (1942) pp. 402–4.

reading extended text; and *reading speed*, in this case the unhurried 'natural' reading speed of passages set in the different typefaces. On the basis of these tests, Luckiesh and Moss rated Memphis Medium highest, followed by Textype, with Caslon Old Face rated much lower.

Gage, however, thought that these results were not credible. In reference to the apparently low rating of Caslon Old Face, Gage quotes the eminent printer Daniel Berkeley Updike's encomium of Caslon as the ultimately readable type. He also criticized the assumption made by Luckiesh and Moss that because, on average, readers completed the fewest lines of texts set in Caslon Old Face, it was the slowest to read. On the basis of character count, which is much higher for Caslon than for the other typefaces, more characters were in fact read, even if fewer lines of text were involved. Subjects therefore read Caslon faster than reported. Gage was also sceptical about the inclusion of Memphis in the comparison, since it was designed for display setting, not text. That a South American newspaper (unnamed) had recently used it for text merely reflected the special printing conditions of newspapers, in which ink might appear thin and grey and was applied to poor-quality paper. In his opinion, Textype was much more readable in text than Memphis Medium. Pointing out that Memphis Medium is distinctly blacker than Textype, Gage raised the question of whether the visibility meter was simply measuring weight, a measure that he believed was not in itself a reliable indicator of readability:

> If we were to be finally bound by these tests, we would say that 10-point Memphis is more readable than 10-point Textype, which is in turn superior in legibility to 11-point Caslon Old Face – provided that each is set 21 picas measure, leaded 3 points, and printed on white book paper.
>
> But we do not yet know further factors which must control any sweeping comment on the general legibility traits of a type family as a whole. Would these tests made with 8-point or 14-point sizes bring similar results?
>
> If the favorable showing of Memphis Medium is due to its weight, then how about the still heavier weights of the same family? The Bold and Extra Bold are far higher in visibility rating. Are we to have blackness of type the determining factor for ease of reading? Common sense says 'no.' But how far does habit control our judgment? Has tradition stopped our use of types that might be easier to read than those normally selected?
>
> Such are the questions we have tossed back to our collaborators, and the further development of this research must inevitably seek the answers.[29]

Luckiesh's response to the questions raised by Gage in his report was based on his own experience in lighting research, as well as his doubts about the role of aesthetics.

> The widespread conflict between utilitarian and esthetic considerations emphasizes the need for scientific data. Often when these become available, esthetic demands are tempered or diminished; and design and practice are more equitably influenced by utilitarian ends. In lighting practice only a decade ago lighting fixtures were designed, sold and bought on the basis of 'beauty,' regardless of the penalties human beings paid for living and working under glaring and inadequate light. Incontrovertible data from sound researches have greatly changed the design of lighting equipment. In a similar way, type-design, typography, etc., must strike a proper balance, and this can only be achieved with certainty if the data are available pertaining to the utilitarian aspects.[30]

Luckiesh did, though, accede to testing the impact of boldness on reading. Linotype supplied him with samples of text in 10-point Memphis, in four weights: light, medium, bold and extra bold (figure 8, overleaf). The results of the tests conducted with them, as plotted graphically, were surprising (figure 9).

The key result was the *divergence* among the measures of visibility, readability (blink rate), and reading speed. Crucially, between medium and bold, there was little difference in reading speed, some difference in visibility, but a significant difference in blink rate. Before these tests, Luckiesh evidently believed that while blink rate was the most sensitive measure associated with readability, visibility and reading speed would still correlate: thus low blink rate would go together with high visibility and higher reading speed. But the tests in fact showed the different measures diverging. While bold showed higher visibility and reading speed than medium, it also showed a significantly higher – not lower – blink rate. Gage's suspicions about the too-simple correlation of weight with readability were confirmed. Luckiesh immediately understood that this implied a separation of

29. Gage (1939), c.
30. Gage (1939), c.

MEMPHIS LIGHT

Meanwhile the plough does its work year by year, the harvests are gathered, the builders build as they are told, the tradesmen work and acquire fresh devices; the knowledge of writing spreads; novel things, the horse and wheeled vehicles and iron, are introduced and become part of the permanent inheritance of mankind; the

MEMPHIS MEDIUM

At a remote period in geological time there is good reason for supposing that there was land where now the Atlantic waters roll, but there is no evidence for and much against any westward extension of Europe or Asia since the Miocene period. But civilization is a matter of at most the last twenty thousand years and probably

MEMPHIS BOLD

Very soon the seafaring men must have realized the peculiar freedom and opportunities the ship gave them. They could get away to islands; no chief nor king could pursue a boat or ship with any certainty; every captain was a king. The seamen would find it easy to make nests upon islands and in strong positions on the main-

MEMPHIS EXTRA BOLD

The trade that was going on in the ancient world before the sixth or seventh century B.C. was almost entirely a barter trade. There was little or no credit or coined money. The early empires got along without coin altogether. The ordinary standard of value with the early

Figure 8. Specimen showing four weights of Memphis: Light, Medium, Bold, and Extra Bold. Luckiesh and Moss (1942), p. 168.

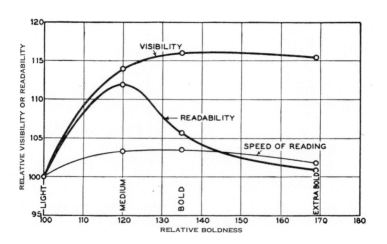

Figure 9. Graph comparing the visibility, readability, and reading speed of four weights of Memphis (Light, Medium, Bold, Extra Bold). Luckiesh and Moss (1942), p. 171.

31. Luckiesh and Moss (1939), p. 652; Luckiesh and Moss (1942), p. 93. 'Ease' is the low end of a scale involving effort, with low effort being 'ease' in reading and high effort 'difficulty' in reading. Luckiesh's definition is apt because the subjective experience readers have of text of poor readability is of having to struggle, to expend more effort in achieving or trying to achieve a normal reading rate. The experience is of ease or difficulty in achieving and sustaining normal reading speed. However, the measures Luckiesh used are of 'strain' or 'fatigue' resulting from heightened efforts in reading. Ease of reading, or high readability, then, is inversely correlated to resulting strain or fatigue – more ease, less resulting strain or fatigue.

32. From the dossier compiled by Chauncey Griffith on Matthew Luckiesh, Margaret I. King Library, University of Kentucky (Lexington), box 8, folder 4; italics here represent underlining in the typescript.

ease of reading from *speed* of reading. Previously, he had included reading speed and accuracy as aspects of readability; from now on he would reserve the term 'readability' for ease of reading alone, and would identify blink rate as the single most reliable measure of readability. Luckiesh henceforth used the term readability to express 'the integral effect of physical factors which influence ease of reading' (in 1939), and 'that attribute of reading materials that governs the relative ease with which different materials may be read by subjects possessing normal vision and exhibiting normal responses' (in 1942).[31]

In addition to the breakthrough to a new definition of readability (figure 10, opposite), Luckiesh was also excited to note that 'the outstandingly important fact revealed by the visibility-boldness relationship is *the definite indication of an optimum boldness*.'[32] The existence of some optimum was suggested by the chart just discussed (see figure 9), and it tempted Luckiesh to read more into it. Undeterred by Gage's scepticism over his claim that the bolder Memphis Medium was more readable than Textype, Luckiesh now asserted that optimum boldness was *the* key factor in readability, and that other stylistic variations were functionally less important, and concerned aesthetics more than utility. The lower blink rate associated with

Figure 10. Report on the importance of blink rate in measuring eyestrain, published in the *Chicago Daily Times*, 19 January 1939. The information and photograph were sent to newspapers by the GE Lighting promotional staff at Nela Park.

Memphis Medium indicated that most text types should be bolder. Luckiesh felt that indeed Memphis Medium hit that level of optimal boldness. Further, he saw that in the range of boldness of normal text types, he might use the visibility meter as a proxy for the blink rate tests involving numerous subjects. Using the visibility meter one could, he believed, quickly measure the visibility of a typeface, and then rule on whether its boldness matched the standard of Memphis Medium.[33]

These assertions were included in what appears to be a final report to Linotype on the results of the research conducted by Luckiesh and Moss. In the 'Conclusions' of the report, Luckiesh wrote:

1. A marked enhancement in the readability of the printed page can be obtained by augmenting the boldness of many types which are now being recommended for body text.

2. An enhancement in readability is decisively less promising by means of alterations in the configuration of modern type-faces than by utilizing the optimum degree of boldness.

3. The design of a type of optimum readability may now be guided with reliability and exactness by measurements of visibility within a range which is now fairly definitely known.

It is emphasized again that all these conclusions are based on the intrinsic visibility of the types studied and upon the facility with which they are actually read, and not upon introspective appraisals of the appearance of the printed page.

.   .   .   .

The design of a superior type – a 'Super Textype' seems to us to be an important future step in our cooperative research program. We are preparing a separate report on the immediate possibilities of further research and of the development of an ideal type-face *in the light of our current knowledge.*[34]

The reaction of Linotype

Although Harry Gage was apparently the guiding hand at Linotype in the collaboration with Luckiesh and Moss, the only record of the company's reaction to Luckiesh's last report is from Gage's colleague, Chauncy H. Griffith, vice president in charge of type design.[35] Griffith was a formidable figure who had, since 1915, brought quality and efficiency to the design and production of Linotype typefaces. His successes included the 'Legibility Group' of types for newspapers. For help in arriving at a considered view of the Luckiesh and Moss research, Griffith turned to his friend and Linotype's foremost type designer, W. A. Dwiggins.

Dwiggins's assessment of the Luckiesh and Moss work was both admiring and critical.[36] He felt they had made important discoveries, but that their conclusions over-reached their test results. Dwiggins began his assessment by agreeing with Luckiesh that 'in the case of any given size of letter, there is certainly an optimum weight for that letter and size, and it's good to have a way for finding it.' But Dwiggins also observed that there were optimums for other variables, too, and that the problem therefore was 'how to hitch it [boldness] up with other "optimums" and make a team – that is what is needed

33. Luckiesh used his visibility meter to test various newspaper types, as he had done with Memphis Medium; several newspapers published letters from him to demonstrate how the visibility and readability of their types had been improved. Luckiesh archives, box 6 (clippings of letters), Western Reserve Historical Society Library.

34. Griffith dossier on Luckiesh, cited above, n. 32.

35. Griffith dossier on Luckiesh, cited above, n. 32.

36. The assessment by W. A. Dwiggins is contained in the Griffith dossier on Luckiesh, cited above. Quotations that follow are from this assessment.

to make the boldness findings valuable in the case of new designs.'
Dwiggins then listed the other four other variables, recommending
that their optimums should also be determined:
 – the ratio of stem weight (breadth of the vertical stroke) to white
   space (i.e. the combined total area of white space of a letter's
   counter(s) and its side bearings);
 – the triple ratio of areas: stem (boldness), to counter, to side
   bearings;
 – the side bearings; and
 – the thick-thin contrast, or 'modeling' ('One would like to know:
   whether monotone and no modeling; or whether modeling, and
   if so how much or how little.')
For Dwiggins, none of these variables, boldness included, operated
independently; instead, 'all these factors interplay; and the investiga-
tor has to keep all the balls in the air at once, as I see it, because each
variable influences all the others. ... Optimum weight alone is not
enough to go ahead with'. He thought that the research should continue since the basis for an ideal text type was far from clear.

> I don't want any of this to make it seem that I am blowing cold on the
> laboratory end of the game. I'm for getting all the facts *via* eye-blinks
> that a feller can get together. ...
>   It's simply that I feel a little shaky about the L. & M. findings because
> I find the investigators so eager and willing to find a Super-Textype on
> 'boldness' alone: '*Now* we've got a sure basis to work on!' They haven't.
> They've built one corner of the foundation very nicely.

Despite its insightful analysis, it seems that Dwiggins's assessment was not shared with Luckiesh and Moss; indeed they seem to
have been quite unaware of the typographic variables Dwiggins listed
and discussed, or their influence on a readers' subjective impression
of boldness. However, Luckiesh was aware that a complex combination of factors influenced readability, and so likely would have been
receptive to Dwiggins's ideas. These circumstances alone certainly
warranted continuation of the research, but that never took place, as
at this point the collaboration between Linotype and Luckiesh and
Moss ended.

The abrupt termination of the collaboration may have resulted
from Griffith's negative reaction to the final report on the research,
or possibly from a change in Gage's role at Linotype. In any case,
the report's dismissal of design factors other than boldness as irrelevant to readability must have struck Griffith as not only lacking an
understanding of type design, but also presumptuous. Writing some
years later, in 1956, Griffith described Luckiesh and Moss's results as
'disappointing'. The pair, he felt, displayed a 'lack of understanding
of the basic principles of type designing which contribute to the ease
and pleasure of reading. Their Conclusions ... were weighted with
theories so abstract and impractical in their broad application to the
subject under consideration as to become of little value in our work,
and the research project was discontinued.'[37]

After its conclusion, Luckiesh nevertheless remained enthusiastic
about the collaboration with Linotype. It represented a culmination
of the work he and Moss had done on ease of reading, which had
begun more than ten years earlier when they began investigating

37. Griffith dossier on Luckiesh, cited
above. Alternatively, it seems equally fair
to suggest that as an applied scientist,
Luckiesh, in his urgency to find practical
applications, was too quick to reach for
single answers and practical measures,
thereby lessening the value his research
might have had for typography.

non-performance indicators of fatigue. Over this period, Luckiesh and Moss had published numerous articles on their work, which they now summarized in the book, *Reading as a visual task* (1942). The book's most important contribution was to present in one place the authors' advances of the previous ten years, namely, the development of a specific, scientifically constructed and validated concept of readability. This presentation was, in turn, supported by the authors' clear sense and understanding of the realities of type and typography. The relative sophistication of the book was no doubt partly enabled by Gage's contributions to the research of Luckiesh and Moss, including preparation of the test samples supplied by Linotype. The analysis of typography that resulted was well informed, notwithstanding the absence of those issues raised by Dwiggins. The book's sophistication is paired with the authors' inventiveness in devising new tests that consider the reader's experience from different angles. Luckiesh and Moss produced two different measures of reading speed, and measures of reflectance, visibility, fatigue in muscles surrounding the eye, blink rate, and many others. These tests and their measures all contribute to an understanding reading as a visual task, both its performance and the costs of that performance.

In retrospect, *Reading as a visual task* holds its own as indeed sophisticated, inventive, well-informed, and of practical as well as theoretical value. But its publication was not entirely well-received. The most important critical review at the time appeared in the *Journal of Applied Psychology*, edited by Donald Paterson. The reviewer was Miles A. Tinker, another leading researcher on typography and reading. In his own work, Tinker relied predominantly on tests of reading speed, tests which he carried out in collaboration with Paterson. Apparently threatened by the minimal importance assigned to reading speed by Luckiesh and Moss, Tinker's review of *Reading as a visual task* dismissed its methodology as unscientific and its results on reading as invalid. It would be the start of a dispute with Luckiesh that would preoccupy Tinker for the next 25 years.

Miles Tinker

Miles Tinker (1893–1969), like Luckiesh, grew up from modest beginnings. One of nine children of a poor Massachusetts farmer, he was the only member of his family to go on to higher education.[38] Tinker completed an undergraduate degree at Clark University in Worchester, at the time one of the leading centers for psychology in the United States; a PhD followed at Stanford University under the leading psychologist Miles Terman. Tinker, the student, struck his teachers as intelligent, academically ambitious, hard working and agreeable, but not particularly original. Terman found Tinker's farm-boy manner of speaking disconcerting and gave him a list of words with which to practice correct pronunciation, so he would not be mistaken as ignorant; Tinker was not offended but grateful. Tinker went on to spend the whole of his career at the University of Minnesota where he was highly productive. There his research focused on measuring eye movements in reading and on the impact of typographic variables on reading speed.

38. Biographical information about Tinker is taken from Sandra Wright Sutherland, 'Miles Tinker and the zone of optimal typography' (PhD thesis, University of Washington, 1989). Here and below, our account of Tinker's family history, education, attitudes to Luckiesh, and reception among typographers (and others) is indebted to Sutherland.

Methodology

Tinker's research methodology followed the philosophy of his teachers, who were doing 'psychometrics', attempting to objectively measure mental qualities, and other human abilities and qualities. One of the pioneers of psychometrics had been his teacher Miles Terman. Terman belonged to the second generation of research psychologists in the USA, many of whom were anxious to show how their field could be of social benefit. His approach was to define a characteristic – most famously, intelligent quotient (IQ) – measure it reliably, and correlate it with other measures such as academic and life achievement.[39] Terman treated the mind as a 'black box' within which he did not seek to understand the causal mechanisms. Instead, he used statistical methods in an effort to ensure that a given trait was reliably measured (i.e. that tests consistently produced the same result for the same person) before doing correlations with other variables.

Tinker's approach to research was also influenced by Paterson, who was a colleague at the University of Minnesota and partner in much of Tinker's work.[40] Like Terman, Paterson had been inspired by Alfred Binet's measurement of intelligence and was similarly devoted to psychometrics. His own research method was criticized by one former student as 'dust-bowl empiricism' – implying that data about empirical relationships, amassed in large quantities but lacking any unifying theory, was barren and unenlightening. Another of Paterson's students named the approach Paterson advocated 'the Minnesota point of view' and characterized it more positively:

> Concepts should be defined; definitions should be operational so that they can be measured; questions should be approached through empirical research; the measurement of individual differences is central; conclusions should be based on objective data rather than on subjective surmise; and research should focus on the search for results that can be applied.[41]

In valuing a narrow focus on the measurement of empirical data, Paterson's method appeared sober and careful. But the aversion to theory meant the method was in fact susceptible to bias and confounding factors. This is because theory unavoidably enters into the choice of what data should be collected and studied, and therefore the effort to avoid a theoretical framework increases the likelihood that one is simply uncritical of the theory that one has (unconsciously) adopted.[42]

In a manner similar to Terman, Tinker would focus on an apparently singular attribute, legibility, and use just one measure of it, reading speed, to determine differences among typefaces and text settings. And although in his career Tinker did do eye movement studies, and occasionally discussed theories of the reading process, in his legibility tests he followed the a-theoretical methodology of Paterson. At the urging of Paterson (who hired him at Minnesota), Tinker embarked on what he felt was a rigorous and methodologically sound program of work to test reading speed against typographic variables.

39. Terman, notably, was the 'Stanford' in the 'Stanford-Binet' intelligence test, which built on the work of Alfred Binet. Terman also defined and measured other qualities such as 'masculinity' and 'femininity'.

40. Paterson's role as 'partner' seems to have been as instigator and guide to Tinker, who then did the work. Tinker published many articles on typography as sole author, including all his articles debating with Luckiesh (discussed below). Paterson published nothing on typography as sole author; rather, he was a frequent collaborator with others on a variety of topics, published many co-authored articles, and supervised numerous graduate students. See Sutherland (1989), ch. 3.

41. Lofquist (1991), p. ix.

42. The measurement of IQ provides an example, where scientists have questioned the concept as too one-dimensional in that it fails to capture a full expression of intelligence, i.e. that the test can measure intelligence in certain areas, such as in mathematics, but not in others, such as social skills. A good theoretical framework could provide a richer view. One troubling outcome of this methodology was Miles Terman's initially racist interpretations of IQ.

Tests, results, reactions

Miles Tinker was one of the earliest researchers to study type and reading systematically. Prior to his work, experiments in legibility had been mostly confined to discerning letters. One previous study focused on reading had used speed of reading as a measure. This study had been carried out by an advertiser, Daniel Starch, in an effort to understand what made advertising copy effective; the study, however, had been done without any systematic controls.[43] Tinker's plan was to adopt Starch's approach (i.e. measure speed of reading), but introduce controls as advocated by Paterson. Tinker would systematically test numerous aspects of typography, from type size and line width in text, to the tabular setting of numbers.

Tinker's first step was to employ a test for reading speed that also controlled for comprehension. To do this, he adopted an existing test, the Chapman-Cook. It involved the measurement of both reading speed and comprehension by inserting into a two-sentence text a 'rogue' word whose meaning was inconsistent with the overall meaning of the text; the reader was required to cross out the rogue word to demonstrate comprehension. For example:

> When I am enjoying anything very much, time seems to go very quickly.
> I noticed this the other day, when I spent the whole afternoon reading
> a very uninteresting book.[44]

(The rogue word is 'uninteresting', which should be 'interesting'.) By ensuring that the text was being read for comprehension, Tinker felt he could then isolate and vary typographic factors to assess and compare their effect on reading speed. To ensure that these factors were indeed isolated, subjects underwent two Chapman-Cook tests, each with a different text, which Tinker then compared. Finding no differences of statistical significance in the results, the tests were declared generally 'reliable'. But at no point did Tinker compare the Chapman-Cook test results against other tests of reading speed – a serious lapse in view of later methodological standards.

This research into reading speed, undertaken by Tinker and Paterson in the late 1920s and throughout the 1930s formed the basis for their co-authored book *How to make type readable: a manual for typographers, printers and advertisers* (1940). On the title page they declared that it was 'based on twelve years of research involving 33,031 persons' (figure 11, overleaf). In their introduction they explained that the book made no reference to earlier research: 'since the bulk of previous investigations are seriously deficient or misleading, due to defects in methodology, references to them would not have been helpful.'[45] They also dismissed as irrelevant the subjective preferences of typographers, since the results of reading tests demonstrated that any variation in the choice of common roman typefaces (of the kind used by typographers) made little difference to 'legibility'.[46] Tinker and Paterson's message, in effect, was a claim of ownership over their subject, a claim that displaced other researchers and typographers, and which was based on supposedly superior methodology incorporating a validated test (Chapman-Cook) and a large number of test subjects.

43. Tinker and Paterson (1928), p. 359.
44. Tinker (1963), p. 21.
45. Paterson and Tinker (1940), p. xvi.
46. In *How to make type readable*, Tinker and Paterson refer to 'legibility' and 'readability' as synonyms; previously, Tinker had referred to 'legibility' alone before adopting 'readability' as the preferred term. The change was possibly influenced by *The science of seeing* (1937), which Tinker reviewed, in which Luckiesh and Moss argue that the term 'readability' was preferable because it would not be confused with visibility (p. 455). Both Luckiesh and Moss, and Tinker and Paterson, claimed responsibility for developing the term. In the late 1940s Tinker reverted back to using 'legibility' alone, ostensibly because 'readability' had also begun to be widely used to characterize the contribution good writing (rhetoric) could make to ease of reading. Tinker's reversion in effect served to distinguish him from Luckiesh, and suppress the specific association of readability with physical factors affecting ease of reading.

How To Make
Type Readable

*A Manual for
Typographers, Printers
and Advertisers*

Based on Twelve Years of
Research Involving Speed
of Reading Tests Given
to 33,031 Persons

Donald G. Paterson
Professor of Psychology, University of Minnesota
and
Miles A. Tinker
Associate Professor of Psychology, University of Minnesota

Harper & Brothers Publishers
New York and London
1940

Figure 11. Title page of *How to make type readable* (1940) by Donald G. Paterson and Miles A. Tinker.

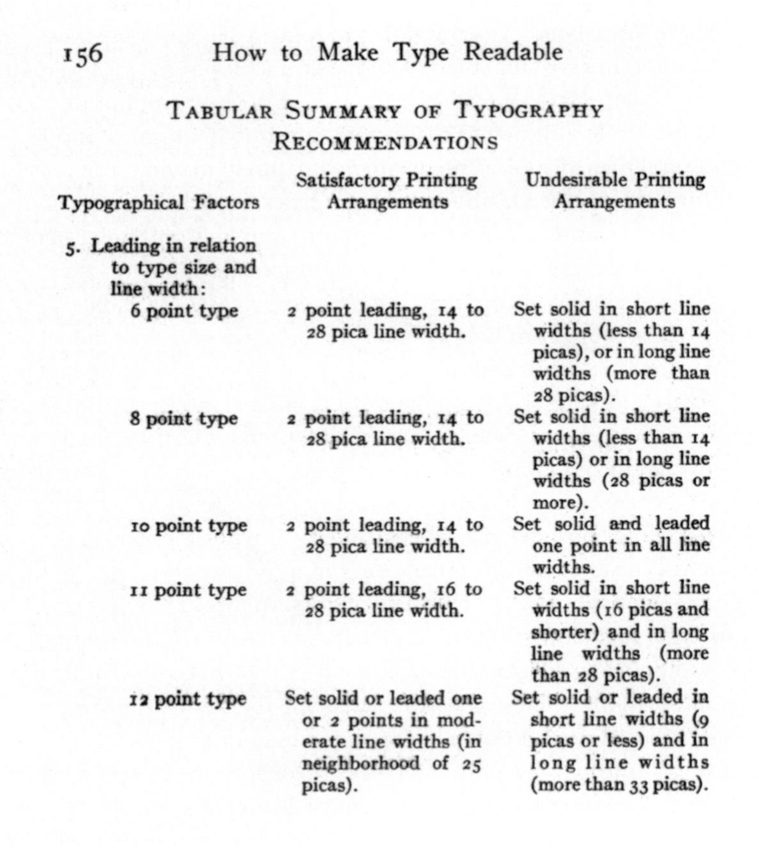

Figure 12. Excerpt from the summary of typography recommendations. *How to make type readable* (1940), p.156.

156   How to Make Type Readable

TABULAR SUMMARY OF TYPOGRAPHY
RECOMMENDATIONS

Typographical Factors	Satisfactory Printing Arrangements	Undesirable Printing Arrangements
5. Leading in relation to type size and line width:		
6 point type	2 point leading, 14 to 28 pica line width.	Set solid in short line widths (less than 14 picas), or in long line widths (more than 28 picas).
8 point type	2 point leading, 14 to 28 pica line width.	Set solid in short line widths (less than 14 picas) or in long line widths (28 picas or more).
10 point type	2 point leading, 14 to 28 pica line width.	Set solid and leaded one point in all line widths.
11 point type	2 point leading, 16 to 28 pica line width.	Set solid in short line widths (16 picas and shorter) and in long line widths (more than 28 picas).
12 point type	Set solid or leaded one or 2 points in moderate line widths (in neighborhood of 25 picas).	Set solid or leaded in short line widths (9 picas or less) and in long line widths (more than 33 picas).

A notable feature of Tinker and Paterson's book is a table of recommendations for (readable) typography. At first glance, the recommendations appear impressively comprehensive, covering kinds of type, size of type, width (i.e. length) of line, size of type in relation to width of line, leading, leading and line width in relation to type size, spatial arrangements of the printed page, black print versus white print, colour of print and background, and printing surfaces. Yet on closer inspection, the recommendations are odd and come across as arbitrary, unsupported or simply ill-advised from the standpoint of typographic practice.

One example may suffice to demonstrate the character of the recommendations; it concerns the arrangement of type that relates leading to type size and line length (figure 12). There is no reference to the impact of typeface variables such as x-height and set width (the length of a lower case alphabet); the recommendations give as 'satisfactory' line lengths of up to 28 picas for any type size between 6- and 11-point; line lengths shorter that 14 picas are (bizarrely) given as unsatisfactory for 6- and 8-point sizes; and so on. Throughout, the recommendations seem to reflect a wish to fix 'optimal' ranges of typographic variables, but without demonstrating the dynamic relationships between them, as might have been shown (for example) by graphing data comparatively (as Luckiesh had done).[47]

How to make type readable was intended by Tinker and Paterson as a manual for practitioners to improve their work. But it appears

47. Sutherland (1989); Sutherland's thesis is that Tinker's work was animated by a search for 'the zone of optimal typography'. Our account here of Tinker's family history, education, attitudes to Luckiesh, and reception in the graphic arts community is indebted to Sutherland's dissertation.

that the 'Typographers, Printers and Advertisers' to whom it was addressed found its recommendations of little or no use, and its publication was met largely with indifference.[48] Among those who ignored the book and the studies that led up to it were Luckiesh and Moss. Although they had earlier quoted Tinker in *The science of seeing*, their discoveries relating to boldness and blink rate apparently led them to regard Tinker's work as of little or no importance, since they now argued that reading speed was a relatively insensitive measure of the quality of a reader's experience, showing only small variations above thresholds for fluent reading.[49] Visibility (as measured by the Luckiesh-Moss meter) and blink rate, on the other hand, showed larger variations and so were more revealing measures of a reader's experience. Luckiesh and Moss's unwillingness to take much notice of Tinker's work – which was invested wholly in reading speed as a measure – and the dismissal that this implied, probably played a significant part in spurring on Tinker's campaign against Luckiesh's work.

The Luckiesh-Tinker dispute

Miles Tinker's review of *Reading as a visual task* by Luckiesh and Moss, in the *Journal of Applied Psychology* (edited by Paterson), was highly critical of the book – indeed so critical that it sparked a seven-year dispute, in print, between Tinker and Luckiesh. Tinker's colleague Paterson stayed out of the debate, but other researchers would also become involved.[50]

In his review, Tinker praised the book's results on visibility but dismissed its account of readability, asserting that other researchers had found blink rate an invalid measure of visual fatigue. He also dismissed Luckiesh's critique of reading speed as an insensitive measure of readability, saying that Luckiesh's failure to control for comprehension invalidated Luckiesh's data on reading rates. He concluded by accusing Luckiesh and Moss of an 'extreme lack of experimental controls', of 'ignor[ing] certain worthwhile research contributions', and of 'inadequate appreciation of certain fundamental principles of reading'.[51] In responding to Tinker's initial attack, Luckiesh pointed out that Tinker failed to cite the evidence he claimed contradicted Luckiesh and Moss's results, and challenged Tinker to do so. As to Tinker's belief that rate of reading is a measure of readability, Luckiesh remarked 'he merely claims this to be.

48. Sutherland (1989), ch. 6, *passim*.

49. Luckiesh (1940), p. 268: 'The normal rate of reading is limited by perceptual phenomena rather than by the physical characteristics of the visual stimuli when the reading is done under the usual supra-threshold conditions.' See also Luckiesh and Moss (1942), p. 121.

50. The exchanges between Tinker and Luckiesh include Tinker (1943a), (1945), (1946), (1948), (1948a), (1949), (1950); and Luckiesh (1943), (1944), (1946), (1947), (1947a), (1948), (1948a), (1948b), (1949). A related exchange between Bitterman and Luckiesh includes Bitterman (1945), (1946), (1947), (1948a); Luckiesh (1946), (1947a), (1948a); and Wood and Bitterman (1950). Luckiesh made no further comment after retiring in 1949; Tinker summarized his case in a review article of 1950 (Tinker, 1950), then recapitulated his arguments in his widely cited book, *The legibility of print* (1963). In the discussion that follows, we are particularly indebted to the research of John Stern and his colleagues who reassessed this complex debate fifty years later, with admirable clarity and insight. See Stern (1994a).

51. Tinker (1943).

He has published no results which prove this.'[52] Luckiesh also (perhaps unwisely) returned some of the insults of Tinker's review, questioning Tinker's own competence as a researcher.

In this first acrimonious exchange, and indeed over the course of the debate that followed, there was nevertheless a lack of full engagement on issues, as Tinker and Luckiesh never agreed on precisely what the actual issues were. One example was the issue of testing actively for comprehension. In all his research Tinker had used the Chapman-Cook test, or an expanded version of it, which included repeated checks on comprehension during the measurement of reading speed. Tinker argued that one had to regularly check for minimum basic comprehension otherwise reading rate measures could be misleading because of 'dawdling' by readers. Luckiesh, on the other hand, believed that when testing for ease of reading, the reading should neither be rushed nor interrupted; instead it should proceed at a 'natural rate' if the test was to be reliable. Luckiesh had been assessing ideas such as Ponder and Kennedy's hypothesis that blinking relieves 'mental tension', and so relieves one kind of fatigue or encumbrance to reading. Rushing the 'natural rate of reading' might increase fatigue, while interrupting reading (for example to test for comprehension) might give time for recovery, thereby reducing the fatigue that had resulted from continuous reading.[53]

For Luckiesh, the consistency and convergence of his results spoke to their reliability. A large part of his work on seeing was not applied research, but rather basic research, which he hypothesized and tested for possible causes of difficulty and fatigue in reading, and the physiological impact of these causal factors. He called this basic research 'axiomatic', stating 'Certain "axiomatic" researches indicate with surprising consistency a qualitative relationship (which is sufficient for our objectives) between decreasing blink rate and increasing readability – ease of seeing. Dr. Tinker completely ignores the extensive coordination and apparent consistency of our results'.[54] In a subsequent response to Luckiesh,[55] Tinker countered by citing the blink rate experiments of McFarland, Holloway, and Hurvitch.[56] These three researchers had found no consistent increase in blink rate relative to time-on-task, and therefore rejected blink rate as an unreliable measure. But in their key experiments, they used just three test subjects who completed only a single (unrepeated) test; as Luckiesh later noted, the (small) sample was 'anything but reliable'.[57]

Throughout the dispute, Tinker never addressed Luckiesh's own claims for his results: that ease of seeing is a different variable from reading speed, and that it has a complex relation to reading speed. This is what Luckiesh was investigating using blink rate. After Luckiesh had repeatedly urged the necessity of using his experimental controls and conditions, Tinker did conduct experiments that he claimed replicated these. Tinker's goal was to determine whether blink rate was both a 'reliable' measure and a 'valid' one. By reliable Tinker meant that if a measurement was repeated, it would produce the same results consistently. In his reliability tests, Tinker repeated blink rate tests on the same individuals and got the same results, confirming that blink rate was indeed a reliable measure. As for

52. Luckiesh (1943), p. 361.

53. In regard to the mitigation of 'dawdling', Luckiesh chose skilled readers for his tests and used what he felt was interesting reading material (*A short history of the world* by H. G. Wells); test subjects were told to read as they normally would.

54. Luckiesh (1943), p. 360.

55. Tinker (1943a).

56. McFarland *et al* (1942). McFarland, Holloway and Hurvitch were researchers at Harvard Business School, which also the published their report.

57. Luckiesh (1947a), p. 267. More recently Stern *et al* (1994a, p. 4) noted that while they 'do not wish to appear unkind' to McFarland and his colleagues, their work 'probably would not have been accepted for publication by a psychological journal, since it contained no statistical evaluation of results but many conclusions.'

validity, Tinker defined it as 'fidelity to an established criterion.'[58] When he measured blink rate against his own criterion measure of reading speed, he found that blink rate gave different results from reading speed, and so concluded that blink rate is not a valid measure.[59]

In this subsequent experimental work by Tinker a variety of problems are, however, evident in the 'proof' that blink rate lacked validity as a measure. The first problem was in the posited criterion itself. Luckiesh had argued that blink rate and reading speed diverge at certain points, with blink rate being the more sensitive measure of the impact of varying typographic conditions on ease of reading. Tinker, by simply positing reading speed as the criterion measure of validity for all aspects of reading, was making an illegitimate circular argument (known as '*petitio principii*' or 'begging the question'). The issue under debate – the validity of using reading speed to measure the impact of typographical factors on ease of reading – is assumed and reasserted, rather than defended by an appeal to independent evidence or principles. Tinker's fallacious approach improperly guaranteed that wherever a measure diverged from reading speed, it would be declared invalid.

There are also specific problems with Tinker's experiments. For example, in a test comparing text set in uppercase with text that mixed upper- and lowercase, Tinker used the Chapman-Cook test, which Luckiesh had pointed out violated the controls necessary for valid results. Again, when comparing newspaper text with book text, Tinker did not control for the x-height or line length of the texts; Luckiesh had found short lines gave lower blink rates, thus undermining the validity of contradictory results Tinker claimed to have got. Finally, in Tinker's experiments on illumination levels, which most closely replicated earlier experiments by Luckiesh, Tinker got seemingly incompatible results in 1945 and 1949.[60] Did the problem lie in Tinker's experimental set-ups, or protocols? In any event, Tinker never acknowledged the problem or sought an explanation.

In addition to Tinker's repeated critical articles over several years, the work of Luckiesh and Moss was also notably challenged by L. Carmichael and W. F. Dearborn in their book *Reading and visual fatigue* (1947). They concluded that sustained reading, even for up to six hours, had no fatiguing effects. Blink rate was tested and no increase was observed, contrary to the results of Luckiesh and Moss. Other researchers, however, raised serious concerns about the validity of Carmichael and Dearborn's work. J. Brožek immediately pointed out that their research involved regular interruptions to reading to test for comprehension, thus violating Luckiesh's control conditions.[61] And later, E. C. Poulton crucially pointed out that Carmichael and Dearborn had made errors in their statistical calculations; when the calculations were done correctly, their data in fact showed increases in blink rate, roughly in line with the results of Luckiesh and Moss – even with the interruptions Carmichael and Dearborn had introduced.[62]

Apart from the contributions and contentions of other researchers, the dispute between Tinker and Luckiesh – a sequence of claim,

58. Tinker (1950).

59. Tinker (1945) and (1946).

60. Tinker (1945) and Tinker (1949)

61. Brožek (1948), p. 420. They also, it seems, did not record food and toilet breaks over a 6-hour period, which would allow significantly more time for recovery from fatigue.

62. Poulton (1958). Luckiesh never responded to Carmichael and Dearborn. There are reasons to suspect that their work did some damage to Luckiesh's subsequent reputation. These include Luckiesh's failure to address their assertions, the prestige of the the authors' association with Harvard, and the passing of ten years before Poulton published his discovery of Carmichael and Dearborn's erroneous statistical calculations. It may also be the case that, with the prestige of its Harvard researchers behind it, *Reading and visual fatigue* played some role in discouraging Linotype from making further reference to Luckiesh's work after 1947, following their publication of *Researches in readability*, which featured and praised Luckiesh's work (discussed below). An example of the persistence of Carmichael and Dearborn's apparent credibility is Sheedy and Larson (2008), who, when discussing blink rate, refer to Carmichael and Dearborn without noting the problems in their methods and subsequent corrections by other researchers.

counterclaim, explanation, and retort – continued until 1949, when Luckiesh retired, after which he made no further comment publicly. By 1950, Brožek, Simonson, and Keys put forward their moderate recommendation that researchers should exercise 'greater caution than at times was present in the controversy regarding the utility of this criterion [of blink rate]'.[63] Tinker, however, without hesitation, continued to discredit Luckiesh both publicly and in private.[64] In his last published articles before retirement, Luckiesh, though irritated by Tinker, seems much less affected by Tinker's criticisms, which he apparently viewed both with contempt and perhaps some resignation; on his part, Luckiesh was confident that the foundation of his work was 'incomplete, but not unstable'.[65] Tinker, unable to let the matter rest, persisted in discrediting Luckiesh even after both had retired, getting in the last word in his *The legibility of print* (1963). By this time Tinker had refined the presentation of himself as an objective and conscientious scientist delivering authoritative judgments based on solid evidence. The book is superficially very persuasive in its dismissal of Luckiesh's work on blink rate – and by extension, Luckiesh's notion of readability. But when one studies the evidence, as fatigue researcher John Stern and his colleagues later did, a quite different picture emerges.[66] Tinker was not actually acting as a fair-minded scientist, but rather as a lawyer assembling a case against Luckiesh, without admitting that much of the evidence cited as authoritative – that of McFarland, Holloway, and Hurvitch, or of Carmichael and Dearborn – either lacked rigour or had been convincingly contested.

Apart from studying the evidence of Tinker's critique of Luckiesh's research, as found in the published record, it is also worthwhile to look more generally at the methodological divide between them. For Tinker's arguments against Luckiesh – and indeed against earlier researchers on reading – were based on his claim that his research methods were 'valid' and others' research methods were not. To understand the issues concerning validity of concepts, we need in our next section to take a brief excursion into developments in philosophy of science, particularly in the field of psychology.

Methodological divide

Tinker and Luckiesh were divided by differing views of good scientific method, in Tinker's case his adherence to the notionally a-theoretical 'black box' approach of psychometrics, and in Luckiesh's, the creative search for immediate causes following Claude Bernard's model for experimental medicine.

For a black box approach to research into a trait or attribute to succeed, a researcher must choose as a variable for testing a factor that is actually a key part of the causal chain of events. But if the variable for testing and quantifying the trait or attribute (IQ, for example) does not correspond to a causal factor, the correlations that the researcher measures are not informative, or worse, are misleading. The weakness of a black-box-and-correlations approach is its vulnerability to 'confounding' factors or variables. If factor A correlates with factor B, it may be that there is another factor, C, that has a causal impact on both A and B, and therefore confounds the claim of a causal

63. Brožek (1950), p. 62.

64. Tinker's son, Gordon Tinker, remembers his father pacing around the house muttering 'that Luckiesh son of a bitch'; he believed his father regarded Luckiesh as a fraud. Sutherland (1989), p. 86.

65. Luckiesh (1948c), p. 931. In his final published comments, Luckiesh observed that Tinker had come to illumination issues 'as a newcomer in this complex field in 1934 [and] took a definite position, based largely upon the inadequate criterion of rate of reading.' (Luckiesh, 1948a, p. 885) Luckiesh also noted that, in correspondence with Tinker, he had made efforts in to clarify Tinker's misunderstandings, but found that Tinker's 'misunderstandings have become misrepresentations.' (p. 885) Unlike Tinker's family, Luckiesh's family was unaware of the dispute; personal communication from Peggy Luckiesh Kundtz and John Kundtz, 4 October 2012.

66. Stern (1994).

connection between A and B.[67] Those using a black-box-and-correlations approach have been very aware of the danger of confounding factors, and have sought to avoid them through the use of good statistical methods, operational definitions, or other techniques that would allow them to form a truthful causal picture. But confounding factors cannot be avoided in a black box approach. Three theorists of scientific method, Karl Popper, Paul Meehl, and Donald Campbell, each studied the problem of confounding factors and all drew the same conclusion: the black box approach is fundamentally flawed because there is no substitute for hypothesizing possible causes; nor is there a routine, or 'algorithm', for avoiding confounding factors. As Claude Bernard had urged, researchers need to hypothesize causes, then rigorously test the hypotheses.

Popper supported Bernard's call for a creative search for immediate causes by pointing out that there is no purely logical path from data to reliable theory, that is to say, no algorithm. Theories, by definition, exceed any finite set of data, and so are fallible. Like Bernard, Popper argued that the only way to eliminate errors and get at the truth is to make bold hypotheses about causes, then seek out data to test them. Hypotheses are searchlights that can locate revealing tests; tests, in turn, are crucial for discriminating among theories that are nearer or more distant from the truth. To attempt an a-theoretical approach by simply gathering data and looking for correlations, which Popper called 'inductivism', is to risk working from a theory in any case, only unconsciously. The notionally a-theoretical approach thus makes a researcher uncritical of theories that may nevertheless be at work. Confounding factors may be overlooked and experimental results vitiated. And, with fewer imaginative theories of causation, fewer searchlights are in play and less of interest or practical use is likely to be discovered.

Tinker believed that by focusing on a single criterion for legibility – speed of reading – he could effectively control for problems of confounding factors entering his experiments. Paul Meehl, however, has shown that Tinker's confidence in such a single criterion was misplaced. Meehl completed his doctorate under Paterson and spent his career at the University of Minnesota, but later became a fierce critic of the Minnesota approach.[68] He pointed out that the claimed benefits of a single criterion for measuring an attribute, even when the criterion was operationally defined, were overblown. He noted that some concepts in physics, whose rigor psychologists were attempting to emulate, could indeed be measured by a single criterion and operationalized. 'Electrical resistance', for example, is defined as the ratio between the measures of voltage and current. However others concepts, such as 'electron', have no single criterion for measurement, and no associated operational definition. To show that 'electron' is a valid concept involved development of a rich theoretical framework, and a whole variety of tests of that framework.

Meehl noted that in psychology as well, many legitimate concepts do not have unitary operational definitions and should instead be regarded as 'hypothetical constructs.'[69] In psychology, these hypothetical constructs include any trait that cannot be measured simply and directly by a single operation; IQ, introversion, and depression

67. The notion of confounding factor has been illustrated by a scenario involving ice cream and drowning. It might be proposed that eating ice cream causes cramps, and that cramps cause people to drown; therefore these two variables appear to correlate. A confounding factor, however, may be outside air temperature: in warm months, people both eat more ice cream and swim more frequently; it may be this variable that is causal, while the correlation of ice cream and drowning is spurious. See 'Confounding', en.wikipedia.org/wiki/Confounding.

68. Meehl (1989). While at Minnesota, Meehl contributed to the Minnesota Multiphasic Personality Inventory (MMPI), an instrument that is still (in revised form) one of the most widely used to assess personality traits.

69. MacCorquodale and Meehl (1948).

are examples. Meehl argued that for these hypothetical constructs 'validation' of their use in scientific experimentation and theorizing was a much more complex process.

Donald Campbell took up Meehl's idea and developed what became the most widely used approach to validation of hypothetical constructs. The problem of confounding factors, Campbell pointed out, goes beyond failure to recognize causal variables that are additional to those being tested. A construct may itself be misconceived or invalid, especially if it bundles two or more factors. For example, 'legibility' (broadly defined) bundles ease of reading and reading speed, so the correlations using that construct will be misleading.

Campbell proposed that to validate a construct, one must show that the construct stands up to different tests which *converge,* showing that the construct (such as legibility) varies in the same way in different situations. There must also be tests that *discriminate* this variable from other variables. Only when a variable that is a hypothetical construct is subjected to convergent and discriminating tests can a researcher draw conclusions about whether the variable labels just one causal factor. Campbell's methodology pushes experimental psychologists to consider competing causal hypotheses, just as Bernard and Popper had recommended.[70]

The guidelines Campbell set out in his important article of 1959 are very similar to those Luckiesh had adhered to twenty years earlier in his 'axiomatic researches'. Luckiesh did different tests of readability whose indicators of ease of reading (or low fatigue in reading) do converge. His measures of general muscular tension, of fatigue in the eye muscles involved in binocular vision, and of blink rate, were each independent and all three converged. Importantly, Luckiesh was also careful to do tests of the second kind identified by Campbell, those that discriminated ease of reading from other variables or constructs, namely visibility and reading speed; here Luckiesh found divergence. Luckiesh's concept of 'ease of reading' therefore exhibited Campbell's notion of construct validity.

In light of Campbell's standards for construct validity, the weakness in Tinker also becomes clear. In his treatment of the term 'legibility', he avoided evaluating legibility as a hypothetical construct. By choosing to use only speed of reading as legibility's measure, he was presuming without any independent check that a single criterion was enough to rank typefaces, type sizes, measures, line-feed, and so on, according to their legibility – which he also assumed is the same thing as readability.[71]

Tinker was well aware that the ability to read text depends on a number of factors being above minimum thresholds, and that these factors may continue above thresholds to have an impact on reader experience. Yet in his discussion in *The legibility of print*, he assumes (without any comment) that a single criterion is needed, then looks at candidates for that single criterion. He writes that 'to a considerable degree, legibility is defined in terms of a specific method of approach to the study of the problem.'[72] He mentions measuring speed of perception, perceptibility at a distance, perceptibility in peripheral vision, visibility, 'rate of work' (reading speed), and

70. It is no accident that Campbell and Popper take similar lines: both studied under followers of the anti-associationist Würtzberg School of psychology; Tinker's influences, on the other hand, were all associationists. For a discussion of how assumptions about human psychology influence research methodology, see Berkson (1984).

71. In 1928, when Tinker began his series of thirteen studies of typographical factors that would later become the backbone of *How to make type readable*, he focused on the impact of different typographic variables on reading speed, that is to say, on 'documenting empirical relationships' specifically (Tinker and Paterson, 1928). But by the early 1930s, he shifted from this narrow focus to the broader one of assessing 'relative legibility' (Tinker and Paterson, 1931). The shift was made without ever addressing questions about the validity of legibility as a hypothetical construct.

72. Tinker (1963), p. 5.

fatigue. This variety of factors suggests that Tinker's 'legibility' quali-fies as a 'hypothetical construct', calling for the kind of (demanding) validation described by Campbell. But after characterizing legibility so expansively, Tinker then goes through a process of elimination, stating the limitations of each measure, as well as of blink rate, con-cluding that 'the large majority of investigators have come to depend upon some aspect of rate of work or speed … for studying the legi-bility of print. … It seems to have high reliability and apparently good validity.'[73] It is thus striking that Tinker makes a claim for 'good validity' in *The legibility of print* since, in his discussion of the speed of reading measure, he does not in fact demonstrate its validity as a criterion measure. Throughout *The legibility of print*, Tinker makes no formal case for the validation of reading speed as a measure of legibility, but instead remained content in his claim that because it is widely used, it is 'apparently' valid.

Tinker's treatment of 'legibility' was indeed muddled fundamen-tally. He wanted the notion of legibility to have a broad scope, includ-ing ease of reading and threshold measures. This would require the kind of complex validation Meehl and Campbell called for in the case of theoretical constructs. But Tinker settled on just a single measure and treated it much like an operational definition, whose meaning was unproblematic and therefore did not require demanding valida-tion. While he settled on a single measure, giving 'legibility' a narrow scope, he continued to use the term in a broader sense. Tinker also failed to explore how reading speed relates functionally to visibility, distance, and other measures; nor did he discuss how ease of reading and speed of reading are related. Instead, he simply ploughed ahead with his own assessments of various typographic layouts, using only his preferred tests of reading speed; other possible approaches were ignored.

How to validate concepts was widely discussed in the 1940's and 1950's, including by Paul Meehl in Tinker's own department at Min-nesota. But consideration of these discussions was consistently neglected by Tinker, with the result that his claims for 'validation' of reading speed as the sole measure of legibility were not well founded, either by the standards of his time or by today's.

Reception and value

In 1948, at the height of the dispute between Luckiesh and Tinker, a particularly astute survey of the state of reading research drew atten-tion (by implication) to the narrowness of Tinker and Paterson's analysis. The popular graphic arts magazine, *Print*, published the article 'What do you mean, – Legibility?' by Irving C. Whittemore[74] (figure 13, overleaf). Whittemore, a psychologist, was also knowledge-able about typography and was aware of the debate. He began the article with a mock dialogue between 'Bruce Rolldike' (a conflation of Bruce Rogers, Carl Purington Rollins, Daniel Berkeley Updike) and 'Tinkerson' (i.e. Tinker and Paterson). The satire is heavy-handed, but Whittemore nevertheless concludes with a series of incisive ques-tions, noting that the issue of 'legibility' (and reading) has many dimensions:

73. Tinker (1963), p. 30.
74. Whittemore (1948), pp. 35–7.

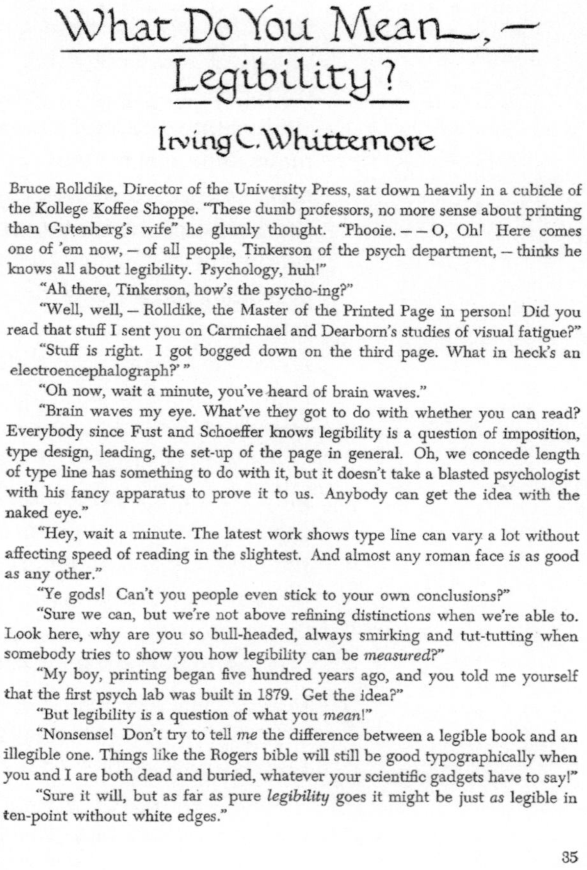

What Do You Mean, — Legibility?

Irving C. Whittemore

Bruce Rolldike, Director of the University Press, sat down heavily in a cubicle of the Kollege Koffee Shoppe. "These dumb professors, no more sense about printing than Gutenberg's wife" he glumly thought. "Phooie. – – O, Oh! Here comes one of 'em now, – of all people, Tinkerson of the psych department, – thinks he knows all about legibility. Psychology, huh!"

"Ah there, Tinkerson, how's the psycho-ing?"

"Well, well, – Rolldike, the Master of the Printed Page in person! Did you read that stuff I sent you on Carmichael and Dearborn's studies of visual fatigue?"

"Stuff is right. I got bogged down on the third page. What in heck's an electroencephalograph?' "

"Oh now, wait a minute, you've heard of brain waves."

"Brain waves my eye. What've they got to do with whether you can read? Everybody since Fust and Schoeffer knows legibility is a question of imposition, type design, leading, the set-up of the page in general. Oh, we concede length of type line has something to do with it, but it doesn't take a blasted psychologist with his fancy apparatus to prove it to us. Anybody can get the idea with the naked eye."

"Hey, wait a minute. The latest work shows type line can vary a lot without affecting speed of reading in the slightest. And almost any roman face is as good as any other."

"Ye gods! Can't you people even stick to your own conclusions?"

"Sure we can, but we're not above refining distinctions when we're able to. Look here, why are you so bull-headed, always smirking and tut-tutting when somebody tries to show you how legibility can be *measured*?"

"My boy, printing began five hundred years ago, and you told me yourself that the first psych lab was built in 1879. Get the idea?"

"But legibility is a question of what you *mean*!"

"Nonsense! Don't try to tell *me* the difference between a legible book and an illegible one. Things like the Rogers bible will still be good typographically when you and I are both dead and buried, whatever your scientific gadgets have to say!"

"Sure it will, but as far as pure *legibility* goes it might be just *as* legible in ten-point without white edges."

35

Figure 13. Satire on legibility by Irving C. Whittemore. *Print* magazine, 1948.

Legibility? What do you mean, *Legibility?* Do you mean:
　(1) easy to read fast,
　(2) easy to read at a distance,
　(3) easy to read in dim light,
　(4) easy to read when you haven't your glasses,
　(5) easy on the brain,
　(6) not tiring to the eyes,
　(7) possible to grasp in big gulps of meaning,
　(8) pleasant to read,
　(9) inviting to the eye, or
　(10) something else?

Before you pick your fights, Mr. Rolldike, Mr. Tinkerson – *answer the question, gentlemen!*

Whittemore's questions both identify the key issues that should be addressed by typographers and scientists, and in hindsight are suggestive of the gap between them. For master typographers (such as Rogers, Rollins, or Updike), enhancing reader experience was a multi-dimensional problem, involving many aspects of accessibility and aesthetics; for certain scientists (such as Tinker and Paterson), only one dimension of reader experience was proving of interest: efficacy of performance as measured by reading speed. Whittemore's challenge – as Dwiggins, too, had articulated earlier – was to understand the many dimensions of reader experience.

Tinker

Among typographers, there is little evidence that Tinker was accepted as an authority on the issues that concerned them. Books on typography sometimes refer to his work, but do not embrace his recommendations.[75] Among experimental psychologists, on the other hand, Tinker's *The legibility of print* is often treated as a standard reference on early research in typography, and is referred to with respect and as a trusted source.[76] But more recently, Tinker's claims to superior methodology and results have not held up well, in particular under the scrutiny of two commentators who are, in effect, the contemporary counterparts of Tinker and Luckiesh. They are Gordon Legge, an influential researcher into reading at University of Minnesota, and Mark Rea, a leading researcher in illumination at the Lighting Research Center at Resselaer Polytechnic (a contemporary equivalent of Nela Park).

In his published work, Legge acknowledges the extensive work of his predecessor, Tinker, which first defined the field of scientific testing of typography's impact on reading. But Legge also draws attention to the numerous problems in Tinker's work, and so, indirectly, throws into relief its flawed influence. The first problem Legge identifies is Tinker's exclusive reliance on the Chapman-Cook reading test, discussed above. Today, the Chapman-Cook test is apparently used only to assess impaired cognition due to brain injury, and is not used as a test of reading speed. Legge confirms the view that the Chapman-Cook, in particular its testing for comprehension, introduces confounding factors. He notes that 'Any measure of reading performance with high cognitive demand may dilute the impact of

75. This judgment is based principally on Sutherland (1989), as well as (e.g.) *The visible word* (Spencer, 1969), and more recently Lund (2004), Beier (2009), and others. Sutherland reviews graphic arts literature from the period during which Tinker and Paterson were active publishing their research, up until 1989, concluding that 'The audience which might have used this information did not embrace it.' Sutherland observes that, with the exception of Whittemore's article in *Print* (1948), the work of Tinker and Paterson on typographical factors and how to make type readable is 'not mentioned in the graphic arts literature of [the] time'; and that more recently Tinker and Paterson's work has 'survived only minimally' (see Sutherland, 1989, pp. 89–100). In *The Thames and Hudson manual of typography* (1980), McLean, who mentions Tinker as an authority, nevertheless maintained that 'no research so far published has been seriously helpful to designers concerned with the design of a straightforward reading matter for literate adults, except insofar as it has, in general, confirmed their practice. Research in legibility, even when carried out under the most "scientific" conditions, has not yet come up with anything

fundamental that typographic designers did not already know – or believe – with their inherited experience of five hundred years of printing history'. (p. 47)
76. Legge (2006) refers, with apparent respect, to the work of Tinker and Paterson as 'influential', and that it 'surveyed the body of research to that time', though he follows this with the critique summarized below. Legge's critical view, however, is an exception. Elsewhere, when Tinker's results and assessment of Luckiesh are mentioned, they are typically just reported, not challenged. A passing comment by Kerfoot (1967, p. 121) – 'an authoritative review of the research on the legibility of print was prepared by Tinker (1963)' – is probably indicative of how *Legibility of print* was then and is still viewed by scientists making reference to typography. In general, Tinker's preferential reliance on reading speed as a measure of legibility, and the tacit acceptance of legibility as a simple, transparent, and unproblematic construct, seems widely shared. And while hardly conclusive, it may be of interest that Google Scholar search results give 126 citations for *How to make type readable* and 517 citations for *Legibility of print*.

visual factors including print legibility. The 'rogue' word method does seem to have substantial cognitive demand.'[77] Legge finds other problems, too, such as Tinker's ignoring of distance to reading material, which affects visual size and is therefore an important influence on reading speed. By doing so, another confounding factor was allowed to entered into his work.[78] Legge faults Tinker more summarily for his 'behaviourist' approach to research, which had 'operationalized the definition of legibility in terms of the measurement process.'[79] The views of Rea on Tinker are given in two articles published in 1986 and 1987.[80] Rea dismembers Tinker's work on illumination (though this lies outside the scope of this essay), pointing out many confounding factors in his experiments. Like Legge, he also takes issue with reading speed as the sole measure of visual experience.

The considerable reputation of Tinker's work grew out of the behaviourist tenor of his times. But in retrospect his work stands up neither to the generally accepted principles of methodology set out Campbell, nor to the critiques of Stern, Legge, or Rea. His reputation as an experimenter is surely unmerited: his methodology was flawed, his results questionable, and he was unjust both to his predecessors and to Luckiesh. His unfortunate influence lies not in so much in his specific claims as in his narrowing of the study of reader experience, which has probably held back progress in the understanding of typography and reading. But if Tinker's work is flawed, it also made a contribution that should be acknowledged. The performance measures he used, such as reading speed and eye movements, *are* important indicators of reader experience,[81] even if a good theory of reading should explain the impact of typographic features on *all* performance levels (reading speed, eye movements, comprehension, and so on) and non-performance costs. Given the likely importance of reading speed in particular, Tinker's data offer a starting point for further inquiry. His reliance on the Chapman-Cook test, however, means that none of his data can be relied on until his tests are repeated with better ones. Tinker's data on typography might still serve as a reference point for researchers, but should not be treated as authoritative.

77. Gordon Legge, e-mail to authors, 12 July 2011. For evidence, Legge cites Crossland (2008), an article in which he collaborated. The article documents a test comparison of reading speeds of sentences, with and without a true-false judgment being required. The true-false judgment was found to alter the reading speeds, including in tests on the influence of typographic features. Since the Chapman-Cook requires a kind of search process, in which (for example) line length might have a strong influence, it seems likely, on the evidence of Crossland, that the results of Tinker's tests would have been misleading.

78. It is worth noting two further examples of probable confounding factors in Tinker's work: he used point size rather than x-height as a measure of type size, and he did not control for illumination.

79. Legge (2006), p. 108. In this article, Legge emphasizes that research into reading requires a wider range of methods than was used by Tinker, which should include the psychophysical study of visual perception.

80. Rea (1986); and Rea (1987), p. 130 f. The latter is cited by the Illuminating Engineering Society as among the one hundred best articles in the field.

81. See, for example, Legge and Bigelow (2011).

Luckiesh

The reception and value of Luckiesh's work is, in several respects, the inverse of Tinker's. There are good reasons to conclude that the persistence of Tinker's attack on Luckiesh's work resulted in its near total disregard among experimental psychologists. Among typographers, however, Luckiesh's influence has been significant and lasting, if obscured. In English-speaking spheres, the notion of readability – ease of reading – he pioneered has been widely endorsed as a goal in the design of text and of typefaces intended for text composition. Luckiesh's name, however, and the experimental basis of readability, have been largely forgotten.

This situation arose in two stages, separated by two decades. In 1942 Harry Gage expressed admiration for Luckiesh's research, whose importance he emphasized in a laudatory foreword to *Reading as a visual task* (1942). Five years later, a handsome, illustrated pamphlet about Luckiesh's work, *Researches in readability*, was published by Linotype (also probably written by Gage).[82] This pamphlet now introduced two different concepts: Luckiesh's 'readability'; and 'legibility', which the pamphlet's author associated with 'quickness of perception' or the 'quick recognition of a word or phrase', such as in reading display type.[83] As already noted, legibility was a concept that Luckiesh had little use for, since it was generally linked to reading speed.[84] But here the two terms came together and were juxtaposed.

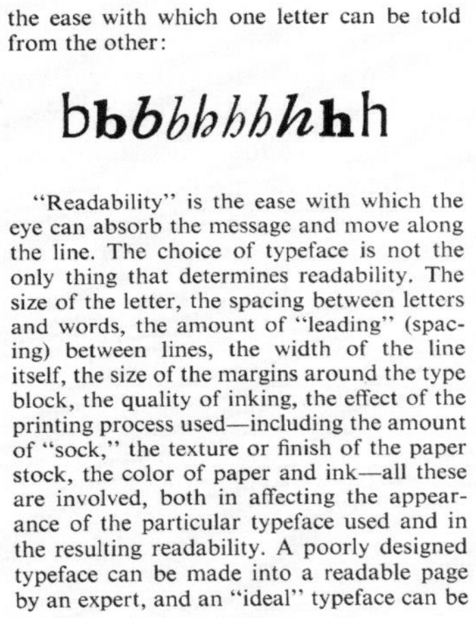

Much later, in 1967, the paired but distinct concepts were taken up by J. Ben Lieberman in his book *Types of typefaces*. Lieberman had consulted Paul A. Bennett who, as director of typography at Linotype between 1932 and 1962, was undoubtedly well aware of the research Luckiesh and Moss had done for the company. Lieberman probably learned from Bennett about the distinction Linotype had made between readability and legibility, but he tried to improve it. He defined legibility as 'ease with which one letter can be told from another'; as an example of a 'legibility problem' he illustrated the confusion that could occur between italic *b* and old face italic *h* (figure 14). His definition of readability drew on Luckiesh: the 'ease with which the eye can absorb the message and move along the line.'[85] But while taking up Luckiesh's definition, Lieberman did not directly cite Luckiesh and Moss. His book therefore seems to be the point at which the readability/legibility distinction was solidified, but the connection to Luckiesh lost. Many subsequent works on typography follow the distinction (with varying phrasing), and recommend

the ease with which one letter can be told from the other:

b**b***b*b*b*b*h*h**h**h

"Readability" is the ease with which the eye can absorb the message and move along the line. The choice of typeface is not the only thing that determines readability. The size of the letter, the spacing between letters and words, the amount of "leading" (spacing) between lines, the width of the line itself, the size of the margins around the type block, the quality of inking, the effect of the printing process used—including the amount of "sock," the texture or finish of the paper stock, the color of paper and ink—all these are involved, both in affecting the appearance of the particular typeface used and in the resulting readability. A poorly designed typeface can be made into a readable page by an expert, and an "ideal" typeface can be

Figure 14. Illustration of 'legibility'. *Types of typefaces* (1967) by J. Ben Lieberman, p. 85.

82. Linotype (1947). The pamphlet focuses on Luckiesh; Moss had died in 1943.

83. Linotype (1947). No tests on reading display type are cited in the pamphlet to support this definition of 'legibility', which seems instead to rely on the conventional view in typography that display typefaces function differently than text typefaces. Linotype sold text as well as display typefaces, and possibly wanted to employ a distinctive term when discussing the latter, in keeping with the conventional typographic distinction.

84. In Luckiesh and Moss (1942), p. 390, legibility is described as 'a term which has been narrowly defined as that characteristic of printed or written material which determines the speed and accuracy with which it may be read. As commonly used, it is indefinite and often ambiguous.'

85. Lieberman (1967), p. 65. Lieberman's definition of legibility may have been influenced by work at that time on letter differentiation; see, for example, Poulton (1965).

readability as a goal in continuous text composition, offering the testimony of practice that Luckiesh's original concept is sound.[86]

Recent and future research

Luckiesh's work can, we believe, inspire new ideas and insights both in the practice of typography and in experimental psychology. For the practice of typography an important insight of Luckiesh was that reader experience is the 'integral effect'[87] of many diverse factors affecting reading:

> 'The various factors determining the visibility and readability of reading material are always encountered in a complex combination. … As none of the factors is ever unaccompanied by others, it is impossible to rank them in a categorical manner.'[88]

This 'integral effect' suggests that different aspects of reading as a visual task may prompt different typographic decisions. Depending on the situation and the designer's goal, different design decisions can enhance one or another aspect of the reader experience.

The Luckiesh boldness chart (see figure 9) begins to capture this complexity in a way that may extend to other performance factors. Bolder types are generally used by typographers to direct the reader's attention or to orient the reader to a document's structure. Luckiesh's identification of visibility as a characteristic of bold typefaces offers a psychophysical explanation for this practice. High visibility seems to counteract the effects of crowding in peripheral vision, effects that make it difficult to isolate a word or words in a field of other words or letters. Similarly, Luckiesh's blink tests reveal that there is a psychophysical reason why medium weights of text are easier to read in continuous settings. There may also be a creative tension between pure performance measures and non-performance costs that typographers can productively exploit. Reading speed and reading comfort may at times be in conflict with one another, where a gain in one (reading speed) might outweigh a gain in the other (by minimizing effort), or vice versa. When this is the case, this can inform decisions about line lengths and column widths, where such a trade-off may be at issue.

Luckiesh's work points to the need to address the complexity of the psychophysical factors in reading, and therefore to consider carefully the intention of any piece of typographic design. Is the most important factor that a piece of text looks inviting, or has a specific visual look or aesthetic mood? Is it most important that readers can read the text with comfort? Is it most important that readers can find a part of the text readily on the page? All of these factors play against one another, and how different aspects of the text relate to each other and to the impression of the whole are of paramount importance. Awareness of the diversity of demands on the reader and their tensions with one another can help guide typographic decisions.

Reading and blinks

In the field of reading research, reading speed as a measure has proven to have more to offer than was revealed either by Tinker's

86. See, for example, Walter Tracy, *Letters of credit* (1986), James Felici, *Complete manual of typography* (2003), and Mitchell and Wightman, *Book typography: a designer's manual* (2005); among these examples, 'legibility' sometimes includes quickness in recognizing words as well as letters. For sources commenting on typeface design and readability, see for example Tracy (1986), pp. 30–2, and Berkson (2010) and (2011).
87. Luckiesh (1939), p. 652.
88. Luckiesh (1942), p. 370.

narrow approach or Luckiesh's downplaying of its significance. The recent work of Pelli, and of Legge, shows that (along with thresholds and critical values) one can identify 'fluent ranges' from graphs of reading speeds; Bigelow and Legge show fluent ranges for type size, using a variety of typefaces.[89] It seems likely, in turn, that graphing factors such as contrast, illumination, time, distance, and size, in order to observe how they compare and intersect, will add to the knowledge of how fluent ranges change. Building on the example of Luckiesh will involve studying the range and diversity of variables associated with the forms of typefaces, taking into account both performance measures that identify thresholds and ranges, and non-performance costs that identify optimums.

Research into spontaneous blinks of readers – Luckiesh's main innovation in research tools – is now more promising than ever, as recent discoveries about eye blinks open new avenues of research.[90]

To better understand the promise of new research into blink rate, it is necessary to briefly review Luckiesh's own research on blink rate. In his early work, Luckiesh tested for fatigue in the muscles controlling the eye, and in strain caused by eyeglasses with deliberately improper prescriptions; he also tested for general muscular strain and changes in heart rate. In tests on typography, he also studied fatigue by measuring blink rates from the first and last five minutes of an hour of continuous reading, and comparing them. But later, when studying typographic variables in detail, he only compared blink rates during a single 5-minute period. He never explained why he thought this shorter period equally valid to the earlier test. One plausible reason, though not stated explicitly by Luckiesh, is that he came to believe that ease of reading for the most part related not to fatigue in eye muscles but to the encumbrance of reading caused by 'mental tension'.[91] Luckiesh also acknowledged that some kinds of demands on the visual system initially reduced, rather than increased blink rate. The diversity of effects these demands produced indicates that different kinds of strain, and different factors inducing fatigue, should be separated and evaluated on their own, possibly by different types of tests involving eye blinks. Here, and in general it seems, Luckiesh was mistaken in putting all causes of strain and all factors inducing fatigue into one bundle.

The differentiation of kinds of strain and factors inducing fatigue has begun to take place in more recent research. James Sheedy and colleagues at the College of Optometry at Pacific University, for example, have studied strain in eye muscles caused by taxing physical conditions associated with reading, including reading from a screen. They have concluded that different conditions can cause strain in different eye muscles.[92] But there is reason to suspect (following Luckiesh) that the typographic issues involve the costs of brain processing rather than eye muscle strain. Further study using blink rate seems warranted.

Yu-Chi Tai and colleagues, also at the College of Optometry at Pacific University, studied the eye movements (saccades) associated with blinks in reading.[93] They found that blinks do not occur randomly, but are 'more associated with interruptions in reading:

89. Pelli (2007), Legge (2011), Legge and Bigelow (2011). Fluent range, as defined by Bigelow and Legge, is the broad but limited size range over which text can be read at the fastest presentation rate yielding a criterion reading accuracy. According to their data, for a reading distance of 40 cm, the fluent range corresponds to type with an x-height between 1.4 mm (4 points) and 14 mm (40 points).

90. Stern *et al* (1994).

91. It is this mental tension that Ponder and Kennedy (1927) claimed was relieved by blinking.

92. Sheedy and Larson (2008); Gowriskaran *et al* (2012). Sheedy and colleagues make reference to the blink rate work of Stern, and thus indirectly to Luckiesh.

93. Yu-Chi Tai (2009), slides 11, 13, 21.

corrective saccades, regressive saccades, and line change saccades.' These kinds of eye movements are interruptions of the normal reading process for 'visual difficulty' or 'interruption in visual acquisition'. The blinks associated with corrective saccades take longer than those during normal saccades, but are still shorter than the time spent in eye fixations. Such results support Luckiesh's theory that increased blink rate reflects some kind of tax on brain processing, specifically in the visual cortex.[94]

Other recent studies on blinking suggest more directly that Luckiesh was right in thinking that spontaneous blinks indeed reflect how visual processing taxes the brain. Volkmann and colleagues showed that visual processing is substantially suppressed during eye blinks.[95] Johns and colleagues showed, using reaction times on a vigilance test, that attention or vision is suppressed before and after both blinks and saccades.[96] This research of both these groups suggests that eye blink provides a physiological opportunity for some kind of recovery mechanism from visual work, in both neural processing and eye movement.

Colzato and colleagues showed an intriguing connection between eye blink and attentional blink.[97] Attentional blink (which is not an actual eye blink) occurs in tasks involving Rapid Serial Visual Presentation (RSVP). When a test subject is asked to identify a particular letter from a series of letters flashed at them, they succeed in doing so, but are unable to identify the next letter after the one identified if it is different and follows at a sufficiently short time interval. The critical interval varies with the individual; as it turns out, the attentional blink interval for an individual is highly correlated with that individual's spontaneous eye blink rate. Colzato and colleagues hypothesize that eye blink is thus connected to the attention processes in the brain and efficient processing in the visual cortex.[98] They also theorize that these processes involve dopamine, a neurotransmitter, suggested by the fact that those who suffer from Parkinson's disease, caused by low dopamine, have reduced eye blink rate, while those who suffer from schizophrenia have both increased dopamine levels and increased blink rates. This theory comes full circle to Ponder and Kennedy's original claim that blinks relieve 'mental tension'.

Colzato's studies suggest the hypothesis that eye blink is specifically connected to the temporary depletion of dopamine or other neurotransmitters, a depletion relieved by the way blinking momentarily shuts down activity in the visual cortex, allowing time for blood circulation to replenish chemicals to the temporarily inactive nerve cells. If this depletion is caused by non-optimal processing, Colzato's and Sheedy and colleagues' findings strongly suggests that Luckiesh's theory of blink rate – that the increase in blink rate over time may be a kind of summative measure of different typographic and environmental factors causing strain or fatigue in continuous reading – is ready to be revived.

For testing typographic variables, blink rate has the advantage of being exquisitely sensitive to brain activity; but it also has the disadvantage of being responsive to *many different* brain activities. It is important, therefore, to carefully separate different factors

94. The most recent work on blink rate by researchers at Pacific University (Gowrisankaran, 2012) shows a reduced total blink rate over a 30-minute period with greater cognitive demands. This work did not, however, compare initial and final blink rates over time, as Luckiesh did in tests that were more thorough-going.

95. Volkman *et al* (1980).

96. Johns *et al* (2009).

97. Colzato *et al* (2008).

98. This is reminiscent of Luckiesh and Moss (1934), which reports on efforts to supply quantitative data pertaining to the 'character or efficiency of the "cortical" integrational process' in the 'occipital' or visual cortex. Luckiesh never integrated this early work into his later research on reading, though the report is included in the bibliography of *Reading as a visual task*.

and their affects on blink rate. By holding potentially confounding factors constant, the impact of typographic variables on reading might be newly tested by blink rate and other aspects of eye blinks, checking Luckiesh's work and extending it to important questions that he did not address, such as the influence of serifs, or differences between reading from printed matter and from screens.

Luckiesh's approach to the study of reading can help bridge the divide in understanding between typographers and psychologists. Seeking to understand the costs of visual performance, and not just the performance itself, opens up many avenues for understanding the reading process and its relationship to typography. Questions of ease and fatigue are probably of key importance in assessing typographic variables at levels above basic thresholds for fluent reading. Luckiesh's concern for multiple factors in reading is also rich with possibilities. Though Luckiesh tended to emphasize one factor, blink rate, he researched many. The comments of his type-aware critics, Dwiggins and Whittemore, indicate how Luckiesh's ideas could be extended to new factors and variables that may affect reading in diverse ways. Investigation of this varied interaction through measures such as blink rate, visibility, and reading speed promises new insights into legibility and readability. The fruits of the collaboration between Luckiesh and Moss and Linotype can be a source of inspiration for typography and reading research well into the future.

Bibliography

Ackerman, P. L. (ed.) (2011). *Cognitive fatigue: multidisciplinary perspectives on current research and future applications*. Washington, DC: American Psychological Association

Beier, Sophie (2009). 'Typeface legibility: towards defining familiarity'. PhD thesis, Royal College of Art

Berkson, William and John Wettersten (1984). *Learning from error: Karl Popper's psychology of learning*. La Salle Illinois: Open Court

Berkson, William (2010). 'Reviving Caslon', part 2 ('Readability, affability, authority'), ilovetypography.com/2010/11/02/reviving-caslon-part-2-readability-affability-authority/

Berkson, William (2011). 'Readability and revival: the case of Caslon', *Printing History*, vol. 10, July 2011, pp. 3–24

Bitterman, M. E. (1945). 'Heart rate and frequency of blinking as indices of visual efficiency', *Journal of Experimental Psychology*, vol. 35, no. 4, pp. 279–92

Bitterman, M. E. (1946). 'A reply to Dr. Luckiesh', *Journal of Experimental Psychology*, vol. 36, no. 2, pp. 182–4

Bitterman, M. E. (1947). 'Frequency of blinking in visual work: a reply to Dr. Luckiesh', *Journal of Experimental Psychology*, vol. 37, no. 3, pp. 269–70

Bitterman, M. E. (1948). 'Lighting and visual efficiency: the present status of research', *Illuminating Engineering*, vol. 43, pp. 906–22; discussion (Matthew Luckiesh): pp. 923–31

Brožek, Josef (1948). 'Visual fatigue; a critical comment', *The American Journal of Psychology*, vol. 61, no. 3, pp. 420–4

Brožek, J., E. Simonson, and A. Keys (1950). 'Changes in performance and in ocular functions resulting from strenuous visual inspection', *The American Journal of Psychology*, vol. 63, no. 1, p. 51–66

Campbell, Donald T. and Donald W. Fiske (1959). 'Convergent and discriminant validation by the Multitrait-Multimethod Matrix', *Psychological Bulletin*, vol. 56, no. 2, pp. 81–105

Carmichael, Leonard and Walter F. Dearborn (1947). *Reading and visual fatigue*. Boston: Houghton Mifflin

Cobb, Percy W. and Frank K. Moss (1928). 'The four variables of the visual threshold', *Journal of The Franklin Institute*, vol. 205, pp. 831–47

Colzato, L. S., H. A. Slagter, M. Spapé, and B. Hommel (2008). 'Blinks of the eye predict blinks of the mind', *Neuropsychologia*, vol. 46, issue 13, pp. 3179–83

Covington, Edward J. (1992). *A man from Maquoketa: a biography of Matthew Luckiesh*. Nela Park, Ohio: General Electric Lighting

Crossland, M. D., G. E. Legge, S. C. Dakin (2008). 'The development of an automated sentence generator for the assessment of reading speed', *Behavioral and Brain Functions*, vol. 4 (www.behavioralandbrainfunctions.com/content/4/1/14)

De Vinne, Theodore Low (1886). *Historic printing types*. New York: The Grolier Club

DiLaura, David L. (2005). *A history of light and lighting: a celebration of the centenary of the Illuminating Engineering Society of North America*. New York: Illuminating Engineering Society of North America

Felici, James (2003). *Complete manual of typography*. Berkeley: Peachpit Press

Gage, Harry L. (1937). 'Research in readability 1 – the program for research', *Linotype News*, September 1937, vol. 16, no. 2, p. 2

Gage, Harry L. (1938). *Linotype News*, a. 'Research in readability 2 – effects of leading' (March 1938, vol. 16, no. 5, p. 2); b. 'Research in readability 3 – effects of color in paper' (May 1938, p. 2); c. 'Research in readability 4 – comparison of Caslon Old Face, Textype and Memphis medium' (July 1938, p. 2); d. 'Research in readability 5 – The quantitative relationship between visibility and type size' (November 1938, p. 2)

Gage, Harry L. (1939). *Linotype News*, a. 'Research in legibility 6 – the visibility of print on various qualities of "white" paper' (Jan 1939, p. 4); b. 'Research in readability 7 – the significance of the blink test' (July 1939, p. 5)

Gowriskaran, S., N. K. Nahar, J. R. Hayes, and J. E. Sheedy (2012). 'Asthenopia and blink rate under visual and cognitive loads', *Optometry and Vision Science*, vol. 89, no. 1, pp. 97–104

Johns, M., K. Crowley, R. Chapman, A. Tucker, and C. Hocking (2009). 'The effect of blinks and saccadic eye movements on visual reaction times', *Attention, Perception, & Psychophysics*, vol. 71, no. 4, pp. 783–8

Kerfoot, James F. (1967). 'Reading in the elementary school', *Review of Educational Research*, vol. 37, no. 2, pp. 120–33

Legge, Gordon E. (2006). *Psychophysics of reading in normal and low vision*. Mahwah, NJ: Lawrence Erlbaum Associates Publishers

Legge, Gordon E. and Charles A. Bigelow (2011). 'Does print size matter for reading? A review of findings from vision science and typography', *Journal of Vision*, vol. 11, no. 5, article 8

Lieberman, J. Ben (1967). *Types of typefaces*. New York: Sterling

Linotype, Mergenthaler (1947). *Researches in readability*. Brooklyn: Mergenthaler Linotype Co.

Lofquist, Lloyd H. (1991). *Essentials of person-environment correspondence counseling*. Minneapolis: University of Minnesota Press

Luckiesh, Matthew, Percy W. Cobb, and Frank K. Moss (1927). 'An investigation of the reliability of the li test', *Transactions of the Illuminating Engineering Society*, vol. 22, pp. 43–51; discussion: pp. 51–78

Luckiesh, Matthew and Frank K. Moss (1929). 'The new science of seeing', *Electrical World*, vol. 93, pp. 15–39; discussion: pp. 39–49

Luckiesh, Matthew and Frank K. Moss (1930). *Transactions of the Illuminating Engineering Society*, vol. 25, p. 15

Luckiesh, Matthew (1932) 'The human seeing machine', *Transactions of the Illuminating Engineering Society*, vol. 27, p. 699 ff.

Luckiesh, Matthew and Frank K. Moss (1934). 'A view of the cortical integrational process through liminal visual stimuli', *Journal of Experimental Psychology*, vol. 17, no. 3, pp. 449–61

Luckiesh, Matthew and Frank K. Moss (1935). 'Visibility: its measurement and significance in seeing', *Journal of the Franklin Institute*, vol. 220, p. 431

Luckiesh, Matthew and Frank K. Moss (1937). 'The eyelid reflex as a criterion of ocular fatigue', *Journal of Experimental Psychology*, vol. 20, no. 6, pp. 589–96

Luckiesh, Matthew and Frank K. Moss (1937a). *The science of seeing*. New York: Van Nostrand

Luckiesh, Matthew and Frank K. Moss (1939). 'The visibility and readability of printed matter', *Journal of Applied Psychology*, vol. 23, no. 6, pp. 645–59

Luckiesh, Matthew and Frank K. Moss (1939a). 'Frequency of blinking as a clinical criterions of ease of seeing', *The Australasian Journal of Optometry*, vol. 22, issue 10, pp. 501–8

Luckiesh, Matthew and Frank K. Moss (1940). 'Criteria of readability', *Journal of Experimental Psychology*, vol. 27, no. 3, pp. 256–70

Luckiesh, Matthew and Frank K. Moss (1940a). 'A summary of researches involving blink-rate as a criterion of ease of seeing', *Illuminating Engineering*, vol. 35, pp. 19–32

Luckiesh, Matthew and Frank K. Moss (1942). *Reading as a visual task*. New York: D. Van Nostrand

Luckiesh, Matthew (1943). 'Some comments on Dr. Tinker's review of *Reading as a visual task*', *Journal of Applied Psychology*, vol. 27, no. 4, pp. 360–2

Luckiesh, Matthew (1944). 'On the rate of involuntary blinking', *Illuminating Engineering*, vol. 39, pp. 69–71

Luckiesh, Matthew (1946). 'Comments on criteria of ease of reading', *Journal of Experimental Psychology*, vol. 36, no. 2, pp. 180–2

Luckiesh, Matthew, Sylvester K. Guth, and Frank K. Moss (1947). 'The blink-rate and ease of seeing', *Illuminating Engineering*, vol. 42, pp. 584–8

Luckiesh, Matthew (1947a). 'Discussion: reading and the rate of blinking', *Journal of Experimental Psychology*, vol. 37, no. 3, pp. 266–8

Luckiesh, Matthew (1948). 'Recommended footcandle levels for prolonged critical seeing', *Journal of the Optical Society of America*, vol. 38, issue 8, pp. 712–18.

Luckiesh, Matthew (1948a). 'Discussion: a reply to Dr. Miles A. Tinker', *Illuminating Engineering*, vol. 43, pp. 882–905

Luckiesh, Matthew (1948b). 'Footcandle levels: threshold, ideal, optimum and recommended', *Illuminating Engineering*, vol. 43, pp. 395–411; discussion: pp. 411–15

Luckiesh, Matthew (1948c). 'Lighting and visual efficiency: The present state of research', *Illuminating Engineering*, vol. 43, pp. 923–31

Luckiesh, Matthew (1949). 'Important concepts underlying lighting for critical seeing', *Illuminating Engineering*, vol. 44, pp. 226–30

Lund, Ole (1999). 'Knowledge construction in typography: the case of legibility research and the legibility of sans serif typefaces'. PhD thesis, University of Reading

Lund, Ole (2004). 'Evidence-based typography or easygoing operationalism?', in *Proceedings of the first international conference on typography and visual communication: history, theory, education: June 2002 Thessaloniki*. Thessaloniki: University of Macedonia Press, pp. 93–8

MacCorquodale, K. and Paul Meehl (1948). 'On a distinction between hypothetical constructs and intervening variables', *Psychological Review*, vol. 55, no. 2, pp. 95–107

McFarland, R. A., A. H. Holoway, and L. M. Hurvich (1942) 'Studies on visual fatigue, part 5: ordinary blinking and visual fatigue', Cambridge, MA: Graduate School of Business Administration, Harvard

Meehl, Paul (1978). 'Theoretical risks and tabular asterisks: Sir Karl, Sir Ronald, and the slow progress of soft psychology', *Journal of Consulting and Clinical Psychology*, vol. 46, no. 4, pp. 806–34

Meehl, Paul (1989). 'Paul Meehl' [autobiography], in G. Lindzey (ed.), *A history of psychology in autobiography*. Stanford: University of Stanford Press, pp. 337–89

McLean, Ruari (1980). *The Thames and Hudson manual of typography*. London: Thames and Hudson

Mitchell, Michael and Susan Wightman (2005). *Book typography: a designer's manual*. Marlborough: Libanus Press

Patterson, D. A. and Miles A. Tinker (1940). *How to make type readable*. New York: Harper Brothers

Pelli, D. G., K. A. Tillman, J. Freeman, M. Su, T. D. Berger, and N. J. Majaj (2007). 'Crowding and eccentricity determine reading rate', *Journal of Vision*, vol. 7, no. 2, article 20, pp. 1–36

Ponder, E. and W. P. Kennedy (1927). 'On the act of blinking', *Quarterly Journal of Experimental Physiology*, vol. 18, pp. 89–110

Poulton, E. C. (1958). 'On reading and visual fatigue', *The American Journal of Psychology*, vol. 71, no. 3, pp. 609–11

Poulton, E. C. (1965). 'Letter differentiation and rate of comprehension in reading', *Journal of Applied Psychology*, vol. 49, no. 5, pp. 358–62

Rea, Mark S. (1986). 'Toward a model of visual performance: foundations and data', *Journal of the Illuminating Engineering Society*, vol. 15, pp. 41–57

Rea, Mark S. (1987). 'Toward a model of visual performance: a review of methodologies', *Journal of the Illuminating Engineering Society*, vol. 16, pp. 128–42

Sheedy, J. and K. Larson (2008). 'Blink: the stress of reading', *Eye*, vol. 17, no. 67, p. 95

Spencer, Herbert (1969). *The visible word*. New York: Hastings House

Stern, John A., Donna Boyer, and David Schroeder (1994). 'Blink rate: a possible measure of fatigue', *Human Factors*, vol. 36, no. 2, pp. 285–97

Stern, John A., Donna Boyer, and David Schroeder (1994a). 'Blink rate as a measure of fatigue: a review', report no. DOT/FAA/AM-94/17, August 1994. Washington, DC: U. S. Department of Transportation, Federal Aviation Administration

Sutherland, Sandra Wright (1989). 'Miles Tinker and the zone of optimal typography'. PhD thesis, University of Washington

Tai, Yu-Chi, J. Sheedy, and J. Hayes (2009). *Blink is not a random event in reading*. http://commons.pacificu.edu/compvision/2009/thursday/11/

Tinker, Miles A. and Donald G. Patterson (1928). 'Influence of type form on speed of reading', *Journal of Applied Psychology*, vol. 12, no. 4, pp. 359–63

Tinker, Miles A. and Donald G. Patterson (1931). 'Studies of typographical factors influencing speed of reading. VII. Variations in color of print and background', *Journal of Applied Psychology*, vol. 15, no. 5, pp. 471–9

Tinker, Miles A. (1934). 'Illumination and the hygiene of reading', *Journal of Educational Psychology*, vol. 25, no. 9, pp. 669–80

Tinker, Miles A. (1935). 'Cautions concerning illumination intensities used for reading', *American Journal of Optometry*, vol. 12, pp. 43–51

Tinker, Miles A. (1943). [Review of *Reading as a visual task*], *Journal of Applied Psychology*, vol. 27, no. 1, pp. 116–18

Tinker, Miles A. (1943a). 'A reply to Dr. Luckiesh', *Journal of Applied Psychology*, vol. 27, no. 5, pp. 469–72

Tinker, Miles A. (1945). 'Reliability of blinking frequency employed as a measure of readability', *Journal of Experimental Psychology*, vol. 35, no. 5, pp. 418–24

Tinker, Miles A. (1946). 'Validity of frequency of blinking as a criterion of readability', *Journal of Experimental Psychology*, vol. 36, no. 5, pp. 453–60

Tinker, Miles A. (1948). 'Readability of book print and newsprint in terms of blink rate', *Journal of Educational Psychology*, vol. 39, no. 1, pp. 35–9

Tinker, Miles, A. (1948a). 'Trends in illumination standards', *Illuminating Engineering*, vol. 43, pp. 867–81

Tinker, Miles A. (1949). 'Involuntary blink rate and illumination intensity in visual work', *Journal of Experimental Psychology*, vol. 39, no. 4, pp. 558–60

Tinker, Miles A. (1950). 'Reliability and validity of involuntary blinking as a measure of ease of seeing', *Journal of Educational Psychology*, vol. 41, no. 7, pp. 417–427

Tinker, Miles A. (1963). *Legibility of print*. Ames: Iowa State University Press

Tracy, Walter (1986). *Letters of credit*. London: Gordon Fraser Gallery

Volkman, F. C., L. A. Riggs, and R. K. Moore (1980). 'Eye blinks and visual suppression', *Science*, 207, pp. 900–2

Whittemore, Irving C. (1948). 'What do you mean, legibility?', *Print, a quarterly journal of the graphic arts*, vol. 5, no. 4, pp. 35–7.

Wood, C. L. and M. E. Bitterman (1950). 'Blinking as a measure of effort in visual work', *The American Journal of Psychology*, vol. 63, no. 4, pp. 584–8

Paul Luna

Picture this: how illustrations define dictionaries

This essays surveys developments in the illustration of English dictionaries from the earliest printed editions to the present. Illustrations both support definitions and provide cultural context, especially in dictionaries for learners of English. A development is traced from the use of individual images depicting objects to the wider use of more complex illustrations that depict actions, processes, and systems. The way that these are integrated with the text of the dictionary is also considered. Competition between learners' dictionaries in recent years has led to the increased use of full-page colour illustrations as marketable 'features'.

Illustrations are an integral part of many dictionaries.[1] Yet the selection, placing, and sizing of illustrations has often been highly conservative, and has appeared to reflect the editorial concerns and technological constraints of previous eras.[2] We might start with the question 'why not illustrate?', especially when we consider the ability of an illustration to simplify the definition of technical terms.[3] How do illustrations affect the reader's view of a dictionary as objective, and how do illustrations reinforce the pedagogic aims of the dictionary? By their graphic nature, illustrations stand out from the field of text on which they are positioned, and they can immediately indicate to the reader the level of seriousness or popularity of the book's approach, or the age-range for which it is intended. Illustrations are also expensive to create and can add to printing costs, so it is not surprising that there is much direct and indirect copying from dictionary to dictionary, and simple re-use. This essay surveys developments in illustrating dictionaries, considering the difference between distributing individual illustrations throughout the text of the dictionary and grouping illustrations into larger synoptic illustrations. The graphic style of illustrations and the role of illustrations in 'feature-led' dictionary marketing are also discussed.

Early attempts at illustration

It is possible to find illustrations in manuscript glossaries, and those in the fifteenth-century *Pictorial vocabulary* (figure 1) seem almost incidental to the text, literally marginal additions: 'a bell, a horse with a saddle and a stirrup, a dragon, a spade, and a scythe [are] agreeable additions to an otherwise unnoteworthy assemblage of words.'[4]

While several early dictionaries have woodcut title-page decorations or devices,[5] Thomas Blount's *Glossographia* (1656) has the first illustrations in a printed English dictionary. The words illustrated in *Glossographia*, as in other early English dictionaries, fall into

Figure 1. *Pictorial vocabulary*, illustrations for *damus* (buck) and *gallina* (hen) (repr. Wright, 1884).

1. The earliest citations in the *Oxford English Dictionary* for 'illustration' in the senses 'pictorial elucidation of any subject' and 'an illustrative picture; a drawing, plate, engraving, cut, or the like' are 1813 and 1816 respectively.

2. 'If today's purchaser of a dictionary expects it to contain many small black-and-white illustrations, his or her expectations derive ultimately from the now obsolete reproductive technology [wood engraving] that made possible the success, almost a century and a half ago, of Blackie's *Imperial Dictionary*.' (Hancher, 1998, p. 158.)

3. McDermott (2005) asks this question of Samuel Johnson's *Dictionary*.

4. Burchfield (1985), p. 79. See Stein (1985), pp. 66–73, for a discussion of the text of the *Pictorial vocabulary*, and Wright (1884, repr. 1976), vol. 2, cols. 745–814, for the full text and reproductions of the illustrations.

5. Listed by McDermott (2005), p. 174.

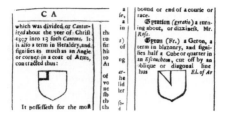

Figure 2. Thomas Blount, *Glossographia* (1656), illustrations for *canton* and *gyron* (from facsimile, linear reduction 50%).

Figure 3. Nathan Bailey, *The Universal Etymological English Dictionary* (1727), illustrations for *angle* (60%).

two distinct categories. The first is heraldry: early editions of *Glossographia* contained two illustrations for the heraldic terms *canton* and *gyron* (figure 2). For the fourth edition (1674) Blount added a third illustration, *bend*; in the next edition (1681) he added yet another, *chevron*.[6] The second category, more loosely defined, consists of scientific and technical diagrams. Nathan Bailey considerably expanded the use of such illustrations in a language dictionary in *The Universal Etymological Dictionary of English* (1727), whose title page promised not just 'Explications, [and] Etymologies' but also '*engraven Schemes, where necessary, for the more easy and clear apprehending them*'. Bailey later described a 'scheme' as

> A Model, Draught, &c. or the Representation of any geometrical or astronomical Figure or Problem, by Lines sensible to the Eye.[7]

This definition is itself taken from John Harris's influential scientific encyclopedia of 1704, *Lexicon Technicum*. Harris adds 'these are otherwise called *Diagrams*'.[8] Bailey includes some twenty-four small diagrams to illustrate geometrical terms (*acute angle*, *right angle*, *plain angle*, figure 3), and two to illustrate astronomical terms (*Ptolemaic* and *Copernican systems*). But they were outnumbered by the 199 woodcuts used to illustrate heraldic terms and crowns – abstract and schematic rather than representational illustrations.[9]

The focus by Blount and Bailey on heraldry (which continued until the nineteenth century) is not surprising: Hancher argues that heraldry is a system that can be regarded as rhetorical as well as graphic, therefore particularly suitable for inclusion in a dictionary:

> Another aspect of heraldic cuts … is their linguistic abstraction. They show signifiers and not signifieds; they are not pictures of physical objects but samples of a code, or (better) samples of segments of a code.[10]

Heraldic illustrations also provided information about a system that was bound up with status and privilege in society, and related to antiquarian and gentlemanly interests. In this sense they were part of the aspirational rather than practical content of the dictionary, much as the elaborate recipes included by Mrs Beeton in her *Book of household management* (which were also illustrated) reflect what a Victorian housewife might be flattered to think she would be called on to prepare.[11] On a more practical level these illustrations were easy to combine with text: the stylized nature of heraldic illustration lends itself to simple, linear, monochrome woodcut illustrations. The linear quality of the illustrations also fits well with the appearance of the

6. Hancher (1992), pp. 1–2.

7. *Dictionarium Britannicum* (1730), cited in Hancher (1992), p. 1.

8. The *Oxford English Dictionary*'s first citation for *diagram* in the sense 'an illustrative figure which, without representing the exact appearance of an object, gives an outline or general scheme of it, so as to exhibit the shape and relations of its various parts', is 1619 (from a text on astronomy). Blount had included the word *diagram*, meaning a musical scale, in *Glossographia*.

9. This information and the citation of Harris are in Hancher (1992). Bailey also

includes a word game, a set of tables to generate Latin hexameters – which seems to run against the concept that an 'objective' dictionary should not simply reflect the lexicographer's interests.

10. Hancher (1992), p. 3.

11. 'Three pages are devoted to an elaborate recipe for turtle soup, … quite beyond the scope of a domestic kitchen. … These are essentially fantasy recipes, included to give the reader something to aim for – talismans of the pleasure that await them at the top of the social tree.' Humble (2000), pp. xxii–xxiii.

surrounding type. The technique of woodcut illustration was at this period efficient but hardly beautiful – the development of a wood-engraving technique that would be both informative and visually elegant would have to wait until Thomas Bewick's work a century later.[12] The technical significance of both woodcut and wood engraving lay in the fact that they were easily integrated with type. Illustrations could be placed exactly in position within dictionary entries, if necessary with type running around them, so that a page containing both text and illustration could be printed in a single operation. Woodcuts were also cheap and quick to produce, though this was less the case with wood engravings.

For larger or more finely detailed illustrations, engraved metal (copper, or later steel) plates were used. This was a finer technique, and it allowed for much greater definition, precision, and control of inking, but it demanded a completely separate printing process. Engraved metal plates were printed by the intaglio method, as opposed to the letterpress method used for text. So any book involving such illustrations would have to be a two-process operation, with the text and illustrations printed on separate sheets of paper, finally coming together only at the binding stage. The inclusion of engravings necessarily made a book more expensive, a significant cost being that of engraving in addition to the cost of printing the plates.[13] Harris's *Lexicon Technicum* and Bailey's *Dictionarium Britannicum* use both techniques. They include small heraldic and scientific illustrations as woodcuts in the text, and full-page engraved plates positioned close to the relevant entry (figure 4).

Unlike many of the dictionaries, encyclopedias, and lexicons from which he drew material, Samuel Johnson's *Dictionary* (1755) eschewed illustrations, and McDermott argues that this caused him difficulties in the definition of technical terms, particularly when he was basing entries on those same, illustrated, sources.[14] The boundary between dictionaries and encyclopedias can be fluid – even a language-focused dictionary such as Johnson's has entries with encyclopedic qualities. Illustrations can be seen positively as a feature that allows encyclopedic material to be incorporated into a dictionary, or negatively as a diversion from the prime purpose of a dictionary to record language in as general a way as possible. The view that the aims of verbal definitions and illustrations are different is well summed up in the introduction to the *Oxford Illustrated Dictionary*: 'Words are often best defined in general terms but a drawing has to be of a particular thing and therefore gives an example of the particular use of a word rather than a generalized statement.'[15] Johnson's 'plain' approach to presentation, concentrating attention on the verbal content, was followed by Noah Webster in his 1828 dictionary, by Charles

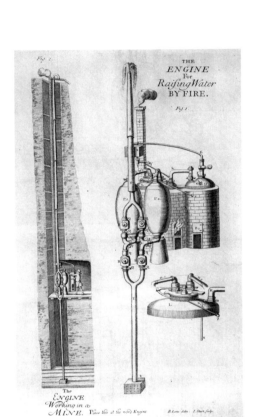

Figure 4. John Harris, *Lexicon Technicum* (fifth edition, 1736), illustration for *engine* (30%).

12. Thomas Bewick (1753–1828) developed the technique of adapting metal-engraving tools to engrave on the end-grain of boxwood. This produced illustrations with a much finer control of both line weight and the representation of light and shade than the earlier method of cutting on the plank of the wood, and which could rival the precision of copper or steel engraving. Bewick did not invent the technique: 'his significance lay in the fact that he was an artist and draughtsman of subtlety and strength, blessed with an imaginative and inventive genius.' (Bain, 1981, p. 18)

13. Ould (2013) discusses the costs of engravings in the eighteenth century.

14. McDermott (2005), pp. 165–8.

15. *Oxford Illustrated Dictionary* (1962), p. viii.

Stalls, Higham Ferrers Church, Northamptonshire.

Figure 5. John Ogilvie, *Imperial Dictionary* (1850, repr. 1876), illustration for *stall*, signed by Jewitt (85%).

Accolade.

Group of the Laocoön.

Tattooing.

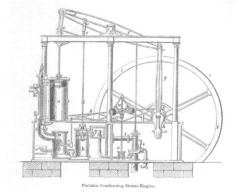

Portable Condensing Steam-Engine.

a, The steam cylinder ; *b*, the piston ; *c*, the upper steam port or passage ; *d*, the lower steam port ; *e, e*, the parallel motion ; *f, f*, the beam ; *g*, the connecting rod ; *h*, the crank ; *i, i*, the fly-wheel ; *k, k*, the eccentric and its rod for working the steam valve ; *l*, the steam valve and valve casing ; *m*, the throttle valve ; *n*, the condenser ; *o*, the injection cock ; *p*, the air-pump ; *q*, the hot well ; *r*, the sniffing-valve, for creating a vacuum in the condenser, previous to starting the engine ; *s*, the feed pump for supplying the boilers ; *t*, the cold water pump for supplying the condenser cistern ; *u*, the governor.

Figure 6. John Ogilvie, *Imperial Dictionary* (1850, repr. 1876), illustrations for *accolade*, *aggroup*, *tattooing*, and *steam-engine* (67%).

Richardson, by the *Oxford English Dictionary* and, elsewhere, by the great European national dictionaries of the nineteenth century; and this despite the use of illustrations in contemporary popular dictionaries.

The *Imperial Dictionary*

The definitive illustrated dictionary of the nineteenth century was John Ogilvie's *Imperial Dictionary* (1850), which in many ways defined what the public would expect of an illustrated dictionary for more than a century. Printed by the Glasgow firm of Blackie & Son, it is in a slightly smaller format than Webster's dictionary of 1828. It added 'about two thousand engravings on wood', which are its main claim to graphic distinction. These were clearly intended to do more than assist in definitions; as stated in the preface, the dictionary aimed to present 'something to interest and instruct ... so that the charge usually preferred against English Dictionaries, namely, that they furnish but *dry sort of reading*, will not apply to this Dictionary'.[16] Illustrations were a feature, part of the overall marketing mix: in keeping with the period of the Great Exhibition of 1851, the preface also stated that 'The Imperial Dictionary will be found to contain, along with etymologies and the definitions of words and terms, a large amount of useful and interesting information connected with literature, art, and science.'

The illustrations were of a high technical and artistic quality. A large number of the wood engravings were by Orlando Jewitt, who has been described as 'virtually the last wood-engraver active at mid-century who still designed the illustrations he engraved, rather than merely reproducing the drawings of others'.[17] Jewitt signed some of these engravings (figure 5). Jewitt's connection with the architect A. W. N. Pugin and the Gothic revival are clear: many of the illustrations are drawn in a style that reflects the medieval interests of that movement. This impression is emphasized by the continuing presence of a large number of illustrations of heraldic terms. Elsewhere a medieval king awards an *accolade* (figure 6), we see a Gothic *aisle* and *arcade*, and a *battle-axe* being wielded by a medieval knight; a *baldrick* and *balistraria* appear side-by-side; a *draw-bridge* is shown. But the middle ages are not the exclusive time-frame of the illustrations: others reproduce classical artefacts (the Laocoön appears at *aggroup*), and the modern technological world is represented by *differential-coupling* and *steam-engine*. Another theme is the exotic and colonial/imperial (*Buddha* is illustrated, and a Maori chief provides the illustration at *tattooing*).

In general there is a historical, naturalistic, and romantic cast to the illustrations that is markedly different from the technical illustrations of eighteenth-century dictionaries. This is emphasized by the quality of drawing that wood engraving could reproduce. Whereas woodcuts were essentially linear, wood engravings, in the hands

16. *Imperial Dictionary* (1850, repr. 1876), p. viii. Emphasis in the original.
17. 'An important exponent of the Gothic revival and the Oxford Movement, who engraved many of the illustrations in polemical and antiquarian works by A. W. N. Pugin and his associates.' (Hancher, 1998, p. 164) Hancher also notes that Jewitt's work for the *Imperial Dictionary* is not mentioned in Harry Carter's *Orlando Jewitt* (London: Oxford University Press, 1962).

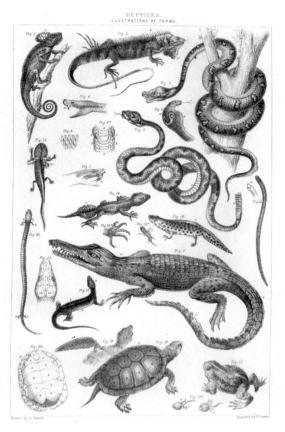

Figure 7. John Ogilvie, *Imperial Dictionary* (1850, repr. 1876), illustrations for *lighthouse* and *reptiles* (50%).

of an expert such as Jewitt, were capable of a dramatic tonal range as well as a high level of detail and fidelity to the original drawing. These illustrations are small and precious, and reinforce the formal and architectural page design. The narrative content of the illustrations – the sense that an object or action is being carefully situated in a place and time, and not being abstracted – adds to the impression that the *Imperial Dictionary* is a 'window on the world' for its Victorian readers.[18] The *Imperial Dictionary* reflects a world-view that gives pride of place to Britain, with its empire bringing tribute to the mother country, as it did for the Great Exhibition.[19]

Jewitt also drew some of the illustrations that were reproduced as full-page engravings. Instead of being distributed throughout the text, these are gathered together, with explanatory letterpress pages, at the beginning of each of the two volumes. We can divide these into two categories, synoptic and taxonomic. Synoptic illustrations are large and detailed, showing component parts of a complex object or system such as *lighthouse* (figure 7). Taxonomic illustrations present an overview of a class of objects such as *birds*, *fishes*, and *reptiles*. Jewitt does not just combine matching individual drawings of whole creatures, but in the case of *reptiles* also includes details and depictions of behaviour. The *Imperial Dictionary* therefore combines highly

18. For a discussion of the value of context in dictionary illustrations, see Hancher (1988).

19. 'They tell us as much about the Victorian reader as they told that reader about the meanings of English words. ...

Emblematic of national pride and global expansiveness, the many engravings marked this new dictionary as "imperial" indeed.' (Hancher, 1998, p. 159). By the 1882 edition, however, many 'medieval' images had been removed.

Figure 8. Robert Hunter, *Enclyclopædic Dictionary* (1879–88). Illustration for *a-hull* (60%).

Figure 9. John Ogilvie, *Imperial Dictionary* (1850, repr. 1876, left) and *Chambers's Twentieth Century Dictionary* (1901, right), illustrations for *ambry* and *andiron* compared (reduced).

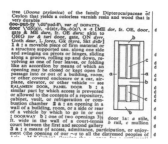

Figure 10. *Webster's Third New International Dictionary of the English Language* (1961), illustration for *door* (60%)

20. An exception is the *Century Dictionary* (1889–91); see Hancher (1996).
21. *Oxford Illustrated Dictionary* (1962), p. v.

individual illustrations, distributed among the range of entries, with plates that bring together visual information about an area of knowledge. The plates enable the taxonomic aspects of the illustrations to be explicit, whereas the effectiveness of a set of illustrations (birds, for example) to explain similarities and relationships is diluted when they are distributed across many hundreds of pages. The balance between these two approaches, and the related balance between linear and tonal techniques, is one that we will see in later dictionaries.

The influence of the *Imperial Dictionary* can be detected in later nineteenth-century dictionaries, often with less impressive results.[20] Robert Hunter's *Encycopædic Dictionary* (1879–88) unusually combined an open and spatially articulated typographic style with wood-engraved illustrations in the text, in a style that is clearly derived from the *Imperial* (figure 8). Similarly, *Chambers's Twentieth Century Dictionary* (1901) includes wood engravings, but these are feeble imitations of the *Imperial* style, losing the subtlty and depiction of depth in Jewitt's work (figure 9). Taking as a sample illustrations for words beginning with the letter A, the indebtedness of Chambers to the *Imperial* is revealed. Of the fourteen words illustrated in Chambers, ten are illustrated in the earlier work, and only three are not; and the one further word illustrated in Chambers does not have an equivalent entry in the *Imperial*. But the pressure to eliminate illustrations from serious, concise dictionaries had begun. The editor of later editions of the *Imperial Dictionary*, Charles Annandale, had eliminated them altogether from his *Concise Dictionary* (1886), in spite of its being nominally a condensation of the *Imperial*.

Modern illustrated dictionaries

The various concise Oxford dictionaries of the early twentieth century took their lead from the *Oxford English Dictionary* and were unillustrated. This meant that a leading range of dictionaries, in the growing concise and smaller sector of the market, had abandoned a feature thought essential at the end of the previous century, and which continued to be treated as important in the United States. There, even the larger 'unabridged' dictionary retained its requirement for illustrations: the controversial *Webster's Third New International Dictionary of the English Language* (1961) was illustrated exactly in the style of the *Imperial Dictionary* of a century before, with individual in-entry line illustrations and separate full-page illustrations (figures 10 and 17). Oxford's view of the place of illustrations in dictionaries was confirmed when, in 1962, it finally published the *Oxford Illustrated Dictionary*. This had been planned since before the Second World War, as a dictionary which would 'combine the essential features of an encyclopedia and of a dictionary in the ordinary sense' and which would be 'copiously illustrated'.[21] It was clearly not a priority in Oxford's dictionary publication programme, as its gestation took nearly 25 years. In spite of its solitary position as an Oxford illustrated dictionary in the 1960s, the book does have some interesting features. While there are some straightforward single illustrations (*aarvark*, *adze*, and *alembic*) that show complete objects

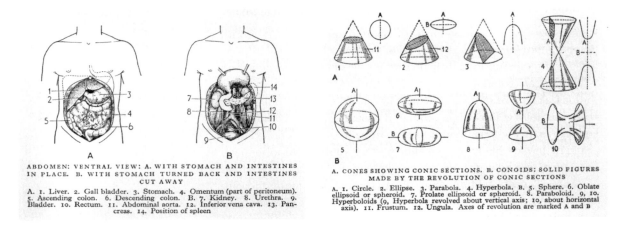

A

B

ABDOMEN: VENTRAL VIEW: A. WITH STOMACH AND INTESTINES IN PLACE. B. WITH STOMACH TURNED BACK AND INTESTINES CUT AWAY

A. 1. Liver. 2. Gall bladder. 3. Stomach. 4. Omentum (part of peritoneum). 5. Ascending colon. 6. Descending colon. B. 7. Kidney. 8. Urethra. 9. Bladder. 10. Rectum. 11. Abdominal aorta. 12. Inferior vena cava. 13. Pancreas. 14. Position of spleen

A. CONES SHOWING CONIC SECTIONS. B. CONOIDS: SOLID FIGURES MADE BY THE REVOLUTION OF CONIC SECTIONS

A. 1. Circle. 2. Ellipse. 3. Parabola. 4. Hyperbola. B. 5. Sphere. 6. Oblate ellipsoid or spheroid. 7. Prolate ellipsoid or spheroid. 8. Paraboloid. 9, 10. Hyperboloids (9, Hyperbola revolved about vertical axis; 10, about horizontal axis). 11. Frustum. 12. Ungula. Axes of revolution are marked A and B

Figure 11. *Oxford Illustrated Dictionary* (1962), illustrations for *abdomen*, and for *cones showing conic sections* and *conoids* (85%).

Figure 12. *The Random House Dictionary* (1966), illustrations for *capuchin* and *capybara* (100%).

22. *Oxford Illustrated Dictionary* (1962), p. viii.

without any further explanation, the majority of illustrations either have details or labelling, or are synoptic illustrations of one kind or another. This is explained in the introduction:

> each of [the illustrations] is independent and self-explanatory.... To avoid wasteful repetition many subjects have been grouped together, especially where the members of a group help to explain one another: the picture of a machine, for example, will not only illustrate the machine itself but will exhibit the nature of its parts, and their relation to one another and to the whole. In some cases illustrations demonstrate how things work, but only where this helps to define the words.[22]

Abdomen shows two views of the human abdomen, with internal organs labelled (figure 11). Labelling, which necessarily illustrates words out of their alphabetic sequence, requires careful cross-referencing. In the *Oxford Illustrated Dictionary* there is cross-referencing to illustrations from words at other places in the dictionary, but there is some inconsistency in this. For example, while the entry for *platelet* correctly has a cross-reference to the illustration at *blood*, the entry for the word *urethra* only has a cross-reference to the illustration at *pelvis* when the word is included in the illustration labels at both *abdomen* and *pelvis*.

The *Oxford Illustrated Dictionary* is at its most interesting when it illustrates groups or classes of objects: it shows three *anchors*, not one, and five *cranes*; a dozen *cones showing conic sections* and *conoids* are illustrated. Its illustrations are also detailed: *corms* are shown with leaves present and removed, and in cross-section. The illustration for *motor-car* is a 'transparent' outline of the bodywork with the mechanics revealed, and with numbered leader lines indicating the relevant parts named in a separate list. This is combined with small drawings of different bodywork styles. Where most dictionary illustrations say nothing about relative scale (because objects are shown out of context and without being juxtaposed against something whose size is familiar), the *Oxford Illustrated Dictionary* shows *string* instruments together so that the relative sizes can be judged. This does not prevent it showing a *tapir* and the much smaller, lemur-like *tasier* with no indication of relative size at all, the definitions simply stating both are 'small'. The *Random House Dictionary* (1966, figure 12) shows how size can be indicated verbally within illustration captions.

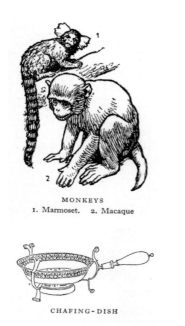

MONKEYS
1. Marmoset.   2. Macaque

CHAFING-DISH

Figure 13. *Oxford Illustrated Dictionary*
(1962), comparison of drawing styles
for *monkey* and *chafing-dish* (80%).

Figure 14. *Oxford Reference Dictionary*
(1986), illustrations for *church
architecture* (40%).

(In relation to explaining scale, the narrative style of the *Imperial
Dictionary*, which frequently included humans in the illustrations,
had some advantages over a nominally 'objective' style.) The *Oxford
Illustrated Dictionary* even attempts to illustrate some physical processes (at *aeronautics*, it shows aircraft manoeuvres, and it illustrates
swimming strokes). Importantly, all these illustrations, whether single
items or grouped, are within entries; there are no separate full-page
plates at the beginning or end of the book.

The drawing style of the *Oxford Illustrated Dictionary* is a spectrum
between technical drawing and relatively freehand pen-and-ink illustration. Usually monoline, with shading indicated by stipples and
hatching, the illustrations have a neutral, impersonal feel, but there
is an inconsistency of line-weight, caused by the varying weights and
sizes at which individual pieces of artwork were drawn, and the varying percentages by which they were reduced. (Compare the heaviness
of the relatively freely drawn *monkey* with the lightness of the 'technical style' for *chafing-dish* in figure 13.) In spite of these imperfections,
this dictionary demonstrates that it is possible to conceive illustrations that do more than illustrate single objects and yet can be integrated into the entries themselves by using a cross-reference system.

The *Oxford Illustrated Dictionary* approach was modified for its
successor, the *Oxford Reference Dictionary* (1986), which abandoned
individual illustrations entirely, relying on full-page illustrations,
each with a theme. This thematic approach was seen as enhancing the encyclopedic qualities of the dictionary, and included
topics such as *church architecture*, *body*, *hallmarks*, and *mathematics*
(figure 14). These composite illustrations both categorize and label
sets of objects and detail the constituent parts of objects. There are
also conceptual illustrations showing organizational relationships,

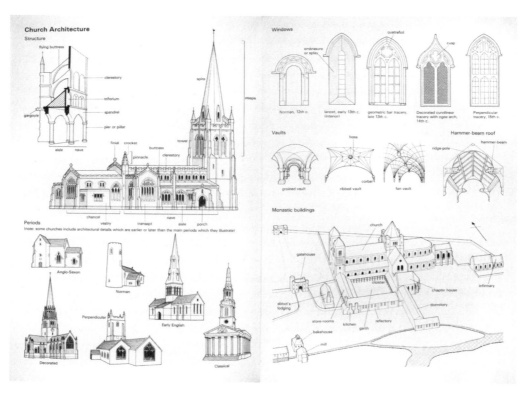

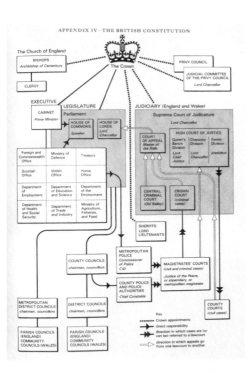

Figure 15. *Oxford Reference Dictionary* (1986), illustration for *British constitution* (40%).

23. *Oxford-Duden Pictorial English Dictionary* (1987), foreword (unpaginated).

sometimes called organigrams, for example *British constitution* (figure 15). All the full-page illustrations are placed close to a relevant entry, distributing them throughout the book, but thereby reducing their impact. While the illustrations themselves are more than competently drawn, the line illustrations have relatively little shading, which creates light-grey pages that are not graphically prominent, and the illustration pages can easily be missed by a casual browser. Furthermore, the reader no longer 'discovers' illustrations while consulting a particular entry, but has to follow a cross reference from a word to the relevant illustration. The costs of researching, planning, and drawing these more complex illustrations was far greater than simply commissioning artists to produce individual in-entry illustrations from standard sources, and heavily restricted the overall number of illustrations. Some illustrations were subsequently combined with a different text in the *Oxford English Reference Dictionary* (1995), where they were relegated to an appendix along with lists of prime ministers and royal genealogies. This concentrated their impact, but also indicated just how peripheral illustration pages had become to the language-based content of the dictionary. The very different approaches of the synoptic, taxonomic, and organizational illustrations, and their juxtaposition with text-based material, added to the impression of a confused collection of items brought together to fill up the last pages of the dictionary.

A different approach is taken by the Duden pictorial dictionaries. These are essentially updated versions of Comenius' *Orbis Sensualium Pictus* (1658) where illustrations are the core of each dictionary rather than an additional feature (figure 16).

> An illustration will help the reader to visualize the object denoted by the word and to form an impression of the way in which objects function in their own technical field or in [everyday life]. ... Each double page of the dictionary contains a list of the vocabulary of a subject together with a picture illustrating this vocabulary.[23]

The Duden dictionaries are certainly thorough, but perhaps not as uniform in their style as this makes it sound: the illustration panels

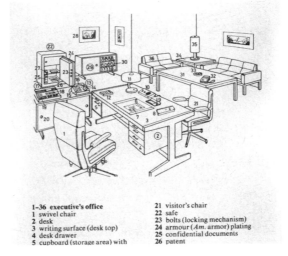

28 dog brush
29 dog comb
30 lead (dog lead, leash); *for hunting*: leash

1–36 **executive's office**
1 swivel chair
2 desk
3 writing surface (desk top)
4 desk drawer
5 cupboard (storage area) with

21 visitor's chair
22 safe
23 bolts (locking mechanism)
24 armour (*Am.* armor) plating
25 confidential documents
26 patent

Figure 16. *Oxford-Duden Pictorial English Dictionary* (1981, repr. 1987), illustrations for *breeds of dog* and *office* (67%).

1 bar	22–23 stereo system (stereo
2 barmaid	equipment)
3 bar stool	22 tuner
4 shelf for bottles	23 amplifier
5 shelf for glasses	24 records (discs)
6 beer glass	25 disc jockey

Figure 17. *Oxford-Duden Pictorial Dictionary* (1981, repr. 1987), illustration for *discotheque* (67%), and *Webster's Third New International Dictionary of the English Language* (1961), illustration for *dogs* (38%).

include collections of objects, drawn in a 'neutral' linear style, but the presentation varies. Some are simply collections of individual drawings on a neutral field, with no indication of absolute scale or whether the individual elements are consistently scaled (*breeds of dog* and *art*). Some are perspective scenes with naturalistic spatial relationships (*bakery* and *office*). Some combine schematic, blueprint-like drawings with perspective drawings (*railway line*). Stability and longevity is important in dictionary illustration, given the tendency for publishers to reissue editions over a long period of time. The more taxonomic or table-like the illustration, the less likely it is to date, especially if the subject is some aspect of the natural world. Technological applications are particularly likely to date, and the lifespan of Duden illustrations, with heavy coverage of areas of technology and industry, is therefore compromised. As time passes, the illustrations that give context by showing street scenes, household rooms, the interior of a discotheque, and so on suffer from precisely the specific allusions to the period of their drawing that originally provided up-to-date appeal and contextualization (figure 17). Perhaps this is the reason for the highly conservative approach to illustration found in dictionaries such as *Webster's Third New International Dictionary of the English Language* (1961), whose illustrations would not have looked out of place in the *Imperial Dictionary*. *Webster's Third* was particularly careful to select topics that would not date for its full-page, taxonomic colour plates. These cover stable categories such as *cats*, *dogs*, *flags* (perhaps not quite so stable but easily correctible) and *gems*.[24]

24. Colour plates had added encyclopedic visual content to nineteeth-century dictionaries. The 1882 (repr. 1896) edition of the *Imperial Dictionary* included a double-page full-colour lithographed plate in each of its eight volumes: *national coats of arms*, *decorations of honour*, *illuminated writing*, *language map of the world*, *architectural ornaments*, *precious stones*, *colour*, and *signal flags*. Other plates were printed in black with a stone background tint. The *Century Dictionary* included sixteen colour plates depicting flora and fauna, *flags*, *signals*, *colors of the spectrum and of pigments*, and *color-types of the races of men* (Hancher, 1996, p. 109).

Beatitude *n* 1 each of the sayings of Jesus Christ in the Sermon on the Mount about the eight groups of people who will receive blessing in heaven (Matthew 5:3–11) 2 a title given to a senior bishop in non-Orthodox churches of the E Mediterranean

The Beatles

Beatles /beèt'lz/ (1959–70) British pop music group
beatnik /beètnik/ *n* a member of the Beat Generation of

Figure 18. *Encarta Concise Dictionary* (2001), illustration for *Beatles* (75%).

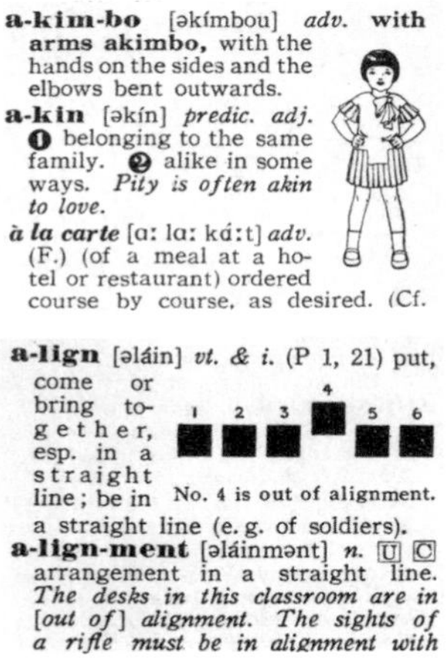

a-kim-bo [əkímbou] *adv.* with arms akimbo, with the hands on the sides and the elbows bent outwards.
a-kin [əkín] *predic. adj.* ❶ belonging to the same family. ❷ alike in some ways. *Pity is often akin to love.*
à la carte [ɑː lɑː kɑːt] *adv.* (F.) (of a meal at a hotel or restaurant) ordered course by course, as desired. (Cf.

a-lign [əláin] *vt. & i.* (P 1, 21) put, come or bring to-gether, esp. in a straight line ; be in a straight line (e. g. of soldiers).
a-lign-ment [əláinmənt] *n.* Ⓤ Ⓒ arrangement in a straight line. *The desks in this classroom are in [out of] alignment. The sights of a rifle must be in alignment with*

No. 4 is out of alignment.

Figure 19. *Advanced Learner's Dictionary of Current English* (1948), illustrations for *akimbo* and *alignment* (75%).

25. 'The likenesses reproduced in the [*Oxford Dictionary of National Biography*] were to be "visually rich as well as informative", so selections were not restricted to head-and-shoulder or half-length studies. Full-length portraits were chosen where these seemed more revealing. Costume, background, accessories, and period stylization were seen, along with likeness, as part of what "constitutes the portrait as a representation of a given individual". Consequently the reproductions included in the Dictionary show in almost all cases

The *American Heritage Dictionary* (third edition, 1992) and the *Encarta* dictionaries demonstrate how publishers respond to the marketing requirement of making dictionaries relevant to their audience – or perhaps of ensuring that there is consumer recognition of the dictionary content. The 'modern' aspect of these dictionaries is the widespread use of photographs. The subjects for photography are chosen to accord with the principle of not dating too rapidly. In the *American Heritage Dictionary*, which has a considerable encyclopedic content, some are portraits of famous people, works of art, or buildings (*Maria Callas*, a De Kooning painting, *Abu Simbel*). These have a high recognition factor, and can be thought of as iconic, saying something about the concern of the dictionary to connect with its readership, rather than being genuinely explanatory. This is reinforced by the choice of specific, familiar portraits for individuals: in the *Encarta Concise English Dictionary* (2001) the *Beatles* are shown in 1963 (figure 18) and *Margaret Thatcher* at her election victory in 1979. These thumbnail reminders, tightly cropped, are an interesting contrast to the rigorously selected images of subjects for the *Oxford Dictionary of National Biography*, which, with far greater resources of time and space, chose to concentrate on the significant but less obvious portrait, or the image which contextualized the sitter.[25]

Illustrations in learners' dictionaries

The development from the alternatives of individual in-entry illustrations or separate, full-page illustrations to something altogether more complex and interesting can be see in the successive editions of A. S. Hornby's *Advanced Learner's Dictionary*.[26] Hornby's original *Idiomatic and Syntactic Dictionary* (1942) was republished by Oxford as the *Advanced Learner's Dictionary of Current English* in 1948, with the title of later editions simplified to *Oxford Advanced Learner's Dictionary*. The 1948 edition claimed to include 1406 illustrations. All but three of these are in-entry line illustrations (the remainder showing the range of the human voice and musical instruments, and soccer, rugby, and cricket pitches as an appendix). They are almost all drawings of objects, and are a relatively conservative basic selection with a few items useful to the target audience of non-native learners of English. Occasionally they are used to discriminate sense (at *bar* chocolate bars and prison bars are shown, at *tablet* both medicinal tablets and a memorial tablet are shown) but mostly they are in the familiar range typified by *abacus, armour, centaur, vaulted roof*, and *woodpecker*. The dictionary's emphasis on current vocabulary does sometimes influence the illustrations, for example *tuxedo* and *cash register*. A few adjectives are illustrated, for example *akimbo* and *upside down. Alignment* is illustrated by one of the few diagrammatic illustrations in the dictionary (figure 19). If we divide the illustrations in the 1948 edition into sixteen general categories,[27] then it becomes

the complete original composition.' 'Selecting the images', from 'Introduction to the Oxford Dictionary of National Biography', available at http://global.oup.com/oxforddnb/info/print/intro/intro4/ (accessed 9 September 2013).

26. See p. 171 for a full list of editions.

Cowie (1999) traces the book's history.

27. The categories are: adjectives, agriculture/technology, architecture, anatomy, astronomy/mathematics, botany/zoology, domestic objects/furniture, dress, food, history/mythology, jobs, military, music, nautical, transport, sports.

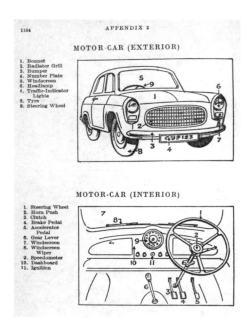

Figure 20. *Oxford Advanced Learner's Dictionary*, second edition (1963), illustrations for *motor-car* (57%).

28. *Oxford Advanced Learner's Dictionary*, second edition (1963), p. vi.

clear that botanical/zoological illustrations are by far the greatest proportion, covering 14 of the 40 illustrations in the letter A, and 54 of the 214 in the letter S. Other well-represented categories in the letter S are technology/tools/agriculture (40), domestic objects/furniture (28), dress (24), architecture (12), and military (11).

The second edition (1963) continued with much the same approach as the first edition, but with a smaller overall number of illlustrations, 'about 1000';[28] these were re-drawn, but in much the same style and with much the same distribution. The appendix retained the illustrations for sports fields and added one for *baseball*, and drawings were added of *full-rigged sailing ship*, *sailing dinghy*, *motor car* (exterior and interior, figure 20) and *aeroplane*, all showing component parts labelled with numbers and leader lines. This reduction in the number of illustrations matched the overall approach to the design of the dictionary: its text content was very much increased, and the typography became both more cramped and less graphically articulated.

In the third edition (1974) the overall number of illustrations was reduced yet again, with the introduction talking simply about 'a large number', so that only about a quarter of the first edition's total remained. In a radical departure, taking advantage of the offset lithography printing process, many of the illustrations were now photographs, and the additional line illustrations were completely redrawn in a much more controlled, mechanical style. As well as this technological change, we can see a more considered approach to illustration. There is a more systematic attempt to disambiguate senses rather than simply identify a headword. For example, *caravan* shows a caravan of camels, a gypsy caravan, and a modern (cardrawn) caravan (figure 21), while *reel* shows a cotton reel, a fishing reel, and a cable reel. Groups of related objects are shown as simple taxonomies at *arachnid*, *mollusc*, and *reptile* (without indication of absolute or relative scale). In a retrograde change, illustrations are sometimes grouped simply to save space, so that a *palette* is shown next to a *paling*, and a *microphone* next to a *microscope*, only because those entries are in the same column. A drawing and a photograph

Figure 21. *Oxford Advanced Learner's Dictionary*, third edition (1974, repr. 1985), illustrations for *caravan*, *microphone*, *microscope*, and *periscope* (80%).

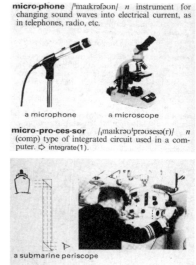

are combined to illustrate *periscope*, the drawing being a linear diagram of the light-path, the photograph showing the way a submarine's periscope is handled by the operator and indicating its scale.

The opportunities that photographs offer to show a higher level of detail in the depiction of an object are not realized in the third edition, however. Through several reprints the quality of offset lithography reproduction is poor, and the contrast of most of the photographs is extreme, so that highlights are bleached out and shadow areas filled in, reducing detail overall. *Concertina* (mostly black) and *maggot* (mostly white) are nearly impossible to decipher. The bleaching out of highlight detail causes particular problems when the photograph is a cut-out, as at *kimono* and *tool*, because it becomes impossible to discern the true outline of the object. Occasionally the reproduction quality makes it impossible to tell if the illustration is a photograph or a drawing (*safety-pin*).

These issues were evidently understood because the fourth edition (1989) abandons photography altogether. While the illustrations still disambiguate senses and provide taxonomies, they are now drawn with a heavier overall line-weight, which combines with the stronger Nimrod typeface and improved printing to give a denser, less contrasty page. The number of illustrations is increased (1,820 are claimed) and an art editor, two illustration editors, and ten illustrators and studios are named as contributors.[29] How the total number of illustrations is calculated is not clear because there are only 58 illustrated entries in the letter S, compared with 172 in the second edition, which only claimed 'about 1000' overall. But if the number of *words* appearing in illustrations is the criterion, this would enable the illustration for *tennis court* to cover *baseline*, *centre mark*, *centre service line*, *double sideline*, *net*, *net judge*, *service line*, *single sideline tramlines*, *racket*, and *umpire*, and that at *turnip* to cover *swede* and *parsnip*. A few more illustrations are added in the appendix, of the synoptic kind with numbered and labelled keys. In this edition their usefulness to the overseas learner is further indicated by captions such as *some typical British homes* and *wild animals common in Britain*. Even a particularly British motorway junction is depicted (figure 22),

29. *Oxford Advanced Learner's Dictionary*, fourth edition (1989), p. vi.

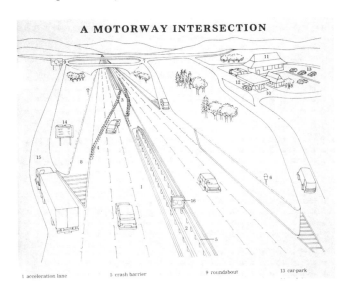

Figure 22. *Oxford Advanced Learner's Dictionary*, fourth edition (1989), illustration for *motorway intersection* (67%).

complete with *cones* and a *contraflow*. The fifth edition (1995), while innovative in its overall design, retains about the same number of illustrated entries as the fourth, but claims, more accurately, '1700 words illustrated' (although there are no more than 500 separate illustrations).

The *Oxford Advanced Learner's Dictionary* faced increasing competition in the 1990s and 2000s. The *Longman Dictionary of Contemporary English* (third edition, 1995) introduced a large number of innovations in illustration, which were matched almost immediately by Oxford and Macmillan in their equivalent dictionaries. The other competitor in the field, the *Cambridge International Dictionary of English*, appeared in the same year as the Longman dictionary, and was visually far less successful.

In the *Longman Dictionary of Contemporary English* illustrations have a function to expand and relate vocabulary as well as to identify objects, disambiguate homonyms, discriminate senses, and (for foreign learners) indicate particularly British instances of familiar objects. The overall graphic style is still linear, with a drawn black line on white ground. There are some single-object illustrations (*acorn*), synoptic illustrations (*aircraft*) and disambiguations (*nucleus*). But there is a noticeable change of graphic style. For illustrations of human actions (at *arm* we are shown *arms folded*, *arm-in-arm*, and *arms akimbo*) the drawings are now more casual and cartoon-like (figure 23). The most prominent innovation is the introduction of full-page illustrations printed as three full-colour sections, each of eight pages, which fall at about one-third and two-thirds through the book. Printed on thicker matt paper than the rest of the dictionary, these sections are visible even when the book is closed because the illustrations bleed, and can be easily spotted even by the casual bookshop browser.

These illustrations are mostly composites, like the Duden pictorial dictionary illustrations, but with a wide range of configurations, each suited to the word-groupings being illustrated. The simplest are naturalistic, perspective composites: *kitchen* has over forty items or actions labelled (actions such as *roast* and *fry* are set in capitals to distinguish them from nouns, and British and US English variants are shown). *Landscapes*, *office*, and *restaurant* follow a similar style. Somewhat less naturalistic are the compositions for *fruit* and *vegetables*. *Verbs in the kitchen* and *driving* are grids of individual drawings. Actions are shown by details of hands with utensils (*chop* and *slice*), or of driver or vehicle actions (*change lanes* and *slow down*) respectively. *Types of walk*, *physical contact,* and *sound* are similar, with naturalistic drawings tightly cropped to the action and with neutral backgrounds, except for some *physical contact* and *types of walk* illustrations where context is required (a river for *wade*). *Patterns and fabrics* and *describing clothes* are naturalistic taxonomies. *Position and direction*, *describing people*, *broken*, and *colours* are altogether more inventive (figure 24, opposite). *Position and direction* consists of a full-page naturalistic perspective drawing, but instead of being a composite of objects, it is a composite of spatial relationships, which are numbered and explained in a text panel on the facing page. The text is a narrative commentary on the bicycle race depicted in the picture,

Figure 23. *Longman Dictionary of Contemporary English* (1995), illustration for *arm* (77%).

Figure 24. *Longman Dictionary of Contemporary English* (1995), illustrations (from top to bottom) for *position and direction*, *broken* and *physical contact 1*, and *house* and *colours/colors* (35%).

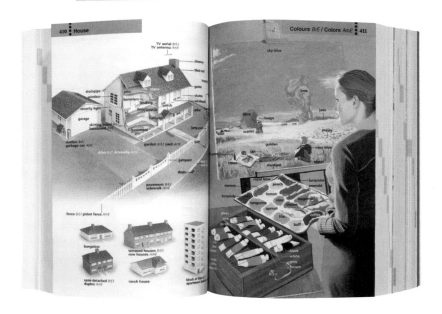

explaining who is *beyond* whom, who is *among* the crowd, and so on. *Describing people* works in a similar way, with a set of family photographs in a *trompe-l'œil* composition, with a narrative text describing each family member. *Broken* again uses the naturalistic perspective to depict a living room where every object has seen better days (such as *ripped* and *crumpled*). *Colours* is a naturalistic perspective of an artist painting a picture, allowing all the colours in her paint-box, and on her palette and canvas, to be labelled. Finally, illustrations with a quite different purpose (and which appear in no other learner's dictionary) are the small histograms showing frequency-of-occurrence data for particular words and combinations. These are placed in small panels next to the relevant entry.

The sixth edition of the *Oxford Advanced Learner's Dictionary*, a direct response to the *Longman Dictionary of Contemporary English*, promised '1,700 words illustrated, many in groups, to introduce you to related vocabulary'. In this role, illustrations are joined by text-only pages that 'show the vocabulary you need for topics such as sport and computing', and by explicit boxed lists of 'word families' in certain entries. Photographs are still avoided, and the most prominent groups of illustrations are those presented, as in the Longman dictionary, on full-colour pages. Again they are separately printed, on smooth coated paper, and inserted together about one-quarter of the way though the dictionary in the middle of letter D. While this is convenient for binding and may achieve impact for browsing readers in a bookshop, it is quite without regard to relating illustrations to specific entries. The paper surface reproduces saturated colours better than the Longman dictionary, and emphasizes the techniques of hyper-realist painting and computer-aided rendering.

The configuration of illustrations differs from Longman's: in the sixth edition of the *Oxford Advanced Learner's Dictionary* there are only taxonomies. *Bread, cakes, and desserts* and *fruit and vegetables* are brightly coloured, and *clothes and fabrics* is rendered in a hyper-realist style. *The animal kingdom* is drawn in the friendlier manner of a children's picture book, while *games and toys* returns to the hyper-realist style. But in a nod to perspective, everything is drawn as a three-dimensional object, casting a shadow on the white ground of the page (figure 25, opposite). The most recent edition of the *Oxford Advanced Learner's Dictionary*, the eighth (2010), re-used some of the sixth edition's illustrations with some reorganization, and developed the computer-rendered hyper-realist style in perspective illustrations such as *living room* (figure 26). The influence of children's infotainment illustration, as practised by publishers such as Dorling Kindersley, is clear.[30] (Dorling Kindersley produced its own subject 'visual dictionaries' from 1991, which consist of double-page spreads of labelled illustrations, figure 27). These were organized thematically, not alphabetically.

In comparison, the black-only line drawings that still appear in the *Oxford Advanced Learner's Dictionary* are relatively conservative, except for illustrations in an informal cartoon style used to show human actions or emotions, for example *trolley rage* in the insert on new words (figure 28), *shrug* (*one's shoulders*), *stamp* (*one's foot*), *wring out*, *wrinkle* (*one's forehead*). Apart from these, almost no illustrations

30. The cut-out style used by Dorling Kindersley publications owes a great deal to the need for illustrations to be reusable from book to book; photographing objects on a white background allows them to be re-contextualized more easily.

Figure 25. *Oxford Advanced Learner's Dictionary*, sixth edition (2000), illustrations for *fruit and vegetables* and *clothes and fabrics* (35%).

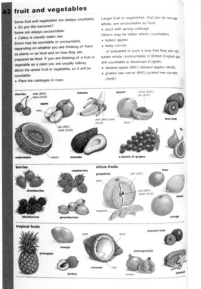

Figure 26. *Oxford Advanced Learner's Dictionary*, eighth edition (2010), illustrations for *fruit and vegetables* and *living room* (35%).

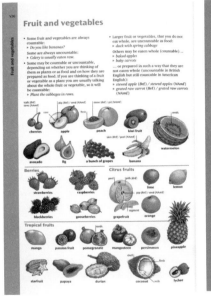

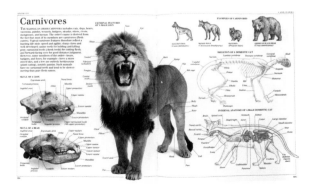

Figure 27. Dorling Kindersley, *Ultimate Visual Dictionary* (1994), illustration for *carnivores* (20%).

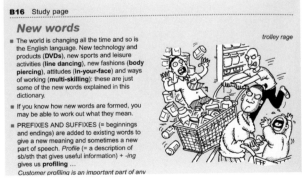

Figure 28. *Oxford Advanced Learner's Dictionary*, sixth edition (2000), illustration for *trolley rage* (60%).

Figure 28. Illustrations for *sundial* in successive editions of *Oxford Advanced Learner's Dictionary* (50%).

Figure 29. *Macmillan English Dictionary for Advanced Learners* (2002), illustrations for *fire* and *catch* (60%).

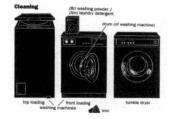

Figure 30. *Cambridge International Dictionary of English* (1995), illustration for *cleaning* (55%).

remain illustrating a single word; some twenty-nine entries in the letter S are illustrated, but almost all are disambiguations or taxonomies. The sole 'single object' illustration in the letter S is the old stalwart *sundial*, possibly included for sentimental reasons, for it has appeared in all eight editions from 1942 to 2010 (figure 28).

The *Macmillan English Dictionary for Advanced Learners* (2002) adopted an approach very similar to the sixth edition of the *Oxford Advanced Learner's Dictionary*: it has a section of glossy, full-page colour taxonomies in a hyper-realist style (again with very similar topics and content, but the lack of colour edge-strip or bleed means that the section is not as visible to the casual browser as Oxford's or Longman's), and a number of in-entry illustrations. These make greater use of tints and shading, and of the second colour (red) used throughout the dictionary. Some are taxonomies (*chair*) or are synoptic (*body*), some disambiguate senses and words (a single illustration group shows *burn*, *light*, and *set fire to*), and some show the sequences of some actions (*catch* and *dodge*) (figure 29). A cartoon-like drawing style is used more freely for these than in other dictionaries. A tiny residue of single-object illustrations remains (for example *bonsai* and *crutch*). The *Cambridge International Dictionary of English* (1995) used the unusual technique of white line on black illustrations, causing problems with the reproduction of fine detail, and leading to the disconcerting presentation of 'white goods' as black at *cleaning* (figure 30).

Reinforcing dictionary content

The leading UK English language dictionaries that are contemporary with these learners' dictionaries (*Collins English Dictionary*, the *Concise Oxford English Dictionary*, and the *New Penguin English Dictionary*) remain resolutely unillustrated. Illustration can therefore be seen as reserved for semi-encyclopedic dictionaries such as the *Encarta* series, children's dictionaries and learners' dictionaries. Children's dictionaries have their own market requirements for a complex mix of graphic elements, dictated by teachers' expectations and the need to support the classroom teaching of English. Similarly, learners' dictionaries have recently developed an approach to illustrations that allows them to have a stronger pedagogic function, so that they can help the reader by expanding vocabulary, reinforcing the connections between words, and embodying semantic networks. The use of colour illustrations, particularly when concentrated in sections printed on coated paper, certainly provides a marketing opportunity to promote the attractiveness and up-to-dateness of the dictionary, but the illustrations still function as reinforcements for the verbal content of the dictionary. In moving away from the discrete, single-object, in-entry illustration that was commonplace from the 1650s to the 1970s, learners' dictionaries have ensured that in-entry illustrations disambiguate as well as depict, have offered new approaches to composite illustrations, and have clearly demonstrated that illustrations can help dictionaries define actions, moods, emotions, and processes as well as objects.

Acknowledgements

Figures 1 and 2 are reproduced from the online and facsimile editions respectively (listed below). Figures 3 and 8 are reproduced from books in the Bodleian Library, University of Oxford (figure 3: 302 f. 42; figure 8: 30254 d. 19). Figure 2 was photographed by Paul Lucas in the *Oxford English Dictionary* library with the permission of the *OED* librarian. All other photography by Laura Bennetto.

Bibliography

Dictionaries consulted (those published from 1850 are arranged by title)

The Advanced Learner's Dictionary of Current English (1948). A. S. Hornby, E. V. Gatenby, and H. Wakefield (eds). London: Oxford University Press (reprint of 1942 Kaitakusha edition)

The Advanced Learner's Dictionary of Current English (1963). 2nd edn, A. S. Hornby, E. V. Gatenby, and H. Wakefield (eds). London: Oxford University Press

American Heritage Dictionary (1992). 3rd edn, [William Morris (ed.)]. Boston: Houghton Mifflin

Bailey, Nathan (1727). *The Universal Etymological English Dictionary*. London: printed for T. Cox

Bailey, Nathan (1730). *Dictionarium Britannicum*. London: printed for T. Cox

Blount, Thomas (1656). *Glossographia: or a Dictionary Interpreting all such Hard Words....* London: printed by Tho. Newcomb (facsimile repr. Menston: Scolar Press, 1969)

Cambridge International Dictionary of English (1995). Paul Procter (ed.). Cambridge: Cambridge University Press

The Century Dictionary (1889–91). William Dwight Whitney (ed.). New York: The Century Co.

Chambers's Twentieth Century Dictionary of the English Language (1901). Thomas Davidson (ed.). London and Edinburgh: W. & R. Chambers

Collins English Dictionary: desktop edition (2004). Sandra Anderson *et al* (eds). Glasgow: Collins

The Concise Oxford English Dictionary (2011). 12th edn, Angus Stevenson and Maurice Waite (eds). Oxford: Oxford University Press

A Concise Dictionary of the English Language (1886). Charles Annandale (ed.). London: Blackie and Son

Encarta World Dictionary (1999). Kathy Rooney (ed.). London: Bloomsbury

Encarta Concise English Dictionary (2001). Kathy Rooney (ed.). London: Bloomsbury

The Encyclopædic Dictionary (1879–88). Robert Hunter (ed.). London: Cassell

Harris, John (1704). *Lexicon Technicum* (5th edn, 1736). London: printed for J. Walthoe

The Imperial Dictionary of the English Language (1850). John Ogilvie (ed.). Glasgow: Blackie and Son; (repr. 1876), London: Blackie and Son

The Imperial Dictionary of the English Language (1882, repr. 1896). John Ogilvie and Charles Annandale (eds). London: Blackie and Son

Johnson, Samuel (1755). *A Dictionary of the English Language*. London: W. Strahan

Longman Dictionary of Contemporary English (1995). 3rd edn, Della Summers (ed.). Harlow: Pearson Education Ltd

Macmillan English Dictionary for Advanced Learners (2002). Michael Rundell (ed.). Oxford: Macmillan Education

The New Penguin English Dictionary (2000). Robert Allen (ed.). London: Penguin Books

Oxford Advanced Learner's Dictionary of Current English (1974, repr. 1985). 3rd edn, A. S. Hornby, A. P. Cowie, and J. W. Lewis (eds). London: Oxford University Press

Oxford Advanced Learner's Dictionary of Current English (1989). 4th edn, A. P. Cowie (ed.). Oxford: Oxford University Press

Oxford Advanced Learner's Dictionary of Current English (1995). 5th edn, J. Crowther (ed.). Oxford: Oxford University Press

Oxford Advanced Learner's Dictionary of Current English (2000). 6th edn, S. Wehmeier (ed.). Oxford: Oxford University Press

Oxford Advanced Learner's Dictionary of Current English (2005). 7th edn, S. Wehmeier (ed.). Oxford: Oxford University Press

Oxford Advanced Learner's Dictionary of Current English (2010). 8th edn, J. Turnbull (ed.). Oxford: Oxford University Press

Oxford-Duden Pictorial English Dictionary (1981, repr. 1987). John Pheby (ed.). Oxford: Oxford University Press

The Oxford English Dictionary (1933). 12 vols, James A. H. Murray, Henry Bradley, W. A. Craigie, and C. T. Onions (ed.). Oxford: Clarendon Press

The Oxford English Dictionary (1989). 2nd edn, 20 vols, J. A. Simpson and E. S. C. Weiner (eds). Oxford: Clarendon Press

Oxford English Reference Dictionary (1995). Judy Pearsall and Bill Trumble (eds). Oxford: Oxford University Press

Oxford Illustrated Dictionary (1962). J. Coulson, C. T. Carr, L. Hutchinson, D. Eagle, H. M. Petter (eds). Oxford: Clarendon Press

The Oxford Reference Dictionary (1986). Joyce Hawkins and Susan Le Roux (eds). Oxford: Clarendon Press

The Random House Dictionary of the English Language (1966). Jess Stein and Laurence Urdang (eds). New York: Random House

Richardson, Charles (1836). *A New Dictionary of the English Language*. London: William Pickering

Ultimate Visual Dictionary (1994). London: Dorling Kindersley

Webster, Noah (1828). *An American Dictionary of the English Language*. New York: S. Converse (repr. New York: Johnson Reprint, 1970)

Webster's Third New International Dictionary of the English Language (1961). Philip B. Gove (ed.). Springfield, MA: G. & C. Merriam

Other works consulted

Bain, Iain (ed.) (1981). *Thomas Bewick: my life*. London: Folio Society

Burchfield, Robert (1985). *The English language*. Oxford: Oxford University Press

Cowie, A. P. (1999). *English dictionaries for foreign learners*. Oxford: Clarendon Press

Hancher, Michael (1988). 'Bagpipe and distaff: interpreting dictionary illustrations', *Dictionaries: journal of the Dictionary Society of North America*, no. 10, pp. 93–109

Hancher, Michael (1992). 'Bailey and after: illustrating meaning', *Word & image*, vol. 8, no. 1 (January–March), pp. 1–20

Hancher, Michael (1996). '[*The Century Dictionary*:] Illustrations', *Dictionaries: Journal of the Dictionary Society of North America*, no. 17, pp. 79–115

Hancher, Michael (1998). 'Gazing at *The Imperial Dictionary*', *Book History*, no. 1, pp. 156–81

Humble, Nicola (ed.) (2000). *Mrs Beeton's book of household management*. Oxford: Oxford University Press

McDemott, Anne (2005). 'Johnson's definitions of technical terms and the absence of illustrations', *International Journal of Lexicography*, vol. 18, no. 1, pp. 173–87

Ould, Martyn (2013). 'The workplace: places, procedures, and personnel 1668–1780', *History of Oxford University Press*, vol. 1, Ian Gadd (ed.), pp. 193–240. Oxford: Oxford University Press

Stein, Gabriele (1985). *The English dictionary before Cawdrey*. Tübingen: Max Niemeyer

Wright, Thomas (1884). *Anglo-Saxon and Old English vocabularies*. 2nd edition, Richard Paul Wülcker (ed.). London: Trübner (accessed at http://www.archive.org/details/anglosaxonoldeng01wriguoft, 7 October 2013)

Titus Nemeth

Simplified Arabic: a new form of Arabic type for hot metal composition

This essay is an investigation into the origins of Simplified Arabic, a typeface developed in the 1950s by the British Linotype company in collaboration with Kamel Mrowa, owner and editor-in-chief of the Lebanese newspaper *al-Hayat*. The essay situates the development of Simplified Arabic within a broader geopolitical context of the Middle East after the Second World War, explains the design concepts underpinning the typeface in relation to the technical requirements of 1950s newspaper production, and assesses the design of the typeface itself. Additional discussion addresses the simplified Arabic typeface introduced subsequently by Intertype, Linotype's competitor, and compares the simplified typefaces of both companies. Brief consideration is given to Simplified Arabic's influence and its lasting impact on Arabic typeface design.

Simplified Arabic was a typeface conceived for the requirements of newspaper production. Introduced by the British Linotype company in the 1950s, the principles underlying its design significantly reduced the number of letterforms typically found in Arabic. The success of the typeface served to establish a novel form of the Arabic script as a *de facto* standard, making Simplified Arabic one of the most important innovations in the history of Arabic typography, and one whose influence can still be felt today. This essay traces Simplified Arabic's context, origins, and development.[1]

The printing trade and the Middle East after the Second World War

In 1908, development work began in New York on the first Arabic Linotype machine.[2] Although the impetus to adapt Arabic to machine composition came from the Arab diaspora in the United States, over the following forty years increased publishing activity in the Middle East created the greatest demand for Arabic typesetting equipment there. This shift in the centre of gravity of Arabic typography reflects far larger changes in the geopolitical fortunes of the Middle East. Two world wars had shaken the European powers and the order they, in turn, had imposed on large parts of the world. In the aftermath of the Second World War and with the emergence of the United States and the Soviet Union as superpowers, European colonial power was eroding. The war had been costly for the United Kingdom and France especially, and throughout their territories they were compelled to give way to increasingly articulate national aspirations voiced by those they governed. The Middle East was fundamentally affected by this changing world order. There the retreating colonial powers left a fragmented region where often artificially defined entities struggled to become nation states on a European model. But the outcome was nevertheless comprehensive: between the withdrawal of French troops from Lebanon and Syria in 1946 and the end of France's war in Algeria in 1962, all the former French and British colonies and protectorates in the Middle East had gained their independence.

1. Two items of terminology need clarification at the outset. First, although the Arabic script is used for languages other than Arabic, this essay refers only to circumstances in which script and language are both Arabic. The second item involves references to companies named 'Linotype'. Linotype & Machinery Ltd, located in the United Kingdom, operated largely independently of the Mergenthaler Linotype Company, located in the United States. For convenience, Linotype & Machinery will be referred to below as 'Linotype', and Mergenthaler Linotype as 'Mergenthaler'.

2. Date from Mergenthaler Linotype Company (1929), p. 4. According to this type specimen, Salloum Mokarzel, editor of *al-Hoda* (The Guidance), a newspaper in Brooklyn, New York, was instrumental in the work of adapting Arabic to the Linotype and the development of the first series of Arabic founts by Mergenthaler.

Later sources suggest that this work was completed by 1910 or 1912, with the installation of the adapted Linotype at the newspaper; see Mokarzel (1968), p. 1, and Anon. (1948). The date of the first edition of *al-Hoda* to be composed on the Linotype has not yet been determined.

These postwar circumstances in the Middle East provided the context for changes in the sphere of typography. The transformation of colonies and protectorates into nation states presented new opportunities to the manufacturers of typesetting equipment. Nationalist sentiments increased the demand for publications printed in local scripts and languages. And with independence and late industrialization came greater demands for printing and typesetting equipment to support growing volumes of communication. To meet the demand, and without indigenous industries to support them, printers and publishers in the Middle East looked to the former colonial powers to supply what they required. The makers of typesetting equipment, principally Linotype and its competitors Monotype and Intertype, sensed both the urgency of the situation and the opportunity, and directed unprecedented levels of resource towards this growing market.[3]

Kamel Mrowa and *al-Hayat*

Simplified Arabic is located in the early phase of these postwar developments. The origins of the typeface can be traced to 1954 when Kamel Mrowa, a Shiah Muslim, asked Linotype to produce a new typeface for the Lebanese daily newspaper *al-Hayat* (figure 1). Mrowa was the owner and editor-in-chief of *al-Hayat*, which he had founded in 1946, the year of Lebanon's independence. The newspaper typified the entrepreneurialism of Lebanon's early years, as the country developed into one of the Middle East's economic hubs, with Beirut an important Arab capital. Lebanon's advantageous geographic position had fostered a long mercantile tradition, attracting foreign investment and turning the country into one of the most prosperous in the region after the war; its literacy rate, the highest in the Arab world, testified to the country's wealth and its place as a centre of Middle East publishing.[4] On-going development in the 1950s, encouraged by liberal economic policies, made Lebanon a fertile ground for business.[5]

Against this background, Mrowa approached Linotype with a proposal for a new Arabic typeface. In a meeting with the Linotype representative Herbert Ellis, Mrowa 'described with enthusiasm the satisfactory and simple form of Arabic script available from a German typewriter he is acquainted with. Mr. Mrowa's belief is that the principle embodied in it could be applied to Linotype composition'[6] (figure 2). This scheme of simplification was based on a reduction of those letterforms required to produce the joined appearance of

Figure 1. Kamel Mrowa, probably in 1966.

Figure 2. Keyboard layout of the German Continental typewriter sent by Mrowa to Linotype. The date stamp of 'Oct 1953' may indicate that Kamel Mrowa approached Linotype that year. 29.2 × 20.5 cm.

3. Sebastian Carter writes that after 1945, Monotype devoted 'a large amount of manufacturing capacity … to cutting non-Latin faces for the newly independent countries of the British Commonwealth', by implication impeding the development of Latin typefaces. See Carter (1997), p. 23.

4. For historical accounts see Ayalon (1995) and Hanebütt-Benz, Glass, and Roper (2002).

5. David Gilmour, *Lebanon: the fractured country*, 2nd rev. edn, 1987, London: Sphere Books.

6. Letter from Walter Tracy to Jackson Burke, 'Arabic', September 17, 1954, 1, box P3640, Mergenthaler Linotype Company Records, 1905–1993, Archives Center, National Museum of American History (hereafter 'MLCR Washington DC'). Tracy is quoting information that Ellis had gathered and passed on to him.

Figure 3. Comparison of Arabic fount extent.

(a) Case arrangement of an Arabic fount containing 470 characters, as used by the Egyptian Government Press in the early twentieth century.

(b) Notional case arrangement of the first Linotype Arabic fount; characters without a direct equivalent to those shown in (a) are placed in the box at lower left. The reduction from 470 to 181 characters is achieved mainly through the removal of ligatures.

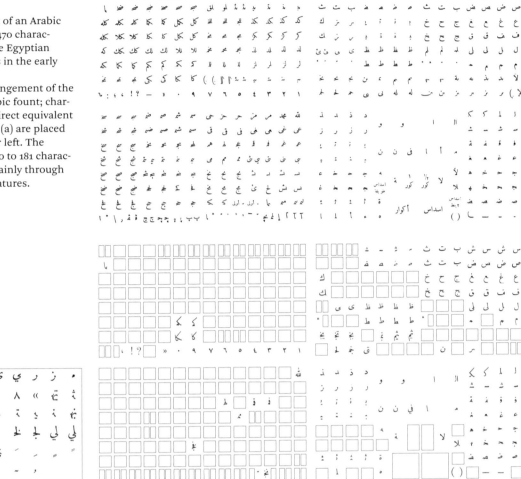

Arabic;[7] broadly speaking, where typographic founts employed a minimum of four shapes for such letters, the typewriter had only two. A typical typewriter character set thus consisted of only 90 characters, including punctuation and figures. Typewriters based on this scheme had been in use for decades,[8] and despite the simplified appearance of their founts, the text they produced had proved acceptable for certain kinds of documents, such as business correspondence and accounts. But for other, typeset, documents any equivalent to a typewriter's simplification of Arabic would have appeared too unconventional[9] (figure 3). Mrowa, however, had exactly this in mind. The simplification he was proposing, which would reduce the number of characters to the 90 available on the typewriter, was intended to increase composition speeds while producing text that was still aesthetically acceptable to a typical newspaper readership. His aim was a pragmatic solution that could be implemented within the constraints of typesetting machines but without upsetting reading habits too dramatically.

7. Of the 28 letters in the Arabic script, all but six are written in joined sequences and therefore require multiple forms depending on their position within a word. The six remaining letters cannot join the following letters, thus creating breaks within the otherwise joined words.

8. There are various claims to the invention of an Arabic typewriter; early evidence includes a patent secured by the Hammond Type-writer Company: 'Improvements in Type-writers', UK patent no. 10,460, 22 June 1901.

9. An approximate analogy in the context of Latin script might, for example, be the use of only capital letters to typeset literary texts. It is important to note the extent to which the typewriter simplified the character set of the Arabic script: Arabic typefaces for hand composition often had up to 470 characters; existing

Arabic typefaces for Linotype composition reduced this number to 180 (the capacity of a Linotype machine fitted with an auxiliary magazine), thereby

profoundly altering the appearance of Arabic (see figure 3); typewriter schemes reduced the number of characters by half again.

Simplified Arabic: proof of concept

When Kamel Mrowa proposed the simplification concept to Linotype, its typographic adviser, Walter Tracy, had been with the company for seven years. Tracy's role was to assess the commercial viability and likely success of new typeface projects. By the 1950s, Linotype (rather than Mergenthaler) handled all machinery and equipment sales and servicing contracts in the Middle East, thus Mrowa's proposal came under Tracy's scrutiny.[10] Tracy's interest and support for simplifying Arabic is evident in his correspondence with Jackson Burke, director of typographic development at Mergenthaler. In a letter of early September 1954 describing Mrowa's proposal, Tracy reasoned:

> To wonder why something of this sort was not done long ago is to conclude that the importance of calligraphy as an Arab [*sic*] art, the complicated nature of a running script, and the necessary 'pointing', have made typefounders anxious to provide printers with everything necessary for acceptance by critical readers, regardless of expense. Mechanical composition is comparatively recent in this field; its 'limitations' are still in process of gaining acceptance (though they could probably be turned to definite advantage if prejudices can be removed).[11]

Tracy then outlined Linotype's plan to develop a trial design 'closely based on our 14-pt double-letter Arabic face' and photographically compose a specimen to assess the interest of potential customers.[12] Mergenthaler's reaction was muted: in an internal memorandum, Chauncey Griffith, Mergenthaler's former director of typographic development, discouraged attempts at *further* simplification of Arabic (i.e. beyond that which had already been implemented in existing typefaces for the Linotype), claiming that it was 'exceedingly difficult, if not impossible, to overcome the inherent prejudice of Arabic thought respecting any material form in the traditional Arabic script'.[13] Griffith's assessment was likely a reflection of Mergenthaler's experience with its customers who used Arabic typefaces in the USA, mainly small, immigrant newspapers and academic publishers. Where Mrowa primarily needed faster composition speeds for a large and growing newspaper, the Arabic press in the USA probably valued the authenticity of conventional Arabic typesetting. For the academic publishers, linguistic precision was a priority, something simplification could not achieve; and in any case, given their small print runs, they would have little to gain from increases in efficiency. For both press and publishers, a simplified Arabic typeface for the Linotype would have held little value.

Despite the doubts raised by Griffiths, Tracy went ahead with the project, as instigated by Mrowa.[14] As mentioned, Mrowa's proposed simplification scheme was tailored to the requirements of a standard

10. Mergenthaler had earlier dealt with Arabic typeface developments, but ceded this responsibility to Linotype in the 1940s.

11. Letter from Walter Tracy to Jackson Burke, 'Arabic', September 3, 1954, p. 2, box P3640, MLCR Washington DC.

12. Letter from Tracy to Burke, 'Arabic', September 3, 1954, p. 3. In the same letter, Tracy also remarked that 'if it came to the point of making a new Arabic fount according to a simplified scheme, I think we should give thought to the creation of a type face which would meet with greater approval than L & M's present series – widely used though it is', indicating Tracy's assessment that high levels of use did not necessarily equate to popularity, only limited choice.

13. Internal memorandum from Chauncey Griffith to Jackson Burke, 'Re: Arabic L. & M. letter of September 3, 1954', September 14, 1954, p. 2, box P3640, MLCR Washington DC.

14. That the drive for Arabic simplification originated in Lebanon rather than in Europe or North America is worth emphasizing. Any notion that compromises in the printed appearance of Arabic were the result of colonial arrogance does not therefore seem tenable. At the same time, the origin in Lebanon of efforts to simplify Arabic may stem in part from the country's historic ties to French and US schools and universities, where many in Lebanon's middle and upper classes were (and continue to be) educated. Western ideas of progress and modernity associated with technological advance encountered in such contexts may have contributed to a readiness to accept the expedience of script simplification for the sake of economic advantage; this would not have been the case in other Arabic countries.

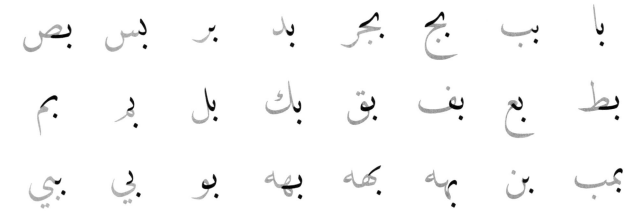

Figure 4. Forms of ب (bā') in different contexts. Typeset in Tasmeem Naskh (DecoType), a typographic model of Ottoman calligraphic practice.

Figure 5. Arabic Series 2 with 3, five characters available for ب (bā'), from an undated specimen, Linotype.

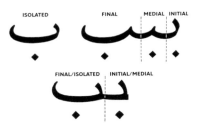

Figure 6. Simplification principle of ب (bā'), detail from a Linotype promotional brochure, 1960/1, reduced.

Linotype, with a single keyboard and without a side magazine.[15] The fount would be restricted to 90 characters, to fit a 90-button keyboard arrangement and the corresponding 90-channel magazine. The character set therefore was determined by the mechanics of the machine, and the design of the typeface would reflect these constraints. Fitting the Arabic alphabet to the limited character set was achieved mainly by assigning multiple roles to single characters. The approach is well illustrated by the character ب (bā'). In its manuscript form, ب is given numerous context-dependent shapes (figure 4). In its typographic form, the number of different shapes of the letter is significantly reduced. One of Linotype's existing Arabic typefaces, for example, employed five characters for ب (figure 5). But Mrowa's scheme would take this further, employing a mere two shapes to render ب in all contexts (figure 6). Similar reductions were applied to the other letters, but to differing degrees and in Tracy's words only 'where this can be done without undue distortion of traditional shapes'.[16] The result was a fount streamlined from 102 to 69 alphabetic characters.[17] (The remaining 21 characters would consist of figures, punctuation, and spaces.)

Although this basic approach to a simplified Arabic typeface was in place in 1954, progress on the project at Linotype was subsequently sluggish. Eventually, in April 1957, an impatient Mrowa accused Linotype of neglecting the project.[18] To push it toward completion, Mrowa sent his staff calligrapher Nabih Jaroudi to the Linotype office in London.[19] During some two weeks of apparently concentrated effort, Jaroudi revised and corrected Linotype's work on the typeface. A proof of 69 characters in regular and bold weights shows the

15. For discussions of linecaster mechanics and their influence on type design and typesetting, see Legros and Grant (1916), Seybold (1984), and Southall (2005).

16. Letter from Walter Tracy to Dawood, January 30, 1964, Walter Tracy correspondence cabinet, folder 18b, Non-Latin Type Collection, Department of Typography & Graphic Communication, University of

Reading (hereafter NLTC Reading).

17. Some of these characters were half-forms, which only produced a meaningful letterform in combination with other characters.

18. During this time, Tracy collected material and pursued his research into Arabic (although he did not learn the language); Tracy (1995), p. 13.

19. Letter from Walter Tracy to Jackson

Burke, 'Simplified Arabic', April 12, 1957, Box P3640, MLCR Washington DC. A 'staff calligrapher' in this context would be a lettering artist who created the large headlines for the daily editions of a newspaper. The skills required were different to those of a traditionally trained calligrapher whose work might be described as more artistic in approach.

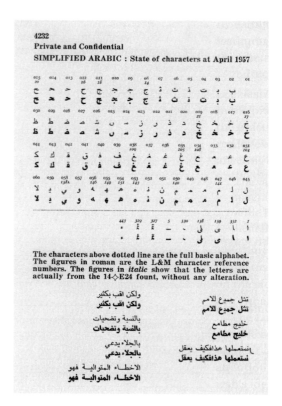

Figure 7. Proof of the 12D size under development, Linotype, April 1957, 25 × 13 cm.

Figure 8. Detail of front page of *al-Hayat*, 13 December 1957, reduced to 66% linear. This is the first known use of a trial version of Simplified Arabic. The type in the decorated frame is the Intertype fount used at this time by *al-Hayat*.

20. Until the introduction of Simplified Arabic, Linotype's founts were assigned a series number but not given a proper name. 'Arabic 2 with 3' describes a duplexed typeface whose regular and bold weights were struck into the same matrices. Individual founts were described by a code denoting point size, depth of strike, and series. The code 14◇E24, for example, denoted a 14-pt Anglo-American type size (14), struck to 'English' depth (◇), in series E24. A capital D following the point size denoted a type size in Didot points; a triangle instead of the diamond denoted matrices struck to 'US' depth.

21. Walter Tracy, '25th April 1957 et seq: Discussion with Nabih Jaroudi on Simplified Arabic, Commentary on Characters as at April 1957', April 25, 1957, Walter Tracy correspondence cabinet, folder 18b, NLTC Reading.

22. It seems very likely that Linotype's interest in developing a simplified Arabic typeface with Mrowa for *al-Hayat* would have been partly encouraged by the prospect of taking over one of Intertype Corporation's customers. Selling machines to a newspaper usually meant securing it as the client for many years, assuring further sales of equipment, servicing contracts, spare parts, and the replacement of matrices.

simplified design at this time (figure 7), based on the 14-pt size of Linotype's existing typeface 'Arabic 2 with 3'.[20] Jaroudi's remarks on the work, recorded in an internal memo, include instructions for the design of characters, their approval or rejection, and advice about the character set.[21] The remarks in particular address design flaws Jaroudi observed in specific characters, such as the oddly sized diacritic dots on characters of ب (bā') and the unsatisfactory shaping of the head of ح (ḥā') in its isolated and final positions.

Linotype revised the design accordingly, and by late 1957 had produced a trial set of matrices for use by *al-Hayat*. On 13 December, the newspaper's front page featured a column of text set in the new typeface (figure 8). This earliest surviving instance of its use is telling, as it shows the design next to the paper's existing typeface manufactured by Linotype's main competitor, Intertype.[22] The Linotype design appears distinctly linear, an effect achieved by minimising curves along its connecting baseline. The result gives a sense of characters connecting and aligning precisely even when the typeface is printed onto absorbent newsprint paper. By contrast, the Intertype typeface has slightly rounded or sagging connections, an unfavourable effect made worse by frequent gaps within letter-groups that interrupt the intended impression of single fused shapes.

But despite these advantages in appearance, several issues can also be observed in this trial. One is the use of a character shape for the ligature لا (lām alif) in all contexts. This produces atypical

Figure 9. Mrowa-Linotype Simplified Arabic, announcement of release, *Linotype Matrix*, 32, November 1959, p. 5 (detail), reduced to 50% linear.

LINOTYPE ARE FIRST IN THE WORLD TO PRODUCE A SYSTEM OF

Simplified Arabic

FOR MECHANICAL COMPOSITION FROM ONE MAGAZINE

THE Arabic script is second only to roman in modern usage; something like one-sixth of the world's people speak languages which are written or printed in Arabic characters. Not all of them are literate; but the development of education is improving the standards of literacy and increasing the demand for printed matter of every kind.

The Arabic alphabet derives from one of the branches of the ancient Semitic alphabet, and is therefore related to Hebrew, Syriac, Ethiopian, and even Greek; there are distinct similarities in the names of some letters in those alphabets, and like Hebrew (and the earliest Greek) Arabic is written from right to left. The Arabic alphabet achieved a distinctive form during the fourth century A.D., but the letters changed their form during the succeeding three hundred years—that is, during the great period of Islamic expansion and scholarship. The script is a particular example of the dictum that 'alphabet follows religion'; it has been adapted to a variety of languages—Persian, Urdu, Malay, some languages of the Polynesian islands, and some in Africa such as Swahili, Sudanese and others.

Like Hebrew, and many Eastern scripts, there is only one basic form of each letter in the Arabic alphabet; that is to say, there are no capitals as in the Latin and Greek alphabets. And a further similarity is that the alphabet is consonantal—the vowel sounds are indicated by signs written over or under the letters, the signs being omitted ('taken as read') in all but educational, religious or classical work.

Calligraphy is an important art amongst Islamic people. The manuscript books by Arabic and Persian artists of the great periods are astonishing to see—the pages an intricate pattern of inscription and decoration, richly gilded and coloured, the text written with evident pleasure in the sensuous freedom of the cursive letter-forms.

Admiration for calligraphy as an art, and the religious significance of it, have prevented the script from attaining one of the chief characteristics of the *printed* roman letter as distinct from the written—the formalising of the letter forms into separate entities. Printed Arabic has had to retain the cursive nature of calligraphy and the flourished final and isolated forms of letters as well as their initial and medial forms. This is rather as if we did all our composition in a joined script and had four kinds of *e*—one for the beginning of the word, one to be used between other letters, another, without a joint-

In the diagram above the first line shows the four forms of the letter ba *in traditional Arabic typography. The second line shows how the four forms of the letter in Mrowa-Linotype Simplified Arabic serve the same functions. Below is a specimen of the new system.*

stroke, when the letter stands on its own, and a swash form for the end of a word—like this:

The effect of this is that, though there are only 28 letters in the alphabet and there are no capitals as in roman or Greek, the printer has to have 104 alphabet characters (four forms of 22 letters and two forms of six) — as well as figures, punctuations, ligatures and signs. This is not an unusually complicated fount—the full Greek fount contains about 180 characters, and most Indian scripts need even more—but it does have a limiting effect on the amount of work accomplished by a compositor or operator in a given time. So it is not surprising that various attempts have been made in recent years to gain economic and productive advantages in printing and publishing by reducing the number of characters in the fount.

Some of these reforms have depended on separating the letters in the word (as in roman composition) thus departing from the cursive tradition. Others have relied on the elimination of the flourished forms, or have reduced them to a standardised appendix. In such reforms the visual result, though intelligible, may be unfamiliar or unattractive; certainly a considerable amount of tolerance is demanded from the reader.

The Mrowa patented system now to be described avoids these hazards.

The system is the outcome of close co-operation between Linotype and Mr Kamel Mrowa, proprietor of 'Dar Al-Hayat' (*The Daily Star*), one of the principal newspapers in Lebanon. His appreciation of the aesthetics of the Arabic script and his grasp of the problems of mechanical composition were invaluable to Linotype in the evolution of the new system.

In the Mrowa system the letters which normally have four forms have been re-designed in two forms—where this can be done without undue distortion of traditional shapes. Similarly, the letters which normally have two forms now have one form only. The result is that the total number of alphabet characters is reduced from 104 to 56.

For Linotype users (and there are very many in the Arab world) the system has tremendous advantages. It means that all the frequent characters—the alphabet, the figures, punctuations, some necessary 'pointed' letters and ligatures—can be contained in one 90-channel magazine instead of the main-and-side-magazines necessary for traditional composition.

The significance of this is obvious. The printer's initial equipment costs are reduced. The operator has an easier keyboard to learn and his output of work is increased. The reader of a newspaper or journal set in Mrowa-Linotype Simplified Arabic finds it no more different from the normal than italic is different from roman. That is to say, there is a *stylistic* difference, but no distortions; letters such as these

which would require considerable alteration if simplified, have been retained in their familiar variety of shapes.

Mrowa-Linotype Simplified Arabic is the result of long study and experiment by Mr Mrowa, the originator, and Linotype & Machinery Ltd. In the columns of 'Dar Al-Hayat' the system has proved notably advantageous in the composing room and entirely satisfactory to readers. It strikes a happy balance between the need for speed and economy on the one hand and the preservation of traditional typographic forms on the other. It is therefore evolutionary rather than revolutionary.

The system is a tribute to the judgment and enterprise of Mr Mrowa and to the typographic resources of Linotype; and it is of the greatest potential benefit to the whole Arab world.

---

word-shapes, analogous to using a Latin uppercase letter in the middle of a word set in lowercase (see, for example, the first word in the headline للاستاذ, li l-ustāḏi, 'for the professor'). Another is this character's pronounced inclination (also found in ل (lām)) that combines unpleasantly with the more upright, isolated ا (alif) with which it is frequently paired. A third issue are the spelling errors found in the text as typeset, possibly related to the new fount scheme that required the composition of individual letters using two successive keystrokes.[23]

Following its trial in *al-Hayat*, work on the typeface continued at Linotype for another two years. Then, in November 1959, in *Linotype Matrix*, the new typeface was finally announced as the 'Mrowa-Linotype Simplified Arabic' (figure 9). An accompanying article highlighted Kamel Mrowa's central role in the project:

> The system is the outcome of close co-operation between Linotype and Mr Kamel Mrowa, proprietor of 'Dar Al-Hayat' ..., one of the principal newspapers in Lebanon. His appreciation of the aesthetics of the Arabic script and his grasp of the problems of mechanical composition were invaluable to Linotype in the evolution of the new system.[24]

In announcing their new typeface, Linotype emphasized the practical advantages of Simplified Arabic. Among these were a greater ease both in learning its keyboard layout and in the actual keying of copy, which contributed to faster composition.[25] These advantages were important selling points in the newspaper industry where production speed and efficiency were crucial. Additionally, the Simplified Arabic scheme allowed the operation of Arabic linecasters to be controlled by coded paper-tape for the first time, resulting in the potential for another three-fold increase in composing speed.[26] Together with these productivity gains, Simplified Arabic also cost

23. See for example the first word of the column احسن (aḥsan; better, best), which lacks a tooth between the medial and final character.

24. Linotype & Machinery Ltd (1959), p. 5.

25. In tests conducted at *al-Hayat* in 1958, a 30 per cent improvement in composing speeds was reported by the newspaper's Linotype operators, and it was speculated that this might increase to as much as 50 per cent once they became better acquainted with the new keyboard layout. Letter from Walter Tracy to Jackson Burke, 'Simplified Arabic', January 13, 1958, box P3640, MLCR Washington DC.

26. 'Teletypesetting' (TTS), in which a paper-tape was coded remotely before being transmitted through wire services and reconstituted by a receiver, eliminated the need to re-key text. Although the most efficient use of TTS required news agencies to provide text already in coded form, agencies in the Middle East rarely did this. However, the technology was used in-house by newspapers in the region to improve their workflows (for example by creating coded tapes to drive multiple composing machines simultaneously).

Figure 10. 'Mrowa Simplified Arabic'
[*sic*], *Linotype Matrix*, 33, May 1960,
cover (detail), reduced to 66% linear.
See also note 31.

CALEDONIA
a brilliant book face
from America

W. A. *Dwiggins*: A type face is good if it is easy to read. No concession that interferes with ease of reading may be made either to beauty of appearance or to mechanical felicity. Legibility is the basic law, the *sine qua* non.
Legibility is helped by keeping the shapes of the characters distinct one from another—so that one easily tells an 'e' from a 'c', etc. Obscurity is the penalty of forcing the characters to fit a too restricted range of body sizes.

Minerva with *italic* and **bold**
a classical display face designed by Reynolds Stone

GOTHIC CONDENSED 25
for news headlines

MROWA SIMPLIFIED ARABIC

لقد حازت طريقة صف الأحرف بالاينوتيب على ثقة الآلاف من اصحاب المطـابع

لقد حازت طريقة صف الأحرف بالاينوتيب على ثقة الآلاف من اصحاب المطـابع

JUBILEE
created especially
for newspaper texts

Jubilee is the first original newspaper text face to have been designed in Great Britain for twenty-three years. Combining practical and æsthetic virtues it stands midway between *Times* and *Excelsior*. It meets the requirements of dry-flong stereotyping and high-speed rotary machining by being as open and sturdy as *Excelsior* and as big on its body. But in setwidth it has almost the same economy as *Times*. Its serifs are blunt but not square.

JULIANA
warmly welcomed
by the
publishing world

The addition of *Juliana* to the type face range marks a further step in Linotype's programme of typographic development. The increasing use of the Linotype system of composition in book production revealed the need for a text type of sixteenth-century Italian character. *Juliana* meets that need—very satisfactorily, too, to judge by the favourable comments of many people who know a good type when they see one. A number of leading printers now have founts of *Juliana*, and it has proved its worth in normal conditions of book production.

BASKERVILLE
Bold and *bold italic* make it even more useful and versatile

PILGRIM : an Eric Gill design

In its general appearance *Pilgrim* is very close to Gill's *Joanna* type, which was made for the Hague & Gill press and in which his *Essay on Typography* was composed. From the study of *Pilgrim* in mass it can be seen that the face is even in colour, with no letter asserting itself against others by reason of awkward design or uneven distribution of weight. The shading in round sorts is vertical; thick and thin strokes are not strongly contrasted; and the capitals are about the same weight as the lower-case.

ADSANS
sans-serif clarity
for small
advertisements

[classified advertisement column, small print]

27. Wear and tear on matrices inside the Linotype linecaster meant that they had to be replaced regularly, resulting in on-going costs for users. Income from the supply and replacement of matrices was an important part of the business models developed by typesetting machine manufacturers.

28. Linotype & Machinery Ltd (1959), p. 5; quotes in the following sentence are also from this source. Two letters to which this applied were ح (hā') and ع ('ayn). Later, ح was simplified; see discussion below.

29. No similar statements are found in earlier articles about Arabic Linotype composition; cf. Linotype & Machinery Ltd (1955), p. 2.

30. Linotype & Machinery Ltd (1959), p. 5.

31. The two lines of Arabic on the cover nevertheless both contain errors in the spelling of 'Linotype'. Notably, too, 'Linotype' has been left out of the typeface name, which is instead rendered 'Mrowa Simplified Arabic'.

less to purchase since it required significantly fewer matrices than other Arabic typefaces.[27]

Apart from the practical and economic advantages Linotype claimed for Simplified Arabic, the article in the *Linotype Matrix* also asserted that 'a reader of a newspaper or journal set in Mrowa-Linotype Simplified Arabic finds it no more different from the normal than italic is different from roman'. Linotype backed up the assertion by pointing out that some characters 'that would require considerable alteration if simplified, have been retained in their familiar variety of shapes'.[28] Customers were assured that the new type would be 'entirely satisfactory to readers' as it 'strikes a happy balance between the need for speed and economy on the one hand and the preservation of traditional typographic forms on the other. It is therefore evolutionary rather than revolutionary.' These statements suggest a perception at Linotype that their new typeface required some explanation because the simplified principle was so far-reaching as to be potentially unsettling.[29] Tracy, probably the author of the article, may not at this point have felt sufficiently well-informed about Arabic typography to justify the radical approach of the new system with full confidence. Instead, responsibility for it is effectively delegated to Mrowa, with Linotype merely providing the infrastructure:

> The system is a tribute to the judgment and enterprise of Mr Mrowa and to the typographic resources of Linotype; and it is of the greatest potential benefit to the whole Arab world.[30]

It may be conjectured that the conspicuous credit given to Mrowa was prompted by a degree of caution on the part of Linotype to embrace the new typeface. But if the company was exercising caution, it was wholly unnecessary in light of the typeface's subsequent success. By the next issue of *Linotype Matrix*, in May 1960, Simplified Arabic featured prominently on the cover as one of the 'New faces of the 50s' and exemplary of Linotype's innovation in type design (figure 10).[31] The company's increased confidence in the new design is

Figure 11. Mrowa-Linotype Simplified
Arabic, proof specimen of three additional sizes, as reproduced in the
Linotype Matrix, 34, December 1960,
p. 2, actual size.

لقد أجمع القائمون على شؤون الطباعة بان طريقة اللينوتيب هي أسرع الوسائل لجمع الحروف.
وقد خلف اختراعها منذ سبعين عاما تغييرا شاملا في دور الطباعة في أكثر من نصف العالم،
لقد أجمع القائمون على شؤون الطباعة بأن طريقة اللينوتيب هي أسرع الوسائل لجمع الحروف.
وقد خلف اختراعها منذ سبعين عاما تغييرا شاملا في دور الطباعة في أكثر من نصف العالم،

10◇E26   Casts on 9-pt Didot

لقد أجمع القائمون على شؤون الطباعة بأن طريقة اللينوتيب هي أسرع
الوسائل لجمع الحروف. وقد خلف اختراعها منذ سبعين عاما تغييرا شاملا
في دور الطباعة في أكثر من نصف العالم، ولا يزال هذا التطور مستمرا في
لقد أجمع القائمون على شؤون الطباعة بأن طريقة اللينوتيب هي أسرع
الوسائل لجمع الحروف. وقد خلف اختراعها منذ سبعين عاما تغييرا شاملا
في دور الطباعة في أكثر من نصف العالم، ولا يزال هذا التطور مستمرا في

14◇E24   Casts on 12-pt Didot

لقد أجمع القائمون على شؤون الطباعة بأن طريقة
اللينوتيب هي أسرع الوسائل لجمع الحروف. وقد
خلف اختراعها منذ سبعين عاما تغييرا شاملا في دور
لقد أجمع القائمون على شؤون الطباعة بأن طريقة
اللينوتيب هي أسرع الوسائل لجمع الحروف. وقد
خلف اختراعها منذ سبعين عاما تغييرا شاملا في دور

18D◇E95   Casts on 18-pt Didot

also demonstrated by the rapid addition of sizes: by December 1960,
10D and 18D founts were available for purchase. The additions were
publicized in *Linotype Matrix*, 34 (figure 11), which noted the 'remarkable success' that Simplified Arabic had achieved 'in the short period
since it was announced.'[32] The release of Mrowa-Linotype Simplified
Arabic, Series 2 with 3,[33] marks the start of a new position of influence Linotype would assume in Arabic typography.

Intertype Abridged Arabic

Soon after Simplified Arabic's entry into the market and its evident
early success, Linotype's competitor, the Intertype Corporation,
began to develop a simplified Arabic typeface of its own. Like
Linotype, Intertype manufactured machines for hot metal type composition.[34] The mechanics of the Intertype linecaster were notably
based on those of the Linotype and its introduction in 1913 soon after
the expiry of Mergenthaler's patents was not coincidental. But the
Intertype also incorporated improvements on its Linotype rival, as
its construction was informed by 'research into the principal defects
and most troublesome features of extant linecasters'. After a difficult
start, the Intertype eventually became a formidable competitor to
the Linotype and by 1957 some 27,000 had been sold.[35]

32. Linotype & Machinery Ltd (1960),
p. 2. The twelve month production time
for the two additional weights seems
quick, given that type development and
the manufacture of matrix founts were
often slowed by the production capacity
of the Linotype works.

33. The addition of 'Series 2 with 3' to
the 'Mrowa-Linotype Simplified Arabic'

name is in reference to the earlier typeface it was based on.

34. The Intertype Corporation was
founded in 1911 as the International
Typesetting Machine Company; see
Wallis (1988), p. 10. The quote that follows
is from this source.

35. Seybold (1984), p. 41. Seybold additionally estimates that 'Intertype's sales

from 1950 on seem to have equalled or
exceeded those of Mergenthaler. In 1956,
for example, Intertype shipped 1,150
units' (p. 41). Wallis states that Intertype
was only able to secure its position in the
market in 1918, helped by an order for
31 linecasters from *The New York Times*;
see Wallis (1988), p. 12.

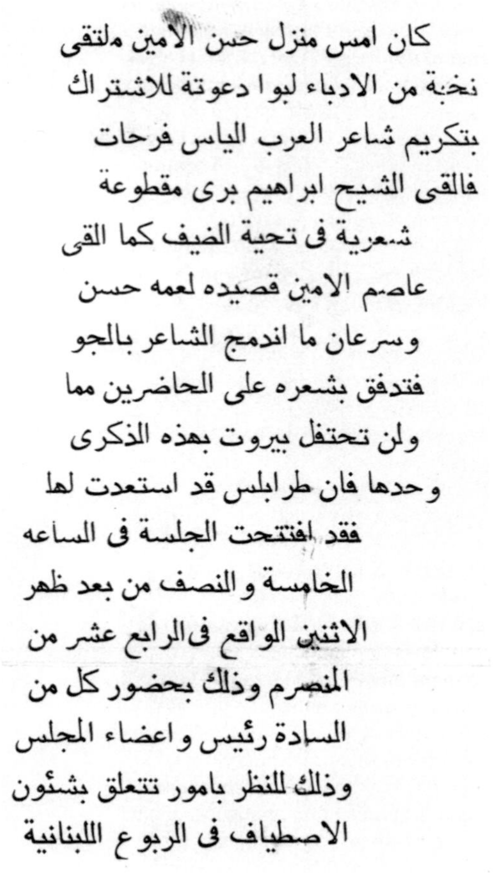

كان امس منزل حسن الامين ملتقى
نخبة من الادباء لبوا دعوتة للاشتراك
بتكريم شاعر العرب الياس فرحات
فالقى الشيخ ابراهيم برى مقطوعة
شعرية فى تحية الضيف كما القى
عاصم الامين قصيده لعمه حسن
وسرعان ما اندمج الشاعر بالجو
فتدفق بشعره على الحاضرين مما
ولن تحتفل بيروت بهذه الذكرى
وحدها فان طرابلس قد استعدت لها
فقد افتتحت الجلسة فى الساعه
الخامسة والنصف من بعد ظهر
الاثنين الواقع فىالرابع عشر من
المنصرم وذلك بحضور كل من
السادة رئيس واعضاء المجلس
وذلك للنظر بامور تتعلق بشئون
الاصطياف فى الربوع اللبنانية

Figure 12. Intertype Abridged Arabic, early proof of the fount under development, Harris-Intertype Ltd, 1960, actual size.

While Intertype's activities in Arabic typography are not well documented, the company had apparently established itself in the Middle East by the 1930s, and counted among its clients the prestigious Egyptian daily newspaper, *al-Ahram*.[36] By the 1950s, Mrowa's *al-Hayat* was also using Intertype machines. After the successful launch of Simplified Arabic, and possibly influenced by *al-Hayat*'s consequent shift to Linotype machines, competition between the two companies intensified. Thus in January 1960, only a few months after Simplified Arabic was made public, a proof of a trial Intertype design on a similar simplified basis was obtained by Walter Tracy (figure 12). Like Linotype, it appears that Intertype derived its design from an existing typeface in its inventory. But the design's overall appearance in proof is crude and is marred by composition errors probably related to the fount scheme adopted. Remnants of a strong horizontal baseline on the right side of numerous characters, retained for composition in medial positions, impede their use at the beginning of words (see, for example, ف (fāʾ) in figure 12, eighth line from top, first word) and increase the type's visual unevenness. For its character set, Intertype's design shows a number of differences from Linotype's Simplified Arabic: ه (hāʾ), for example, is represented by two rather than three distinct characters, omitting a dedicated character for medial positions (an omission that was later reinstated); لا (lām alif), by contrast, retains two distinct characters for isolated and final positions, where Linotype employs only one. Issues such as these show that despite copying a concept already established by Linotype, Intertype's design process was not without difficulties and did not at first produce a convincing result.

By June 1960, Intertype was able to provide its Middle Eastern customers with a more advanced specimen of a single size of their simplified typeface (16-pt), and announced a further three sizes in development (9-, 12-, and 18-pt)[37] (figure 13, opposite). The typeface shows improved alignment between characters and less noticeable right-hand joining strokes. A pronounced horizontality in the lines of text and the shapes of some characters such as د (dāl) suggest a move toward the Mrowa-Linotype design. But in the typeface finally released by Intertype, additional styling and character set features were incorporated that are distinctive and that indeed improve on Linotype's simplification scheme. Notably, Intertype reduced the

36. According to Hišām Baḥarī, a long-time employee of *al-Ahram*, the newspaper helped to develop Arabic Intertype machines and first introduced them in 1932; Baḥarī (1968), p. 138. The date is confirmed by a 1933 issue of the Intertype journal, *Interludes*: 'Intertypes equipped for Arabic composition are now being installed'. Intertype Ltd (1933), p. 9. *Al-Ahram*'s prestige initially derived from its status as one of the oldest Arabic dailies (founded in 1875). It attained particular political significance in the 1950s when Mohamed Hassanein Heikal, a well known journalist and friend of Gamal Abdel Nasser, became its editor-in-chief. Although *al-Ahram*

was government-aligned and played an important role in disseminating Nasser's ideology, Heikal is also credited for making *al-Ahram* the most objective and accurate source of political news in the Arab world during his tenure (1957–74).

37. This specimen was apparently obtained by Linotype surreptitiously through its agent Michael Nahas in Beirut, who explained in an accompanying letter: 'This only specimen copy was obtained from our friend mechanic, which should be returned back, as soon as possible, to the customer from whom he borrowed it'. Letter from Michael A. Nahas to Walter Tracy, June 7, 1960, Simplified Arabic box, NLTC Reading.

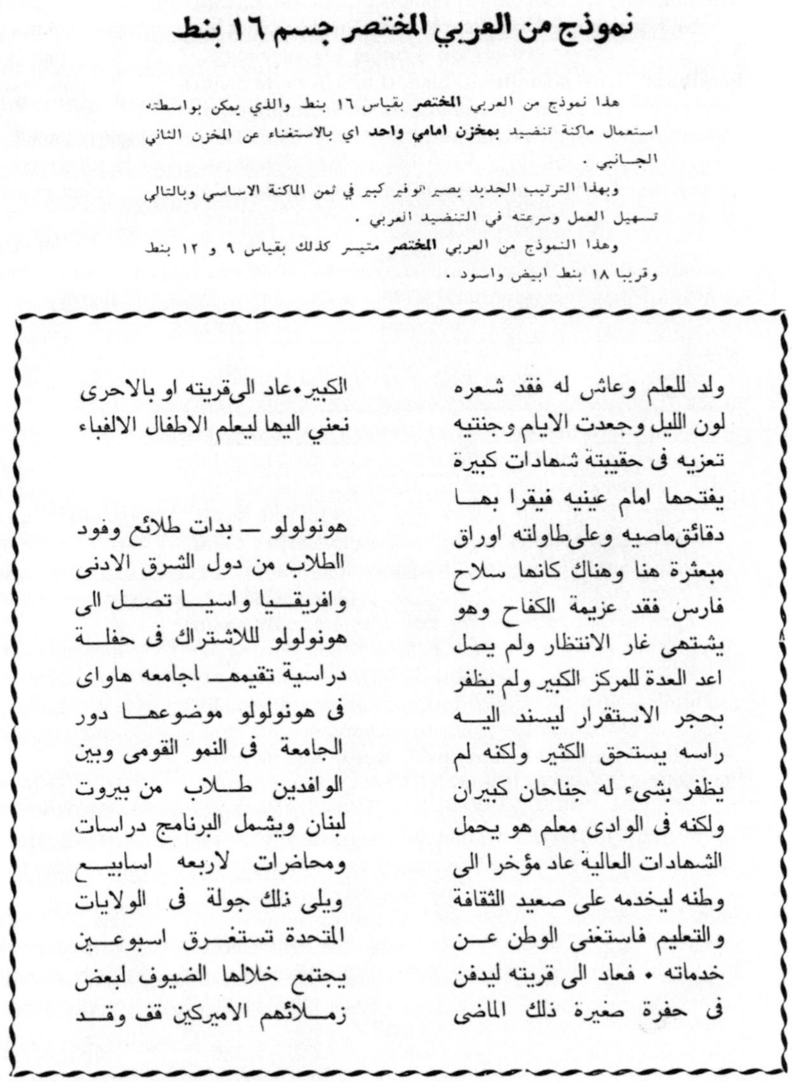

Figure 13. بنط ١٦ جسم المختصر العربي من نموذج (Namūḏaǧ min al-ʿarabiyy al-muḫtaṣar ǧism 16 bunṭ; *Sample of the Abridged Arabic 16-pt body*), advance specimen, Harris-Intertype Ltd, June 1960, reduced to 75% linear.

number of characters required for ح (ḥāʾ) to just one, for both initial and medial positions. The letterform devised for this purpose was better integrated stylistically than the trial version. The reduction of the ح characters also freed up positions in the magazine and on the keyboard for other characters. Among these were two for ي (yāʾ), in final and isolated positions whose inclusion helped bring words closer to their conventional shapes.

In the latter half of 1960 or sometime in 1961, the new design was released as 'Intertype Abridged Arabic' in four sizes[38] (figure 14, overleaf). And by the beginning of 1962, *al-Ahram* was using the typeface for large quantities of text (figure 15). In retrospect, the development of the Abridged Arabic can be seen as consistent with Intertype's

38. It has not been possible to establish a more precise release date.

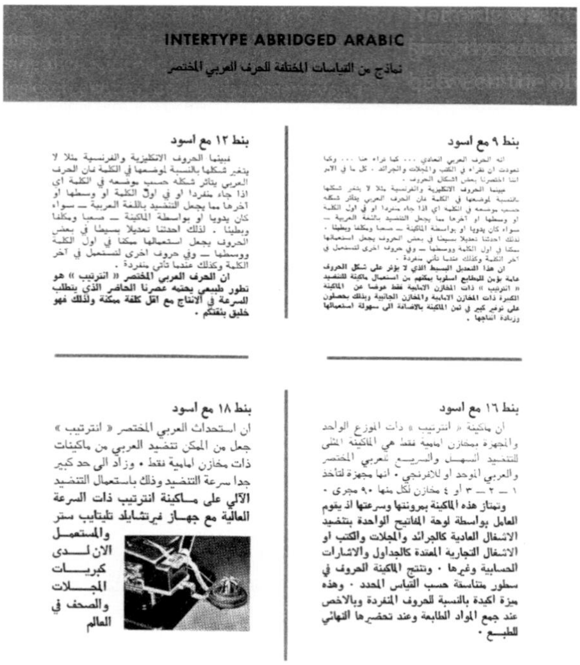

Figure 14. Intertype Abridged Arabic, specimen, undated, Harris-Intertype Ltd, p. 3, 28 × 21 cm.

Figure 15. Detail of *al-Ahram*, February 5, 1962, p. 1, reduced to 66% linear. This cutting from the newspaper shows the bold weight of Intertype Abridged Arabic alongside a larger size of Intertype's normal Arabic fount (opening paragraph), together with hand-lettered headlines.

policy of adapting competitors' typefaces, a policy that today might be considered unethical, and indeed competitors at the time found it objectionable.[39] But if Intertype Abridged Arabic was to a large extent based on the Mrowa-Linotype Simplified Arabic, it also brought new and different qualities to the simplification of Arabic that were recognized by Linotype as improvements.

A new design

Despite the substantial investment in research and development made by Linotype and Mrowa in Simplified Arabic, the patents reportedly registered for its simplification scheme, and Intertype's putative infringement of the system, no legal action was taken by Linotype.[40] While Linotype's resentment towards Intertype was apparently shared by others in the industry, the differences in Intertype's simplification scheme and in the design of the typeface

39. Reporting on the new Intertype Arabic typeface to C. A. Ainsworth, a member of Linotype's management, Walter Tracy was unambiguous in his characterization: 'It is obvious that the Intertype Abridged Arabic is substantially the same scheme as Linotype Simplified Arabic. In view of the fact that we have taken the trouble to apply for patents for our own scheme in a number of countries, it seems necessary to consider whether action should be taken against Intertype'. Letter from Walter Tracy to C. A. Ainsworth, July 5, 1960, Simplified Arabic box, NLTC Reading.

40. Linotype promotional material and business correspondence make reference to patents associated with Simplified Arabic, though no such patents have been located; cf. following note.

Figure 16. Mrowa-Linotype Simplified
Arabic Series 8 with 9, specimen (and
detail, at right) of 12D size, Linotype,
1962, 29.2 × 20.5 cm.

itself were apparently sufficient to make the success of a lawsuit for infringement too uncertain.[41]

At the time Intertype released its Abridged Arabic, Linotype had further sizes of Series 2 with 3 in development. This apparent commitment to the design would seem to make the prospect of an immediate successor unlikely. And yet Linotype embarked on exactly this course when it commissioned a new version of the Mrowa-Linotype Simplified Arabic from Nabih Jaroudi.[42] While there is no confirming evidence, the timing of the initiative suggests that it was in part prompted by the introduction of Intertype's Abridged Arabic.[43] Now, however, Linotype would pursue an entirely new design rather than adapt an existing typeface. Work on this new design progressed much faster than had been the case with its predecessor and by 1962 a first 12D size was ready. A specimen of the 'new design in Mrowa-Linotype Simplified Arabic' credited the typeface to Jaroudi, and announced that additional sizes were underway (figure 16).

Linotype's new design was linked to a new keyboard layout. A diagram dated September 1962 shows how the layout varied from its predecessor, and where characters had been added or repositioned (figure 17, overleaf). Ironically, the changes reflect exactly those improvements Intertype had introduced to their Abridged

41. In 1962, the Monotype Corporation approached Linotype to establish the reach of its patents, and to obtain permission to adopt the Simplified Arabic scheme to it composing machines. An internal Monotype memorandum quotes John Dreyfus, the company's typographical advisor: 'Intertype has stolen the system and have introduced one improvement into their version. To Tracy's regret Linotype decided not to go to law against Intertype over this piracy …. As a member of A. Type. I. [sic], I naturally cannot agree that it would be right for the Corporation to steal this patented system from Linotype. The fact that the system has been patented is proof of the fact that it is intrinsically worthy of protection. It would also be unseemly for the Corporation (as a member of A. Typ. I.) to infringe the Linotype Company's rights in this design, despite the fact that Intertype have done so'. Internal memorandum, 'Simplified Arabic (Mrowa-Linotype)', June 7, 1962, p. 1, correspondence folder Arabic (Egyptian 2), archives of the Monotype Drawing Office, Monotype, Ltd, Salfords, UK (hereafter 'MDO Salfords'). When the Monotype Corporation entered negotiations with Linotype to obtain the rights to copy the system of Simplified Arabic for use on their equipment, an internal company memorandum noted: 'We are satisfied that Linotype have taken over the patent rights from the inventor of the

system and we are negotiating with them regarding the cutting by us of a simplified Arabic.' Internal memorandum, 'Simplified Arabic, Mr D. Stevens letters BEY/41 and 43 of 31st May and 5th June', August 10, 1962, correspondence folder Arabic (Egyptian 2), MDO Salfords.

42. This new version would become known as 'Series 8 with 9'.

43. Recalling his work on Arabic typefaces, Walter Tracy makes no mention of a competitor, suggesting that the decision to revise the first Simplified Arabic was quality driven: 'There was a mixed reception [of the first version], and we were urged to hire a professional scribe to design a new face according to the simplified principle'. Tracy (1995), p. 13.

Figure 17. Keyboard layouts for
Mrowa-Linotype Simplified Arabic,
original (above) and revised (below),
Linotype, 1962. Keys marked (x) in
the revised layout (enlarged in boxes)
indicate character set changes copied
from Intertype's scheme.

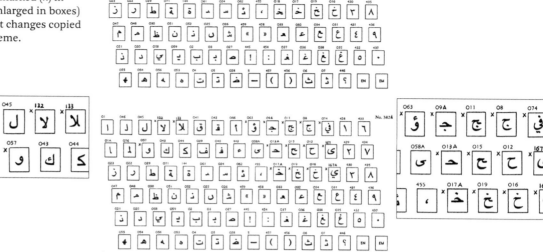

Arabic: for example, in lieu of four forms of ح (ḥāʾ), only three are
employed, allowing additional characters for ى (yāʾ) and ل (lām alif)
to be introduced. But overall, the new design benefitted a great deal
from being wholly conceived within the now well understood limitations that simplification placed on character set and composition
scheme. The design of the characters also changed: rounded and
curved elements were reduced in favour of sharper and more angular
ones, producing a more linear and even effect; text settings looked
streamlined and efficient – appropriately so for a newspaper. The new
typeface also benefitted from apparently improved manufacture that
resulted in precise alignments that minimized gaps between characters, giving the desired impression of fused letter groups.

In the succeeding years, additional sizes of the 'new design'
Mrowa-Linotype Simplified Arabic became available. A specimen
from 1963 showed founts in 9D and 10D; an 18D size followed in 1965,
and in 1966 a 7D fount. The continuous expansion of sizes indicates
that the typeface was indeed popular.[44] But if so, the road to popularity was not entirely straight. The profound differences in appearance
between Simplified Arabic and other Arabic typefaces that more
closely resembled manuscript letters, ensured that Arabic readers
would not embrace the concept of simplification universally. In a
letter of December 1969, some ten years after the introduction of
Simplified Arabic, Linotype's Middle East representative Ralph Goodman listed those places where the system had been accepted (Dubai,
Lebanon, Kuwait, Syria, Tunisia, Bahrain, Libya, Sudan, Aden, Egypt),
where Simplified Arabic founts had been sold but were not wholly
accepted (Algeria, Iraq, Saudi Arabia), and where Simplified Arabic
had 'not yet broken in' (Jordan, Morocco).[45] The factors Goodman
identified as crucial to the acceptance of Simplified Arabic were
pragmatic ones:

> Of course, where we have broken in, as with Tunisia a few years back,
> it is mainly for newspapers, and there is still some resistance to using

44. Walter Tracy claimed that it was
'amongst the most popular of all Arabic
types'. Tracy (1995), p. 13.

45. Letter from Ralph Goodman to
Barnard, December 10, 1969, p. 1, Walter
Tracy correspondence cabinet, folder 18a,
NLTC Reading; The following quote is also
from this source (p. 2).

Figure 18. Yakout, the typeface
formerly known as Mrowa-Linotype
Simplified Arabic, specimen,
Linotype, not dated, Arabic
language cover, 24.5 × 13 cm.

46. Ross (2002). The general commercial
printing market would include products
ranging from magazines to packaging.

47. For example, the founts of the first
version of Mrowa-Linotype Simplified
Arabic Series 2 with 3 were designated
10◊E26, 14◊E24, and 18D◊E95 for its 10D,
14D, and 18D sizes, respectively; for the
successor design, Series 8 with 9, the
designations were 7D◊G69, 9D◊G43,
10D◊G44, 11D◊G41, 14D◊G15, and 18D◊G48
for its range of sizes.

48. Linotype's Simplified Arabic is still
marketed as 'Yakout' today. Monotype
GmbH (2013). The change of name also
served to disguise the type's origins in
hot metal machine composition. The
adoption of the name Yakout for 'Series
8 with 9' and the discontinuation of
'Series 2 with 3' have both caused some
confusion about the history of Simplified
Arabic. Hrant Gabeyan was never credited by Linotype for conceiving the
name of one of the best selling and most
widely read and copied Arabic typefaces.
Elsewhere, Gabeyan did pioneering work
on the first computer-aided Arabic typesetting system installed in the Egyptian
al-Ahram newspaper in 1969. See Gabeyan
(2002).

Simplified for bookwork or for Government work, and certainly for the Koran. But the overwhelming pressure of price, speed and ability to move from hot-metal manual on to tape and eventually photocomposition systems, all work in favour of Simplified. It is considerably cheaper to buy a machine using Simplified, a fount of matrices is cheaper in Simplified – the operator can obtain greater speeds when he no longer has the side magazine Keyboard to think about, he can be trained to touch-type as in Roman, … the printer can move on to tape, and even computers … and one day photocomposition.

Goodman's remarks indicate that the case for Simplified Arabic mainly revolved around the economics of production, as indeed it had for Kamel Mrowa initially. The implication is that gains in effi-ciency, speed, and cost savings would eventually overcome concerns about aesthetics and stylistic appropriateness. And indeed most newspapers in Arabic countries did eventually adopt simplified type-faces, whether by Linotype or by other manufacturers, making this form of printed Arabic widely read throughout the Middle East.

There is little doubt that Simplified Arabic was crucial to the suc-cess of Linotype's Arabic typography programme. Continued devel-opments together with technical advances and increased resources meant that by the 1980s Linotype commanded a 95 per cent share of the Arabic newspaper market and an 80 per cent share of the gen-eral commercial printing market.[46] Simplified Arabic's popularity was supported by on-going refinements, though a change of name may have helped, too. As noted above, prior to the making of Simpli-fied Arabic, Linotype's Arabic typefaces had been identified only by series numbers that for some were probably confusing or difficult to remember and which in any case hampered effective marketing.[47] To address the situation, in 1967 Linotype's Egypt representative, Hrant Gabeyan, sought out suitable names for all the company's existing Arabic typefaces, following the practice long established for Latin script typefaces. Mrowa-Linotype Simplified Arabic Series 8 with 9 became 'Yakout', after the 13th-century calligrapher Yāqūt al-Mustaʿṣimī (figure 18).[48]

Looking forward, looking back

Simplified Arabic was conceived in the particular postwar circum-stances of the Middle East. The efforts of many emerging nations to modernize, often by adopting Western technology, were also accom-panied by attempts to shape progress in appropriate and authentic ways. Industrialization and imported expertise were necessary and pragmatic but needed to be balanced with expressions of national, cultural, and linguistic identity, and the requirements of education. These dynamics were not always or easily compatible and so their co-existence required compromise and often a re-ordering of priori-ties. This was certainly true of the Arabic typographic scene in the postwar period, part of whose legacy is Simplified Arabic. Given the circumstances, Kamel Mrowa's role in Simplified Arabic was crucial, as he brought to the project technical expertise and foresight, expe-rience of commerce and trade in the region, and a cultural aware-ness and sensitivity that enabled him to (correctly) gauge whether

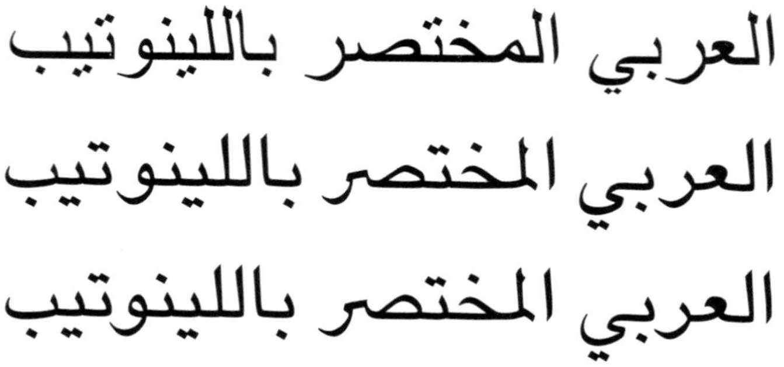

Figure 19. Sample of digital typefaces based on simplification principles.
(a) Arial/Times New Roman Arabic, Microsoft.
(b) Yakout, PostScript version, Linotype AG.
(c) Yakout, OpenType version, Monotype GmbH, redesigned by Tim Holloway and Fiona Ross.

العربي المختصر باللينوتيب

العربي المختصر باللينوتيب

العربي المختصر باللينوتيب

a simplified Arabic typeface would be acceptable for a prominent national newspaper.

The practical achievement of Simplified Arabic is located in the concept established by Kamel Mrowa to make the composition of Arabic better suited to the needs of newspaper production. The advantages it held over earlier typefaces made it a compelling choice when production efficiency, speed, and costs were given priority over aesthetic concerns, linguistic precision, or script conventions. More broadly, the typeface conveyed a sense of modernity and technical progress, and was a timely answer to the urgent needs of a fast evolving newspaper world and of national presses responding to change and upheaval in the Middle East.[49]

Despite the spirit of modernity and progress caught by Simplified Arabic, the type composition system it was developed for – the Linotype linecaster – was nevertheless soon superseded by photocomposition. But Simplified Arabic proved immune to obsolescence, as it was adapted largely unchanged to the new typesetting technology. More recently, Simplified Arabic has again been similarly adapted to digital technology as the basis for default Arabic system fonts on most computers (figure 19).[50] Here its influence continues to grow, despite the fact digital typography would readily allow Arabic typefaces to regain their uncompromised appearance. Instead, the features and principles of Simplified Arabic, born of the mechanical constraints of the Linotype, proliferate and impose a legacy of technical compromise that might have been dispensed with.[51] In turn, Arabic simplification, a product of the 1950's, continues to shape the experiences and expectations of Arabic readers in contexts far removed from where it began.

49. Nevertheless, as Simplified Arabic became more popular, the roles played by Mrowa and to a lesser degree by Jaroudi gradually fell from view in Linotype's promotional materials. While early specimens for the 'Mrowa-Linotype Simplified Arabic' gave full credit to Kamel Mrowa, and as late as 1964, in his article 'The flourishing reed', Walter Tracy acknowledged Mrowa by name for his work on Simplified Arabic (see Tracy (1964), p. 145), by 1965–6 neither Mrowa nor Jaroudi are mentioned in specimens for new sizes of the typeface, which was now also referred to only as 'Simplified Arabic'. Much later, in Tracy's recollections of work on Simplified Arabic (1995, p. 13), Mrowa is not mentioned by name, though Tracy does refer to his assassination: 'not long after [the development of Simplified Arabic], he [Mrowa] was shot dead as he left his office one day; for political reasons, not typographic'. The apparently flippant remark suggests that Tracy did not fully appreciate the political importance of Mrowa's death, which occurred at the start of a series of events that culminated in the outbreak of civil war in Lebanon in 1975. Historian Charles Winslow argues that the assassination, on May 16, 1966, although 'not usually emphasized in these accounts, may well have begun the "hostility-reaction formation" that brought on the protracted civil chaos that wracked Lebanon for nearly

two decades'. Charles Winslow, *Lebanon: war and politics in a fragmented society*, 1996, London & New York: Routledge, p. 152.

50. Arial and Times New Roman, two of the most widely installed Latin system fonts, both include an Arabic character supplement whose design is based on the principles of Simplified Arabic. Despite the distinctive designs of the two typefaces, both share the same Arabic glyphs. The use of a single Arabic design for two stylistically unrelated Latin typefaces is suggestive of the low priority major software providers have long assigned to Arabic typography. Recent original Arabic typeface designs for Microsoft's

Windows 8 may, however, point to changing priorities. While Linotype's Yakout has undergone numerous revisions, most recently in 2002 when the typeface was redesigned and enlarged to take advantage of a new font format (OpenType), its overall design remains defined by the principles of simplification.

51. Ross similarly remarks that 'the unfortunate, but not uncommon, practice of replicating font synopses of the past, which were constrained by previous technologies, is often inappropriate to current typographic possibilities', here referring to the evolution of Bengali printing types. See Ross (1999), p. 77; also Ross (2012), pp. 132–3.

Sources and references

This essay draws mainly on three archives. The Non-Latin Type Collection in the Department of Typography & Graphic Communication, University of Reading, holds most of Walter Tracy's correspondence during his time as typographic adviser at Linotype. The Mergenthaler Linotype Company Records 1905–1993, held at the Archives Center, National Museum of American History, Washington DC, complement Tracy's correspondence, as in many cases they contain the other side of exchanges between the British and US Linotype companies. The archive of the Monotype Drawing Office, located at Monotype Ltd, Salfords, UK, offers the perspective of a competing business.

Anon. (1948). 'Arabic paper here now 50 years old; Editor of *Al-Hoda* recalls first Linotype installed in 1912 as significant milestone', *The New York Times*, August 9, 1948

Ayalon, Ami (1995). *The press in the Arab Middle East: a history*. New York and Oxford: Oxford University Press

Baḥarī, Hišām Tawfīq (1968). *Ṣaḥāfä Al-Ġadu* (Tomorrow's press). Cairo, Egypt: Dār Al-Maʿārif Bimiṣr

Carter, Sebastian (1997). 'The Morison years and beyond: 1923–1965', in A. Boag & L. W. Wallis (eds), *The Monotype Recorder*, centenary issue ('One hundred years of type making, 1897–1997'), new series, no. 10, pp. 14–25

Gabeyan, Hrant (2002). 'Modern developments in Arabic Typesetting', in Hanebütt-Benz, Eva, Dagmar Glass, and Geoffrey Roper (eds), *Middle Eastern languages and the print revolution: a cross-cultural encounter: a catalogue and companion to the exhibition*. Westhofen: WVA-Verlag Skulima, pp. 216–21

Hanebütt-Benz, Eva, Dagmar Glass, and Geoffrey Roper (2002). *Middle Eastern languages and the print revolution: a cross-cultural encounter: a catalogue and companion to the exhibition*. Westhofen: WVA-Verlag Skulima

Intertype Ltd (1933). 'With the editor', *Interludes*, vol. 3, no. 2, April, pp. 8–9

Legros, Lucien Alphonse, and John Cameron Grant (1916). *Typographical printing-surfaces: the technology and mechanism of their production*. London: Longmans, Green and Co.

Linotype & Machinery Ltd (1955). 'Millions of people benefit from the advantages of Linotype composition in Arabic', *Linotype Matrix*, vol. 2, no. 23, October, p. 2

Linotype & Machinery Ltd (1959). 'Linotype are first in the world to produce a system of Simplified Arabic for mechanical composition from one magazine', *Linotype Matrix*, vol. 2, no. 32, November, p. 5

Linotype & Machinery Ltd (1960). 'Now available: 3 sizes of Mrowa-Linotype Simplified Arabic', *Linotype Matrix*, vol. 2, no. 34, December, p. 2

Mergenthaler Linotype Company (1929). 'Al-Munaḍḍadä Al-ʿArabiyyä (Typeset Arabic)

Mokarzel, Mary (1968). Al-Hoda, *1898–1968: the story of Lebanon and its emigrants taken from the newspaper al-Hoda*. New York: Al-Hoda

Monotype GmbH (2013). 'Yakout font family', www.linotype.com/1618/yakout-family.html (6 April 2013)

Ross, Fiona (1999). *The printed Bengali character and its evolution*. Richmond, Surrey: Curzon

Ross, Fiona (2002). 'Non-Latin type design at Linotype', stbride.org/friends/conference/twentiethcenturygraphiccommunication/NonLatin.html (6 April 2013)

Ross, Fiona (2012). 'Non-Latin scripts: key issues in type design', in *Non-Latin scripts: from metal to digital type*. London: St Bride Library, pp. 125–53

Seybold, John W. (1984). *The world of digital typesetting*. Media, PA: Seybold Publications

Southall, Richard (2005). *Printer's type in the twentieth century: manufacturing and design methods*. London & New Castle, DE: The British Library & Oak Knoll Press

Tracy, Walter (1964). 'The flourishing reed', in R. S. Hutchings (ed.), *Alphabet: International Annual of Letterforms*, vol. 1. London: James Moran, pp. 139–46

Tracy, Walter (1995). 'Composing room days', *Printing Historical Society Bulletin*, no. 40, winter 1995/96, pp. 3–15

Wallis, L[awrence]. W. (1988). *A concise chronology of typesetting developments 1886–1986*. London: The Wynkyn de Worde Society in association with Lund Humphries

Images

Figure 1: reproduced with the kind permission of Dar Al-Hayat Information Center, Beirut, Lebanon

Figures 2, 5–8, 11–18: Non-Latin Type Collection, Department of Typography & Graphic Communication, University of Reading

Figure 3a: reproduced with the kind permission of Monotype Ltd, Salfords, Surrey, UK

Figure 9, 10: reproduced with the kind permission of Monotype GmbH, 61352 Bad Homburg, Germany

Figure 19: courtesy Fiona Ross

Acknowledgements

This essay results from doctoral research at the Department of Typography & Graphic Communication, University of Reading, supported by a studentship from the Faculty of Arts, Humanities and Social Sciences, which is gratefully acknowledged. I would like to thank Fiona Ross, my supervisor, for her help throughout the period of work on the essay, and Diane Bilbey for making the Non-Latin Type Collection readily accessible. During my research I consulted a number of other archives. These included the records of the Mergenthaler Linotype company held at the Archives Center, National Museum of American History, Washington DC; I would like to thank Cathy Keen, who facilitated my research there. I would also like to thank Carrol and Karl Kindel for generously hosting my stay in Washington DC, and Alice Savoie for her company and help during our long working hours. In addition, I would like to thank Robin Nicholas of Monotype Ltd for providing access to the archives of the Drawing Office in Salfords, Surrey, and Ian Bezer for sharing information about Monotype's history. I am grateful to Hrant Gabeyan for welcoming me to his home, and for the long interview he granted me, and his efforts at reconstructing past events. I am indebted to Frank Romano for his gift of a rare Arabic specimen from Mergenthaler Linotype, and for his readiness to help in my research. My thanks to Paul Luna for reading a draft of this essay and making valuable suggestions; and a special thank you to Eric Kindel, without whose thorough and thoughtful editing this essay would not have been possible. While I am indebted to all those named above, any errors, omissions, or inaccuracies found here are entirely my own.